Human Nature:
the Categorial Framework

Recent books by P. M. S. Hacker published by Wiley-Blackwell

Wittgenstein's Place in Twentieth-Century Analytic Philosophy (1996)

Philosophical Foundations of Neuroscience (2003), co-authored with
M. R. Bennett

Wittgenstein: Understanding and Meaning, Volume 1 of An Analytical
Commentary on the *Philosophical Investigations*, Part I – Essays (2005),
co-authored with G. P. Baker, second, extensively revised edition by
P. M. S. Hacker

Wittgenstein: Understanding and Meaning, Volume 1 of An Analytical
Commentary on the *Philosophical Investigations*, Part II – Exegesis
§§1–184 (2005), co-authored with G. P. Baker, second, extensively
revised edition by P. M. S. Hacker

History of Cognitive Neuroscience (2008), co-authored with
M. R. Bennett

Wittgenstein: Rules, Grammar, and Necessity, Volume 2 of an Analytical
Commentary on the *Philosophical Investigations* – Essays and Exegesis of
§§185–242 (2009), co-authored with G. P. Baker, second, extensively
revised edition by P. M. S. Hacker

Human Nature:
the Categorial Framework

P. M. S. Hacker

Fellow of St John's College · Oxford

WILEY-BLACKWELL

This paperback edition first published 2010
© 2010 by P. M. S. Hacker.

Edition history: Blackwell Publishing Ltd (hardback, 2007)

Blackwell Publishing was acquired by John Wiley & Sons in February 2007.
Blackwell's publishing program has been merged with Wiley's global Scientific,
Technical, and Medical business to form Wiley-Blackwell.

Registered Office
John Wiley & Sons Ltd, The Atrium, Southern Gate, Chichester, West Sussex,
PO19 8SQ, United Kingdom

Editorial Offices
350 Main Street, Malden, MA 02148-5020, USA
9600 Garsington Road, Oxford, OX4 2DQ, UK
The Atrium, Southern Gate, Chichester, West Sussex, PO19 8SQ, UK

For details of our global editorial offices, for customer services, and for information
about how to apply for permission to reuse the copyright material in this book
please see our website at www.wiley.com/wiley-blackwell.

The right of P. M. S. Hacker to be identified as the author of this work has been
asserted in accordance with the UK Copyright, Designs and Patents Act 1988.

Library of Congress Cataloging-in-Publication Data
Hacker, P. M. S. (Peter Michael Stephan)
   Human nature : the categorial framework / P. M. S. Hacker.
      p. cm.
   Includes bibliographical references and index.
   ISBN 978-1-4051-4728-6 (hardback : alk. paper) — 978-1-4443-3248-3
(paperback : alk. paper)   1. Philosophical anthropology.   I. Title.

   BD450.H2355 2007
   128—dc22

                                                                2006103171

A catalogue record for this title is available from the British Library.

Set in 10.5/12.5pt Sabon
by Graphicraft Limited, Hong Kong
Printed and bound in Singapore
by C.O.S. Printers Pte Ltd

1   2010

For

Hans Oberdiek

Contents

Chapter 3   Causation

Chapter 4   Powers

Chapter 5   Agency

Chapter 6   Teleology and Teleological Explanation

Preface

Philosophy is of little worth unless it aspires to give an overview of a whole domain of thought, to display the ramifying network of conceptual relationships that characterize it, and to resolve problems and puzzlements that characteristically accompany reflection on it. As I reached the end of my academic career, I felt a powerful urge to paint a last large fresco that would depict, sometimes with broad brush, sometimes in fine detail, themes which I had studied and reflected on for the last forty years. The domain I have striven to portray in this book is that of human nature. I have tried to give a perspicuous representation of the most fundamental concepts and conceptual forms in terms of which we think about ourselves. These range from the most general categorial concepts of *substance, causation, power* and *agency* to the more specific and specifically anthropological concepts of *rationality, mind, body* and *person*. This book, *Human Nature: The Categorial Framework*, sketches the structural background and paints the central landmarks of the panorama I have in view. I intend to continue my endeavours in a volume entitled *Human Nature: The Cognitive and Cogitative Powers* that will add to the fresco more and finer detail. If time and fortune permit, I hope to write a concluding volume, *Human Nature: The Affective and Moral Powers*.

To enable readers, especially students, to take in at a glance some parts of my argument and some of the classifications elaborated, I introduced the occasional tree diagram and comparative list. These are often no more than illustrations to the text, sometimes over-simplifying for purposes of surveyability. They are meant to illuminate the argument, as a picture illustrates a story, not to be a substitute for it.

Many friends and acquaintances have encouraged me and given me moral support in the course of writing this book. One of the delights of philosophy is discussion with others who toil on the same rocky pathways and jungle trails, and who not only hold out a helping hand when one slips, and correct one when one takes a wrong path, but also help one blaze a trail. I have been blessed with such friends. If, in the course of these numerous discussions, merriment kept breaking through – as indeed it did – I never found this an impediment to philosophy, but a mark of shared delight in the common pursuit of understanding.

I am grateful to Maria Alvarez, Erich Ammereller, Hanoch Ben-Yami, Stephan Blatti, John Dupré, Hanjo Glock, the late Oswald Hanfling, John Hyman, Wolfgang Künne, Anselm Müller, Bede Rundle, Constantine Sandis, the late Peter Strawson, and David Wiggins, who all read one or more (and some read many more) of the chapters and gave me the great benefit of their criticisms and suggestions. I should like to record my gratitude to Anthony Kenny, whose encouragement in this enterprise, as in others in the past, spurred me on. I have learnt more from his luminous writings and incisive remarks than I can say. I owe a special debt to Hans Oberdiek and to Herman Philipse, who kindly read the whole draft, and whose detailed comments and suggestions were invaluable. I am, as I have so often been in the past, much indebted to Jean van Altena for her expert copy-editing and judicious advice.

I am happy to record my gratitude to my college, St John's, which is unstinting in its support of scholarship, the pursuit of knowledge and the quest for understanding.

Chapter 2 of this book is a modified version of the paper entitled 'Substance: Things and Stuffs', published in the *Proceedings of the Aristotelian Society*, suppl. vol. 78 (2004), pp. 41–63. A much shortened version of chapters 8 and 9 was delivered as a plenary lecture at Kirchberg, August 2006, and is to be published in the *Proceedings of the 29th International Wittgenstein Symposium*. A variant of the same paper was delivered as the opening address at the meeting of the British Society for the Philosophy of Education in Oxford, March 2006. A part of chapter 7 is to be published in Constantine Sandis (ed.), *New Essays on the Explanation of Action*.

P. M. S. Hacker
St John's College, Oxford
July 2006

. . . les principes sont dans l'usage commun et devant les yeux de tout le monde. On n'a que faire de tourner la tête, ni de se faire violence; il n'est question que d'avoir bonne vue. Mais il faut l'avoir bonne, car les principes sont si déliés, et en si grand nombre qu'il est presque impossible qu'il n'en échappe. Or l'omission d'un principe mène a l'erreur. Ainsi il faut avoir la vue bien nette pour voir tous les principes, et ensuite l'esprit juste pour ne pas raisonner faussement sur des principes connus.

. . . the principles are found in common use, and are there for all to see. One has only to look, and no effort is necessary; it is only a question of good eyesight, but it must be good, for the principles are so subtle and numerous, that it is almost impossible but that some escape notice. Now the omission of one principle leads to error; so one needs very clear sight to see all the principles, as well as an accurate mind to avoid drawing false conclusions from known principles.

Pascal, *Pensées*, I, 1

1

The Project

1. Human nature

Human beings are animals with a distinctive range of abilities. Though they have a mind, they are not identical with the mind they have. Though they have a body, they are not identical with the body they have. Nor is a human being a conjunction of a mind and a body that causally interact with each other. Like other animals, human beings have a brain on the normal functioning of which their powers depend. But a human person is not a brain enclosed in a skull. A mature human being is a self-conscious agent, with the ability to act, and to react in thought, feeling and deed, for reasons.

Animals, like inanimate objects, are spatio-temporal continuants. They have a physical location and trace a continuous spatio-temporal path through the world. In this sense, they are, like familiar material objects, *bodies* located on, and moving on, the face of the earth. They are substances, persistent individual things that are classifiable into various substantial kinds according to their nature and our interests. (What counts as such a classifying noun will be examined in chapter 2.) Animals are *animate* substances – *living* things. So, unlike mere material objects, they ingest matter from their environment and metabolize it in order to provide energy for their growth, their distinctive forms of activity, and their reproduction. Unlike plants, animals are *sentient* agents, and all but the lowliest forms of animal life are also *self-moving*. Their sentience is exhibited in their exercise of the sense-faculties they possess: for example, the perceptual faculties of sight, hearing, smell, taste and feeling, and in the actualization of their passive powers of sensation: for example, susceptibility to pain, kinaesthetic sensation and liability to overall bodily feelings, such as feeling tired, and feelings of overall condition, such as feeling well. The perceptual faculties are cognitive. They are sources of knowledge about the perceptible environment. It is by the exercise of these sense-faculties, by the use of the sense-organs that are their vehicles, that animals learn about the objects in, and features of, their environment. Being sentient and being self-moving are complementary powers of animal agency. For an animal that can learn how things are in its vicinity exhibits what it has apprehended both in its finding the things it seeks (such as food, protective environment, a mate) and in its avoiding obstacles and dangers. The criteria for whether an animal has perceived something lie in its responsive behaviour – so perception, knowledge and belief, affection, desire and action are conceptually linked.

The abilities distinctive of human beings are abilities of intellect and will. The relevant abilities of intellect are thought, imagination (the cogitative and creative imagination rather than the image-generating faculty), personal (experiential) and factual memory, reasoning and self-consciousness. Human beings have the ability to think *of* (and imagine) things that lie beyond their present perceptual field – to think of things as encountered in the past and of the encountering of them, of past things learnt about and of the learning of them, of future things that do not yet exist and of eventualities and actions that have not yet occurred or been performed. To the extent that other higher animals possess comparable abilities, then they do so only in rudimentary (pre-linguistic) forms. Humans can think both of what does and also of what does not exist or occur, of what has or has not been done, and of what will and what will not be done. We can believe, imagine, hope or fear that such-and-such is the case, irrespective of whether things are so or not. In short, thought, both in rudimentary form in animals and in developed form in humans, displays *intentionality*. Not only can we think *of* and *about* such things, and think *that* things are thus-and-so, but we can *reason* from such premises to conclusions that follow from or are well supported by them. And we can evaluate such reasoning as valid or invalid, plausible or implausible. Because the horizon of human thinking is so much wider than that of non-human animal thinking, so too the horizon of human feelings and emotions is far wider than that of other animals. Both humans and animals can hope and fear things, but many of the things that humans can hope for (such as salvation, or good weather next week) and fear (such as damnation, or bad weather next week) are not possible objects of corresponding animal emotions.

Like other animals, we are conscious creatures. When conscious (as opposed to being asleep, comatose or anaesthetized), we may be *conscious of* those items in our perceptual field that catch and hold our attention. Unlike other animals, we are also *self-conscious*. We have not only the power to move at will and to perceive how things are in our environment, but also the power to be reflectively aware of our doing or having done so. We can not only think and reason, but can further reflect on ourselves as having thought or reasoned thus-and-so. We can not only have reasoned desires in addition to animal appetites, feel emotions and adopt attitudes, deliberate upon goals and purposes, but we can also realize and reflect on such facts. Being self-conscious creatures, we are subject to a variety of emotions of self-assessment, such as pride, shame and guilt, that are foreclosed to non-self-conscious animals (see fig. 1.1).

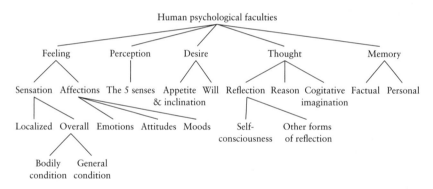

Figure 1.1. *A possible ordering of human psychological faculties*

Human beings can reason from given premises to theoretical or practical conclusions. We can take such-and-such to be *a reason* for thinking that things are thus-and-so. We can also take things' being thus-and-so to be a reason for acting or reacting in a certain way. For we do not merely behave and act as our appetites and fancies incline us, we do much of what we do *for reasons*. We have not only animal desires and passing inclinations, we also have reasoned goals and purposes rooted not merely in our biological make-up, but in reflection on the desirability of objects and objectives relative to our conception of our good and of the good. Rationality is Janus-faced, incorporating both backward- and forward-looking reasons. Inasmuch as we possess an articulate memory, we can take past facts as reasons for present actions and attitudes – as when we act out of gratitude, punish or reward desert, harbour indignation or resentment, or feel ashamed or guilty. Because we can think about and come to know truths or probabilities concerning the future, we can take future facts or the likelihood of future eventualities as reasons for us to act in certain ways here and now. Our behaviour can accordingly be evaluated as rational or reasonable, as well as irrational or unreasonable. And so too can our emotions and attitudes.

These capacities and their exercise give to human beings the status of persons. While *human being* is a biological category, *person* is a moral, legal and social one. To be a person is, among other things, to be a subject of moral rights and duties. It is to be not only an agent, like other animals, but also a moral agent, standing in reciprocal moral relations to others, with a capacity to know and to do good and evil. Since moral agents can act for reasons, and can justify their actions by reference to their reasons, they are also answerable for their deeds. To be a human being is to be a creature whose nature it is to acquire such capacities in the course of normal maturation in a community of like-natured beings.

2. Philosophical anthropology

The above thumbnail sketch in one sense locates human nature in the scheme of things – but the scheme in which it locates it is our conceptual scheme. So much of the sketch is also an indirect description of the network of concepts in terms of which we articulate our nature. It locates the forms of description of human nature in the general conceptual scheme in terms of which we describe all else. The methodical description of the structure of this finely woven network and the examination of some of the ways in which it has been and is commonly misconstrued is the objective of the following studies in *philosophical anthropology*. This term of art has a wider scope than 'philosophy of mind' or 'philosophical psychology', although, as I shall use it, it incorporates these. Philosophical anthropology is the investigation of the concepts and forms of explanation characteristic of the study of man. The systematic description of this network of concepts will enable us to shed light on a multitude of philosophical problems and controversies about human nature and the forms of explanation of human behaviour. Prior to commencing the present task, some methodological reflections are necessary to characterize the task and to defend the methods that will be used.

It would be misguided to suppose that the concepts invoked and their complex relationships are the concepts and conceptual network of a theory of some kind (sometimes referred to contemptuously as 'folk psychology') that might be abandoned if the theory were found defective. Theoretical concepts can indeed be jettisoned with the theory to which they belong, if the theory is radically awry. The concepts of phlogiston and caloric are now of mere historical interest. Non-theoretical concepts include the numerous concepts that are employed, *inter alia*, merely to describe phenomena. The phenomena thus described may or may not stand in need of explanation. In some cases, the explanation needed may be theoretical; but not all explanation is theoretical. Non-theoretical concepts do not fall victim to the falsity of an explanation or falsification of an explanatory theory.

The concepts of a human being, of a person, of the mind and body of a person, of the intellect and the will, perception and sensation, knowledge and belief, memory and imagination, thought and reason, desire, intention and will, feelings and emotions, character traits and attitudes, virtues and vices, are not theoretical concepts. They are not concepts that we could abandon after the manner of *phlogiston* or *caloric*. They *are* used, a-theoretically, to describe phenomena that are the subject matter of numerous theories in the study of human beings, in psychology, anthropology, sociology, history and economics. But that is not their sole role.

These anthropological and psychological concepts do not stand to what they *can* be used to describe merely as representation to what is represented. For our use of many of these concepts and their congeners itself moulds our nature as human beings, as concept-employing, self-conscious creatures. So their use is partly constitutive of what they can also be invoked to describe. The availability of these concepts *gives shape* to our subjective experience, for it is by their use, in the first person, that we are able to *give it articulate expression*.

In learning the vocabulary of psychological concepts, a child is not learning a theory of anything. He is, on the one hand, learning *new forms of behaviour* – learning to replace his cries of pain by 'It hurts' or 'I have a pain' and his cries of indignation with 'No!' and 'I don't like it'; to herald his deliberate actions by 'I'm going to' and later his plans by 'I intend', to prefix an 'I think' to, or interpolate an 'I believe' or an 'as far as I know' in, his unconfirmed assertions; and to preface his fearful but false descriptions on waking from a night-mare with 'I dreamt'. On the other hand, he is learning to describe other people and to describe and explain their behaviour in these terms. But there is nothing theoretical about describing others as being in pain, listening to this or smelling that, wanting this and thinking that, intending, liking, loving and so forth. The mental is not *hidden behind* behaviour; but, one might say, metaphorically speaking, that it infuses it. We must not confuse the possibility of not exhibiting or express-ing it, or of suppressing its manifestation and concealing it, with the idea that it is *unobservable* by others. To be sure, this is not to endorse any form of behaviourism. It is often possible *not* to show that one has a headache; but when one is injured and writhing in agony, one's pain is patent. That is what is *called* 'showing one's pain'. One can think something to be the case, and not say what one thinks; and it is often possible to keep one's thoughts to oneself. But when one says what one thinks, one's thoughts are patent, and when one sincerely confesses one's thoughts to another, one's thoughts are laid bare. Nor should we suppose that the mental is *observable* by the subject, as if one enjoyed privileged access to one's 'domain of consciousness'. There is such a thing as introspection, but it is not a kind of inner perception – it is a form of self-reflection. Such confusions and suppositions concerning psychological concepts incorporate deep and ramifying errors which infect empirical sciences of man, such as psychology and cognitive neuroscience.

Furthermore, the characteristic forms of explanation of human behaviour in terms of reasons are not to be found in the natural sciences and are not proto-scientific explanations. Teleology is, to be sure, also appropriately invoked in the study of non-human, biological phenomena. So too are the concepts of goal, purpose and function. But explanation in terms of reasons and motives is distinct-ive of human behaviour. This too is not part of a proto-science, although it is true that these forms of explanation characterize the study of man in history, psychology and the social sciences. But, like the psychological and anthropological concepts that are involved in such explanations, the explanations themselves are typically partly constitutive of the phenomena that they explain. To learn, as every human being does, to give such explanations at the homely level of personal action and relations is not to learn the rudiments of a science. It is to learn to be a rational human being and to particip-ate in the human form of life that is the birthright and burden of the children of Adam.

3. Grammatical investigation

So, the theme of the following philosophical investigations is human nature. But it is simultaneously the *grammar* of the description of what is distinctively human. And it is the former because it is the latter. For the investigations are purely *conceptual*. They explore the concepts and conceptual forms we employ in our thought and talk about ourselves, and examine the logico-grammatical relationships between these concepts and conceptual forms.

The study of the nature of things, in one sense, belongs to the empirical sciences. It is the task of physics, chemistry and biology, of psychology, economics and sociology to discover the properties and relations, the regularities and laws, of the objects that fall within their domain. Empirical observation leads to explanatory theory, commonly with predictive and retrodictive power. Theories involve abstraction and generalization from observed data, and the confirmation or infirmation of conjectures in experience. The truths discovered are empirical truths, and the theories confirmed are empirical theories.

The study of the nature of things, in another sense, belongs to philosophy. This investigation has sometimes been characterized as the quest for the *essential* nature of things, and contrasted with the empirical sciences that are conceived to study their *contingent* nature. In past ages such investigation was allocated to the Queen of the Sciences – metaphysics. The *de re* essences of things provided the subject matter of metaphysical philosophy, and their disclosure its sublime task.[1] This, however, was an illusion. There is no such thing as metaphysics *thus conceived*, and no such subject matter for philosophy to investigate.

It is one thing to grant that substances of a given kind have essential as well as accidental properties, or that the instantiation of certain properties or relations entails the instantiation or exclusion of certain other properties and relations. It is quite another to hold that propositions that state the essential properties of a given substance or the relations of inclusion or exclusion that hold between properties and relations describe *mind-independent, language-independent, metaphysical necessities* in reality. What appear here to be descriptions of *de re* necessities are actually norms of representation. That

---

[1] A conception taken up again at the end of the nineteenth century by Husserl and the Munich circle of phenomenologists, who abandoned psychologism for a quest for *Wesensschau*.

is, they are not descriptions of how things are, but implicit *prescriptions* (rules) for describing how things are. Consider the following four propositions:

(i)   A material object is a three-dimensional space-occupying entity that can be in motion or at rest and consists of matter of one kind or another.
(ii) Every event is temporally related to every other event.
(iii) Nothing can simultaneously be red all over and also green all over.
(iv) Every rod has a length.

Such propositions appear to be descriptions. They are what we think of as *necessary truths*, for, to be sure, nothing can be a material object that is not a space-occupant or that does not consist of material stuff; it is inconceivable that there be an event that is neither earlier nor later nor yet simultaneous with, or a constituent phase of, any other event, or that something be both red all over and green all over simultaneously; and it is not a contingent matter that we shall never find a rod without a length.

Appearances are deceptive. These sentences express *rules* for the use of their constituent terms *in the guise of descriptions*. If we characterize something as a material object, then it follows without more ado that we may characterize it as a space-occupant made of matter of some kind. We do not have to check to see whether perhaps *this* material object is *not* made of some matter or other, or whether it may have *no* spatial location. These *internal* (defining) properties and relations are *constitutive* of what it is to be a material thing: they are part of what we mean by 'material object'. If reference is made to some event, we can infer without more ado that it is either earlier than, later than, simultaneous with, or a constitutive phase of any other event. If something is described as being red all over, it follows that it is not also green all over – this is not something that we need to confirm by looking. And if something is said to be a rod, it follows that it can be described as having a certain length. What appear to be descriptions of *meta*-physical necessities in nature are norms (rules) for describing natural phenomena. We would not *call* something a material object if it occupied no space or did not consist of matter; we would not *deem* something to be a genuine event if it were not simultaneous with, earlier or later than, or a phase of, any other given event; we would not *describe* something as being red all over if we were willing to describe it as green all over; and we would not *hold* something that lacked a length to be a rod. These are not discoveries about things, but the commitments consequent on employing a certain form of representation or description.

While the truth of an empirical proposition excludes a possibility, the truth of such necessitarian propositions as that nothing can be red and green all over, or that there cannot be a rod without a length, or that every material object must be located somewhere, somewhen, does not. A logical or conceptual impossibility is not a possibility that is impossible. So what is excluded is not a possibility that has been described by a form of words, but only the form of words that appears to describe a possibility. And the form of words is excluded as sense-less, inasmuch as it describes neither a logical possibility nor a logical impossibility. For *there is no such thing* as describing a logical impossibility, *since there is nothing to describe*. So what we are doing is *in effect* excluding a form of words from the language inasmuch as it lacks sense.[2] It makes no sense to say that something is both red and green all over, or that there is a rod with no length; that is, to utter the words 'A is both red all over and green all over' or 'A is a rod but it has no length' is not to say anything intelligible, but to utter a kind of nonsense. What appear to be necessary truths about the world – for example, that nothing *can* be red and green all over simultaneously, or that every rod *must* have a length – are actually no more than *grammatical propositions* that are implicitly about the use of words. These 'can-s' and 'must-s' are marks of norms of representation.

To use the term 'grammar' to refer to any sense- or meaning-determining rules for the use of words is a harmless Wittgensteinian extension of the grammarians' use of the word. I shall follow Wittgenstein's usage and apply the term 'grammar' and its cognates to rules that are not merely syntactical.[3] In this extended use, apparently metaphysical propositions about *de re* necessities are merely *grammatical propositions* – that is, propositions about the usage of expressions

[2] This does not mean that it cannot occur in indirect speech to report someone's words. What it does mean is that if someone is reported as having spoken thus, we know that what he said was a form of nonsense.

[3] The grammarian will say that the rule that 'identical' cannot form a comparative or superlative is a grammatical one, but that the rule that excludes prefixing the phrase 'north-east of' to 'the North Pole' or to 'the South Pole' is not. For our purposes this distinction is unnecessary.

in the form of descriptions of the properties and relations of things. So too, the description of the essential properties and relations of some thing (an F) is a specification of the grammar of 'F'. For it will specify the properties and relations of an F, the loss of which will be tantamount to the destruction of an F or to its degeneration (to its constituting a borderline or limiting case of being an F). Something that lacked these-and-these properties, or did not stand in such-and-such relations, would not be *called* 'an F' (unless we changed the meaning of the word 'F'). Since such propositions are commonly not *especially* concerned with the language in which they are expressed, but apply equally to any language that contains expressions used in the relevantly same way, they are also commonly and correctly said to express *conceptual* truths. So 'Red is darker than pink' is a grammatical proposition that in effect says that anything that can truly be said to be red can also truly be said to be darker than anything that can be said to be pink, and it characterizes the *concepts* of being red, pink and darker than (and not only the English *words*).

However, it would be mistaken to suppose that any clarification of the nature, as opposed to the essence, of an F must adduce characteristic marks of the concept of F – that is, conditions necessary and sufficient for being an F (for the application of the expression 'an F'). For the concept may not be so moulded, and the clarification of what it is to be an F may proceed differently; for there are many different ways of explaining what 'F' or 'an F' means. Some expressions are explained by specification of criteria (i.e. logically good evidence, as opposed to inductive evidence) for their application. Others may be explained by ostensive definition by reference to a sample, as when we point at a certain thing and say, 'That (colour) is Brunswick green' or 'That (length) is one metre' or 'That (animal) is an elephant'. Some expressions are typically explained by enumeration of examples together with a similarity rider: so, if asked what a game is (what the word 'game' means), one might reply that football, bridge, chess, hide-and-seek and suchlike are games. Such expressions, following Wittgenstein, are held to express 'family-resemblance concepts'. And other forms of explanation are licit too. It should be noted that different forms of explanation are not necessarily exclusive: that is, some expressions may be explained correctly in more than one way.

The *philosophical* study of human nature, by contrast with psychological, social-scientific and neuroscientific studies, is *grammatical* or *conceptual*. Philosophical anthropology, as I am using the term, is an investigation into *the conceptual scheme* in terms of which we describe ourselves and our complex moral and social relationships, give expression to our inner life, explain, justify or excuse the thoughts, feelings and actions of human beings. Its product will directly or indirectly be a description of a web of words and the delineation of their forms of connectedness, as well as a characterization of forms of explanation appropriate to and distinctive of the domain. It will not, however, produce a *theory* of human nature.

This book, *Human Nature: The Categorial Framework*, investigates the fundamental categories in terms of which we think about ourselves: the two related categories of substance (for we *are* a substance of a certain kind, and *are made of* substances of various kinds); the category of causation (for we are creatures with causal powers to effect changes to things in the world around us, and causal susceptibilities to be affected by them); the category of power (for we have a wide range of different kinds of active and passive powers); the category of agency (for we are agents with the ability to act or refrain from acting, and to act on things around us). These categorial themes are commonly deemed metaphysical. If by 'metaphysics' one means not a study of the *de re* 'essence of the world' – its allegedly language-independent necessary features – but rather an investigation into the most general structural concepts that inform our thought, then so indeed they are. In *this* sense our investigation can be deemed metaphysical.

Having clarified these very general conceptual forms, I shall then turn to investigate the distinctive forms of understanding and explanation that characterize our thought and talk about ourselves – the various forms of teleological and reason-giving explanation. This elucidation of the categorial framework is preparatory to an investigation of the concepts of the body and the mind that human beings are said to have, and of the relationship between being a human being and being a person.

4. Philosophical investigation

It is not the task of philosophy to compete with the psychological or neuropsychological sciences. It is not its business to come up with empirical theories and conjectures that stand in need of experimental confirmation. That is the business of the empirical sciences. It is not the task of philosophy to produce non-empirical theories either – for there are no such things for philosophy to produce. What would a non-empirical philosophical *theory* look like? And how might it be confirmed or disconfirmed? What the non-empirical sciences of arithmetic, geometry and formal logic can do is produce concepts and conceptual relationships for the empirical sciences to deploy in *their* theories and reasoning about phenomena. These mathematical and logical tasks are *concept formation by proof construction* and *determination of formal canons of validity*. To be sure, the term 'theory' *is* used in this domain. Mathematicians speak of the mathematical theory of functions, for example, and logicians speak of quantification theory. But this invokes the term 'theory' in a quite different sense from that which it has when we speak of empirical theories in the natural sciences. The concepts formed by the mathematical sciences have their *primary* use, directly *or indirectly*, in the transformation of empirical propositions concerning magnitudes and quantifiable attributes of things and in the transformation of descriptions of spatial relations between things, and so forth. But the task of philosophy is not to generate *novel* concepts and conceptual connections for use in the empirical sciences or for use in everyday discourse. Rather, it is to *clarify* existing concepts and conceptual connections and to discern the very general patterns they exhibit. To be sure, this does not imply that in the course of fulfilling that task and ordering the concepts it investigates with the aim of obviating confusions, philosophy may not introduce new distinctions among concepts or classes of concepts, or between different kinds of proposition for purposes of philosophical illumination.

Philosophy is, of course, a *theoretical*, not a practical, *activity*. But there is nothing hypothetico-deductive or predictive, on the model of theories of natural science, about its methods or results. Nor is there any novel concept formation for the purposes of the natural sciences, on the model of many theories in mathematics. But this does not mean that philosophy is not, or cannot be, *systematic*. Nor does it mean that it cannot aspire to whatever degree of *generality* its conceptual elucidations admit of.

The motivation for philosophical concept clarification may be twofold.

First, especially when operating at a high level of generality, there is an intrinsic interest in detecting the most general structural features of our thought. For the ways in which we think about ourselves and our fellow human beings, the concepts we use in expressing or reporting our inner lives and describing those of others, and the distinctive forms we invoke in explaining our own behaviour and that of others, have very general structural features of which we are not ordinarily aware. Indeed, there is no reason why we should be, since the *realization* of affinities and differences, analogies and disanalogies, between different concepts and concept types is not a condition for mastering the uses of those concepts. But achieving an understanding of such general structural features is simultaneously achieving a certain kind of understanding of human nature. For what we come to understand are the *forms* of our understanding of ourselves.

Secondly, the psychological and anthropological concepts and forms of explanation with which we are concerned are the source of deep, widespread and perennial conceptual confusions. Although the concepts are ordinary, everyday ones, which we employ unthinkingly and correctly in the stream of our lives, reflection upon them generates puzzlement. Although the forms of explanation are altogether familiar, and constantly invoked in our daily discourse, they are subject to widespread misconstrual in philosophy, in the human sciences, and in cognitive science and neuroscience, being typically viewed as epiphenomenal, or forms of causal explanation, and so no different in principle from the forms of explanation characteristic of the sciences, or as reducible to such forms.

Many of the most general and problematic concepts, such as *mind*, *soul*, *body*, *self*, *person*, were moulded by, and in some cases generated in the course of, centuries of Greek, Jewish and Christian philosophico-theological reflections in the ancient and early modern world. Some of the resultant misconceptions still cling to our thought about what they signify. The employment of many psychological concepts in the human and zoological sciences is characteristically confused and riven with misconceived scientific theory, precipitously hypothesized without the conceptual clarification that should precede theory construction. So misconceptions and incoherences are masked under the rubrics of theological doctrine and its vulgarization in the understanding of religious believers, on the one hand, and scientific as well as pseudo-scientific theories of psychology, of the mind and the brain, on the other. For the puzzlements often masquerade as mysteries, which, it is alleged, it is not given to man to comprehend, or as forms of empirical ignorance, which will allegedly be solved by the march of science. Whereas in fact the puzzlements and apparent mysteries are knots that we have tied in our understanding. The disentangling of such knots and the explanation of how we tied them and why they hold us captive are primary goals and a full justification for the activity of philosophical clarification. What are clarified are concepts and forms of explanation. What the clarification aims to achieve is the dissolution of misconceptions about our nature and the attainment of a correct conception. The method of clarification is primarily, though not exclusively, an examination of the uses of words and patterns of reasoning.

5. Philosophy and 'mere words'

Is a philosophical inquiry into human nature, then, primarily lexico-graphical? Is it just a matter of language? Surely we are interested in the nature of mankind, not in mere words! To suggest otherwise seems repulsive – a trivialization of a profoundly important subject.

It is inappropriate to denigrate such an interest in words. We do not condemn the investigations of theoretical linguists as trivial because they are concerned with 'mere words'. Why should a corresponding philosophical concern seem of lesser importance? A philosophical inter-est in language is anything but trivial. Of course, it differs from the grammarian's. The questions that engage our attention are of no con-cern to linguists. But it is possible to be interested in language and word usage for many different reasons. Even philosophy of language is not a branch of linguistics, although it focuses upon such linguistic concepts as *name, referring expression, predicate, quantifier, sentence, logical connective*. Philosophical anthropology and philosophy of mind are obviously not branches of linguistics either; but they too are concerned with the elucidation of a segment of language – with the anthropological and psychological vocabulary.

Philosophical elucidation of a segment of language, however, is not a form of glorified lexicography. We do not need to engage in socio-linguistic surveys to establish how the expressions that concern us are used. Being competent speakers of the language, we know per-fectly well how to use the relevant expressions, and at most need to be reminded of the familiar. We may take usage (ordinary or technical, as the case may be) for granted, just as the competent chess-player may take the moves of the game for granted, and the competent math-ematician may take the use of numerals for granted. But we may not have *realized* similarities between different kinds of expression and differences between apparently similar kinds of expression. Such fail-ures of realization may be a source of far-reaching conceptual baffle-ment and error. We commonly construe substantives on the model of names of substances, and run into dire confusion over 'mind', 'self' or 'substance'. We typically construe verbs on the model of names of actions and activities, and lose our bearings when confronted with 'to mean', 'to think' or 'to intend'. We assume unreflectively that adjectives name properties, and become confused by 'true', 'real' or 'good'.

The words and phrases we use, and the complex network of relationships between their uses, are, to invoke Kleist's metaphor,[4] the spectacles through which we view ourselves and the world. It would surely be foolish to suggest that only lense-grinders should be interested in the lenses through which we look, that only grammarians should be interested in the linguistic forms by means of which we articulate our understanding of ourselves and of the world around us. If the lenses are dirty and obscure clear vision, if it is all too easy to mistake reflections on the lenses for things seen, if the curvature of the lenses leads to certain distortions, then careful attention to the spectacles through which we view the world is imperative.

To put the same point less metaphorically, what is thinkable is what is expressible. The primary means for the expression of thought, and the only means for the expression of the kinds of thoughts that we are concerned with, is linguistic. If, in subtle and unnoticed ways, we misuse the words of our language, we shall, often in subtle and unnoticed ways, talk nonsense. We may pose problems that need not solution but dissolution (e.g. 'How is my mind related to my body?'); we may make assertions that transgress the bounds of sense (e.g. 'I am my brain'); we may fall into confusion (e.g. 'If I have a mind, a body, a soul and a self, what is it that has all these things?'). Such misconceived questions, misguided assertions and bewildering confusions are *conceptual*, not empirical. They can be eradicated not by empirical discoveries but only by conceptual investigations. But these transgressions of the bounds of sense are not to be cursorily dismissed as nonsense. They must be explored in detail in order to expose the *roots* of the nonsense, which can *then* be extirpated. The philosophical interest in language – in our forms of representation – *is* an interest in our conceptual scheme. For it is the grammar of our language that determines what it makes sense to say – what we can render intelligible to ourselves.

Usage, the rules or conventions for the correct use of expressions, determines what does and what does not make sense. And in thus determining the bounds of sense, the bounds of what is logically

---

[4] H. von Kleist, *Geschichte meiner Seele*, ed. Helmut Semdner (Insel, Frankfurt am Main, 1977), pp. 174ff. In a letter to Wilhelmine von Zenge (22 March 1801), Kleist used this as a metaphor for Kant's transcendental idealism.

possible are also fixed. So what it makes sense to say and think about human nature, about the mind, about the relationship between mind and body, about the person and about the survival of the person after death, depends upon what we mean by these words. What we mean by them and what they mean must generally coincide. And what they mean depends upon the rules for their employment. For the meaning of a word is what is given by an explanation of meaning. And to explain what an expression means *is* to give a rule for its use. So the kind of grammatical investigation in question is not distinct from an investigation into the a priori nature of mankind. For the nature of a thing just is the range of attributes and powers (possibly related only by a family resemblance) which that thing possesses in virtue of which it may be counted as the kind of thing it is. Possessing those attributes and powers is a ground for characterizing the thing as being of such-and-such a kind. It should be borne in mind that what we now deem the nature of a thing may have originated in empirical discovery, which was subsequently hardened into a rule.

Our investigations are conceptual. This does not mean that they are not *also* linguistic. The philosophical inquiry into human nature is an inquiry into the general concepts we employ to characterize humanity and the distinctive powers of man. Concepts are best thought of as no more than abstractions from the uses of words. For to possess a concept *is* to have mastered the use of a word or phrase. (It is not a mere recognitional ability, a power to distinguish, e.g. F-s (or things which are F) from things which are not – which non-language-using animals possess.) The conceptual investigations in question *are* investigations into the uses of those words we employ to characterize ourselves and our powers. So they are, in the extended sense, grammatical investigations. We are interested in the concepts of agency, mind, body, person, consciousness self-consciousness and so forth; we are interested not in the English words *per se*, but in the *role* of those words and any equivalent words in any other languages.

Of course, different cultures may employ a distinctively different conceptual scheme to talk and think of human beings and their nature. We are much given to representing ourselves and features of ourselves in the faculty terminology that we have inherited from the Greeks. But other forms of representation may eschew this mode of description and classification, or may group human faculties differently. It is a striking fact that German (like many other languages) has no word that corresponds exactly to the English expression 'the mind', but makes do with 'Geist' and 'Seele'. All this means is that the confusions and unclarities that bedevil the thought of English speakers in this domain *may* differ in subtle ways from those of German speakers.

We are trying to elucidate *our* conceptual scheme, a conceptual scheme largely shared by many cultures and manifest in many languages. Such elucidation is not merely conceptual cartography for its own sake, interesting though that may be. It is intended to help us find our way around when we encounter conceptual puzzlement and fall into confusion. The clarification of our concepts, of our uses of words, contributes to the eradication of *our* conceptual confusions. These, to a large degree, are rooted in the grammars of our languages. But this does not mean that our investigation is not really into human nature. Nor does it mean that there are not other roots of conceptual confusion than deceptive features of language.

6. A challenge to the autonomy of the philosophical enterprise: Quine

In the second half of the twentieth century some American philosophers, led by Quine, argued that there is no distinction between conceptual and empirical truths (truths of reason and truths of fact), that the propositions we believe, typically conceived conjunctively to constitute a theory, confront reality for their confirmation as a totality.[5] Any and every proposition within a given theory, including what are conceived (wrongly in Quine's view) to be a priori and necessary propositions (e.g. truths of logic and mathematics) can be relinquished in order to adjust the theory as a whole to the deliverances of experience and experiment. Were this correct, then there would be no categorial distinction between philosophy and science, and philosophical reflection would be a part of general theory construction concerning the world – as indeed Quine argued. So philosophical reflection on human nature would be a part of the human sciences, subject to their jurisdiction, and confirmed or infirmed with them. It is, however, incorrect.

Quine's holistic picture depended on repudiating Carnap's articulation of a distinction between analytic and synthetic propositions (disregarding Kant's, Bolzano's and Frege's different construals of analyticity). It is correct that from his reflections on his distinction between analytic and synthetic propositions, Carnap drew the misguided

---

[5] W. V. O. Quine, 'Two Dogmas of Empiricism' (1953), repr. in *From a Logical Point of View*, 2nd edn. (Harper & Row, New York, 1963).

conclusion that analytic truths *followed* from conventions. But whether his distinction between analytic and synthetic truth itself is irremediably flawed, as Quine argued, is debatable. Quine's accusation was contested by Carnap himself,[6] and arguably successfully deflected by Grice and Strawson.[7] Whether the rejectability of Carnap's distinction between analytic and synthetic propositions implies the rejectability of the different analytic/synthetic distinctions drawn by Kant, Bolzano, Frege and others is also debatable. But, more importantly for present purposes, the distinction between a priori conceptual truths and a posteriori empirical propositions does not depend on the viability of any distinction between analytic and synthetic propositions. Among a priori conceptual truths we should distinguish truths of logic and mathematics, and both from general grammatical truths, no matter whether these are analytic truths (appropriately explained in logical terms) or other non-analytic grammatical truths (e.g. that red is darker than pink, or that nothing can simultaneously be only 2 metres long and also 3 metres long). It should be evident that the distinction between conceptual (including grammatical) truths and empirical ones, unlike the distinction between a priori and a posteriori truths, is *not* epistemic, even though conceptual truths are, of course, a priori. It is a distinction between different roles and uses of propositions. Such differences of role are, of course, connected with differences in grounds for assertion, and with differences in criteria of understanding, misunderstanding and not understanding. Furthermore, the distinction between grammatical and empirical truths is not exhaustive, for there is a class of diverse propositions that constitute the inherited background against which one distinguishes truth from falsehood (e.g. 'The world has existed for many years', 'Cats don't grow on trees', 'My name is NN'). Such propositions are empirical – concern the world and what is in it, yet have a role similar in certain respects to that of grammatical propositions, since they may function as rules for testing other propositions. They are neither self-evident or evident to the senses or reason, nor inferred from such propositions as are; yet they are not supported by any evidence that

---

[6] R. Carnap, 'Quine on Analyticity', in R. Creath (ed.), *Dear Carnap, Dear Van* (University of California Press, Berkeley, 1990), pp. 427–32.

[7] H. P. Grice and P. F. Strawson, 'In Defence of a Dogma', *Philosophical Review*, 65 (1956), pp. 141–58. It is noteworthy that Quine himself rehabilitated at least *a* version of the Carnapian distinction in *The Roots of Reference* (Open Court, La Salle, Ill., 1973), sect. 21.

is more certain than they are in themselves. They are held in place by what surrounds them, like the keystone of an arch.[8] The kinds of proposition which we have been discussing are represented in Figure 1.2 (many further kinds of proposition, such as ethical, aesthetic and religious propositions are excluded).

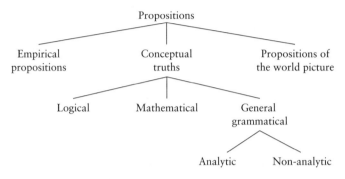

Figure 1.2. *Proposition types*

Contrary to Quine's view, truths of logic and mathematics do not 'face the tribunal of sense' for confirmation or infirmation conjunctively with the empirical theories in which they have been utilized. Their truth is established by deductive proofs, and the acceptance of a proof is tantamount to insulating the propositions in question from empirical fact. No logical or mathematical theorem is shown to be false by the rejectability of the empirical theory in which it is invoked. Nor does confirmation of such a theory (e.g. Newton's theory of gravity) render more certain the mathematics which it employs (e.g. the theorems of the differential calculus were not rendered more certain by the success of Newton's physics).[9] Nothing will *count* as showing that a proven arithmetical proposition is true only for the most part, or only under certain specifiable conditions. But this, *contra* Quine, is not because we shield such propositions from disconfirmation more than others out of considerations of simplicity of theory. Rather, such propositions are given a quite different *role* from empirical propositions

---

[8] Wittgenstein characterized such propositions as propositions of one's 'world picture'; see his *On Certainty* (Blackwell, Oxford, 1969). For illuminating discussion, see A. J. P. Kenny, *Faith and Reason* (Columbia University Press, New York, 1983), lecture 2.

[9] See D. Isaacson, 'Quine and Logical Positivism', in R. F. Gibson, Jr. (ed.), *The Cambridge Companion to Quine* (Cambridge University Press, Cambridge, 2004), p. 254.

– they are normative, not descriptive. What we hold rigid in the face of experience is not a truth about the world, but *the expression of a rule* – for example, a rule for transforming descriptions of how things are in the world. To say that an arithmetical proposition such as 25 × 25 = 625 is true is to characterize it as licensing the transformation of other, in particular empirical, propositions concerning quantities or magnitudes of things. '25 × 25 = 625' licenses one, for example, to transform the proposition that there are 25 boxes of 25 marbles in the drawer into the proposition that there are 625 marbles in boxes in the drawer, without counting afresh.[10]

Non-mathematical and non-logical conceptual truths (i.e. grammatical truths) are equally a priori. To distinguish these from a posteriori empirical truths does not depend upon a Carnapian (or any other) distinction between analytic and synthetic propositions. It depends upon a distinction between implicit statements of rules for the use of words and applications of words in accordance with the rules thus stated. That vixens are foxes (which is analytic, i.e. transformable into a logical truth by substitution of a definitional synonym), that red is more like orange than like yellow (which is not an analytic truth thus understood), that a person is a subject of rights and duties, that to have a mind is to have a certain range of abilities, are specifications of *the nature of their subject* and simultaneously *expressions of rules for the use of their constituent terms*. They license redescriptions of phenomena and inferences from their description.

Analytic truths such as 'Vixens are foxes' or 'Bachelors are unmarried' are a subclass of conceptual truths. It was an error of Carnap and the logical positivists to characterize such truths as true *in virtue of* conventions, and to claim that their truth *followed* from the meanings of terms and laws of logic alone. They do not follow from the meanings of their constituent terms (nothing follows from the meaning of a word, but only from a proposition), but are partly *constitutive of* the meanings of those terms. So it would be more correct to characterize them as *conventions* – as expressions of rules for the use of their constituent words in the misleading guise of descriptions. Of course, to say that such propositions are true is not to say that the rules

[10] To be sure, there are many kinds of arithmetical propositions that are not, or not *directly*, rules for the transformation of empirical propositions about quantities or magnitudes, e.g. the proposition 'There are more primes between 1 and 20 than there are between 20 and 40'. It does not follow that such propositions are not normative. They are the result of applying arithmetical techniques to arithmetic itself, and they forge constitutive connections within the body of arithmetic.

they express are true – for there is no such thing as true or false rules. It is merely to confirm their role as expressions of rules. Similarly, we say that 'The chess king moves one square at a time' expresses a rule of chess, and we also say that it is true that the chess king moves one square at a time. To say the latter is merely to affirm that this is the chess rule for the movement of that piece. For an empirical proposition to be true is for things to be as it says they are. But for a grammatical proposition to be true (no matter whether analytic, like 'Vixens are foxes', or non-analytic, like 'Red is darker than pink') just is for the proposition to express a constitutive rule for the use of the constituent terms. A false empirical proposition is intelligible – it describes a possible state of affairs that does not actually obtain. What we *call* a 'false' grammatical proposition (e.g. that pink is darker than red) does not describe a possibility that does not happen to obtain. It does not describe anything. Nor does it state a false rule for the use of its constituent terms, since rules are not true or false. Indeed, it conjoins words in a manner inimical to the rules for their use. So one might say that it is a peculiar form of nonsense. Of course, rules for the use of words are not immune to revision. But if we revise them, then the words the use of which they determine will have a different meaning – that is, be used in a different way.

In the sequel, I shall not rely on any analytic/synthetic distinction. But I shall constantly invoke the distinction between grammatical or conceptual propositions and empirical ones, even though there are uses of sentences on an occasion, the status of which is unclear; there are sentences the status of which has changed with time ('Acids turn litmus paper red' was once used to define what an acid is, but is no longer so used); and there are sentences that may be used on one occasion to express a grammatical proposition and on another to express a quite different kind of proposition (Doris Day's song 'Que sera, sera' was not a celebration of a theorem of tense-logic). For the distinction between the grammatical and the non-grammatical (including the empirical) is not a distinction between type-sentences, but between uses of sentences.

7. The Platonic and Aristotelian traditions in philosophical anthropology

It is fruitful to view philosophical reflection on human nature as following one or the other of two great paradigms: Platonic and

Aristotelian. The Platonic paradigm is dualist, although its post-Cartesian forms are prone to degenerate into one or the other of its duals (e.g. idealism, on the one hand, and behaviourism or physicalism, on the other). The Aristotelian paradigm is predominantly (non-degenerate) monist.

Dualism has roots in religious doctrine, in the human fear of death and irrational craving for immortality, and in the character of misunderstood experiences, such as dreams or delusions (e.g. of ghosts, of 'out-of-the-body' experiences), on the one hand, and in features of the grammar of personal pronouns, logico-grammatical asymmetries between first- and third-person psychological utterances, and grammatical and idiomatic peculiarities of discourse about mind, soul and body, on the other. Platonic dualism takes a human being to be a creature composed of body and soul. The soul is conceived to have existed prior to birth and embodiment, and to survive the death of the body. The identity of a Socrates turns on the identity of his soul, and the survival of Socrates despite the death of his body is the survival of his soul.[11]

The Aristotelian tradition, as one might expect of its originator, is inspired primarily by biological reflection. The Aristotelian concept of the *psuchē* (a term commonly translated, somewhat misleadingly, as 'soul') is a biological concept, not a psychological, let alone a theological or ethical, one. The *psuchē* is conceived to be the source of the distinctive activities of a living thing – the 'principle' of life that makes it the kind of being that it is. The soul, as Aristotle conceived it, is the set of potentialities the exercise of which is characteristic of the organism. Consequently, it is not only human beings that have

---

[11] . . . either this or something very like it is a true account of our souls and their future habitations – since we have clear evidence that the soul is immortal – this, I think is both a reasonable contention and a belief worth risking, for the risk is a noble one. . . .

We shall try our best to do as you say, said Crito. But how shall we bury you?

Any way you like, replied Socrates, that is, if you can catch me and I don't slip through your fingers.

He laughed gently as he spoke, and turning to us went on, I can't persuade Crito that I am this Socrates here who is talking to you now and marshalling all the arguments. He thinks I am the one whom he will see presently lying dead, and he asks how he is to bury me! . . . you must assure him that when I am dead I shall not stay but depart and be gone. . . . you must keep up your spirits and say that it is only my body that you are burying, and you can bury it as you please, in whatever way you think proper. (*Phaedo* 114d'–116a)

a *psuchē*, but all living creatures, including plants. What is distinctive about the human soul is that it incorporates not only the vegetative powers of growth, nutrition and reproduction, and the sensitive powers of perception, desire and motion, but also the uniquely human rational faculties of will and intellect. The soul is not an entity attached to the body, but is characterized, in Aristotelian jargon, as the 'form' of the living body. The soul stands to the body of a human being roughly as the power of sight stands to the eye. The powers of a thing cannot survive the death of the thing itself. However, Aristotle equivocated, sometimes arguing that the rational soul, in particular the capacity to reflect on necessary truths (later denominated 'the agent intellect'), is itself immortal. This, not obviously coherent idea, was to be the handle that Aquinas seized in order to accommodate Aristotelian philosophy to Christian doctrine.

The Platonist conception of human beings as combinations of body and soul, conceived as two separable entities, was transmuted and transmitted by Plotinus, and synthesized with Christian doctrine by St Augustine. Augustine's conception was to inform the philosophy of the most influential of thinkers of the modern era – Descartes. However, a major and long-lasting period of Aristotelian dominance intervened in the High Middle Ages, as a result of the rediscovery and translation of the bulk of Aristotle's surviving works in the twelfth and thirteenth centuries and of Aquinas's great synthesis of Christian and Aristotelian thought. Aristotelian dominance waned with the rise of Renaissance Neoplatonism consequent upon the rediscovery and translation of the bulk of the surviving Platonic dialogues. It was destroyed by the rise of modern science in the seventeenth century, which disproved a host of Aristotelian empirical hypotheses and replaced a teleological and normative conception of nature with a causal, mechanistic one.

Descartes's philosophy marks a dramatic break in Western thought. On the one hand, he, like Bacon, was the ideological spokesman for the principles of the scientific revolution. The natural sciences had undergone a qualitative change through the mathematicization of physics and its extension from the sublunary sphere to the solar system (including the comets) as a whole, and through its espousal of meticulous observation, experiment and testing of hypotheses by means of newly invented instruments. Cartesian metaphysics sharply divided the study of nature from the study of human thought and consciousness. In opposition to the Aristotelian tradition, Descartes advocated the ontological, nomological and methodological unity of all the natural sciences. *All* natural phenomena (other than human thought and action) were to be explained in terms of the mechanical laws of matter in motion. Hence, contrary to Aristotelian and scholastic thought, the operations of what had been conceived to be the vegetative and sensitive souls were held to be explicable in wholly mechanical terms and required no separate principles for their explanation. While Aristotle thought above all as a biologist (and was, indeed, the greatest biologist until Darwin[12]), Descartes thought as a physicist. It has been a major misfortune for philosophy in the modern era that no great philosopher was a biologist.

Descartes shaped the modern conception of the mind. While the Aristotelian tradition conceived of the human mind primarily in terms of the intellect and the will (all that pertains to the 'rational soul', which is distinctive of mankind), Descartes characterized the mind in terms of thought. But he redefined *thought* to incorporate 'everything which we are aware of as happening within us, insofar as we have awareness of it'.[13] To have a mind, according to Descartes, is to have experience and to be aware of oneself as having experience. So the mind is defined in terms of *consciousness*, narrowly conceived as the awareness of 'thoughts' or experiences 'within us'. So he denied that non-human animals are conscious or have experiences at all, taking them to be mere biological mechanisms. To have a mind, according to Descartes, is to feel sensations as if in the body, to seem to perceive, to feel emotions, to have mental images, desires and likings, as well as to exercise the powers of rational thought and will. This conception of the mind and of the mental still bedevils contemporary thought.

With modifications, Descartes reinstated the Augustinian conception of the mind. So he continued the Platonic tradition. A human being, he argued, is not a unitary substance – an *ens per se*, as the scholastics had held[14] – but a composite entity consisting of mind and body. The soul, contrary to the Aristotelian conception, is not the principle of life in its various forms, but a separate substance – a *res cogitans*. Although united with the body, it is separable from it. The mind and the body interact causally. Impact of corpuscles upon

---

[12] Ernst Mayr, *The Growth of Biological Thought* (The Belknap Press, Cambridge, Mass., 1982), p. 87.

[13] Descartes, *Principles of Philosophy*, I, 9.

[14] Aquinas, in his *Commentary on St Paul's First Letter to the Corinthians*, remarked: 'My soul – that's not what I am (*Anima mea non est ego*).' Hence the orthodox Catholic requirement of the resurrection of the body.

the body generates sensation (feeling sensations as if they were in the body) and perception (seeming to perceive) in the mind, and the mind causes the body to move by the exercise of the will. Mind and body are closely 'intermingled'. For one is not 'in one's body' as a sailor on a ship – one *feels* the impact of the world upon one's body in the form of sensations and apparent perceptions; one does not have to examine one's body as the sailor has to examine his ship to find out how it is affected.[15] The human person, the *ego*, is to be identified with the *res cogitans*. The mind has no parts, and since destruction of an entity is decomposition into component parts, the mind – the person – is immortal.

Cartesian dualism provided the framework of thought about the nature of mankind for the modern era, not merely in the sense that the dominant trend was some form or other of dualism (which is true as far as both popular and scientific thought was concerned until the middle of the twentieth century), but in the much deeper sense that it set the categories in terms of which reflection took place.

Locke, agnostic about man's being composed of two distinct substances, demanded only a duality of a body, on the one hand, and a set of psychological properties (ideas) annexed to it, on the other. Identity of a person, he thought, required only psychological unity and continuity annexed to some substance or other (and not necessarily the same substance throughout the lifetime of the same person). Berkeley abandoned the notion of material substance, but retained the idea of a spiritual substance. Hume jettisoned the concept of substance altogether, denied the intelligibility of material things, and held a human person to be no more than a mere bundle of impressions and ideas bound together by causal and mnemonic relations. This bizarre idealist conception was a *reductio ad absurdum* of the Cartesian world picture, but it displayed quite amazing lasting power, surviving into the middle of the twentieth century. The materialist trend, exemplified by Hobbes, La Mettrie, D'Holbach and Diderot, which involved jettisoning the other side of the Cartesian duality, was very much a minority movement until the twentieth century. Its heirs were behaviourism and various forms of physicalism.

Twentieth-century behaviourism too was an attempt to jettison the immaterial substance while retaining the material one of the Cartesian duality. *Ontological behaviourism*, as espoused by Watson, was a

---

[15] Ironically, the simile is Aristotle's, *De Anima* 413ᵃ9, in what is apparently an allusion to a lost Platonic analogy.

dogmatic assimilation of the mental to the status of mythical entities
or misguidedly postulated entities (such as witches). Its crudity was
noteworthy, and it infected empirical psychologists with a deleterious methodological behaviourism until the equally misconceived,
though slightly less crude, cognitivist revolution of the 1960s. *Logical
behaviourism* was a programme, espoused by a few philosophers (e.g.
Carnap in the early 1930s[16]), for the *logical* reduction of all psychological attributes to behavioural attributes and dispositions to behave.
It correctly stressed that certain psychological concepts (e.g. knowing,
believing, understanding) had often been misconstrued as signifying
mental states, acts or activities. It rightly insisted upon *a* conceptual
nexus between psychological attributes and behaviour. But the crude
reductionism was misconceived, and the character of the conceptual
nexus with behaviour was misunderstood.

One reaction to the failure of the behaviourist programme was to
identify the mental with states and activities of the brain. This took
various physicalist forms. Central state materialism held types of mental state to be identical with types of brain state. Anomalous monism
held 'tokens' of mental states to be identical with 'token' brain states.
Advances in cognitive neuroscience led scientists to jettison the Cartesianism of their teachers (such as Sherrington and some of his pupils),
and to ascribe psychological attributes to the brain in order to explain
how human beings exercise their cognitive and perceptual faculties.
It was unfortunate that the cognitivist revolution in psychology in the
1960s opted for a computationalist, modular conception of the mental,
which identified perceptual and intellectual powers with information
processing familiar from the latest technology of the era. This in turn
encouraged the idea that it is the brain that processes information,
hypothesizes, computes and so forth, and that human perception is

[16] But *not*, despite a mythology fostered in the USA, Gilbert Ryle, who wrote, 'we
employ for saying things about the mental life of people many active verbs which
do signify acts of mind . . . correctly list[ing] *calculating*, *pondering*, and *recalling to
mind* as mental acts or processes'. What Ryle objected to was adding to the list such
verbs as *believing*, *knowing*, *aspiring*, and *detesting* (see 'Phenomenology versus "The
Concept of Mind" ', repr. in his *Collected Papers*, vol. 1 (Hutchinson, London, 1971),
p. 189.
   It has been argued by S. Soames (*Philosophical Quarterly* 56 (2006), p. 430) that
'Ryle was clearly a logical behaviourist. Since he was neither a dualist nor an elim-
inativist, and he rejected the view that mental states are brain states, his views left
nothing else for [mental attributes] to be but behavioural dispositions.' This is like
arguing that if someone is neither a Republican nor a Democrat, then he must be a
Communist.

to be explained in terms of the computations and hypotheses constructed by the brain. These developments in cognitive science led to the emergence of various forms of functionalism in philosophy of mind (see fig. 1.3).

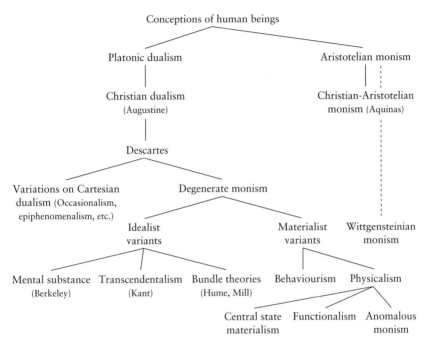

Figure 1.3. *A rough schema of conceptions of human beings and their constitution*

What is most noteworthy about the evolving tale is the extent to which it took place within the shadow of Descartes. For, by and large, responses to Descartes involved rejecting one or the other side of the Cartesian duality of mental substance and material bodies and the attempted reduction of one or the other type of property that Descartes had allocated to the mind or the body. What is most important about current neo-Cartesian views, espoused by many cognitive neuroscientists and self-styled cognitive scientists, as well as by many philosophers, all of whom conceive of themselves as adamantly anti-Cartesian, is the extent to which the Cartesian conception of the relationship between the inner and behaviour remained intact despite abandonment of the Cartesian conception of the mind. For what was characteristically done was to ascribe cognitive and perceptual attributes to the brain, in the course of trying to explain the generic cognitive and perceptual activities and achievements of human beings.

The deepest challenge to the dominance of the Cartesian tradition and its degenerate offshoots came in the mid-twentieth century from Wittgenstein's philosophical psychology.[17] For Wittgenstein did not merely reject one or another of the Cartesian principles and dichotomies. He wiped the board clean of Cartesian doctrines. In an important sense, he unwittingly revived (breathed fresh life into) the Aristotelian tradition. Like Aristotle, he held that such attributes as consciousness, perception, cognition and volition are attributes of the living animal, not of its material parts, such as the brain, let alone of its alleged immaterial parts, such as the mind. He repudiated the Cartesian *res cogitans*, but also denied that the mind is just an aspect of the body ('I'm not that hard up for categories', he remarked drily[18]).

This Gigantomachia will doubtless continue, as each generation struggles to find its way through the jungles of metaphysical speculation, and religious and scientific myth-making about human nature. The following chapters do not aim to contribute a new pathway, but to clear old pathways from overgrowth and to uproot misleading signposts misguidedly placed by recent travellers.

---

[17] But also, less perspicuously and systematically, Heidegger in *Being and Time*.

[18] Wittgenstein, *Remarks on the Philosophy of Psychology*, vol. 2 (Blackwell, Oxford, 1980), §690. He was here objecting specifically to Nietzsche's remark to this effect in *Thus Spake Zarathustra*, Pt 1, chap. 4.

2

Substance

1. Substances: things

Human beings are animate substances – sentient, space-occupying, spatio-temporal continuants of a certain animal kind. They possess a distinctive array of powers, some characteristic of animal kind in general, others unique to rational natures. Their powers of action include a wide range of efficient causal powers to bring about or prevent change by acting on objects in their environment, as well as powers to make other people do things by affording them compelling (obliging) reasons. The categorial concepts of *substance, causation, power* and *agency* provide a large part of the general framework for our thought about the world and about ourselves. For substance concepts, concepts pertaining to the active and passive powers of inanimate and animate agents, and causal concepts provide a large part of the intricately woven network that constitutes our conceptual scheme. The first task is to clarify this general framework. This chapter is concerned with elucidating the concept or, more accurately, the concepts of substance, and extirpating their degenerate offshoots. (There is nothing novel about the latter project, but the task of weeding in the gardens of philosophy never ends.)

We conceive of the natural world as populated by relatively persistent material things of many different kinds. These are spatio-temporal continuants consisting of matter, occupying space, excluding other things of the same kind from the space they occupy, and standing in spatio-temporal relations to each other. They come into existence, exist for a time, and then pass away. We locate them relative to landmarks and to other material things in the landscape

which they, and we, inhabit. We characterize them as things of a
certain kind, and identify and re-identify them accordingly (fig. 2.1).
The expressions we typically use to do so are, in the technical terminology derived from Aristotle, names of *substances*.[1] To be sure,
Aristotle was hunting a different quarry from ours. What we are
concerned with is isolating a category of nouns and noun phrases
that play an important and distinctive role in our conceptual scheme
– not with identifying the ultimate structure and constituents of
reality, as was Aristotle. But precisely because Aristotle typically began
his reflections with meticulous observations on 'what is said', his
ideas shed valuable light on *our* present concerns, and provide a convenient point of departure for my purposes.

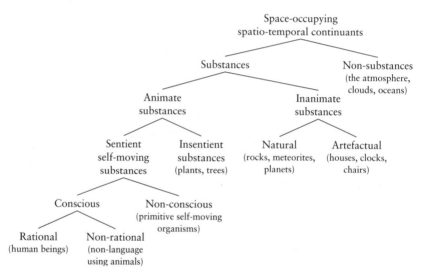

Figure 2.1. *Categories of space-occupants*

The term 'substance' has two distinct, but importantly linked, meanings. In the Aristotelian sense, a substance (more accurately, 'a primary
substance') is a concrete individual thing of a given kind, such as a
particular human being (Socrates), a given tree (Gautama's Bo-tree)
or a certain gemstone (the Kohinoor). The general kind (the 'secondary

[1] Aristotle's most accessible discussion of substance is in the *Categories*, chs 1–5.
His discussion in the *Metaphysics* is much more problematic, and his hylomorphism
questionable. A major contributor to modern discussion of this difficult topic is David
Wiggins: see e.g. his *Sameness and Substance Renewed* (Cambridge University Press,
Cambridge, 2001). I am much indebted to his writings on this theme.

substance' in Aristotle's terminology) to which the individual substance belongs is specified by a substance name ('human being', 'pipal tree' (*ficus religiosa*), 'diamond'). Individual substances are the basic objects of reference and subjects of predication in our conceptual scheme. They *are* things of one kind or another (specified by a substance name, as when we say that Socrates *is a man*). They are *qualified* by numerous properties, specified by non-substantial predicates. So we may say, for example, that Socrates *is in the agora, is snub-nosed,* or *is a philosopher.* But Socrates cannot be said *to qualify* anything (as opposed to *being like Socrates,* which is a relational property that some rare people may have). Nor can the proper name 'Socrates' be said *to be true of* anything (as opposed to the identifying phrase 'is Socrates', which is true of the teacher of Plato and tells us *who he is*), and the proper name does not signify a quality of anything.

Characterizing an individual as a thing of a given kind by using such a (secondary) substance name answers the question of *what the thing is.* Grasp of the substance name implies knowledge of what *being a such-and-such* consists in, in so far as that is logically (or, in the extended sense of the term, grammatically) determined. The substance name provides a covering concept for statements of identity concerning individual things of the relevant kind (Tully is the same *man* as Cicero, Hesperus the same *planet* as Phosphorus, Zeus the same *god* as Jupiter). To have an adequate grasp of what a thing is – that is, that it is such-and-such a substance, is to know (in more or less detail) how to distinguish one such thing from substances of other kinds. It is typically, but by no means uniformly, to know how to count such things – and so to differentiate one such thing from others of the same kind. It is also commonly to know, sometimes as a result of a scientific discovery that has led to a conceptual change, what kinds of change or metamorphosis any individual of the kind in question can undergo compatible with its continued existence and persistent identity (e.g. that maggots turn into flies). How much of such information is to be deemed constitutive of the meaning of the substance term is often indeterminate.

Substances lend themselves to hierarchical classification. Human beings are a kind of anthropoid ape, anthropoid apes a kind of mammal, mammals, in turn, being a kind of vertebrate. If a species name (such as 'human being') applies to an individual substance, and a generic name applies to the species (as 'animal' applies to human beings), the generic name also applies to the individual (primary) substance. Generic names, no less than their subordinate species names, signify kinds of substance. But the species name is more specific and hence more informative than the generic one. The specific differentia signified by the species name characterize the nature of members of the species.

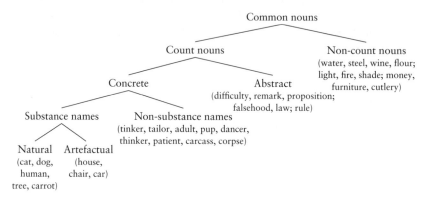

Figure 2.2. *Varieties of count nouns*

Substance names are a subclass of concrete (as opposed to abstract) count nouns (see fig. 2.2). For we must distinguish between 'tinker', 'tailor', 'soldier', 'sailor', which are concrete count nouns but not substance names, and concrete count nouns that are substance names, such as 'man', 'dog', 'cabbage'. One difference is that a non-substantial count noun may cease to apply to an individual thing, without the thing ceasing to exist, whereas a substance name cannot. So, for example, NN can cease to be a tinker or a tailor, yet continue to exist and be the very same human being; but he cannot cease to be a human being and continue to exist. Another is that non-substantial count nouns that apply to substances are themselves explained in terms of the substance name. So, a tinker is *a man, who repairs pots and pans*; a tailor is *a man, who makes clothes*; neither noun signifying a species of man as 'man' (a substance name) signifies a species of animal. Nouns such as 'tinker', 'tailor', 'soldier', 'sailor' attribute to a substance – a human being – the property of engaging in, or being qualified to engage in, a certain activity. Some non-substantial count nouns that apply to substances are explicitly or implicitly relational – for example, 'ancestor (or, descendant) of X', 'mother of Y', 'a parent', 'a grandfather'; but substance names are not, in any such sense, relational. Concrete count nouns such as 'man', 'horse' or 'tree' have both singular and plural forms, take number words as adjectives, and their plural forms take the quantifiers 'many', '(a) few', 'several', as well as phrasal quantifiers such as 'a great number of' and 'a large number of' (see table 2.1 on page 36).

Artefacts (if we admit them among substances, as I shall urge we should) are similarly classifiable. A *chaise longue* is a kind of settee, a settee a piece of furniture made for sitting or reclining on, pieces of furniture are a kind of artefact.

Scientific classification aims to be systematic, guided by clearly statable and applicable principles of classification. These, wherever possible, aim to ensure exclusion of cross-classification, and to determine categories that are fruitful for explanatory purposes and scientific generalization. Non-scientific classification is typically less systematic, guided by a multitude of different purposes, often non-explanatory ones, characteristic of human societies. Even when the purposes are explanatory, the forms of explanation may not be those of the sciences, but pertinent to one form or another of human practice (cuisine, agriculture, manufacturing, architecture, etc.) or to social concerns and interests (including those of morality, criminology and law). These are no less substance-invoking than the explanatory vocabulary of the sciences.

With respect to any substance, we can typically distinguish between properties that are essential for the thing to be the kind of thing it is and properties that are inessential (the *accidents*), even though we may be forced to recognize a degree of indeterminacy in the essential properties and hence borderline cases of being a such-and-such. A cat or a dog must be warm-blooded (or, more generally, mammalian) – this is an essential property. The animal may be large or small of its kind, black or white, agile or clumsy – these are accidental properties. A tree must be a perennial, and have a woody trunk; it may be deciduous or evergreen, have smooth or rough bark. But the boundaries between what to count as a tree and what to count as a shrub or bush are not, and need not be, clearly determined. How high must a mature specimen be? Must it have branches? No decision is normally necessary. To be sure, the concept of a tree is not part of botanical taxonomy. But it would be mistaken to suppose that the substance names of scientific taxonomies are *always* sharply defined. Given the evolution of species, it is evident that the boundary lines determining one species and differentiating it from an emerging species are not always sharp, and borderline cases are commonly to be found. I shall revert to this point below.

Since the accidents of a substance can vary without the substance ceasing to exist, individual substances, as Aristotle noted, may admit of contrary accidents at different times. So, for example, a substance the identity of which does not require it to have a given colour, may have one colour now and another later, and persist through such change. A living substance may have such-and-such a size and weight now and a different size and weight later. But living substances persist throughout such accidental changes.

2. Substances: stuffs

In a different, but ordinary and familiar, sense of the term 'substance', a substance is one kind or another of material stuff. It is in this sense that we speak of sticky substances and of chemical substances, and say that iron and steel, sand and water, bread and butter, are different kinds of substances. Just as substances, understood as kinds of things, can be classified into genus and species, so too can substances, understood as kinds of stuffs or materials. Iron, brass and copper are species of metal; mutton, venison and beef are kinds of meat; cotton, wool and nylon are types of fabric.

Substances in the sense of stuffs are named by a subclass of concrete *non-count nouns* (see fig. 2.3). For we must distinguish between concrete non-count nouns that are names of kinds of stuff and those that are not. The latter class includes such mass nouns as 'light', 'sunshine', 'shade', 'fire', on the one hand, as well as pseudo-mass nouns such as 'furniture', 'money' (coins or notes), 'cutlery', 'clothing', on the other.[2]

Concrete mass nouns of the class that concerns us, such as 'wine', 'metal' or 'glass', do not have a genuine plural form save when used generically to refer to general types (as in 'the wines of France' or 'the metals of the earth'). They take the quantifiers 'much' and 'a little', and phrasal quantifiers such as 'a great deal of' and 'a large (or small) quantity of'. They can be transformed into singular referring expressions by partitives that confer countability, such as 'nugget of', 'pool of', 'grain of' prefixed by an article or indexical, to yield 'the

---

[2] 'Pseudo-mass nouns' because, by contrast with mass nouns signifying stuffs, it is not the case that every part of a piece of furniture (money, cutlery, clothing) down to some limiting level of dissectivity is a piece of furniture (although it may be a piece (i.e. a fragment) of a piece of furniture (e.g. of a chair)); nor is it the case that a piece of furniture consists of furniture. Finally, dividing a piece of furniture into arbitrary parts does not yield quantities of furniture.

nugget of', 'that pool of', 'this grain of' that form particular-designating expressions when affixed to them. An alternative transformation is by means of quantity-designating partitives, such as 'litre of' or 'pound of', which lend themselves to a different kind of particular reference, as in 'the litre of milk in the bottle', 'the pound of butter in the fridge'. Specific quantity reference here allows numerical quantification, but not countability. 'Five litres of petrol', unlike 'five nuggets of gold' or 'five puddles of water', does not specify a number of things, but a quantity of (liquid) stuff (see table 2.1).

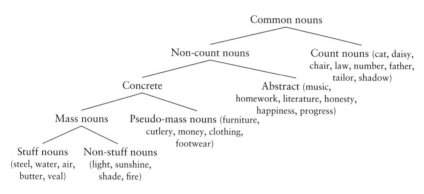

Figure 2.3. *Varieties of non-count nouns*

What marks out the category of substance (stuff) nouns less formally than adjectives of quantity, and differentiates them from pseudo-mass nouns like 'furniture', 'money' or 'cutlery', are three further characteristics that were intimated above.

First, these nouns signify kinds of matter of which space-occupying things consist. Material things, whether they be substances, partitions of stuff (such as chunks, nuggets, lumps or grains), or specific quantities of stuff (such as pints, pounds, litres), consist of stuff (at any rate down to the level of atoms, which consist of particles but not of stuff).

Secondly, every arbitrary division of a partition or specific quantity of a substance (stuff) yields a further partition of that stuff down to the level of *non-dissectivity*. So, for example, any division of a chunk of gold will yield further partitions – nuggets, grains, shavings – of gold down to the atomic level (at which point dissectivity ceases, since atoms of gold do not consist of gold). Similarly, every pool, puddle or glass of water can be further divided into quantities of water, down

	Count nouns		Non-count nouns
	singular	*plural*	
1. The possessive (my, our), whose, which, what; some (stressed), any, no	✓	✓	✓
2. Zero article, some (unstressed), any (unstressed), enough	✗	✓	✓
3. This, that	✓	✗	✓
4. These, those	✗	✓	✗
5. A(n), every, each, either, neither	✓	✗	✗
6. Much	✗	✗	✓
7. One	✓	✗	✗
8. Cardinals greater than one	✗	✓	✗
9. Ordinals	✓	✓	✗
10. Many, (a) few, several	✗	✓	✗
11. Much, (a) little	✗	✗	✓
12. Enough	✗	✓	✓
13. Plenty of, lots of, a lot of	✗	✓	✓
14. A great (good) deal of, a large (small) amount of	✗	✗	✓
15. A great (large, good) number of	✗	✓	✗

Table 2.1 *Count nouns compared with non-count nouns*

to the molecular level. Blood, unlike water, ceases to divide into further quantities of blood at the molar level, since lymphatic fluids, red and white blood corpuscles, are not themselves blood.

Thirdly, the specific quantity of stuff of which a given partition consists (the water of which the glass of water consists), as well as the specific quantity of stuff of which a given object is made (the gold of which a gold ring is made) can retain its identity *qua* specific quantity despite change of form specified by the partitive (e.g. 'glass of') or destruction of the object made of the stuff (e.g. the melting down of the gold ring). So, the puddle of water on the floor may be the very same water as was previously in the glass, and the gold of which the brooch is made may be the very same gold as that of which the ring was made. Quantities of stuff are, in respect of their identity, *form-indifferent* (the gold that was a ring is now a brooch), *fusible* (as when we pour two glasses of water into the same jug, which then contains the very same quantities of water, although no longer separable or separately identifiable) and *dispersible* (as when we scatter ashes to the wind, or pour a pint of water into the sea).

Partitions and specific quantities of stuffs, like things, may undergo *qualitative* (or *accidental*) change and yet remain the same. Just as a plant may turn from green to yellow or an animal change from being fat to being thin, so too *this* quantity of cold water may be heated and change from being cold to being hot, and *this* slice of raw meat may be cooked. Qualitative change stands in contrast to *substantial* change. Substantial change involves the ceasing to be of the substance in question – which happens both to individual substances and to partitions and quantities of stuff. When an oak is chopped down and cut into logs, it undergoes substantial change, for the oak tree no longer exists. Similarly, when wine turns into vinegar, it undergoes substantial change, for the wine no longer exists. In the case of the destruction of things – for example, the oak tree – the stuff of which it consisted (the constitutive wood) may and often does continue to exist. But in the case of the transformation of stuffs, as in the case of the wine turning into vinegar, it is the stuff itself that undergoes essential change.[3]

The logico-grammatical features of substance (stuff) nouns will be important when we come to disprove the claim that a person stands to his body in a relation akin to the relation between a substance (thing) and the stuff of which it consists; that is, that a person is distinct from, but is constituted of, his body (see chapter 9).

3. Substance-referring expressions

We classify individual things in indefinitely many ways. For some purposes, adjectival classification is useful: for example, classifying things by colour, shape, size or weight. For other purposes, nominal classification is what is needed. As already noted, not all our classificatory nominals are substance names. A human being may be a child or an adult, a parent, a doctor, an Englishman, a stamp collector and so forth. The concept of a human being is a substance concept, while that

---

[3] For more extensive treatment, see P. M. S. Hacker, 'Substance: The Constitution of Reality', *Midwest Studies in Philosophy*, (1979), pp. 239–61.

of a child is not – it signifies a human being *at a certain phase* (viz. childhood) in the natural development of human beings. Similar phased substance concepts are 'youth', 'kitten', 'sapling', as well as metamorphic phased concepts such as 'pupa', 'tadpole', 'maggot' – concepts that signify a thing of a given kind at a phase through which every thing of that kind must pass if it survives for long enough. A human being may cease to be a child, while continuing to exist, and whereas the adult Sir Richard Roe is not the same boy as little Dick Roe, since he is not a boy, he *was* once that very boy and *is* the very same human being as him. 'Parent' and 'doctor' are not substance concepts, since a human being can become a parent without loss of identity, and cease to be a doctor without ceasing to exist. But, avatars and gods of mythology and religion apart, nothing that is not a human being can change into one, and, mythology, fairy tales and surrealist fiction apart, a human being cannot cease to be a human being (change into a swine or a frog) and continue to exist.[4] 'Englishman', 'Frenchman', or 'German' are terms by which we may classify human beings, but are not substance concepts, since they merely signify the location of birth (or country of citizenship) of a human being. We might, indeed, say that they signify a property of a substance: namely, the property of having been born in a certain country or of being a citizen of a certain country. Similarly, 'student', 'doctor' or 'balletomane' are not substance concepts. The role of such terms when they occur predicatively, we might say, is to indicate what a person does, or is qualified to do, or likes doing, etc.

Substance terms do, of course, also occur predicatively – obviously so when we characterize a 'primary substance', such as Socrates, as being a 'secondary substance', namely, a human being. Whether that warrants conceiving of *being a human being* as a *property* depends upon how one chooses to mould the vague category of *property*. There is little to be gained, and much to be lost, from failing to segregate predicates in the category of substance from other kinds of predicates that we naturally conceive of as used, directly or indirectly, to ascribe properties to things. Using a sentence in which a proper name occurs predicatively (as in 'The man sitting on the sofa is John Smith') does not attribute to a substance the 'property' of being John Smith, but says *who* that man is. Similarly, to use a sentence in which a

---

[4] Human beings do not change into frogs. But if a human being were to change into a frog, this would be a substantial change. There is no substance here that is first a human being and then a frog.

substance noun occurs predicatively (as in 'Socrates is a man') is not to attribute to Socrates the 'property' of being a man, but to say *what* Socrates is (what *kind of thing* he is).[5] By contrast, to say that Socrates is a philosopher is to say what he does; to say that he is snub-nosed is to say what he looks like; to say that he is in the agora is to say where he is; and so forth.

There are, of course, many things and kinds of thing that are to be found in the world around us to which we refer by means of singular referring expressions, and by reference to which we may explain various phenomena that call out for explanation, that are not substances. We refer to rainbows, reflections and shadows, to sounds and smells, to holes, gaps, knots and lumps, to waves, currents, lakes and oceans, to valleys, passes, gulfs and deltas, to the atmosphere and stratosphere. We also refer to heaps and bundles, to groups and teams, to armies and to peoples; and, of course, to the indefinite variety of events, states and processes. These are clearly *not* substances, although they are objects of singular reference typically with a rough spatio-temporal location.

Other things (or better, concepts of other things) are more difficult to classify: Is a perennial river a substance? Perhaps not. Is an ephemeral river (that flows once every three years)? Surely not. What of a mountain? A hill? A hillock? Or a bump? If a bump is merely a disturbance on the surface of a solid, then a mountain is nothing more than a large bump. If the Kohinoor is a substance, then so too are the stones on the garden path, and if stones, why not lumps of ice, and if lumps of ice, then why not pools of water? – But it would be fruitless to let the concept of substance, the philosophers's term of art, drift thus.

Substance (thing) names are count nouns, but it is not uniformly the case that clear criteria for counting individuals are implicit in the meaning of any given substance name. Given the various forms of vegetative, asexual reproduction, it is obvious that there can be no clear and unequivocal way of distinguishing one such plant of a given kind from another. There is surely no answer to the question of how many plants there are on one's lawn, even if one's lawn is nothing but grass; nor can there typically be any answer to the question 'How

[5] For a highly illuminating discussion of this and related matters, as well as a profound criticism of the Frege–Russell assimilation of common nouns to predicates, see Hanoch Ben-Yami, *Logic and Natural Language: On Plural Reference and its Semantic and Logical Significance* (Ashgate, Aldershot, 2004).

many daisies (not flowers, but plants) are there on the daisy lawn?'
It is unclear how to count the number of individual trees in a copse
grown from root suckers, and although it is easy to count the number
of daffodils (flowers, not plants) in a given clump in the spring, it is
not clear how to answer the question of how many plants there are
in the clump.

The concept of substance (thing) is one of the *most* general categorial concepts, and like other such concepts it is exceedingly vague and
flexible. Our general categorial concepts are not akin to variables in
a formal calculus taking a sharply defined range of values as their
values. On the contrary, they tend to be elastic, not rigid, frayed at the
edges, not sharply circumscribed. They have their uses, to be sure, but
one should not expect greater precision from them than they are capable of delivering – and that is not very great. Given the multiplicity
of needs in response to which our rich and refined languages have
evolved, and given that languages are dynamic, it should be altogether
unsurprising that the boundaries between different classes of word
should be blurred, that the categories of types of expression are often
not sharply circumscribed.

To say that an S is a substance informs us of the logical character
of the concept of an S rather than telling us further distinguishing
material features of S-s. Cabbages and cauliflowers, cats and dogs,
are kinds of things, just as wine and water, iron and steel, are kinds
of stuffs. But the concept of a substance (thing) is not the concept
of yet another kind of thing, and the concept of a substance (stuff)
is not the concept of yet another kind of stuff. It was ill-advised of
Descartes to suggest that matter is a kind of substance, and at best
confusing to suggest that mind is another. *Matter* is simply the formal *summum genus* of stuffs. The totality of matter is not, in any
useful sense, a kind of substance at all, and the assimilation of matter
to space (the denial of the intelligibility of a vacuum) was a blunder.
'Mind', to be sure, does not signify a kind of stuff (nor indeed did
Descartes think it did) – it is a count noun, not a mass noun. So,
unlike 'matter', it admits plurality. Descartes claimed that matter, on
the one hand, and minds, on the other, are sempiternalia. The totality
of space-matter, given the principle of conservation, and individual
minds, given their absolute simplicity, causally depend for their
existence on nothing other than the concurrence of God. Matter is
indestructible, and minds are immortal. But irrespective of whether
the principle of conservation of matter is true and of whether minds

Cartesian matter	Matter	Cartesian minds	Minds[a]
essentially extended	essentially space-occupying	essentially thinking (conscious)	essentially the possession and exercise of rational powers by living beings
not distinguished from space	distinct from space	a non-spatial substance	not substances
infinitely divisible	not infinitely divisible	indivisible	neither divisible nor indivisible
a totality (the plenum), not a plurality	stuffs of multiple kinds consisting of particles	plurality; unspecified criteria of identity	plurality; identity-dependent on the identity of the animal
indestructible (principle of conservation of matter)	destructible through substantial change or transformation into energy	indestructible because indivisible	destructible with the destruction of the animal

[a] See further, ch. 8.

Table 2.2 *Cartesian and non-Cartesian matter and minds*

are simple, characterizing mind and matter as two kinds (the only two kinds) of *substance* is at best misleading. For, first, 'mind' and 'matter' do not signify two species of a common genus – the one allegedly signifies individual things of a certain kind, the other allegedly signifies a totality. So even in Cartesian terms they are surely *categorially* distinct even if they have the common property of being sempiternalia. Secondly, as we shall see (ch. 8), 'mind', though a count noun, does not signify a kind of thing, let alone a substance, in *any* sense of the term (see table 2.2).

In trying to delineate the boundaries of the categorial terms of 'substance' (thing) and 'substance' (stuff), we are not endeavouring to classify everything there is (as if the philosopher were a 'metaphysicist'). Our purposes are as different from Descartes's as they are from Aristotle's. We aim to differentiate between kinds of concepts or kinds of expressions. We are trying to attain a synoptic view of our conceptual scheme, of the ways in which we think and speak about objects of our experience and of ourselves as subjects of experience – not to steal a march on natural science. Of course, this does not mean that we are not *also* trying to attain a synoptic view of the formal features of substances and constitutive stuffs of which the world consists.

4. Conceptual connections between things and stuffs

The two senses of the term 'substance' – that is, substance as a persistent thing of a certain sort and substance as stuff of a certain kind – are systematically related. For a concrete individual thing of a given kind is a space-occupying, spatio-temporal continuant, and is made of, constituted of, matter of some kind: that is, a quantity of one sort or another of substance (stuff) or substances (stuffs).

It is important not to conflate the relationship between a thing and its constitutive stuff with the relationship between the thing and its parts. The stuff of which a thing is made is neither larger nor smaller nor the same size as the thing itself, although it weighs the same. The parts of a thing are smaller than the whole of which they are parts. If a thing is wholly made of such-and-such stuff, then all the parts of the thing consist of that stuff. But if a thing is made of such-and-such parts, it does not follow that its parts are made of such-and-such parts. One may destroy the thing and its parts without destroying the stuff of which it is made, but one cannot destroy the stuff of which a thing is made without destroying the thing itself.

It is not necessary for the continued identity of a substance (thing) that it consist of the same specific quantity of stuff throughout the whole of its existence. This is most obvious in the case of living beings. Since they metabolize food from their environment, they may change all of their constitutive matter in the course of their lives while remaining the same being.

Artefacts, on the whole, do not change the totality of their constitutive stuff, and if, under the touch of a Midas, they did so instantaneously, the continued identity of the artefact would be called into question. For it is not at all obvious that the china vase, transformed into gold, is the very same vase as hitherto, any more than a gold vase, miraculously transformed into a transparent glass one, would count as the very same vase. However, some of the parts of an artefact can be, and often are, replaced without loss of identity. To that extent, then, change of some of the constitutive matter of which an artefact is made is compatible with its continued identity. Whether gradual replacement of *all* of the parts over a prolonged period of time (as in the famous example of Theseus' ship) is compatible with continued identity or not is contentious. Every rotten plank of the ship that is lovingly rebuilt on shore is identical with a plank of the original vessel, but it is clear which way the marine insurance company should decide if the question of which ship is the one insured should arise. In this case, the identity of the artefact is not impugned by the complete change of its parts, and hence its specific (as opposed to generic) constitutive stuff, over a prolonged period of time.[6]

Among the attributes of an individual substance, there are some that are attributable to the constitutive material of the thing – for example, its plasticity, hardness, weight, solubility or insolubility in this or that solvent, commonly also its smell, taste and texture. So, for example, that this bronze statuette is soluble in hydrochloric acid, is hard and weighs more than two pounds is due to the fact that the bronze of which it is made dissolves in such acid, is a hard material, and that the specific quantity of bronze from which it is made weighs more than two pounds. The colour of a thing is typically the colour of its exterior surface (its bark, skin, peel, etc.), which, in the case of many artefacts, may be no more than a layer of oxides, or maybe a decorative or protective coat of paint, varnish, tar, etc. on its surface. But we would not deem the table to be *made* of wood and varnish or of wood and stain. Rather, it is made of wood, and it has been varnished or stained (see table 2.3).

Other attributes of things are determined by the kind of substance the thing is. If it is an artefact, for example, its size, shape and parts are typically determined by the purpose of the artefact. If it is a living being, its morphological features, characteristic organs, pattern of development, and characteristic modes of behaviour are non-derivative properties of the creature, and are determined by the nature of the organism which it is.

---

[6] It is interesting that we would not, I think, say the same about the continued identity of a painting, all the pigments (and even the plaster, panel or canvas of which) were gradually replaced over time. At some stage, one might suppose, Leonardo's *Last Supper* may well cease to be Leonardo's *Last Supper*, even though *a* painting continues to exist on the wall of the refectory of Santa Maria della Grazie.

	Attributable to the constitutive materials	Attributable to the thing and its nature	Can be attributable to the surface of the thing and its constitution
Plasticity	✓		
Weight	✓		
Solubility	✓		
Smell	✓		✓
Taste	✓		
Colour	✓		✓
Size		✓	
Shape		✓	
Parts		✓	

Table 2.3   *Dependence of the properties of things on the constitutive stuff or on the nature of the thing*

5. Substances and their substantial parts

Are the substantial parts of an individual living substance, such as a leaf or a flower, a head or a tail, themselves substances? There is no need to claim that. Of course, the parts may be detached from the substance of which they are parts. In that sense, the constitutive parts of a substance *can* enjoy independent existence. But, in another sense, they *cannot*. For such parts are functionally defined, and they do not fulfil their defining function once they have become detached. The amputated leg is no longer used by an animal to walk, and the eye removed from the sighted animal is no longer an organ of vision. (But one need not follow Aristotle in holding that it is no more an eye than a painted eye,[7] since, unlike a painted eye, it *was* once an organ of vision.) Furthermore, these functional parts do not long survive detachment from the organism of which they were a part. Independently of human interference, they wither or decay. Of course, human beings can graft shoots and transplant organs. But this does not significantly affect the point being made, since although these parts

[7] Aristotle, *De Anima* 412b20–24.

of an organism *are* transferable, they still only fulfil their defining function as constituent parts of a living plant or animal.

Matters are less clear with regard to parts of an artefact. To be sure, they fulfil a function in the whole of which they are a part (although we sometimes distinguish parts that fulfil a function from parts that are 'merely decorative'). But, unlike the parts of an organism, they are created independently of the artefact of which, on assembly, they become a functioning part. They are detachable from the whole of which they are parts without detriment to the possibility of their re-employment in the same functional role either in the same artefact duly reassembled or in a different one. Unlike parts of an organism that grow as the organism matures, and decay when detached from the organism, they can be stored without decay or deterioration independently of the mechanism for which they are made. So it is difficult to see any overriding reason for denying that parts of an artefact can be considered as substances – *if* we resolve to consider artefacts to be non-natural substances.

Among the attributes which a substance, a concrete thing of a certain kind, has, some are actualities, such as its size, shape, colour, location, and some are potentialities or dispositional properties, such as its mobility, hardness, brittleness, solubility, inflammability. These potentialities include the wide range of active and passive powers of a substance. In the case of living things, in particular animals, the active powers include their numerous different kinds of abilities to do or refrain from doing those things they *can* do. For many of the active powers of animals, unlike those of insentient substances, are two-way powers. This will be discussed in chapter 4.

6. Substances conceived as natural kinds

It would be mistaken to take the two very general categories of substances – that is, things and stuffs – to be two super-categories of *natural kinds*, where natural kinds are conceived to be discovered rather than stipulated, and subject to natural laws concerning those kinds. The salient properties of natural kinds thus conceived are sometimes held to be causally determined by a real essence constituted by their microstructure or microstructural properties. The natural kind, it is argued, is defined by microstructural similarity to an ostended or otherwise located paradigm. This sample, in its role as a paradigm of the (often yet to be discovered) microstructural real essence,

Substance

is conceived to be partly constitutive of the *meaning* of the natural kind name. Accordingly, scientific discovery holds a blank cheque from semantics, which it can fill in as science progresses.[8] This conception of the explanation of what natural kind terms mean is the contemporary heir to the venerable idea of 'real definition'. It is rooted in Locke's distinction between real and nominal essence but, unlike Locke, holds the real essence of a thing to be both discoverable and partly constitutive of the meaning of its name. It draws support from the discovery of the periodic table of elements, and, even more questionably, from the discovery of DNA and its genetic role.

It is doubtful whether the categories found to be useful in the natural sciences are themselves natural kind terms *thus understood*. For this conception of natural kinds is a metaphysical rather than a scientific one, rooted in a form of metaphysical essentialism, on the one hand, and misconceptions concerning meaning and explanation, on the other.[9]

It is an illusion that scientific discovery can disclose what the words we use, such as 'gold' and 'water', 'fish' and 'lily', *really* mean. For what a word means is determined by convention, not by discovery – although, of course, discovery may be elevated into convention by agreement on a new rule for the use of a word. What a word means is specified by the common, accepted explanation of its meaning. Such an explanation of meaning functions as a rule or standard of correctness for applications of a term. Accordingly, our terms for kinds of things and stuffs do not draw blank cheques on future discoveries – for if they did, the explanations of what they mean could not also function as guides to and standards for correct use as they do. Science can discover what the structure of a gold atom or a water molecule really is and why gold and water behave as they do. It can explain how vertebrate sea-dwellers evolved and distinguish many different kinds among them, or what lilies have in common

[8] For the view that natural kinds have an essence and are defined by reference to similarity to a paradigmatic sample, see H. Putnam, 'The Meaning of "Meaning"', repr. in his *Mind, Language, and Reality* (Cambridge University Press, Cambridge, 1975), pp. 215–71. For illuminating refutation of this conception of natural kinds, from which the following discussion is derived, see J. Dupré, *The Disorder of Things* (Harvard University Press, Cambridge, Mass., 1993), Part I, and his *Humans and Other Animals* (Clarendon Press, Oxford, 2002), esp. Parts I and II.

[9] For examination of the semantic misconceptions, see P. M. S. Hacker, *Wittgenstein's Place in Twentieth-Century Analytic Philosophy* (Blackwell, Oxford, 1996), pp. 250–53, 329f.

with garlic, and it can then accept or reject the usefulness of these categories (fish, *Liliaceae*) for purposes of biological explanation and classification. However, in discovering that pure water, ice, steam and snow consist of two parts hydrogen and one part oxygen in chemical combination, scientists did not discover what the word 'water' *really* means. If chemists and educated laymen now choose to define 'water' as 'a substance (solid, liquid or gaseous) that consists of two parts hydrogen and one part oxygen in chemical combination', that merely shows either that 'water' now has a harmlessly fluctuating meaning, or that what was inductive evidence for water, ice (water in its solid state) or steam (water in its gaseous state) has been elevated to being part of the meaning of the word 'water' in scientific parlance.

It is a mistake to suppose that natural kind terms are defined by reference to unspecified microstructural similarity relations to a paradigm. In so far as paradigms play any role in explaining the meaning of a word, as indeed they do when a word is defined by means of an ostensive definition involving a sample, they must be usable as objects of comparison to guide the use of a word. For the role of the paradigm is as a standard for the correct application of the definiendum F: something which is *this* ☞ (and here one points at the paradigm) or is *what this* ☞ *is*, is rightly said to be F, or an F. So the relevant features of the paradigm must be both known and evident – otherwise the paradigm has no normative role. But if the putative 'similarity relation' concerns microstructural properties, the paradigm can play no normative, standard-setting role. For if the microstructure instantiated by the paradigm is unknown and still awaiting scientific discovery, the paradigm can provide no guidance in applying or withholding 'F'. But if the requisite microstructure *is* known, the paradigm is redundant. For one can find out directly by appropriate chemical tests what the microstructure of the entity under investigation is and so determine, independently of any paradigm, whether it is F or an F.

No doubt we are prone to be mesmerized by the example of the periodic table in chemistry and its bearing on the determination of the nature of stuffs. But it is unrepresentative; and even in this case it would be mistaken to suppose that all essential properties are derivable from the atomic number of what is classified. The behaviour of iron atoms, for example, is very unlike that of ferric or ferrous ions, even though all have the atomic number 26 and are rightly classified as belonging to the same natural kind. Moreover, it would be absurd to suppose that the nature of scrambled egg or Yorkshire pudding is something that is determined, independently of their nominal essences, by the atomic numbers of their constituent elements, or that we need to wait upon scientific discoveries to find out what 'beef' and 'venison', 'paper' and 'glass', really mean or really are (as opposed to discovering what their chemical analysis is). Yet names of cooked and manufactured substances are no less substance (stuff) nouns than names of the chemical elements or of compounds that are to be found in nature.

Whatever plausibility this conception of the real essence of substances has with respect to stuffs rapidly evaporates when we consider things. Clearly, the nature of artefacts is not defined by reference to their constitutive matter, even though being made of such-and-such materials may well be necessary for an artefact to fulfil its defining functions. What differentiates a gold ring from a gold watch, a mahogany bookcase from a mahogany desk, is not their particulate (molecular) structures. Similarly, although the DNA of cats differs from that of dogs, and that of cabbages from that of cauliflowers, we do not *define* different animate substances by reference to their genetic make-up. We may indeed explain what a cat or a dog is by an ostensive definition, but not by reference to any microstructural similarity relationships to the ostended paradigm. Moreover, the nature of an animate substance – that is, what it is to be a so-and-so – does not follow from a description of its genetic make-up and the laws of physics and chemistry. The relationship between a gold ring and the gold of which it consists is altogether different from the relationship between an organism and the DNA that is contained within its cells – remember that nothing is *made* of (or *consists* of) DNA. So too, the relationships, both logical and causal, between the properties of gold objects and the structure of their constitutive gold atoms is altogether different from the relationship between the properties of organisms and the structure of the DNA molecules within their cells.

With the triumph of Darwinism, the idea that biological species are determined by a common essence, as was supposed by Aristotelian scientific conceptions, was rejected. For the theory of evolution showed the untenability of the idea of the fixity of species, and phylogenetic classification proceeded without any such assumption – often yielding equivocal and optional results. Furthermore, the latter classification is by no means uniformly the most useful in the biological sciences, and morphological classifications are often called for to satisfy explanatory needs. But evolutionary (historical) classifications, on the one hand, and morphological (structural) classifications, on the other, may generate taxa of different kinds. There is no uniquely correct and omni-explanatory classificatory scheme, and Plato's distasteful metaphor of carving nature at her joints is more apt at the butcher's than on the agenda of science. Of course, not anything goes; but how we should classify things when engaged in a given science depends upon our scientific purposes, upon the peculiarities of the thing we are investigating, and upon the features we wish to explain. There is no reason to suppose a priori that there is only one scientifically fruitful way of classifying natural phenomena.

One may grant that scientific taxonomy is fruitful. It is subservient to the explanatory enterprises of science. The fruitfulness of such a taxonomy is evident in the range and explanatory powers of the ensuing generalizations. So many of the features of things and stuffs that are individuated in terms of common-or-garden concepts are explained by scientific theories that rely on more specialized and often very different classifications. But, first, not all the things that interest us and for which we have coined general names stand in need of any explanation. Secondly, not all explanation is scientific explanation. So although many phenomena that concern us do call out for explanation, the requisite explanations may involve reference to human activities and interests, to custom, law, economics and history, and may employ classifications quite distinct from, but no less useful within their domains than, those of the natural sciences. Thirdly, there is no such thing as Science, but only a multitude of different natural sciences, on the one hand, and social and human sciences, on the other. The reductive ideal of unified science was rightly abandoned by its twentieth-century progenitors, the members of the Vienna Circle. There is no absolute, final classificatory scheme for everything there is, but only a multiplicity of taxonomies that the various sciences, natural and social, find fruitful, and the multitude of more or less unsystematic substance terms, in both senses of the word, that mankind in general finds useful for the manifold purposes that inform our lives.

7. Substances conceived as a common logico-linguistic category

It is evident that our ordinary classifications of material and animate things into substances of different kinds were not designed for purposes of scientific taxonomy or for scientific explanatory power, but for purposes of humdrum identification and re-identification relative to a multitude of different human concerns. Relative to our purposes and interests, it can hardly be said that we err in distinguishing between onions and garlic, or between both and lilies, even though all belong to the *Liliaceae* family, or that we have made a mistake in segregating moths from butterflies,[10] even though Macrolepidoptera include all butterflies and some moths. Our interests and concerns are numerous and very varied. The fact that *tree* has no place in botanical taxonomy does not mean that this term is not a substance name of a natural kind of thing (and we may begin to harbour doubts about the usefulness of the philosophers' term of art 'a natural kind'). The fact that *angiosperm*, which subsumes daisies, cacti and oak trees (since they all produce seeds in ovaries) but excludes pine trees, has no place in ordinary classifications does not show anything other than the fact that the interests of botany differ from those that underlie the classifications of ordinary language.[11] The great majority of farm animals (cows, sheep, goats), of domestic animals (pets such as cats and dogs), and the vast majority of crops and flowering plants to be found in our gardens are not *natural* but *unnatural* kinds – the result of massive human intervention, of cross-breeding, artificial insemination and fertilization, and, more recently, of genetic engineering.

Similarly, it is clear that the logico-grammatical category of concrete mass nouns signifying stuffs of one kind or another is indifferent to whether the designated stuff is natural or not. Wine is no less of a substance than water, even though it is manufactured by human beings, and honey is as much a stuff as helium, even though it is made by bees. Wool or silk are natural kinds of stuff, but by the time we have finished with the natural material, the resultant wools and silks are very different from anything found on the back of a sheep or constituting the chrysalis of a silk worm. Bread and butter are no less kinds of stuffs than wheat (or indeed the flour that is produced from it) and milk. The general concepts of substances (stuffs) that we employ in our daily discourse were not introduced as part of a taxonomy for scientific (e.g. chemical) purposes; they do not involve a systematic hierarchy of kinds of stuffs, and they invoke very different principles of classification suited to the numerous different purposes that we have. From a logico-grammatical point of view, however, there is no significant difference between natural and manufactured stuffs.

---

[10] The lepidopterous insects, not their final mature phase.

[11] See Dupré, *Disorder of Things*, ch. 1.

General names of artefacts are, as suggested above, no less substance names than general names of natural things. Artefacts are enduring features of the landscapes and cityscapes we inhabit, commonly long outlasting many of their natural inhabitants. Most of the salient objects around us are, by now, artefactual. We refer to artefacts, often locate ourselves by reference to certain kinds of them, sometimes trace the provenance of other kinds, identify and re-identify them. Material artefacts (by contrast with such artefacts as works of literature or music) consist of the stuffs of which they are made. They possess active and passive powers, and they undergo various forms of change compatible with their continued identity. Artefactual names serve to identify and re-identify a persistent thing as *that* particular thing of such-and-such a sort; they typically provide principles for counting things of the relevant kind, and they determine, as part of their meaning, a tolerably clear array of properties the possession of which is essential for the thing in question to be said to continue to exist. St Paul's is still the same building, despite having been extensively refaced, but the Winter Palace is a meticulous reconstruction of the building destroyed by the Nazis. A table can tolerate scratches and stains and the replacement of a leg or two compatible with its continued identity, but not being chopped into small pieces. A motor car can be repainted, have a new set of tyres, even a new engine, yet remain the same car; but it will not remain the same car after being squashed into a cube preparatory to being melted down. Of course, there is a fair degree of indeterminacy at the borderlines, but then that is true of concepts of natural objects too.

8. A historical digression: misconceptions of the category of substance

Three strands in the classical Aristotelian account were seriously misconstrued in the seventeenth-century debate concerning substance, with long-lasting effects upon philosophical reflection. Aristotelian primary substances were rightly conceived to enjoy *independent existence* in a sense in which properties do not. They were correctly conceived to be subjects of predication, *bearers of properties*. And they were rightly held to be subjects of changing accidents, capable of bearing contrary properties at different times, and hence *persisting through change*. The seventeenth- and eighteenth-century thinkers, their thoughts focused to a large extent on the scientific revolution through which they were living and to which their philosophies were trying to do justice, knotted these simple strands into an unprecedented tangle.

As we have already noted, the idea of substance as an independent existence was drastically reinterpreted by Descartes, removing it from its Aristotelian context and from its categorial status as a general form of our thought about material objects, on the one hand, and about their constitutive matter, on the other. For Descartes understood *independent existence* in causal, rather than logical terms.[12] A substance, according to him, is 'a thing that exists in such a way as to *depend on no other thing* for its existence' (emphasis added).[13] He held that only God is completely independent of everything else, and is therefore the only substance *stricto sensu*. In a derivative sense, minds (a plurality) and matter (a totality: the plenum, the totality of space-matter) are also substances, since they depend for their existence only upon the concurrence of God (whose sustaining activity, Descartes thought, was necessary for the continued existence of all things). But God apart, the plenum is indestructible, since the total quantity of matter in the universe is, Descartes believed, conserved throughout all change. Minds are sempiternal, since, lacking parts, they are simple, and all destruction is decomposition into, and rearrangement of, constituents. The Aristotelian sense of independent existence, by contrast with the Cartesian, was non-causal. The sense in which the properties of a thing, such as its motion, shape or colour, are not independent existences is that (with qualifications for shadows, holes, gaps, shafts of light, etc.) there can be no movement that is not the movement of some thing, no shape unless there is something that has that shape, and no colour unless there is something coloured. To say that a particular substance exists is to say that there is a thing of a certain kind somewhere, somewhen. To say that a quality exists is to say that some thing (or things) somewhere, somewhen, is (or are) qualified in a certain way. So the existence of substances was not held to be independent *of any other substances*, let alone of *conditions* such as heat and cold, rain and snow, as well as other atmospheric circumstances and environmental accompaniments.

[12] There is some equivocation in Descartes as to whether the form of independence or relative independence is causal or ontological. The former is evident in his claim that matter and mind need only the concurrence of God in order to exist; the latter is to the fore in his remark in the Fourth Set of Replies that substances, but not properties, 'exist through themselves' (*res per se subsistentes*).

[13] Descartes, *Principles of Philosophy*, I, 51.

Similarly, the Aristotelian conception of the persistence of substances through change simply meant that particular things can change their accidents and yet persist – that, contrary to what Hume later averred, change (accidental, as opposed to substantial, change) is compatible with continued identity. It did *not* mean that there is, throughout all change, something that remains unchanged. (*That* doctrine is to be found in Aristotle's hylomorphism, in his (mis)conception of 'materia prima'.)

Matters were further exacerbated by Locke, who seized on the idea of substances as bearers of qualities – a thought fostered by the etymology of 'substance' (*substantia* – that which stands under or supports). Properties of a thing are, in Aristotle's jargon, '*in* a subject' (as we might say that they are '*had* by a subject'), a thought that was transmitted in the confusing jargon of '*inhering in* a subject'. This, in Locke's hands, yielded the misconception of *substance in general* as something that possesses properties but is distinct from them – a bare unqualified particular, a something 'I know not what' in which qualities inhere.[14] Substances, far from being conceived to be kinds of persistent spatio-temporal things, were taken to be the *substrata* of properties – something that 'supported', 'united together' the properties a thing possesses, the carcasses of the furniture of the world on which a veneer of properties is stuck. 'All our *Ideas* of the several sorts of Substances', Locke wrote, summarizing his conception, 'are nothing but Collections of simple *Ideas*, with a Supposition of something, to which they belong, and in which they subsist; though of this supposed something, we have no distinct *Idea* at all.'[15] Being a mere *something* in which properties inhere, it seemed that substance 'in and of itself' must *lack properties*. Locke confused the bare idea of a subject of predication with the idea of a bare subject of predication.[16] The former is the perfectly coherent thought of something,

[14] Locke, *An Essay Concerning Human Understanding*, II. xxiii. 1–6, 15, 37; III. vi. 21.

[15] Ibid., II. xxiii. 37; see also I. iv. 18: 'We have no clear idea at all, and therefore signify nothing by the word *Substance*, but only an uncertain supposition of we know not what; (i.e. of something whereof we have no particular distinct positive) *Idea*, which we take to be the *substratum*, or support, of those *Ideas* we do know.'

[16] A point nicely made by David Wiggins in his 'Substance', in A. C. Grayling (ed.), *Philosophy – A Guide through the Subject* (Oxford University Press, Oxford, 1995), p. 227.

as yet unspecified, which . . . The latter is the incoherent idea of a thing without qualities. The idea that qualities are *collectable*[17] (other than, in a Pickwickian sense, by words) is an altogether misleading metaphor, as are the thoughts that they can, like twigs, be *bound together* or, like billboards, be *supported*.[18]

Small wonder that Hume washed his hands of the morass, declaring the very idea of material substance an 'unintelligible chimera' and that of a spiritual substance 'absolutely unintelligible'.[19] But nothing could have been further from Aristotle's mind than this Lockean confusion. An Aristotelian (primary) substance was anything but a bare particular – it was a persistent thing of a given kind, with an essence determined by its essential properties, a subject of accidents that may change without affecting the identity of the substance. To specify only the qualities of a thing will, Aristotle insisted, tell us *what the thing is like* or *what condition it is in*. But if we want to know *what it is*, we must be told, by specification of a secondary substance, what kind of thing it is.

Descartes, opposing the scholastic Aristotelian tradition, had declared that there are only two kinds of substance. Berkeley held that there is only one kind. Spinoza insisted that there is only one substance, Leibniz that there are infinitely many. And Hume denied that there are any substances at all (unless one counts each idea and impression as a substance). More than a century of philosophical reflection had reduced the subject to incoherence.

Kant sapiently attempted to rehabilitate the concept of substance. He emphasized a fundamental point that will preoccupy us in the sequel: namely, that the concepts of substance, agency and causation are intimately interwoven.[20] Unfortunately, however, he married the legacy of Descartes to the confusions of Locke. For, like Descartes, he associated substance in experience with what is 'abiding in its existence', and misguidedly identified it not with the relatively abiding familiar things around us, but with the supposed permanent totality

---

[17] Locke, *Essay*, IV. vi. 7.

[18] Ibid., II. xxiii. 4.

[19] Hume, *A Treatise of Human Nature*, I. iv. 3 and I. iv. 4.

[20] Kant, *Critique of Pure Reason*, B 249–50. For a helpful discussion of the flaws in Kant's treatment of substance, see P. F. Strawson, 'Kant on Substance', repr. in his *Entity and Identity and Other Essays* (Clarendon Press, Oxford, 1997), pp. 268–79.

of matter in space (unlike Descartes, he differentiated matter from space). 'In all change of appearances', he wrote, 'substance is permanent; its quantum in nature is neither increased nor diminished. . . . the substratum of all that is real, that is, of all that belongs to the existence of things is *substance*; and all that belongs to existence can be thought only as a determination of substance.' Substance, he held, 'as the substrate of all change, remains ever the same'; it is 'something *abiding* and *permanent*, of which all change and co-existence are only so many ways (modes of time) in which the permanent exists'.[21] So, like Descartes, Kant thought of the various individual material substances (in the classical sense of the term 'substance') that we encounter around us as no more than passing modes of the underlying substrate of all change. Elsewhere, echoing Locke and compounding confusion, he averred that 'in all substances the true subject – namely that which remains after all the accidents (as predicates) have been removed – and hence the *substantial* itself, is unknown to us.'[22]

There is irony in all this, since what Kant needed in order to undermine the empiricism against which he warred, and to establish the conditions of the possibility of an objective spatio-temporal framework within which objects of experience can be distinguished from the experience of objects, was precisely the notion of Aristotelian substances as the *relatively* abiding, but impermanent, independent objects of our experience.[23] Such objects of reference and subjects of predication perfectly adequately fulfil the Kantian requirements necessary for the unity of time, on the one hand, and for a stable background against which we can apprehend change, on the other. That such objects of experience themselves come into existence and pass away does not impugn the unity of the spatio-temporal framework in which we encounter, identify and re-identify them – as long as they do not all pass away simultaneously. Nor does the demand that in every change some thing should persist require that something should persist through every change. All that is necessary is that there be Aristotelian substances among phenomena (see list 2.1).

[21] Kant, *Critique of Pure Reason*, B 224, 225, 226.

[22] Kant, *Prolegomena to any Future Metaphysics*, §46.

[23] See P. F. Strawson, *The Bounds of Sense* (Methuen, London, 1966), pp. 128–32.

List 2.1 Degeneration since Aristotle: the increasingly incoherent demands placed on the idea of substance

1 **That substances be independently existing things**
   That substances depend on nothing else for their existence
   That substances be indestructible

2 **That substances be subjects of predication**
   That substances be bearers of properties
   That substances be bare bearers of properties

3 **That substances be subjects of changing accidents**
   That substances be unchanging persistents through change
   That substance be the permanent substrate of all change

4 **That specification of a (secondary) substance answer the question 'What is it?'**
   That reference to a substance answer the question 'What binds these phenomenal properties together into an individual thing?'

3

Causation

1. Causation: Humean, neo-Humean and anti-Humean

Primary substances, individual things of a kind, are paradigmatic agents with active and passive powers. The active powers of inanimate and animate substances alike include causal powers. Such agents act on other things, including other substances, and thereby bring about changes in those things that are susceptible to change in response to such action. These changes in turn may trigger a further sequence of events that are often attributable to the initiating agent, who can then be said to have brought them about. Whatever one thus brings about, one brings about by doing something.

Identifying the cause of something is like saying 'That ☞ is what was responsible for it'. It is no coincidence that the Greek word *aition*, translated into Latin by *causa*, from which our word 'cause' derives, originally meant 'guilt', 'blame', 'accusation'. When *aition* was first used in an explanatory sense, it was restricted to something or someone's affording a person or persons a reason for acting – as when bad weather causes us to abandon a picnic, or the Prime Minister's speech caused the adjournment of the House. The Latin *causa* retained this association with *a reason*, *motive* or *inducement*, and so does this use of our verb 'to cause' and the cognate noun. This linkage is manifest in legal parlance when lawyers speak of *having cause to*, or of requiring the plaintiff to *show cause why*.

A similarly hermeneutically informed use of the verb and its cognates is also manifest in the most common use of 'cause' in description and explanation of human affairs, including history, economics and sociology, as when we debate the causes of the Second World War and ask what caused the rise in the rate of inflation. It is a different kind of cause from efficient causes, but it is not obvious that we need think of it as a different *sense* of 'cause'. It has a manifest connection with making things happen and bringing about changes, with conditions *sine qua non*, with explanation, and with the action and reaction of agents with active and passive powers – only here the agents are typically human beings acting or reacting for reasons, often in pursuit of goals, often making patients, who are other human beings, do things, or inducing them to do things, by threats and incentives. Here too identification of the cause or causes commonly involves assignment of responsibility and consequent praise or blame.

Philosophical reflection of the last three centuries on causation has been focused largely upon the analysis of efficient causation. It has been guided by Hume's account in the *Treatise*. On the one hand, Hume was taken to have repudiated the rationalist conception of causality as a form of *de re* necessity, criticizing our idea of a necessary connection between cause and effect as an illicit projection of our own associatively generated expectations onto reality. On the other hand, he proposed an analysis of singular causal connection in terms of instantiation of a regularity of succession of paired events, taking a cause to be a necessary and sufficient condition for the occurrence of an event.[1]

Some of Hume's successors, including Kant, tried to defend the idea that cause and effect *are* necessarily connected. 'The concept of cause', Kant wrote, 'involves the character of necessity, which no experience can yield.'[2] He denied the correctness of Hume's projectivist

---

[1] The traditional interpretation of Hume has been challenged in recent years by Galen Strawson, in his *The Secret Connection: Causation, Realism, and David Hume* (Oxford University Press, Oxford, 1989). He argued that Hume was a closet realist about anankastic causation, and merely expressed scepticism about our capacity to discover the objective necessitation that is intrinsic to causation. Given our limited faculties, we have to rest satisfied with regularity of succession and remain ignorant of the hidden necessitating causes of things. Against this interpretation, see Jonathan Bennett, *Learning from Six Philosophers*, vol. 2 (Oxford University Press, Oxford, 2001), §§273–5. There is no reason for us to take sides in this exegetical controversy. What matters is that Hume was generally understood for more than two centuries to have analysed causation in terms of constant conjunction, contiguity and temporal priority, and to have tried to explain away the idea of necessary connection.

[2] Kant, *Critique of Pure Reason*, A 112.

explanation of the necessity imputed to a causal sequence, insisting that 'The concept of cause . . . , which expresses the necessity of an event under a presupposed condition, would be false if it rested only on an arbitrary subjective necessity, implanted in us, of connecting certain empirical representations according to the rule of causal relation.'[3] Against Hume's regularity account, Kant was adamant that 'the very concept of a cause . . . contains the concept of a necessary connection with an effect'.[4] Present-day support for an anankastic (necessitarian) conception is to be found in the attempts of Harré and Madden to articulate a conception of non-logical *natural necessity* that is distinct from mere regularity.[5]

Other successors of Hume, such as Mill, attempted to refine his account. More aware than Hume of the multiplicity of causal conditions, Mill held a cause to be *stricto sensu* the totality of conditions *sufficient*, rather than *necessary and sufficient* (as Hume had suggested) for the effect. 'The cause is then philosophically speaking the sum total of the conditions positive and negative taken together; the whole of the contingencies of every description which being realized the consequence invariably follows.'[6] So he recognized that the same kind of event may be produced by quite different independent causes, each such cause consisting of a plurality of conditions jointly sufficient for the event. Invariable sequence of antecedent conditions and consequent, however, is insufficient for a causal connection. It needs to be supplemented, Mill insisted, by the requirement of *unconditionality* in order to exclude counteracting causes.[7] Mill held that a cause is 'the sum total of conditions' sufficient for the occurrence of an event, and asserted that 'we have philosophically speaking no right to give the name of cause to one of them exclusively of the others'.[8] Nevertheless, he noted that in common discourse we select one condition out of the total set and denominate it 'the cause', and he took some preliminary steps towards clarifying the principles of selection

[3] Ibid., B 168.

[4] Ibid., B 5.

[5] R. Harré and E. H. Madden, *Causal Powers* (Blackwell, Oxford, 1975); see also R. Harré, *Laws of Nature* (Duckworth, London, 1993).

[6] J. S. Mill, *A System of Logic*, Bk. I, ch. v, sect. 3.

[7] Ibid., Bk. III, ch. v, sect. 6.

[8] Ibid., Bk. III, ch. v, sect. 3.

we employ. Modern support for a variant of Mill's conception, which pays much more careful attention to our selection of 'the cause' from among a set of conditions held to be jointly sufficient for an event, is given by John Mackie. He argued that a cause is an INUS condition: that is, an insufficient but necessary component of a set of conditions that are unnecessary but jointly sufficient for the occurrence of the effect.[9] And he elaborated in some detail the variable, context-dependent and purpose-relative principles whereby we identify a factor as the cause.

A quite different neo-Humean account of causation was suggested by Davidson, who held that every singular causal statement implies a strict (exceptionless) causal *law*.[10] Unlike the Humean regularity conception, however, this nomological one holds that the implied causal law may be unknown, since what 'E_1 caused E_2' implies is only that there is *some* causal law connecting the two individual events, not that there is a law that whenever an event of type E_1 occurs, it is followed by an event of type E_2. (The wind may have caused the apple to fall from the tree, but there is no law of nature connecting wind with apples falling from trees. There may, however, be a law concerning tensile strength of materials and the force needed to break them, which applies to the stem of an apple and the force exerted by the wind.)

In reaction to such Humean and neo-Humean analyses of causation there have been various, very different attempts, by Collingwood, Gasking, Hart and Honoré, Anscombe, von Wright and others, to link the concept of causation neither to regular sequences of events nor to nomologically connected events *simpliciter*, but rather, directly or indirectly, to human agency or to human action and to the possibility of manipulation – of bringing about events through human intervention in the normal course of events. This conception of causation is a descendant of a much older notion, prominent among the Cambridge Platonists, dominant in Berkeley's metaphysics and in Reid's criticisms of Locke and Hume, of rightly associating causation with agency, correctly linking agency with activity, but denying that 'brute matter' can be active or can possess powers. Berkeley denied that there are any causes *in rerum natura*, and held that science discovers regularities (laws) of nature, but not causes. 'The true use and end of Natural

[9] J. L. Mackie, *The Cement of the Universe* (Clarendon Press, Oxford, 1974).

[10] D. Davidson, 'Causal Relations', repr. in *Essays on Actions and Events* (Clarendon Press, Oxford, 1980), pp. 149–62.

Philosophy', he wrote to Johnson, 'is to explain the phenomena of nature; which is done by discovering the laws of nature, and reducing particular appearances to them. . . . This mechanical philosophy doth not assign or suppose any one natural efficient cause in the strict and proper sense.' On this venerable picture, activity is a prerogative of spirit (thought and volition): 'A proper efficient cause I can conceive none but Spirit; nor any action, strictly speaking, but where there is Will.'[11] Reid did not deny that there are efficient causes in nature, but held that our conception of the relation of cause to effect is modelled on the relation between ourselves and our actions. 'If it be so that the conception of an efficient cause enters into the mind, only from the early conviction we have that we are the efficients of our own voluntary actions (which I think is most probable)', he wrote, 'the notion of efficiency will be reduced to this, That it is a relation between the cause and the effect, similar to that which is between us and our voluntary actions.'[12] *These* misconceptions, rooted in the traditional restriction of powers *stricto sensu* to two-way powers of animate beings with a will,[13] are not present in the reflections of

---

[11] Berkeley, letter to Johnson, 25 Nov. 1729, repr. in *The Works of George Berkeley*, ed. T. E. Jessop, vol. 2, p. 279; see also *The Principles of Human Knowledge*, sects XXX–XXXI.

[12] Thomas Reid, *Essays on the Active Powers of Man*, Essay I, in *The Works of Thomas Reid*, ed. Sir William Hamilton (Maclachlan and Stewart, Edinburgh, 1863), vol. 2, p. 524. Locke had side-stepped the issue of 'Whether Matter be not wholly destitute of *active Power* . . . and whether the intermediate state of created Spirits be not that alone, which is capable of both *active* and *passive Power*' (*An Essay Concerning Human Understanding*, II. xxi. 2), but held that 'Bodies, by our Senses, do not afford us so clear and distinct an *Idea* of *active Power*, as we have from reflection on the Operations of our Minds' (ibid., II. xxi. 4), since bodies transfer but do not initiate motion, and so give us but 'a very obscure *Idea* of an *active Power* of moving'. Reid went further, holding that 'From the consciousness of our own activity, seems to be derived not only the clearest, but the only conception we can form of activity, or the exertion of active power' (*Essays*, p. 523).

[13] Thus Reid: 'Power to produce any effect, implies power not to produce it. We can conceive no way in which power may be determined to one of these rather than the other, in a being that has no will', hence 'of the manner in which a cause may exert its active power, we can have no conception, but from consciousness of the manner in which our own active power is exerted' (*Essays*, p. 523). To be sure, inanimate causes do not *exert* their powers, but rather manifest them when the appropriate conditions for their actualization obtain. Animate beings do not *exert* their causal powers either, but use or exercise them. Whether we are the causes of our own actions or movements is questionable, and will be questioned in ch. 4.

twentieth-century philosophers who link causation with action and manipulation. We shall examine their conception below.

2. On causal necessity

It is very tempting to think that causes necessitate their effects, that if the cause is present, the effect *must* occur – that is, that there is a necessary connection between cause and effect.[14] So Spinoza, for example, held that 'From a given determinate cause the effect follows necessarily; and conversely, if there is no determinate cause, it is impossible for an effect to follow.'[15] It was against such rationalist conceptions that Hume argued, conceding that the idea of necessary connection is part of our complex idea of a causal relation, but imputing the idea of necessary connection not to an antecedent impression of an objective anankastic connection but to our associative propensity resulting from observation of previous such successions of paired events. 'Either we have no idea of necessity', he wrote, 'or necessity is nothing but that determination of the thought to pass from causes to effects and from effects to causes, according to their experienc'd union.'[16] The supposition that effect E_2 *must* follow the occurrence of its cause E_1 is, according to Hume, a projection on to reality of our felt associative propensity. Necessary connection, *properly speaking*, he held, is 'a relation of ideas' – a conceptual relation between concepts, propositions or judgements, not an objective relationship between events.

Hume rightly insisted that causal *relations* are contingent. But it does not follow that all causal *statements* are synthetic. That footprints in the sand are caused by feet, that sunburn is caused by sunshine, that raindrops on the window-pane are caused by rainfall, are examples of the indefinitely many analytic causal propositions that we can produce. In such cases, the description of a phenomenon – of marks in the sand as footprints or of drops of water on the window-pane as raindrops – incorporates specification of its cause, just as

---

[14] The following two sections are much indebted to Bede Rundle's lectures on causation at Oxford, 2003, which provided the stimulus for this chapter.

[15] Spinoza, *Ethics*, Part I, Axiom 3.

[16] Hume, *A Treatise of Human Nature*, Part III, sect. XIV, ed. L. A. Selby-Bigge, rev. P. H. Nidditch (Clarendon Press, Oxford, 1978), p. 166.

describing an act as keeping a promise implies an antecedent act of making a promise. So there is an internal relation between footprints and their cause, between raindrops and rainfall, sunburns and sunshine. Internal relations appear to be objective relations between things, but that appearance is no more than the shadow cast by logico-grammatical relations between concepts. For internal relations are determined by grammar – by rules for the use of expressions. So *this* form of connection, wholly unmysteriously, is *verbal* – and it is between descriptions. But *causal relations*, including causal relations between events, are external – contingent, not necessary.

Hume's criticisms of the rationalist anankastic conception of causal relations was liberating, even though his psychologist diagnosis of the source of the error in projection is surely not the whole story and sometimes not even part of it. That we have observed a number of causally related, paired events in the past may well lead us to expect E_2 to follow the currently observed E_1 if the circumstances are relevantly similar. We may indeed say that in these circumstances E_2 *must* occur, that it is *inevitable* that E_2 should occur, given what we know about the items involved, that there *is no other possibility*, given the available data, than that E_2 should occur. The *natural necessity* that we impute to the occurrence need not be derived from our projecting our feeling of expectation on to reality. It may well be derived from our knowledge of the *natures* of the items and operative mechanisms involved, our knowledge of the *circumstances* at hand and our knowledge of the *possibilities* that are (or were) open. But if we think that in speaking of what is naturally necessary we have disclosed a form of *de re* necessity in nature, then we are subject to illusion.

We are indeed inclined to say that if we immerse this lump of zinc in this bath of hydrochloric acid in solution, then the zinc *must* dissolve, that it will *unavoidably* dissolve, or that it is *bound* to dissolve. And that is indeed true – but potentially misleading. It is misleading inasmuch as the necessity is not a feature of the event of the zinc's dissolving. We legitimately invoke modal terms in such contexts. But rather than jumping to the conclusion that we have come across a special, non-logical form of objective necessity, we should reflect on the use of the modal terms that we thus invoke. What work is the 'must' doing? Does it signify a *de re* necessity in nature? Or is its role quite different? This is one of the cases in which, *mutatis mutandis*, Frege's remark on apodeictic judgements was right: 'What distinguishes the apodeictic from the assertoric judgment is that it indicates the existence of general judgments from which the proposition may be inferred – an indication that is absent in the assertoric judgement. If I term a proposition "necessary" then I am giving a hint as to my grounds for judgment.'[17]

If it is true that whenever such-and-such a quantity of zinc is immersed in such-and-such a quantity of hydrochloric acid solution, it dissolves, then it follows that if *this* lump of zinc is immersed (in such circumstances), then it *will* dissolve. Moreover, such a generalization is not an accidental one. But *that* it is not accidental does not imply that it is *necessary*. Any necessity in the matter is associated with the inference, not with its conclusion. Given these established truths, then it *follows* (logically, necessarily) that the zinc *will* dissolve – but it does not follow that the zinc will *necessarily* dissolve.

We may go further and insist that the zinc *must* dissolve – that *it has no other alternative*, that *it cannot help* dissolving. But this is mere anthropomorphizing. We may licitly say that the zinc must dissolve, but not because *it has no other options*, for lumps of zinc are not the kinds of things to which it makes sense to assign options. So why *must* it dissolve? What work is the 'must' doing here?

Let us suppose that the only (pertinent) conditions in which the lump of zinc might not dissolve are that there is an inhibitor in the acid, or that the bath of acid is about to be emptied, or the lump of zinc is going to be removed. Suppose further that all these possibilities can, for one reason or another, be excluded. Then we may say that *on these assumptions* the zinc *must* dissolve – that there is no other possibility. For we are in a position to exclude the other possibilities on good grounds. The *must* is relative to the premises. It is not that *the event is necessary*, but rather that *the conclusion is inescapable*.

Similarly, knowing what we do about the inner constitution of zinc atoms, we may rightly say that the zinc is *bound* to dissolve. Given that zinc ions have a greater affinity to chloride ions than do hydrogen ions, then it *follows* that zinc chloride will form in the solution. There is no *necessary* connection between the event of the zinc's immersion in the acid and the event of its dissolving – but that, *pace* Hume, does not mean that there is no *connection*. The connection is fully explained by ionic theory, which describes the invariable behaviour of such-and-such ions with such-and-such features.

---

[17] G. Frege, *Begriffsschrift – A Formalized Language of Pure Thought Modelled upon the Language of Arithmetic* (Halle, 1879), §4, trans. P. T. Geach.

Causal relations are not a kind of necessary relation between events. It is not even as if the antecedent event *makes* the consequent event happen *by doing something to it* – events are not agents and do not act on each other. If we wish to continue to speak of 'natural necessity' (which is, in principle, unobjectionable), then we should do so with full awareness that the distinction between what is naturally necessary and what is not is between what is invariably so *given such-and-such conditions and operative mechanisms* and what is only coincidentally invariably so or not invariably so at all, rather than between what is necessary and what is merely invariable.[18]

3. Event causation is not a prototype

Neo-Humean philosophers take as the prototype (that which is basic in the order of understanding) of the causal relation that needs to be scrutinized propositions of the general form 'E_1 caused E_2': for example, the flood caused the collapse of the river banks, the eruption caused the destruction of the town, the stone's hitting the window caused the breaking of the window. Here two singular event-designating expressions (which may be de-verbal nouns, gerundive nominalizations, etc.) are linked by the verb 'to cause', and causation is held to be a relation between individual events. Taking this form of causal statement to be the prototype is misleading and problematic.

It is misleading inasmuch as singular event-designating phrases are *typically* results of nominalization of sentences.[19] We describe the outcome of a causal operation by means of a sentence that states what happened as a result or consequence of the operation of the cause: for example, the cup broke, the town was destroyed, the wood burned. We can then transform the sentential description into an event-designating noun phrase: for example, 'the breaking of the cup', 'the

---

[18] B. Rundle, *Why there is Something rather than Nothing* (Clarendon Press, Oxford, 2004), pp. 50–5.

[19] There is no *need* to go further than this qualified claim. Even if there are event names that are original rather than derived, we cannot coherently entertain the thought of a language in which reference to an objective domain were possible and in which a distinction could be drawn between the objective world and our experience of it, that was bereft of substance-referring expressions and consisted instead of original event-referring expressions.

destruction of the town', 'the burning of the wood'. But it is evident that the description of the effect is given by the sentential description, and that the event designator, being a nominal transform of the verb in that description, is parasitic on it. Of course, neither events nor substances enjoy any form of *ontological* priority relative to each other. For unless there can be a world without change (a dubious idea), there cannot be substances without events. And unless there can be a dynamic world without any substances changing, there cannot be events without substances. Certainly, in our world, substances and events are ontologically co-ordinate. Nevertheless, it is substances, rather than events, that are the primary particulars in *our* conceptual scheme. They are the primary objects of reference and subjects of predication. It is by reference to them that we determine the spatial framework within which we non-deictically refer to objects and describe what befalls them. Reference to individual substances by means of definite or indefinite descriptions incorporating substance names is *logico-grammatically* prior to reference to events by means of event designators, precisely because event designators characteristically presuppose substance names either for their generation or for their explanation. So it is misleading to suggest that event causation, as given by statements of the form 'E$_1$ caused E$_2$', are prototypical, inasmuch as their two event designators are generally parasitic on substance-referring expressions, and are transforms of descriptions of the outcome of causal operations.[20]

Taking event causation as prototypical is problematic for a number of reasons, all of which surfaced in Hume's famous discussion. Above all, the causal relation becomes opaque. If we focus on events as the prototypical causal relata and on statements of the form 'E$_1$ caused E$_2$' as the prototypical causal statements, we shall find it puzzling and difficult to specify *what that relation is*. 'All events seem entirely loose and separate,' Hume observed; 'One event follows another; but we never can observe any tie between them. They seem *conjoined* but never *connected*.'[21] Famously, all Hume could find was the relation of temporal priority, spatial contiguity (which he

---

[20] Of course, one may say that 'A's V-ing P caused P's X-ing' is derived from 'P X'd *because* A V'd it'. But the latter sentential form is an explanation of *why* P X'd, and we can give this explanation because we know that the agent A X'd the patient P by V-ing it.

[21] Hume, *An Enquiry Concerning Human Understanding*, Sect. VII, Part II, ed. L. A. Selby-Bigge, 2nd edn (Clarendon Press, Oxford, 1902), p. 74.

abandoned in the *Enquiry*), and instantiation of a regularity (necessary connection having been dissolved into illicit psychological projection).

When our mind is focused on statements of event causation, it seems obvious that the causal relation itself is unobservable. We cannot *see* that one event causes another, we cannot *see the causing* – or so, in our Humean moments, we are inclined to think. That thought, to be sure, does not come from observing, let alone from engaging in, causal interactions, but from reflecting on causal sentences of this form and wondering what the verb that links the two event designators *stands for*. When we so reflect, it seems that one event happens, and then another happens. What makes the one the cause of the other is not actually visible in what is observed – the verb 'caused' in the sentence 'E_1 caused E_2' does not stand for anything observable in the succession of designated events. For all that can be observed, it seems (and seemed to Hume), are relations of temporal priority and of spatial contiguity.

In virtue of what, then, is one event the cause of some other event? Temporal priority is not sufficient for causation (and not necessary either, as we shall see below). Contiguity of events is a questionable notion inasmuch as events are not space-occupants. They lack spatial boundaries (they may need space in which to take place, but do not fill any space) and so cannot *touch* each other. So, we 'beat about the bush' with Hume, and conclude that what makes the relation causal is that *it instantiates a regularity*. This idea strengthens the bizarre thought that one cannot observe that one event causes another, since one cannot *observe* that E_1's being followed by E_2 instantiates a regularity. If one follows Hume's footsteps thus far, then debate will unavoidably ensue as to whether the causal relation between events is such that the occurrence of the cause is a necessary condition, or a sufficient condition (Hume moved from one to the other in the same breath[22]), or a sum total of conditions jointly sufficient for the occurrence of the effect (as Mill held), or an INUS condition (as Mackie proposed).

Given the importance, here and in the sequel, of the categories of (material) objects and events, it may be helpful to bear in mind the logico-grammatical differences between them (see table 3.1).

---

[22] '[W]e may define a cause to be *an object, followed by another, and where all objects similar to the first are followed by objects similar to the second. Or in other words where, if the first object had not been, the second had never existed*' (ibid., Sect. VII, Part II, p. 76).

Material objects	*Events*
exist	happen, occur, take place
persist, endure	go on, continue, unfold
have three spatial dimensions	lack spatial dimensions
occupy space	typically have a location;[a] may need space in order to occur, but do not occupy (fill) space
have parts, ordered in space	may have phases, ordered in time
the parts are smaller than the whole	the phases are briefer than the whole
consist *of* matter of one or more kinds	do not *consist of* anything (other than phases)
characteristically have size, shape, texture, colour and degrees of solidity	have size only in the sense that the event occurs over extensive space; cannot have shape, texture, colour or degree of solidity
can *emit* sound (if active or acted on) and can *have* a smell	can *make* sounds or smells
can move from one location to another – one and the same object occupying successive places	can move only in so far as successive phases, but not the whole event, may be located at different places (as when a party moves from garden to ballroom, a battle from hill to vale)
can change in accidental properties	can change only in character of successive phases (growing louder or fiercer)
have powers to act on other objects to produce change	cannot *act on* objects, but only affect them, and cannot *act on* other events, but only produce them

[a] So-called Cambridge events, like Xanthippe's becoming a widow, do not have a spatial location as the death of Socrates does. Similarly, legal and economic events, such as the rise in the price of butter, or a company's going bankrupt, or the outbreak of war, have a spatial location only in a derivative sense.

Table 3.1 *A logico-grammatical comparison of material objects and events*

4. The inadequacy of Hume's analysis: observability, spatio-temporal relations and regularity

We may have started by beating about the bush, but we ended by barking up the wrong tree. The meagre materials at hand are not only insufficient to elucidate our concepts of causation and causal relations, they positively lead us in the wrong direction. We must remind ourselves of the obvious: we observe and participate in causal transactions constantly. We feel the fire warm our hands (why else would we go over to the fireplace?). We feel the blow that hurts us and know that it is what makes us stagger. We move things about by picking them up and putting them down elsewhere. We slice bread with a bread knife, pour water into or out of a jug, open or shut a door, pick an apple off a tree, tear a piece of paper in half, write a letter with a pen, and put a match to a fire. We watch the rain soaking the laundry, observe a car flatten a tin can, see a stone break a window-pane.

So, we observe agents acting on patients and bringing about change. Sometimes we are the agent, and we make things happen by doing something to a patient. Sometimes we are the patient, and can feel or see that an agent is acting on us and bringing about a change in us. At other times, we are neither agent nor patient. We may be mere idle observers. Or we may intently watch the outcome of an experiment, having engineered the occurrence for a purpose. In myriad such cases, we observe an agent bringing about a change in a patient by *acting on* the patient, and we may actually see the mode of operation whereby the change is produced. It may well be that the observed change instantiates a regularity, but the idea that one cannot observe an individual transaction to be causal is misconceived; the idea that what renders the transaction a causal one is that it instantiates a regularity is mistaken; and the thought that we know the transaction to be a causal one only because we know that it instantiates a regularity is false.

With such examples before our eyes, we can also note that the idea that a cause must precede its effect is wrong. For there are innumerable examples of simultaneous production of effects. The razor blade cuts the piece of paper – but it is not as if the movement of the razor on the paper precedes the cutting of the paper. If a stone drops into a pond, it causes a splash – but it is not as if the dropping of the stone into the pond occurs first and *then* the displacement of the water takes place. The railway engine pushes the carriage before it (we may disregard the buffers and assume contiguity) – but the engine does not move before the carriage. One reason for demur is the thought that unless the event denominated the cause preceded the event held to be the effect, it would be impossible to identify which caused which – a thought that is bound to occur to those who conceive of a cause as a condition or set of conditions both necessary and sufficient for the occurrence of the effect. For if so, the effect is both sufficient and necessary for the occurrence of the cause. So how could we distinguish cause from effect other than by reference to its temporal priority? But this merely highlights the extent to which primary focus upon causation as a relation between events is awry, since there is no difficulty whatsoever in identifying the *agent* of change – for example, the razor that cuts the paper, the stone that falls into the pond, and the engine that pushes the carriage. Even where the events are simultaneous, as they often are, the agent that brings about the change commonly sets events in motion prior to acting on the patient. The person who cuts the paper picks up the razor before putting it to the paper, the stone that displaces the water begins to fall before it penetrates the surface of the pond, and the engine that pushes the carriage is started up by the engine driver before it begins to move. The impression that the event that is the cause must precede the event that is the effect is partly derived from those cases of human agential causation where we know or find out *what we have to manipulate* in order to bring about the desired effect – we have to pick up the bread knife before putting it to the bread and cutting, to throw the stone, engage the lever, and so forth.

Hume's demand for spatial contiguity is similarly awry. This is obvious when we speak of the causes of such events as the decline in the national birthrate, of the rise in the rate of inflation, or of outbreak of the Second World War – here any talk of spatial contiguity of cause and effect is patently out of order. But a much more general point is involved. As noted above, talk of contiguity of *events* is, quite generally, anomalous, because events are not spatial continuants and lack spatial boundaries (see table 3.1). They may need space in order to occur, but they do not occupy or fill a space. A wedding may fill a church, but not as water fills a glass – rather as an audience fills a theatre (taking up all the seats). Parking a car needs space, but does not fill a space – only the car does that. Lacking spatial boundaries, one event cannot *touch* another. Indeed, two distinct events may occur at the very same place, but it would be mistaken to think that they are then contiguous. A poker placed in the fire may turn red and grow hot, but the event of its turning red is not *contiguous* with the event of its growing hot – not because it is distant, let alone because it is the same event, but because it makes no sense to speak of contiguity here. So, one event may indeed cause another although they are not, and could not be, contiguous. Is there, then, no problem concerning action at a distance? Were Newton's worries groundless? Are the tides, the rise and fall of the oceans, not caused by the moon's exerting gravitational force *at a distance*? That is misleading. To describe the moon as '*exerting* gravitational force' is merely to show a preference for a *form of description*. For *exerting gravitational force* is not an action of the moon upon the oceans. Here our causal explanation has shifted away from the paradigm, while retaining its preferred form. We might, less misleadingly, say that the rotation of the earth in the vicinity of the orbiting moon causes the tides – a phenomenon that is described by, and that instantiates, the inverse square law. However, the event of the earth's rotating is neither contiguous with nor not contiguous with the moon's orbiting the earth at a distance of 400,000 kilometres.

Does every singular causal connection instantiate a causal generalization? Perhaps the question should be approached obliquely. Does our knowledge that a causal relation obtains depend on our knowledge of a regularity which it instantiates? It is evident, from the many examples of our own action upon things and our observation of other substances acting on things (including ourselves), that this need not be so. In innumerable cases of acting on another thing by mechanical contact and manipulation, we see and feel ourselves changing its position (by pushing, pulling, lifting, depositing, throwing), changing its form (by crumpling, moulding, chiselling), changing its size (by squeezing, compressing, inflating, cutting), changing its colour (by painting or polishing), or indeed putting an end to its existence (by breaking, burning, melting, eating), and so forth. Of course, in many cases, including some of the kinds of cases just mentioned, it may not be obvious, at the first occurrence, that it was our voluntary action that brought about the change in question. So we may repeat the action. But this is done in order to *confirm* that it was our V-ing that brought about the change, not in order to try to discern a regularity from which it would follow that our action was the cause of the change. Similarly, when an inanimate agent acts on a patient and a given change follows, it may not be evident that the change resulted from the action of the agent rather than from some other cause. So we may seek a repetition of the occurrence, or engineer an experiment that will repeat it. But again, the regularity merely confirms that it is the agent's action that causes the change to the patient. To be sure, the elementary case of observable agent-causation is but one form of causal relation. Many causal connections are discovered only after laborious experimentation, and are rendered intelligible only in the framework of a complex scientific theory. But the elementary case suffices to show that to discover that a causal relation obtained in an individual case, that an agent made something happen by acting on a patient, we need not always first establish that such-and-such actions or events are uniformly followed by such-and-such other events.

Is a cause not a necessary condition for the occurrence of the effect? Hume was surely mistaken here, since a given effect may be brought about in all manner of different ways. Was it not necessary on *this* occasion? Not necessarily so; something can cause a certain event on an occasion without being a necessary condition of its occurrence on that occasion. In certain circumstances we can confidently say that had *this* event not occurred, something else would have occurred with exactly the same effect. Indeed, sometimes we *know* (because we designed the mechanism) that the occurrence of C_1 actually *prevents* C_2 (which would cause E) from occurring, so that had C_1 not occurred, then C_2 would have occurred and *it* would have caused E (that is the point of fail-safe devices).

Is a cause not a sufficient condition, or a sufficient condition in the circumstances? If E happens whenever C happens, is not the occurrence of C the cause of E's happening? No, we must be careful not to confuse a *sufficient condition* of a given change E with a *condition sufficient to cause* such a change. For something may be a sufficient condition of the occurrence of E without causing it. To be sure, if C causes E, then C is a sufficient condition for E. But the converse does not follow, since C may be a non-causal, invariable accompaniment of E, and provide adequate grounds (a sufficient condition) for inferring that E will occur or is occurring, without being the cause (as glowing red is an invariable accompaniment of a lump of iron's reaching *n* degrees Centigrade without its causing the iron to be hot).[23]

Does a singular causal statement not nevertheless imply a causal *law*? Not so. All that follows is a presumption that if the same action or event does not, on a subsequent occasion, produce the same result, then there is a difference between the cases that will explain the different outcomes. So the generalizations that follow from a singular causal proposition are not, or not typically, and certainly not necessarily, nomic. Rather,

[23] Rundle, *Why there is Something*, pp. 57–60.

they may be, and commonly are, low-level generalizations, qualified by a *ceteris paribus* clause or by open conditionals ('throwing stones at windows breaks them, *if* one throws hard enough, *if* the glass is not reinforced'), more akin to recipes than to laws of nature.[24] Having found out that doing *this* to *that* brings it about that *p*, then, if you want to bring it about that *p*, *this* is what you should do. Of course, the further away we move from quotidian causal knowledge in the direction of scientific investigations, the closer we are likely to be moving to the nomic generalizations that mesmerize philosophers and characterize *some* parts of science. But it is not these that are implied by the humdrum causal statements that pervade our discourse. The idea that every singular causal statement implies a causal law is no more than a groundless commitment to an inchoate form of determinism.

5. The flaw in the early modern debate

Schopenhauer insisted that only events can be causes of anything.[25] Ducasse followed suit, insisting that 'nothing can, in strict propriety, ever be spoken of as a cause or an effect, except an *event*. . . . objects themselves (in the sense of substances, e.g. gold; or things, e.g. a tree) never can properly be spoken of as causes or effects, but only as agents or patients . . .'.[26] But this is not true. A tree may cause a wall to

[24] See D. Gasking, 'Causation and Recipes', *Mind*, 54 (1955), pp. 479–87, for elaboration of the analogy between causal statements and recipes. Though, I think, it is taken too far, it is a salutary reminder of the evident.

[25] A. Schopenhauer, *The Fourfold Root of the Principle of Sufficient Reason*, trans. K. Hillebrand (George Bell, London, 1907), pp. 38ff.

[26] C. J. Ducasse, 'On the Nature and the Observability of the Causal Relation', repr. in E. Sosa (ed.), *Causation and Conditionals* (Oxford University Press, Oxford, 1975), p. 115. It is noteworthy that G. H. von Wright, for very different reasons, similarly held that 'causal relations exist between natural events, not between agents and events' (*Causality and Determinism* (Columbia University Press, New York, 1974), p. 49). The relation between an agent's act and the upshot or *result* of his act, von Wright argued, is logical, not causal (the result of opening the window is that the window is open). The result of an action (thus construed) may itself be the cause of further consequences of the action. We may concede that this is so for causative verbs the applicability of which to an agent entails that the correlative change has occurred. But this does not imply that there is no such thing as agent causation. That if A opened the door, then he caused the door to be open by opening it, is analytic – for one cannot open a door without the door's being open, at least momentarily. But one can, non-analytically, say that the agent opened the door (brought it about that the door is open, caused the door to be open) by pushing it.

collapse – by undermining its foundations. The sun may cause a photographic plate to darken, by shining on it. Substances (things) are agents,
not events or classes of events, but that does not preclude their causing things. Are they not caus*ers* rather than caus*es*? No, not *rather
than*: a causer is the agent by which or by whom an effect is produced. It is indeed paradigmatically such agents that cause, bring about,
sustain, prevent or suppress change in patients, and do so by acting
on them. (Events, to be sure, are causes too, but not causers.) Is it,
then, that although substances (things) cause changes to patients
upon which they act, they cannot be said to *be* causes? That would
be wrong too. It is true that we more readily speak of the agent as
causing, rather than as *the* (or *a*) *cause*, but there is nothing awry in
saying with the OED that women are the cause of much mischief
(and men of even more). The tubercle bacillus is the cause of tuber-
culosis, the spirocete bacterium *Trepona pallidum* is the cause of
syphilis, and the Hansen bacillus is the cause of leprosy. And the cause
of a fire, we may discover, was a faulty gas valve. Similarly, there is
nothing wrong with identifying substances – stuffs – as causes. Gold,
in a thin film on the surfaces of satellites, is the cause of their very
high degree of reflection of incident infra-red radiation. The acid in
urban rain is the cause of the erosion of building stone. In short, it
is substances and particularized, or specific quantities of, stuff of a
given kind that paradigmatically possess causal powers, and indeed
substances, in both senses of the term, are partly defined by their
causal powers. It would be curious indeed if things and stuffs were
excluded a priori from the category of causes or denied the power
to bring about change by acting on other things. It would be very
strange to *discover* that human beings *cannot* (logically) make things
happen or prevent them from happening, or cannot be identified as
the causes (and causers) of the various disasters they bring about by
their actions. They are makers and breakers, creators and destroyers.
It would be equally strange to suppose that our rich and variegated
vocabulary of causal verbs is *improperly* applied to ourselves and to
other substances.[27]

[27] One may grant that we do not readily speak of one substance *causing another
substance*. We would not say (as Aristotle did) that a father is the cause of his child
or that a carpenter causes his chair. Nor would we say that the child is the effect of
his father or the chair of the carpenter. But we would say that the father begat the
child and that the carpenter made the chair.
   One may equally grant (cf. R. Squires, 'On One's Mind', *Philosophical Quarterly*,
20 (1970), pp. 349–51) that although we may say that an agent A (a certain

How did philosophers come to think otherwise? Partly through the loss of control over the Aristotelian categorial concept of substance, which, as we saw in chapter 2, begins, in the early modern period, with Descartes, is patent in quite different, but equally disastrous, ways in Locke and Spinoza, is glaring in Hume and – despite his efforts to salvage the concept – prominent in Kant. What none of these great thinkers did – to their cost – was to go back to Aristotle and attempt to recover from his discussion of *ousia* a correct account of one of the most basic categories of our thought and talk. It is noteworthy that this sorry confusion from Descartes to Kant was rife at the very time that, in response to the advances in the physical sciences, extensive philosophical investigation into the concept of efficient causation and causal explanation was commenced. Much of the confusion that ensued did indeed stem from excessive preoccupation with what were conceived to be the deliverances of the new science of matter in motion, and too little attention to the demands of reference and predication, identification and re-identification. Hence too, excessive attention was paid to the conceptual character of laws of nature and their role in explanation of natural phenomena, and too little to the use of causative verbs and to humdrum causal judgements and explanations. But philosophy is not the handmaiden of science. It is the tribunal of sense – for both science and common discourse. The concept of cause is at least as fundamental a category of ordinary thought and talk as it is of scientific thought and talk. The former is prior to the latter in the order of understanding.

6. Agent causation as prototype

'Im Anfang war die Tat' ('In the beginning was the deed') Goethe wrote (and Wittgenstein liked to quote). It is to action and passion,

---

substance) was the cause of a certain outcome (e.g. an accident), we would not say that, since A (the thing that caused the accident) was freshly painted and cost £5, the cause of the accident was freshly painted and cost £5. But this does not imply that substances (objects) cannot be causes. To say that A – a substance – was the cause is to identify *the object* that brought about the outcome, typically by doing something. But to predicate things *of* the cause is typically to speak of *the explanation* of the outcome, and it is not the agent that is the explanans, but rather *that it did* whatever it did. We switch here from speaking of the 'natural relation' of causation to speaking of the 'rational relation' of causal explanation (cf. P. F. Strawson, *Analysis and Metaphysics* (Oxford University Press, Oxford, 1992), pp. 109–13).

in the first place, that we should look to clarify our concept of causation. The rationale for this claim is twofold. First, we have already noted that substance concepts are used to signify the basic objects of reference and subjects of predication in our conceptual scheme. Only thus can an objective, public, spatio-temporal system of reference be determined. Active and passive causal powers are characteristic marks of our concepts of substances. Substances are *agents*: that is, things of certain kinds that act on other things. Since there can be no (empirical) agents that cannot also be *patients*, they are also things that can be acted on. So the primacy of agent causation in our conceptual scheme is a correlate of the primacy of concepts of substances in it.

A second rationale for looking, in the first instance, to action and passion for the elucidation of our general concept of causation and for our conception of causal relations is an analytic-genetic one. We may concede that it is not the task of philosophy to speculate on the empirical order of concept acquisition or to trespass upon the territory of psychological learning theory. But it is perfectly licit to reflect upon the needs that call these concepts into existence, and to clarify the roles that they fulfil in the transactions of a language-using animal. To do so, it is profitable to start with a rudimentary language-game in which the moves are clearest. It is no coincidence that the two rationales converge.

The most elementary way in which human beings, as patients, are acted upon is by impact of objects and, in childhood, by parental manipulation. A child is picked up, put down, turned over, pushed, pulled, bathed, dried, warmed, fed, and so on and so forth – subjection to the causal ministries of parents and others being part of the neonate's natural condition. The most elementary way in which human beings, as agents, act upon objects in their environment, both intentionally and non-intentionally, is by impact and manipulation. We move, stop, stretch, compress, lift, put down, drop, place, replace, displace, pluck, pick up, fold, pleat, tear, cut, slice, saw, break, snap, crack, scrape, polish, shake, rotate, spin, dip, immerse, insert, extract, cover, disclose, bury, dig up, open, close an endless variety of things.

Among the earliest things we learn are ways of making things happen (and keeping them happening), of stopping things from continuing, and of preventing things from happening, by our active intervention. We observe how causal agents around us bring about changes, and we commonly apprehend how we ourselves can intervene to stop things from happening or to make things happen. The background to the child's earliest mastery of causal discourse consists in his activities of reacting, often defensively and suppressively, to the cause (e.g. when it hurts or threatens) and in his tentative 'experimental' interventions in the course of things (by poking, pushing, pulling, etc.). When the cause of a salient event is not patent, the child naturally looks for the cause, tries to trace the cause, and gradually learns to experiment, in rudimentary fashion, to find the cause. For that will enable the child, in many commonplace household cases, to discover how to produce or prevent the effect. Mastery of the rudiments of causal discourse is interwoven, from the very beginning, with productive and preventive *control*, with *expectation*, and, as the language of causative verbs is mastered, with *prediction* and then with *explanation*.

The child's induction into the language-games of cause and effect is by way of mastering the use of elementary causative verbs. He could not begin with such forms as 'the X-ing of (agent) A caused the Y-ing of (patient) P'. Rather, the most rudimentary causal vocabulary consists of simple transitive verbs signifying acting on a patient, simple causal verbs implying a result of action, and substance names. 'Do it!' and 'Make it . . . !' belong here too. So too do 'Who did it?', 'What made it . . . ?', and 'Why did it . . . ?'. 'Cause' and 'effect', the generic concepts, do not. For, in the rudimentary cases of agential causation, to cause something to happen is paradigmatically to bring about a change in something by acting on it. Hence specific concepts of action and of changes effected are presupposed by the general concepts of 'to cause', 'to bring about' as well as 'effect', 'consequence' and 'result'. For the general concepts are exemplified by, and hence too explained by, the specific ones.

Impact and manipulation – hitting, pounding, pushing, pulling, tugging, pressing, knocking, picking up, putting down, rolling, squeezing, rubbing, stretching, etc. – enjoy a prominence in the primitive language-games of *ordering someone to make things happen*, of *obeying orders to make things happen*, of *describing someone as making things happen*, and of *asking who or what made things happen*. For we are agents, whose primary and most primitive mode of affecting other things is by way of impact and contact, pressure and traction. No less importantly for the intentional agents that concept-exercising creatures must be are *preventing things from happening* and *stopping things that are happening*, as well as *sustaining* change. For just as we bring about changes by moving in various ways and thereby acting on other things, so too we can interfere in what is going on around us and prevent things from happening, arrest them while they are happening, or keep them going on. In this connection a host of causative verb phrases such as 'to stop P', 'to slow P down', 'to hold P open (closed, taut)', 'to hold P up (down, still)', 'to keep P . . . (hot, cool, wet, dry)' find an obvious role in orders, questions and descriptions.

Here, in a human being's most basic forms of interaction with the environment, the very idea that causal connections are opaque, are not observable – indeed that causes and effects are not, in themselves *connected* at all, but, as Hume wrote, are 'loose and separate' – is absurd. There is nothing opaque about what causes us to fall when we are pushed, and nothing unknown about the cause when we knock over a jug of water, throw a ball, blow a whistle, and so on. The connections between being pushed and falling, between knocking over a receptacle full of water and the water's spilling, or between blowing into a whistle and producing the sound are patent. For these are but so many modes of operation of an agent (often an intentional agent, such as ourselves) upon a patient whereby a change is produced, the change being the result of the action.

Often the mode of operation of one thing on another is evident. One billiard ball makes another billiard ball move by hitting it, a branch breaks a bush by falling on it, a stone crushes a snail by rolling over it. In other cases, the agent is evident, but the mode of operation is not perspicuous: water dissolves sugar, but theory is needed to explain how; salt corrodes iron, but developed chemistry was required to explain the process. In some cases – for example, of 'insubstantial agency' – the mode of operation is inseparable from the agent: the wind breaks the tree by blowing it over (the wind, one might say, is an event in substantial clothing); the river deepens the riverbed by flowing over it.[28] In yet other cases, the causal agent possesses *no* mode of operation – as when a banana skin causes a person to slip and fall, or ice on the road causes a car to skid, or fog causes traffic disruption. But in such cases, we are moving away from the paradigm of agent causation. For here the causal agent does not *act on* the patient, thereby bringing about a change.[29] Rather, the presence of the agent is more akin to a causal condition.

---

[28] What else could a wind do (as opposed to effect) other than blow? or a river do, other than flow? These, one might say, are pseudo-modes of operation, a product of our preference for a form.

[29] Does the banana skin *make* the person slip, or the ice *make* the car skid, without *doing* anything to him or it? One need not regiment usage here. If we choose to say so, then we are detaching the notion of *making something happen* from that of *doing something*. We may do so – but then we must distinguish the two cases, and note that when *making something happen* is thus detached from acting on another thing, it amounts to no more than 'bare causing'. Certainly the banana skin (the agent) caused the person to slip (without acting on him) – other things being equal, he would not have slipped had he not stepped on it.

So, the prototype of causation is of a substantial agent making something happen by acting on a patient. Substantial agent causation provides the *centre of variation*, or better, the *centres* of variation, around which we can order the variety of concepts of causal connection. For there is not one single form of agent causation, but a number of different forms. So far we have emphasized elementary human agency, inasmuch as it is evident that the language-games with causal concepts find their most primitive and perspicuous form there. But not all agency is animate, or even substantial.

Not all causal agents are primary substances. Some are partitioned stuffs – a grain, nugget, chunk, puddle, pool or pond of such-and-such can be a causal agent no less than a thing of a given kind. So too can specific quantities of stuff – this millilitre of acid can burn a hole through the tablecloth, just as that litre of water will remove this stain, and these few milligrams of cyanide suffice to kill someone. We go further, casting things that are neither substances nor partitions or specific quantities of stuff in the role of agents of change. For we speak, perfectly correctly, of the wind blowing down a tree, of light darkening a photographic plate, and the summer's heat turning the milk sour (see fig. 3.1).

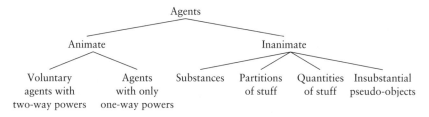

Figure 3.1. *Kinds of causal agents*

Agents act on patients, thereby bringing about a change to the patient (or preventing a change that would otherwise have occurred). So powerful agents are causally related to the patients upon which they act. But, of course, we must take care to clarify what is meant by 'a causal relation' in these cases: are we referring simply to the relation between agent and patient that consists in the agent's *acting on* the patient – that is, what the agent does to the patient in order to bring about a change? Or are we referring to the relation between the agent and the patient that is specified by the causative verb (e.g. A *broke, twisted, moved*, P)? Or are we referring to the relation between the agent and the event or state of affairs that the agent brought about or made happen (as when we say, 'He caused the breakage (the staining, the cooling)' or 'He caused the P to V' ('the vase to break', 'the room to cool down') or 'He made the P V' ('the brass shine', 'the room tidy')? All are legitimate, and a choice is available, but we must be clear what we have in mind when we speak of a causal relation in this context.

Among agents of change that are primary substances, we distinguish animate from inanimate ones. The former include voluntary agents, such as ourselves, with two-way powers to act or refrain from acting at will. Even within the scope of human causal agency there is, as previously noted, important diversity. For we distinguish between human efficient causation, as when we act on something and bring about (or prevent) change, and interpersonal motivational causation, as when we make someone do something by threats, lies or inducements. (This leaves aside such forms of causation, sometimes called 'mental causation', as making someone laugh or cry, on the one hand, and making someone do something under hypnosis, on the other.)

So even our basic prototypes are richly variegated. The derivative forms that provide further centres of variation are even more so.

7. Agent causation is *only* a prototype

Agent causation in its various forms provides the prototypes of causal relations. From these general prototypes, which look both to inanimate causation and to animate causation (which includes efficient causation by action as well as intentional, rational-teleological causation), the prodigiously diverse forms of causal discourse branch off. Some anti-Humean philosophers have exaggerated and distorted the role of control in our conception of causation. Collingwood went so far as to declare that a cause is an event or state by producing or preventing which *we* can produce or prevent the effect – happily embracing the consequence that it would be a contradiction in terms to speak of discovering a non-manipulable cause, such as the cause of sunspots, of supernovae, of non-curable cancers, of earthquakes or volcanic eruptions.[30] But justice can be done to the centrality of controllable causes in our primitive language-game without embracing a conclusion that flies in the face of our use of the term 'cause' in our fully-fledged language-games. For to be sure, we crave *causal* explanations of

[30] R. G. Collingwood, *An Essay on Metaphysics*, rev. edn, ed. R. Martin (Clarendon Press, Oxford, 1998), Part IIIC.

endless non-preventable phenomena, and much that cannot be prevented (earthquakes, tidal waves) can be *avoided* if duly understood,
and predicted on the basis of correct aetiological understanding in
the particular case. What makes an explanation or prediction causal
is not that the phenomenon is accessible to human control.

Von Wright too argued that the concept of cause presupposes that
of human action – in two ways, epistemically and logically. The only
way to establish that a regular sequence is causal (nomic) rather than
accidental, he held, is to validate a counterfactual conditional statement. We need to find out whether, had the putative cause not occurred,
then the effect would not have occurred. But the only way to establish such counterfactuals is by action – by experimental interference
in the course of nature. So our *knowledge* of causes depends on our
manipulative and experimental action. But the dependence he saw
was also a *logical* one, between the causal counterfactual conditional
and action. Over and above the regular sequence, if we could produce (or have produced) the first state on an occasion when it does
or did not obtain, we should bring about (or have brought about)
the second in consequence.[31] So, he averred, '*p* is a cause relative to
q, and *q* an effect relative to *p*, if and only if by doing *p* we could
bring about *q* or by suppressing *p* we could remove *q* or prevent it
from happening'.[32] More generally, he argued that if man 'stood quite
"passive" against nature, if he did not possess the notion that *he* can
do things, make a difference to the world, then there would be no
way of distinguishing the accidental regularity from the causal one.
. . . Man would simply not be familiar with the notion of counter-
factuality, with the idea of how it would have been, if – *This* is the
ground for saying that the *concept* of causal connection rests on the
concept of [human] action.'[33]

One may concede that only an active being could acquire causal
concepts and the general concept of causation. But only an active
being could acquire a language of *any* kind, no matter whether it included causal concepts or not. It is doubtful whether the thought that
man might stand 'passive' against nature is intelligible. Among other
things, such a being would not be a language-using, self-conscious

[31] von Wright, *Causality and Determinism*, p. 51.

[32] G. H. von Wright, *Explanation and Understanding* (Routledge & Kegan Paul,
London, 1971), p. 70. This is not meant as a definition.

[33] von Wright, *Causality and Determinism*, pp. 52f.

creature (as we are). The preconditions for concept acquisition in general are not evidently constitutive elements in the rules for the use of causal verbs. Even if it is true that only intentional agents possessed of causal powers can acquire causal concepts, this does not show that every use of a causal concept implies the (logical) possibility of intentional intervention or manipulation.

It is not evident that it is part of the rules for the use of causal concepts that the cause of a given change must be something that 'we' could suppress or bring about. Astronomical investigation into the causes of the explosion of supernovae is not rendered incoherent just because they are not something that human beings could ever generate. The claim that the Gulf of Mexico was formed by the impact of a large meteor is not invalidated merely because no human being could have prevented it. Of course, we may say that 'if we *could* produce the first state on an occasion when it does not obtain, we should bring about the second in consequence', but all that amounts to is that if E_1 had occurred, then E_2 would have occurred in those circumstances (E_2 would not have occurred 'by itself'). 'We' are strictly superfluous.

Finally, although the hypothesis that the regular sequence of E_2-type events upon E_1-type events is not accidental, but causal, is often validated by experimental confirmation of a counterfactual conditional, this is surely *not* the only way. For, as noted, innumerable causal generalizations are established simply as generalizations of observed singular causal sequences. These may indeed not be *nomic*. Hence they are not results of scientific theory, but the data for such theorizing. But they are causal generalizations, not descriptions of accidental regularities, and they are based on patent singular causal connections that we observe around us. People, we observe, catch cold from standing in a draught; manure is good for crops; wine intoxicates; and so on. We often know that E_1 caused E_2 (we observed it happen, or we made it happen). We do not assume that *whenever* an E_1-type event occurs, an E_2-type event will follow, any more than we assume that *whenever* we act on P by x-ing it, P will V – only that if E_2 does not follow, if P does not V, then there we look for some reason *why* it doesn't, some difference in the circumstances that explains this.

8. Event causation and other centres of variation

If an agent A acts on a patient P by x-ing it, and thereby brings about a change to P, then, in innumerable cases, we can redescribe the causal interaction as A's causing a change to P or as making P change or as bringing about the event of P's V-ing. So, for example, the hot-plate may act on the butter in the frying pan by heating it, thereby melting the butter – so, the hotplate caused the butter to melt, it made the butter melt, it brought about the melting of the butter. Similarly, the stone may act on the window by hitting it, thereby breaking it – so, the stone caused the window to break, it made the window break, it brought about the breaking of the window. In such cases, we describe an agent acting on a patient and causing the occurrence of an event. But, of course, we can carry our transformations fur-ther, and swallow up the reference to the agent and the description of its action by a further nominalization: *the hotplate's heating up* caused the melting of the butter, and *the stone's hitting the window* caused the breaking of the window. Here we have passed from the agential (and, in these two cases, substantial) to the eventual mode of description in which agent and patient alike are swallowed up in event designations (see Table 3.2).

Here too we find a simple paradigm around which are clustered different but related conceptual forms. The centre of variation is the case of one event consisting of a substance acting on another substance and a consequent event consisting of the change to the second sub-stance. The former event is characterized as the cause of the latter, precisely because the constitutive substance is the agent that acted on the patient the change to which is what the second event consists in. A number of features of this simple paradigm of event causation are noteworthy.

First, causation here is a simple binary relation between events. This stands in contrast to the variety of causal relations exhibited by agent causation, where the agent *acts on* the patient *thereby producing* a change *in it*, or, what amounts to the same thing, where the agent does something to the patient, *by doing which* it brings about a change in or to the patient. One may say that if A V's P (the stone breaks the window, the cat kills the mouse, the man lights the stove), this is a binary causal relation between two substances signified by a causal verb that entails a change to the patient brought about by the agent. But one may also say that in cases in which A X's P thereby V-ing it (as when the stone hits the window thereby breaking it) or A V's P by X-ing it (the cat kills the mouse by breaking its neck), we have a more complex relation. Similarly, A may V P, thus preventing P's acting on B and thereby changing B – so A prevents B's X-ing by V-ing P – an even more complex relation.

1. *Two event descriptions linked by a causal connective*

A V's P	as a consequence of which	P X's
The hotplate heats the butter		the butter melts
The stone hits the window		the window breaks
NN opens the door		the room cools

2. *A statement of agent causation supplemented by a specification of a mode of operation*

A X's P by V-ing it (A makes P X by V-ing it; A brings it about that P X's by V-ing it)
The hotplate melts the butter by heating it
The stone breaks the window by hitting it
NN cools the room by opening the door

3. *An event description linked to an infinitive effect-description*

A V's P	thereby causing	P to X
The hotplate heats the butter		the butter to melt
The stone hits the window		the window to break
NN opens the door		the room to cool

4. *Event causation: two event designations linked by the causal operator*

A's V-ing P	caused	P's X-ing
The hotplate's heating the butter		the melting of the butter
The stone's hitting the window		the breaking of the window
NN's opening the door		the cooling of the room

Table 3.2 *Transforms of elementary causal descriptions*

Secondly, the causal responsibility for the change in question is now assigned not to a 'powerful particular' – that is, a substance with an array of causal powers that were manifest in its interaction with the patient – but to an individual event.

Thirdly, events are not *agents*. Precisely because they are not space-occupying temporally persistent particulars, events do not possess *latent* powers explicable by reference to their constitutive nature, as substances do. They are, as noted, causes, but not causers.

Fourthly, and consequently, in descriptions of event causation the explanatory weight of the causal ascription shifts. If E_1 caused E_2, we cannot intelligibly ask what E_1 *did to* E_2 – for one event does not *act on* another event (although we can, of course, ask what an event did to a substance or thing – as when we ask what the heating of the solution did to it, or what the earthquake did to the city). Often we can ask *how* the first event caused the second – but the answer, where we can give one, is not by mentioning what the first did to the second, but by specification of an 'intermediate mechanism' or intervening steps in a 'causal chain'. So if we are asked how the flipping of the light switch causes the turning on of the lights, we may answer by explaining that it closes an electrical circuit, which makes the current flow, which heats up the filament, which . . .

Fifthly, the causal relation between events is formal, its content having been swallowed up in the event descriptions. What the agent did to the patient, and what the result of its so doing was, has been incorporated in the event descriptions, leaving the causal relation contentless. Small wonder that Hume found it problematic to say what it is for one event to cause another, merely gesturing, rather unsuccessfully, at spatio-temporal priority and contiguity, and suggesting, wrongly, that it resides in something unobservable in the individual succession of the two events: namely, instantiation of a regularity. The consequent bewilderment is not unlike the puzzlement over what a substance S can possibly be, given that a substance is a bearer of properties, including the property of being an S. Then, like Locke, we may wonder what the bearer of the property of being an S can possibly be. Similarly here, if we replace the simple description 'The stone hit the window and broke it' (in which what the stone did to the window and what the effect of its thus acting on the window was is evident) by the event description 'The stone's hitting the window caused the breaking of the window', we may then wonder what exactly the causal relation between the events consists in or what the verb 'cause' in this context stands for.

The simple paradigm of the X-ing of A causing the V-ing of P is itself a further centre of variation for another array of types of causal statement. For this paradigm is obviously subject to all the variation we noted in the case of agent causation. Not all agents are substances, so not all events that qualify as causes are changes to substances: for example, the downpour may cause flooding, just as the flash of light may cause the darkening of a photographic plate. Similarly, not all effects are transformations of substances: an explosion may cause a flash of light just as it causes a noise.

There is further, much more extensive conceptual variety consequent upon the polyvalency of the categorial concept of an event. For not all event designations signify simple substance or agential transformation. 'Habitat destruction is the cause of species' extinction', 'The decrease in the infection rate is caused by dietary improvements', 'The rise in the rate of inflation is due to the lax monetary policy', 'The decline in the value of Crook's shares caused the collapse of the market' are all respectable causal statements (though not all are instances of efficient causation). But they are ones that are far from the simple prototype of one 'atomic event' (an action of one substance upon another) causing another (the transformation of that substance). As causal description and attribution are extended from powerful agents to simple 'atomic' events, and then to mass events (such as the French Revolution, the collapse of the gold standard, the outbreak of the First World War, global warming, the extinction of the dinosaurs), we move further and further away from the idea of an active cause that *acts on* a thing and *makes* it change.

An even deeper shift in our causal talk arises when we identify the cause of a change as being neither an event (atomic or otherwise) nor a substance (animate or inanimate) nor a mere insubstantial agent, but rather a *state*, a *condition*, a *property*, or even a *fact*. The icy state of the road can be said to have caused the accident, just as the presence of oxygen (an untoward condition that may have accidentally obtained in an oxygen-free laboratory) may be said to have caused the explosion. The weight of the vault can be said to have caused its collapse, and the tension in the string may cause it to emit a certain sound when plucked. So too, we may say that the fact that the river flooded caused the crops to rot. Here we have moved away from the paradigms, the centres of variation, of agent causation and of event causation alike. If viewed from the perspective of agential and eventual causation, it might seem bizarre that we can speak of *states* of things, *properties* of things, let alone of *facts* as being causes. How can a state *do* anything? How can a property *act on* anything? How can a fact, which is not a spatio-temporal item at all, *bring about a change*? But it is perfectly natural and intelligible that we should speak this way, as we shift our focus from the causal agent or event to a causal *explanation* that does not so much describe what happened as render it intelligible *that* it happened. But for the icy state of the road, the car would not have skidded; had the vault been lighter, the transept would not have collapsed. Had the string not been so taut, it would not have emitted a sound. But for the fact that the river flooded, the crops would not have rotted in the fields. So we *explain* the one in terms of the other: '*q*', we say, 'because *p*', and the explanation we offer is a causal one. But the terms of a correct causal explanation, the *explanandum* and *explanans*, need not be the terms of a causal relation – and when we cite facts or properties, for example, they are patently not.[34] We might say that every causal description is also a causal explanation, but not every causal explanation is a causal description. But it is obvious why our language should have evolved to accommodate both within the rubric of causation.[35]

Once it is realized that our causal discourse incorporates this degree of conceptual diversity, including in the family of causes substantial agents, insubstantial agents, events, processes, properties, states, conditions and facts, it is easy to see why we should also incorporate among explanatory causes the *non-occurrence* of events and the *absence* of conditions. The lack of rainfall is the cause of the failure of the crops, vitamin B deficiency is the cause of beri-beri, and the signalman's failure to pull the lever is the cause of the accident. Here our

[34] The idea that facts are causal relata was proposed by D. H. Mellor, *The Facts of Causation* (Routledge, London, 1995), and duly refuted by W. Künne, *Conceptions of Truth* (Clarendon Press, Oxford, 2003), pp. 142–4. The claim that facts are spatio-temporal items (as events evidently are) was mistakenly asserted by J. L. Austin in 'Truth' and 'Unfair to Facts', repr. in *Philosophical Papers* (Clarendon Press, Oxford, 1961), and disproved by Strawson in 'Truth', repr. in *Logico-linguistic Papers* (Methuen, London, 1971). More recently, J. R. Searle repeated Austin's error, arguing that 'facts can function causally' ('Truth: A Reconsideration of Strawson's Views', in L. E. Hahn (ed.), *The Philosophy of P. F. Strawson*, Library of Living Philosophers, 26 (Open Court, Chicago and Lasalle, Ill., 1998), p. 389), and was corrected by Strawson, who pointed out that Searle's Austinian examples merely show that facts can be causally explanatory, i.e. can be cited in causal explanations, but this does not mean that they can be causally efficacious or stand in causal relations ('Reply to John Searle', ibid., p. 404).

[35] See P. F. Strawson, *Analysis and Metaphysics*, ch. 9.

use of the concept of cause has parted company altogether from the idea of action on something, from the notion of the manifestation of active power. But it retains its connection with the thought of what is, in the circumstances, a condition *sine qua non*. But for the lack of rainfall, the crops would not have failed – and rain normally falls; but for the vitamin B deficiency, the patients would not have fallen victim to beri-beri – and human beings normally obtain sufficient vitamin B for their health; but for the signalman's failure to signal, the train would not have crashed – and it is the signalman's duty to signal. Of course, many other conditions *sine qua non* could be cited. So why pick on the *absence* of a condition or event and cite it as the cause? Typically because it is this that was abnormal, or unexpected, or a breach of duty in the particular case – hence reference to it explains the occurrence in question and assigns causal responsibility (and often personal liability too).[36]

9. Overview

The above discussion has not explored the idea of causal conditions, and has not mentioned the idea of a causal law. These, though of great interest, are not pertinent to our general enterprise. What I have tried to do is to press the case for the conceptual diversity of our common notion of causation. We should look upon substance causation – that is, one substance's acting on another and bringing about a change by its action – as a prototype for our general concept of cause. But it is only one among a variety of centres of variation around which we can fruitfully organize the forms of our various kinds of causal attributions.

Substance causation widens to incorporate agents of change that are not primary substances, both those that are partitions of stuff and those that are specific quantities of stuff, on the one hand, and insubstantial agents of change, such as light, electricity, rain and wind, on the other. Syntactic transformations of many kinds of statements of agent causation yield statements of event causation that link event designations. Here the notion of active power attributable to the intrinsic nature of the cause slips from sight, and the mode of operation is commonly swallowed up in the event designations. (But, as noted,

[36] H. L. A. Hart and A. M. Honoré, *Causation in the Law* (Clarendon Press, Oxford, 1959), ch. 5.

the idea of an agent *acting on* a patient thereby bringing about a change already vanishes in the case of certain forms of substance causation itself (as when a banana skin causes someone to slip).)

Event causation provides a further centre of variation for another array of forms of causal statement. The conceptual diversity of our general category of events is, unsurprisingly, mirrored in the conceptual diversity of event causation.

Once event causation is added to the simpler forms of agential causation, it is natural to extend causal statements to various kinds of causal conditions, determining causes from among such in accordance with various principles of selection. For clearly, any case of event causation presupposes a set of conditions *sine qua non* for the occurrence of the effect. Consequently, not only events are denominated causes, but also states, properties and other conditions that feature in causal explanations. What circumstance from among the antecedent conditions of a particular event we denominate the cause is highly purpose-relative and context-dependent – being determined by our interests, by what is normal and what abnormal in the circumstances, by what is expected, and so forth.

Once we allow categorially varied kinds of conditions to be cited in causal explanations, there is no reason to exclude the absence of expected or normal events, processes and conditions or the omission of acts or activities that might have been expected or required.

The salient pitfall in philosophical scrutiny of our concept of causation and of the forms of our causal statements is to suppose that usage is conceptually homogeneous, and hence to seek to reduce all forms to one single form. But our general category of causation is as unruly, multifaceted and frayed at the edges as our other characteristic categorial concepts. It is, in short, well-adapted to the conditions of our life.

The concept of substance, of action and causation, and hence of powers to act and to act on other things are among the categorial struts in the scaffolding of our thought and talk. So the next theme to which we shall turn is that of agential potencies, liabilities, tendencies and dispositions.

4

Powers

1. Possibility

Since substances are agents, they can *do* things and *act on* other things. The first-order powers of agents are their abilities to do things and to bring about (sustain or prevent) change, on the one hand, and their liabilities to change or to resist change, on the other. The philosophical investigation of such powers of substances in general and of human beings in particular is an investigation into the concepts and conceptual relationships pertaining to their potentialities (and lack of potentialities) for doing and undergoing things.

We distinguish the *actuality of possibilities* ('existential possibility') from the *possibility of actualities* ('problematic possibility').[1] The linguistic forms that pick out the actuality of a possibility are 'It is possible to . . .', 'It is possible for . . .' and 'It is possible that A should . . .' (i.e. 'possible that . . .' followed by a subjunctive). The characteristic form appropriate to discourse concerning the possibility of an actuality is 'It is possible that . . .' followed by an indicative. So, for example, 'It is possible that she is in London today' asserts the possibility of an actuality, whereas 'It is possible for her to be in London today' asserts the actuality of a possibility. The two quite different kinds of statement are differently tensed. When discussing what can or could be done or befall, we tense the possibility: 'It is, was, will be, would be, would have been, possible to . . . (for . . . , that A should

---

[1] See A. R. White, *Modal Thinking* (Blackwell, Oxford, 1975), ch. 1, to which I am indebted for the following discussion.

. . .).' By contrast, when discussing what may be or may have been so, we tense that which is possible: 'It is possible that A did V, is V-ing, will V.' So we can say that it was once possible for A to V, but it no longer is (the opportunity having been missed), but we cannot say that it was once possible that A did V, but no longer is. Rather, we assert that it once seemed possible that A did V, but now that possibility can be excluded. The possibility of an actuality implies the actuality of the corresponding possibility, but that a certain possibility exists does not imply that it is possible that it is, was, or will be actualized (see table 4.1).

A possibility that is actual may itself be a logical, physical, technical, psychological, economic, moral or legal possibility (and doubtless others too) – depending on which aspects or features of a situation are taken into account. What is logically possible is what makes sense. A logical impossibility, as we have noted, is not a possibility that is impossible. It does not exclude anything other than a form of words – which is excluded as lacking any sense. What is physically possible is what is consistent with the laws of nature and the intrinsic natures of things. What is physically impossible is what is inconsistent with the laws of nature or beyond the physical powers of things. It is therefore not logically impossible, for the description of what is physically impossible *makes sense* – it describes a (logical) possibility that is not, as a matter of fact, available to a substance, including such substances as human beings, due to limitations on their physical powers. What are technically possible are courses of action made available by existing skills, techniques and machines. What is psychologically possible is what a person can bring himself to do in the face of his revulsions, terrors, compulsive neuroses, etc. What is legally possible for a legal subject is what he is empowered or permitted by law to do.

The modal auxiliary 'can' is the most commonly used instrument to indicate the actuality of a possibility, whereas one role of the auxiliary 'may' is to indicate the possibility of an actuality. 'A can be in London tomorrow' signifies that it is possible *for* A *to be* in London tomorrow, whereas 'A may be in London tomorrow' signifies that it is possible *that* A *will be* in London tomorrow. There is no need to insist (as some have done) that this auxiliary verb has many different meanings or senses. But, depending upon the agent and the context under consideration, very different features of situations and agents may be picked out by its use. 'A can V' commonly ascribes a (generic) *ability* to an agent (e.g. 'He can speak German / play cricket

Actuality of a possibility (*existential possibility*)	*Possibility of an actuality* (*problematic possibility*)
It is possible to . . . It is possible for . . . It is possible that A should be // have . . .	It is possible that *p*
It is possible to . . . // for . . . // that . . . should . . . It was possible to . . . // for . . . // that . . . should . . . It will be possible to // for . . . // that . . . should . . . It would be possible to // for . . . // that . . . should . . . It would have been possible to . . . // for . . . // that . . . should . . .	It is possible that A is V-ing It is possible that A V'd It is possible that A will V It is possible that A would V It is possible that A would have V'd
It was once possible for A to V (but no longer is)	It once seemed possible that A V'd (but no longer seems so)
'It is possible for A to V' does not imply 'It is possible that A V's'	'It is possible that A V's' implies 'It is possible for A to V'
Can, in certain cases, ask *how* it is possible	Can ask only what evidence there is for the possibility that A is V-ing, V'd, will V, would have V'd
Contrasts with necessity: if it is necessary to . . . // for . . . // that . . . should // then it is not possible that . . . not V (there is no way to avoid V-ing)	Contrasts with 'It is certain that *p*' and with 'It is probable that *p*'
Can be qualified as logical, physical, technical, psychological, economic, moral, legal, etc.	Cannot be thus qualified; but is evidence-relative

Table 4.1 *The actuality of a possibility and the possibility of an actuality compared*

/ ride a bicycle', 'It can dissolve metals / stick any surfaces / pick up radio signals'). In other contexts it may be used to ascribe the possibility of a specific *accomplishment* on an occasion (e.g. 'He can get a First', 'It can stick this to that', 'I can hole this in three'). 'A can V' may be used to attribute *perceptual and intellectual powers* (e.g. 'Bees can see', 'He can understand Chinese').[2] It may indicate a *regulation* ('He can take a fortnight's holiday each year'). It can indicate an *objective opportunity* (e.g. 'The shop is open, so you can get some widgets'), the availability of appropriate means that renders a given end *attainable* ('Now that I have a knife, I can cut it') or a *subjective opportunity* ('I am free next Friday afternoon, so I can meet you then'). 'A can be F' may be used to ascribe the possibility of *exhibiting general characteristics* (e.g. 'She can be very charming', 'It can be dangerous'). Our concern in the sequel will be exclusively with the actuality of possibilities, and not with the possibility of actualities.

Note that the fact that A V's (V'd or will V) implies that it is (was or will be) possible for A to V (hence the scholastic tag 'ab esse ad posse'), but, in the case of human and animal agency it may not imply that A has or had the ability to V – since in some kinds of cases A may V or may have V'd by sheer fluke or beginner's luck.[3] Of course, an inanimate agent too may V by a fluke, but then the fluke will lie in the obtaining of the circumstances required for A to V despite the low probability of their occurrence. If an inanimate agent V's, then it can, is able or has the power to V, whereas a human being may V even though he lacks the ability to V.

2. Powers of the inanimate

Inanimate stuffs and things have powers – potentialities to change, bring about change, be changed or resist being changed. Dynamite is

---

[2] Rather curiously, it can also be used to describe their actualization: e.g. 'I can see him walking across the road', 'I can understand your predicament' – and here *that I can* implies *that I do*.

[3] But not in any kind of case. If V-ing is so easy that any able-bodied adult can do it (e.g. open a door), it cannot be a fluke that A (a normal, able-bodied adult) did it. If it is so difficult that only an expert could do it (e.g. put ten consecutive shots in the bull), then by and large it could not be a fluke that A did it (he must be a marksman).

explosive, steel resilient, wood inflammable, sand insoluble and arsenic poisonous. Hence too partitions (e.g. a stick of dynamite, a bar of steel) and specific quantities (this pint of milk, that ounce of arsenic) of such stuffs can be said to have those powers (although in some cases a threshold quantity may be needed for the stuff to possess the power). Similarly, inanimate natural and artefactual substances (things) have powers – the sun has the power to radiate light and heat, stones of appropriate size and hardness have the power to break windows, candles have the power to illuminate the darkness, and motor cars (these days) generally have the power to do 100 mph. To specify the powers of an inanimate agent is to describe what behaviour *is physically, chemically, etc. possible for it*, given its nature.

The powers of inanimate things require conditions for them to be actualized. Among the conditions necessary for the actualization of the power of an inanimate object we can, from case to case, distinguish *enabling conditions* from the *stimulus condition* – the latter being the condition that initiates the action (winding up a spring-driven watch is a stimulus condition for the action of the watch, whereas winding up a long-case clock is only an enabling condition, and it is setting the pendulum in motion that is the stimulus condition). Where the power in question is to generate or undergo a process, we can further distinguish accelerating from decelerating conditions, sustaining conditions, impeding and terminating conditions.

The conditions necessary for the actualization of the power of an inanimate thing may be internal (but not intrinsic) to the substance, or external (circumstantial). Internal conditions concern the accidental properties of the substance – a piece of wood can burn, for example, only if it is dry; a quantity of hydrochloric acid can dissolve zinc only if it is in solution; and a car can run only if there is petrol in the tank. External conditions concern circumstances – a piece of wood can burn, but only if there is oxygen, and a standard eighteenth-century table clock can keep time accurately only if there is no significant fluctuation of temperature. If such internal and external conditions were to be satisfied, then, if agent A has the power to V, it would V, and if they are satisfied, then it will V. In this sense, the powers of an inanimate agent are dispositional properties.

It is striking that, unlike *distinctively* human dispositions, an inanimate substance may, and most commonly does, possess natural dispositions which are never actualized. Obviously, not every poisonous substance (thing, or partition or specific quantity of stuff) poisons anything, not every brittle substance breaks, and not every soluble thing dissolves. For the vast majority of things, the conditions and circumstances for some of their various powers to be actualized are never fulfilled. Human dispositions (of temperament and character), by contrast, are possessed only if what they are dispositions to do is, from time to time, done. One cannot be timid unless one acts timidly from time to time, or of a cheerful disposition unless one is cheerful occasionally. If someone manages to go through life without ever being confronted by danger, he cannot *be* courageous – the most one can say is that *had* he been so confronted, then *he would have acted* courageously and *would have been* a courageous man. But human abilities, unlike dispositions of temperament and character, *are* like dispositions of the inanimate in *this* respect: they can be possessed but never exercised. For an ability and an opportunity do not imply action. We all have the ability to kill other humans, but, mercifully, few of us choose to exercise it.

The powers of the inanimate, being dispositions in the above explained sense, are one-way powers – if the conditions for the actualization of an agent's power to V are satisfied, then the agent V's – for the agent does not have the power not to V in those circumstances. There is no such thing as an inanimate substance's having a choice, hence no such thing as its refraining or abstaining from V-ing when the conditions for V-ing are satisfied. Because the powers of the inanimate are one-way powers, there are no *opportunity conditions* for an inanimate substance to actualize its powers, but only *occasions*. For inanimate substances do not have *opportunities* which they can either avail themselves of or pass by, as human beings and other animals do.

Not all the active powers ascribable to inanimate substances are essentially powers to produce change. For inanimate things can not only *act on* other things, they can also simply *do* things – as the river may flow, the wheel may turn, and the pendulum may swing back and forth. Nevertheless, the causal powers of things loom large in our concepts (and conceptions) of (secondary) substances. Causal powers are patient- and circumstance-relative. Arsenic is poisonous for some creatures, but not for others (and a lethal dose for one animal, or kind of animal, may not be such for another); a kitchen knife can cut bread or vegetables, but not iron or glass. Similarly, substances have characteristic powers at normal temperatures, but quite different ones at extremes of heat or cold; some things have their characteristic powers when in solution, but not when dry, or at atmospheric pressure, but not in a vacuum.

3. Active and passive powers of the inanimate

An inanimate substance has an active power to act on a patient in appropriate circumstances if and only if it can act on that patient or type of patient, and its being able to do so is attributable to its intrinsic properties or its essential nature (or both). The distinction between active and passive powers goes back to Aristotle, but there is a long tradition in early modern philosophy of denying that inanimate substances have active powers at all. Thus Locke, for example, argued that

> there are instances of both [motion and thinking], which, upon due consideration, will be found rather *Passions* than *Actions*, and consequently so far the effects barely of passive Powers in those subjects, which yet on their account are thought *Agents*. For in these instances, the substance that hath motion, or thought, receives the impression whereby it is put into that *Action* purely from without, and so acts merely by the capacity it has to receive such an impression from some external Agent; and such a *Power* is not properly an *Active Power*, but a mere passive capacity in the subject. Sometimes the Substance, or Agent, puts itself into *Action* by its own Power, and this is properly *Active Power*. . . . the *Active power* of motion is in no substance which cannot begin motion in it self, or in another substance when at rest.[4]

This, in effect, conflates the case in which a substance that has been caused to move can make another substance move by virtue of its own movement (as in the case of the impact of one billiard ball upon another) with mere passive power to be moved. More generally, it fails to recognize inanimate active powers to make certain things happen, a power possessed by inanimate substances despite their motion not being *self-initiated*, acknowledging only the active power to *initiate* a happening, in particular the power to do so at will – as possessed by animal and human agents. But we do want to distinguish between the billiard ball, that *can*, if set in motion, move another billiard ball by impact, and a ping-pong ball that, if moving at similar speed, *cannot* do so. (Similarly, we want to deny that hydrochloric acid has the power to dissolve gold and affirm that aqua regia does have such a power.)

---

[4] Locke, *An Essay Concerning Human Understanding*, II. xxi. 72.

Others, such as Thomas Reid, denied the intelligibility of passive powers, taking active powers to stand in contrast to *speculative* powers. 'I conceive passive power is no power at all', he wrote, 'To call [the possibility of being changed] *power*, seems to be a misapplication of this word. . . . I see no propriety at all in passive power; it is a powerless power, and a contradiction in terms.'[5] This objection carries little weight, since the distinction is meant to be a quasi-technical one between different kinds of potentialities, and is not meant to reflect the customary use of the English word 'power' (although Reid's nineteenth-century editor, Sir William Hamilton, pointed out that it does reflect a grammatical distinction among ancient Greek adjectives). 'Power' thus used includes both potentialities to do things and act on other things, on the one hand, and the potentialities to react to being acted on, on the other. The words 'liability' and 'susceptibility', in their ordinary use, manifest the recognition in English of (a part of the range of) the category of passive powers. A liability of an inanimate thing is a passive disposition: a substance is liable to V (undergo a certain change) *if* acted on by another agent in appropriate circumstances. A susceptibility is a sensitivity (vulnerability) to a certain agent or condition that brings about change. That something is liable to V if conditions C obtain does not imply that it will ever V. But something is prone to V or has a tendency to V only if it V's with some regularity – the concepts of a proneness and a tendency being frequency concepts. Liabilities and susceptibilities are among the *reactive* passive powers of substances. These may be contrasted with *resistive* passive powers, such as insolubility, non-inflammability, being bullet-proof or earthquake-resistant, and so forth.

We have already remarked that there are no substances in nature that are only agents or only patients. There is commonly causal reciprocity in the interaction of agent and patient. The agent that acts on a patient may be destroyed in effecting the change it brings about – as is a stick of dynamite or a bomb; or the agent may be destroyed *by the patient* in the course of the interaction – as when the antibiotic acts upon the bacteria of the illness that it was taken to cure; or the agent may itself be changed by the patient in certain ways – as when the saw is blunted by the wood it is cutting.

[5] Thomas Reid, *Essays on the Active Powers of Man*, Essay I, in *The Works of Thomas Reid*, ed. Sir William Hamilton (Maclachlan and Stewart, Edinburgh, 1863), vol. 2, p. 519.

4. Power and its actualization

A power, no matter whether active or passive, is a kind of potentiality. Hence, contrary to what has sometimes been claimed, it is not a state. Nor is possessing a power the same as being in a certain state. To be sure, a substance may be in a certain state for a period of time, and it may also possess a given power for a period of time – but being in the state is not the same as having the power, even if the existence of the state explains the possession of the power. Wittgenstein made this point forcibly in the Brown Book:

> There are . . . various reasons which incline us to look at the fact of something being possible, someone being able to do something, etc., as the fact that he or it is in a particular state. Roughly speaking, this comes to saying that 'A is in the state of being able to do something' is the form of representation we are most strongly tempted to adopt; or, as one could also put it, we are strongly inclined to use the metaphor of something being in a peculiar state for saying that something can behave in a particular way. And this way of representation, or this metaphor, is embodied in the expression 'He is capable of . . .', 'He is able to multiply large numbers in his head', 'He can play chess': in these sentences the verb is used in the *present tense*, suggesting that the phrases are descriptions of states which exist at the moment when we speak.
>   The same tendency shows itself in our calling the ability to solve a mathematical problem, the ability to enjoy a piece of music, etc., certain states of mind; we don't mean by this expression 'conscious mental phenomena'. Rather, a state of mind in this sense is the state of a hypothetical mechanism, a mind model meant to explain the conscious mental phenomena . . . In this way also we can hardly help conceiving of memory as a kind of storehouse. Note also how sure people are that to the ability to add or to multiply or to say a poem by heart, etc., there *must* correspond a peculiar state of the person's brain, although on the other hand they know next to nothing about such psycho-physiological correspondences. We regard these phenomena as manifestations of this mechanism, and their possibility is the particular construction of the mechanism itself.[6]

The point applies no less to powers of the inanimate. One can commonly (but by no means uniformly) perceive the state a thing or a

[6] Luding Wittgenstein, *The Blue and Brown Books* (Blackwell, Oxford, 1958), pp. 117f.

quantity of stuff is in – whether it is liquid or solid, whether the spring is wound up or run down, whether the garden is tidy or overgrown, etc. For the state is an actuality. But one cannot see the powers of a thing any more than one can see the sounds it makes, for the power is a potentiality. To be sure, in some cases, one can see *that it has* certain powers – for example, that this round peg can fit into that hole, that this doorstop can keep the door open, that this spring can drive the clock. Sometimes a state of the possessor of the power shows that it possesses the power, and commonly the possession of a power is explicable by reference to a state of the substance in question. If the going-train is wound up, then it can drive the movement; if the sealing wax is hot (and hence liquified), then it can seal the parcel – but the state is not identical with the power.

A power is not only distinct from the state, if any, that explains its possession, but it is also distinct from its actualization. Being able to V is one thing, V-ing is another. A power is typically possessed over time, but it is actualized (if at all) at a time or at certain times (and perhaps, for a time). Of course, some powers, by their nature, can be actualized only once – a stick of dynamite or a bomb can explode only once, an aspirin is not for multiple use, and although a cigarette can be shared, it cannot be smoked a second time. Nevertheless, such objects, if they do not degenerate, may possess the power for as long as they exist, which may be for many years. Although the power can be actualized only once, it can be actualized at any time during which the substance possesses it.

The relationship between a power and its actualization has bred three distinctive philosophical confusions: scepticism concerning powers, reduction of powers to their exercise, and reification of powers (see fig. 4.1).[7]

Scepticism about powers has been generated by the thought that one can perceive the actualization of powers, but not the powers themselves. To extreme empiricists, this has suggested that talk of powers is mere mystification, and that the very concept (or idea) of power is vacuous. Thus Hume wrote, 'It is impossible . . . that the idea of power can be derived from the contemplation of bodies, in single instances of their operation, because no bodies ever discover

---

[7] See M. Ayers, *The Refutation of Determinism* (Methuen, London, 1968), and A. J. P. Kenny, *Will, Freedom and Power* (Blackwell, Oxford, 1976). To the latter, here, as elsewhere, I am much indebted.

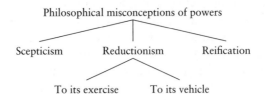

Figure 4.1. *Standard misconceptions about powers*

any power which can be the original of this idea.'[8] And, 'We never
have any impression, that contains any power or efficacy. We never
therefore have any idea of power.'[9] But even if we grant that powers
are not perceptible – that is, that there is no such thing as perceiving the potency of a thing, but only *that* it has it – it does not
follow that we have no genuine concept of power. The expressions
'possibility', 'potentiality', 'power', 'ability', 'liability' all have determinate uses in our language. Moreover, that one cannot perceive a
power does not imply that we lack adequate grounds for applying
the concept. There are various criteria, some logical and others
empirical, for the possession of a power by a thing. The logical
criteria for whether a spatial object *fits* into another spatial object
or into a given space are its shape and size. That a long-case clock
has a huge bob, a heat-compensating pendulum, a spring-and-shutter
winding mechanism, and is in good working order is an empirical
warrant that it can keep good time. And so on.

Scepticism about powers leads readily to *reductionism*. No one,
presumably, would wish to claim that there are *no* possibilities at all
– that no substance or agent has the power to do *anything*. But one
might claim (and rash determinists do claim) that the only things that
can happen are those things that do happen, and hence that the only
power a thing has is the power to do exactly what it does. And so
indeed Hume proceeded to argue: 'The distinction we often make
betwixt *power* and the *exercise* of it, is . . . without foundation' and
'is entirely frivolous'.[10] Accordingly, only what is actual is possible,

---

[8] Hume, *An Enquiry Concerning Human Understanding*, Sect. VII, Part 1, §50,
ed. Selby-Bigge, 2nd edn (Clarendon Press, Oxford, 1902), p. 64.

[9] Hume, *A Treatise on Human Nature*, I. iii. xiv.

[10] Ibid.

and whatever happens is the only thing that can happen. This form of reductionism is indeed ancient, having been embraced in antiquity by the Megarians. The incoherence of the position was already exposed by Aristotle.[11] For if a thing *can* do only what it in fact *does* do, then we can no longer speak of skills, since a man cannot do what he is not doing; nor can we speak of learning (acquisition of skills). We should be deemed blind when we are not seeing, and deaf when we are not hearing. Moreover, if what *is* not V-ing *cannot* V, as the Megarians (and Hume) held, and if what cannot V will not V, then nothing can ever happen. And this is patently absurd.

A third kind of confusion is to *reify* powers. It was a confusion of alchemists to suppose that they could get the powers of one substance to migrate to another, as if the powers of a thing were ingredients that could be distilled and then transferred. If one thinks of powers as being kinds of things, then one will be prone to view the relation between a power and its actualization as a causal, rather than a logical, relation, as if the power of an agent to V could make the agent V. It is instructive to learn that opium has the power to put people to sleep, but, as Molière mocked, foolish to explain *why* or *how* opium puts people to sleep by reference to its power to do so. The reification of powers is particularly rife in faculty psychology, in which the actions of sentient agents are attributed to their faculties. Locke noted that although understanding and the will are two faculties of the mind, one must not suppose these words 'to stand for some real Beings in the Soul, that performed those Actions of Understanding and Volition. . . . this way of Speaking of *Faculties*, has misled many into a confused Notion of so many distinct Agents in us, which had their several Provinces and Authorities, and did command, obey, and perform several Actions, as so many distinct Beings.'[12] And he warned wisely that 'if it be reasonable to suppose and talk of *Faculties*, as distinct Beings, that can act . . . 'tis fit that we should make a speaking *Faculty*, and a walking *Faculty*, and a dancing *Faculty*, by which those Actions are produced . . .'.[13] The dangers against which Locke warned have not disappeared, and distinguished thinkers still succumb to these confusions. Noam Chomsky, for example, writes:

[11] Aristotle, *Metaphysics*, Bk IX, ch. 3.

[12] Locke, *Essay*, II. xxi. 6.

[13] Ibid., II. xxi. 17f.

The language faculty is a component of the mind/brain, part of the human biological endowment. Presented with data, the child, or, more specifically, *the child's language faculty, forms a language*, a computational system of some kind that provides structured representations of linguistic expressions that determine their sound and meaning. . . . Universal grammar attempts to formulate the principles that enter into the operation of the language faculty. The grammar of a particular language is an account of *the state of the language faculty after it has been presented with data of experience*; universal grammar is an account of the initial state of the language faculty before any experience.[14]

'This way of talking', as Locke noted in 1690, 'nevertheless, has prevailed, and, as I guess, produced great confusion.' Nowhere does it produce more confusion than in attributing powers to the mind and conceiving of the mind as the agent that exercises the distinctively human powers of intellect and will.

Powers are not themselves agents, but rather the potencies of agents. The possessor of the power to V is the agent that has the ability to V. The identity of the owner of a power does not determine the identity of the power. What distinguishes A's powers from B's powers (if they are distinct) is not the difference in the possessor. (Similarly, what distinguishes *this* colour from *that* colour, or my pain from your pain, is not who has it.) Nor is it the aetiology of the acquisition of the power by its possessor. How one acquired a power, or what caused one to have a certain power is one thing, *what* power one has is another. The identity of a power is determined by what it is a power to do, whether it is a one-way or a two-way power (see below), the extent of the power (the range of its possible patients), the conditions under which it can be actualized, and the degree of the power.

The possession of a power by a substance is determined by various criteria. The most obvious is, of course, its actualization. But, as already noted, there are others. Some pertain to overt features of the substance (as size and shape are criteria for an object's fitting into a space, for whether a screwdriver will fit a given screw or a key open a given lock). Others pertain to the constitutive matter (whether it is made of steel or clay), or some specific ingredient of a stuff or thing (whether it contains an antibiotic), or the structure and relations of

---

[14] Noam Chomsky, *Language and Problems of Knowledge: The Managua Lectures* (MIT Press, Cambridge, Mass., 1988), pp. 60f; emphasis added.

the parts of the thing (a motor or engine of one kind or another). In some cases, a criterion for a specific substance's having a power to V may simply be that it is a *normal* S, the ability to V being a defining feature of S's.

5. Power and its vehicle

It is often useful to distinguish between a power and its vehicle.[15] The vehicle of a power, if it has one, is the ingredient, constitutive matter, form or structure in virtue of which the substance that has the power to V can V. In some cases, how the substance V's is explained by reference to the operation of its vehicle. The vehicle of a power is an actuality, not a potentiality. It is something that can, for example, be weighed (in certain cases) or its dimensions measured (in others).

The vehicles of the powers of many stuffs are ingredients. So, for example, the vehicle of the power of whisky to intoxicate is the alcohol that is one of its ingredients, the vehicle of the power of hemlock to poison is coniine, and the vehicle of the power of fresh lime juice to prevent scurvy is vitamin C (ascorbic acid). Adequate knowledge of physiology and neurophysiology will explain the operation of molecules of C_2H_5OH on the relevant parts of the brain that renders the whisky-drinker drunk, just as physiological and chemical theory will explain the operation of 2n-propylpiperidine in poisoning anyone who drinks hemlock, or the operation of ascorbic acid in the prevention or cure of scurvy. But note that the distinction between the possessor of a power and the vehicle of the power cannot be drawn with reference to the intoxicative power of alcohol itself or to the poisonousness of coniine, or to the curative power of vitamin C. Nevertheless, the distinction is clear and important in discourse concerning medicines, drugs and foodstuffs, where we wish to know the so-called *active ingredient* in the substance or partition of stuff.

The vehicle of the power of a substance (thing) may also be its constitutive stuff – the vehicle of the power of a steel jack to support the weight of the car is the hardened steel of which it is made. But it may also be the shape of a thing – the vehicle of the power of the key to open a door is not only the metal of which it is made

---

[15] Kenny, *Will, Freedom and Power*, pp. 10f.

but also the particular shape it has that fits the wards of the lock. And it may be the structure and dynamics of a mechanism – as the vehicle of the power of a motor car to do 120 mph is its engine with its structure of cylinders, pistons, etc. I shall defer for a moment the application of the distinction between power and vehicle to human powers.

Once the distinction between power and vehicle is drawn, the error of yet another form of reductionism is readily exposed. Central state materialism was prone to reduce a power to its vehicle, and to think of a power, thus reduced, as the cause of its actualization or manifestation. Thus it has been argued that

> . . . to speak of an object's having a dispositional property entails that the object is in some non-dispositional state or that it has some property (there exists a 'categorical basis') which is responsible for the object manifesting certain behaviour in certain circumstances . . . if brittleness can be identified with an actual *state* of the glass, then we can think of it as a cause, or, more vaguely, a causal factor, in the process that brings about the breaking. Dispositions are seen to be states that actually *stand behind* their manifestations. It is simply that the states are *identified* in terms of their manifestations in suitable conditions, rather than in terms of their intrinsic nature.
>
> Our argument for a 'Realist' account of dispositions can equally be applied to capacities and powers. They, too, must be conceived of as states of the object that has the capacity or power.[16]

This form of reductionism, as Anthony Kenny pointed out, is no less misconceived than Megarian and Humean reduction of powers to their exercise. It is striking how much more tempting vehicle reductionism appears to be at the micro-level of molecular, atomic and ionic theory than it is at the gross level of observable mechanisms. No one would identify the horsepower of the car with the state of its engine. Nor would anyone look for its horsepower under its bonnet, save in jest. But many are prone to identify powers of stuffs, things and of animals (including humans) with the molecular structure of their ingredients, constituents or parts. (Materialist philosophers and cognitive neuroscientists are particularly prone to identify psychological and intellectual powers – such as knowledge or memory – with neural

---

[16] D. M. Armstrong, *A Materialist Theory of the Mind* (Routledge & Kegan Paul, London, 1968), pp. 86, 88.

structures.) But this is confused. Although many powers may indeed have a 'categorical basis' in their vehicle, nevertheless the potency is distinct from, and not reducible to, the structure or form of the vehicle. One and the same power, in different artefacts (e.g. in different computers or calculators operating with different systems, or in clockwork and electronic watches), may have an entirely different vehicle or categorical basis. If the powers were reducible to their vehicles, they could not be identical – but they often are. The possibility of a substance's V-ing cannot be *reduced* to what makes it possible for the substance to V, but only *explained* by reference to it.

Furthermore, although it is an ideal of science to explain powers in terms of underlying structures, it is not logically possible that *all* powers should be so explained. At the ultimate level of scientific explanation at any given epoch, we find an array of basic individuals, properties and relations. The powers of *those* individuals cannot be *further* explained in terms of yet another level of different individuals, properties and relations – for there is, in our present scientific conceptual scheme, no further level (and if there were, there would be no further level behind that one). That the basic individuals in our scientific conceptual scheme have the powers they have is just a brute fact.

6. First- and second-order powers; loss of power

Some things may lack a certain power but be able to acquire it. To have the capacity to acquire a power is itself a power, a second-order one. So, for example, iron or steel can be magnetized – that is, acquire the power to attract metal. If a piece of iron or steel is placed inside a solenoid through which electric current is flowing, it will become magnetized. Wood, by contrast, has no such second-order power.

Corresponding to the second-order power to acquire a power is the liability or susceptibility to lose or be deprived of a power. A sharp blow to a magnet will deprive it of its powers of magnetic attraction; blunting a knife will deprive it of its power to cut well. Foodstuffs are liable to deteriorate over time due to bacterial growth and chemical transformation, thus losing their nutritive powers (and acquiring noxious powers to poison which they lack when fresh). Machines tend to become less powerful or to lose some of their powers through the wear and tear of use.

Just as there are second-order powers to acquire active powers, so too there are second-order powers to acquire passive ones. Many materials (and hence any partitions or specific quantities of the stuff) and artefacts are sensitive to ageing, use and exposure of one kind or another, acquiring liabilities and susceptibilities they did not have when new. So metals such as steel and certain artefacts made of steel are susceptible to metal fatigue consequent on use, thus acquiring a liability to fracture. Damage to the surface of some treated metals and artefacts made of such metals may render the material susceptible to rusting. Oxidation, due to exposure to air and to sunlight, may make rubber or a rubber band lose its elasticity.

Liability to lose a power through degeneration or through the action of some agent is a second-order passive power. Degeneration is intrinsic change. It may be accelerated through extrinsic conditions. Loss of power through extrinsic action of another agent may be through damage or environmentally induced deterioration (in the case of inanimate things) and injury and infection (in the case of animals). To lose a power is to be (relatively) incapacitated. Some powers are either possessed or not possessed; others admit of degrees. Substances that have powers that admit of degrees may suffer partial loss of power – be weakened. To undergo partial loss of power is to suffer impairment. Incapacitation and impairment may be temporary or permanent. Substances that possess a power that admits of degrees may lose that power immediately or gradually. Drugs, for example, typically lose their effectiveness gradually, and machines tend to deteriorate slowly through use, more rapidly through over-use. But breakage of critical parts typically involves complete loss of functionality. Loss of power may be ameliorated naturally (recovery through a period of disuse) or by intervention (repair). The loss of powers by animate beings and humans will be discussed below.

7. Human powers: basic distinctions

Humans are living beings and share many powers with other animate creatures. We are self-moving creatures with a variety of perceptual powers; we can feel affections and have desires; hence we pursue goals, and can feel pleasure and pain. The particular ranges and degrees of many of these powers are characteristic of us as a species – part of our nature, as are their vehicles. Many can be enhanced by training. The innate distribution of the natural powers of human beings is unequal. So is the distribution of the second-order powers to acquire first-order powers by learning.

The possibility of exercising these powers and their roles in our lives greatly concern us. For, unlike all other animals, we are language-using, self-conscious creatures. So we are aware of our possession of powers, often take pleasure in their exercise, and fear their loss or diminution. We are aware, and often conscious, of our powers of movement, perception and sensation, of our affective capacities and susceptibilities (e.g. of our sensibility and sensitivity), of our cognitive and cogitative powers (e.g. of our erudition, memory and intelligence, of our abilities to learn and to reason), of our physical strength, powers of endurance, sexual potency, and of our liability to various forms of impairment, deterioration or loss of power. What counts as a normal human being is determined in part by possession of distinctive ranges and degrees of passive and active powers.

Distinctions that apply to the powers of inanimate and insentient substances also apply to the powers of man, but often with important differences and modifications. For many of our powers are voluntary ones, which we can exercise at will. This fact, the varying degrees and forms of voluntariness, and their various consequences, carry in their wake a far more complex network of subtly differentiated concepts apt for the description of human possibilities of changing, bringing about change, being changed or resisting change than is required for the description of the inanimate.

i. *One-way and two-way powers*

As we have seen, insentient objects have only one-way powers. Many of our powers are also one-way, such as our powers to digest food, to salivate, to grow (in childhood) – in short, all those things that we *can* do, but which we cannot do at will and cannot refrain from doing or directly control. Two-way powers, by contrast, are powers of voluntary action. They might be called 'volitional powers', being powers to do things that we can do or refrain from doing at will. One can refrain from (forbear or omit) V-ing only if there is an opportunity to V. What one cannot do for lack of an opportunity, one cannot forbear either – omission presupposes ability and opportunity. One may be unable to omit, forbear or refrain – when one acts under inner compulsion. Although doing and forbearing are reciprocal, one may have to learn how to V, but it does not follow that one has to learn how to forbear V-ing (although one may need to be trained to resist temptation).

It is only inasmuch as we have the two-way power to V or not to V that we can be said to V voluntarily, to V because we want to, or to V intentionally, and hence too, to choose to V, to try to V, or to V on purpose. (Of course, if V-ing is a one-way power, we may voluntarily *bring it about* that we V.) Clearly, two-way powers are not, as such, dispositions, although, of course, many human dispositions are exhibited in the exercise of two-way powers. That a person has the ability to V or refrain from V-ing at will, does not imply that he has a disposition or proneness to V, or indeed that he ever will V. Indeed, not everything a person is able to do or refrain from doing at will, and which, under certain circumstances, he would do (e.g. commit suicide *in extremis*), qualifies as something that he has or could have a disposition or tendency to do.

We possess the power to imagine, to think and to reason, and these powers too we can exercise at will. To do so is, in one sense, not to *act* at all (hence we contrast thought and action). In another sense, one might say, these are 'mental acts'. But mental acts are not without qualification a species of act of which overt acts are another species. They need involve neither bringing about nor preventing changes in the world (acting on another thing), or indeed even moving. But we should distinguish between cases of voluntary action and thought, where we could have refrained or abstained from doing whatever we did, and cases in which we could not help doing what we did. It is a marked feature of our powers of thought and imagination that although we can typically think and imagine things at will, it is also *common* for us to think and imagine things without wanting to – thoughts come to us unbidden, and our imagination often runs away with us. By contrast, humdrum movement-involving human actions, such as eating, drinking, walking, playing, are normally performed voluntarily. These can be involuntary only in abnormal circumstances. But they may be non-voluntary, when one is forced to do them.

Between the extremes of one-way and two-way powers are cases of powers the exercise of which is not *wholly* under our control.[17] These include actions of a kind that we can initiate, but cannot stop once begun, such as blinking, actions that we cannot initiate at will, but which we can stop or inhibit once begun (sneezing, weeping),

---

[17] See B. Rundle, *Mind in Action* (Clarendon Press, Oxford, 1997), pp. 159f.

and actions which we can initiate or stop at will, but over which we nevertheless have only partial control, like breathing. The spectrum of different kinds of cases that stretches between one-way powers such as the power to digest, on the one hand, and two-way powers, such as the power to move one's legs, on the other, is not simply linear. There are many different kinds of differences.

Perception occupies an interesting position in respect of its voluntariness and the degree to which it is under our voluntary control. In one sense, which impressed the British empiricists, seeing, hearing and feeling are not voluntary. If one's eyes are open, one normally cannot fail to see the salient things before one. One has no choice but to hear the loud noises in one's locality; and one typically cannot but feel the heat of the fire in one's vicinity or the cold of the ice that one touches. But one can, of course, shut one's eyes, block one's ears, or walk away. It is noteworthy that seeing and hearing are not actions. But looking, glancing, gazing, scrutinizing, peeking, watching, looking for and looking at are; and so is listening to and listening for. These are things that one can typically do or refrain from doing at will.

Understanding is a quite different kind of ability. One can try to understand and come to understand something – for example, by assiduous study or careful attention. But someone who understands English cannot choose to understand or not to understand the English speech of others that he hears. His understanding whatever he thus understands is not an act of his. On the other hand, if he understood what was said, then he can act on it, explain it, react to it – and these are things he *can* typically do at will.

Knowledge is yet another kind of case. Knowledge that something is so (including knowing where, when, who, why, what and how) is an ability. But it is not rigidly tied to a single act category, performance of which is the exercise of the ability. Someone who knows that such-and-such is thus-and-so is able to do a variety of very different things, such as answer the appropriate WH-questions, act in certain ways (if he knows where . . . , he will, in certain cases, be able to e.g. find . . . , or find his way to . . . , if he knows how he will, in some cases, be able to . . . , in others be able to explain how to . . .). *These* are typically voluntary powers. He will also understand various things the understanding of which depends on possessing the relevant knowledge. One cannot know at will, only acquire knowledge in a variety of ways, some of which are under the control of the will and others of which are not. One cannot try to know as one can try to understand something, only try to acquire the desired knowledge by observation, learning or reflection.

ii. *Abilities*

When discussing human powers, we speak much more readily of *abilities* to do or refrain from doing things, as well as of abilities to react to and respond to things, than we do when speaking of the powers of the inanimate and insentient (indeed, in some languages, e.g. German, one would not extend the term 'ability' (*Fähigkeit*) to the inanimate at all). It is noteworthy that we speak of abilities only where there is a standard to be reached.[18] A marksman may have the ability to hit the bull nine times out of ten, but the novice cannot be said to have the ability to miss the bull nine times out of ten (save as a joke), although it may well be possible that he should do so, and probable that he will.

Abilities are inherently general. To have the ability to V means that V-ing is an act of a kind that one can perform. Hence I may have occasion to say that I couldn't V at *t*, since I was prevented, or lacked the opportunity; but I could have V'ed had I not been prevented, or had I had a chance to V. It is important not to confuse the generic 'can' of ability with the 'can' of achievement that is tied to an occasion. If a person has the ability to V, then given an opportunity and volition, he will, more often than not, V. Occasional failure is compatible, in many cases, with being able to V, but it is a criterion for the possession of the ability to V that when we *set ourselves* to V, we *normally* succeed. Note that the generality of an ability is compatible with a very high degree of specificity: the generality concerns possible occasions for its exercise, whereas its degree of specificity concerns the character of the performance that constitutes its manifestation or exercise. As noted above, even abilities that can be exercised only once are general, in the sense that they *can* be exercised whenever an opportunity arises.

We speak of *having*, or *possessing*, abilities – this is the picture we use. But to possess an ability is not to own anything – it is to be able to do something. It is important not to be confused by the form in which we present reference to abilities. Possessions that are not in use can be stored. But when one is not exercising an ability, it is not in storage. Nor is it located anywhere, even though its vehicle, if it can be said to have one, may have a location (e.g. the sense-organs are the vehicles of the perceptual powers). Knowledge is an ability, and memory is knowledge retained. It is a common error among psychologists and neuroscientists to suppose that memories are, need to be, or can be, stored in the brain. But the knowledge that is an ability – namely, knowing something to be so – or the knowledge that amounts to a skill or mastery of a technique (such as knowledge of English) is not storable. *What is known* (also denominated 'knowledge'), in the case of knowing that something is so, *is*, of course, storable – for example, in books, filing cabinets and computers – if it is inscribed, encoded or photographed, etc. But there is no such thing as storing knowledge *in the brain*.[19] Memory is only metaphorically a storehouse of ideas. (Of course, this does not mean that there are no neural conditions for remembering something.)

iii. *Being able to and knowing how to*

There is an obvious relationship between being able to do something and knowing how to do it. But it would be mistaken to think that to be able to V is to know how to V, for neither implies the other. This is obvious in the case of plants and machines that can do, are able to do, all manner of things, but cannot be said to know how to do them. But it is equally obvious with human beings in the case of activities that involve no know-how, such as seeing, breathing, blinking, moving one's limbs and so on. Someone with good sense-faculties can see objects in the far distance, hear faint noises, and smell the faintest whiff of scent, but does not know how to do these things. Some people can go without sleep for 24 hours, and others are able to drink large quantities of alcohol without becoming drunk, but no question of knowing how arises. Contrariwise, one may know how to do many things that one cannot do, either through lack of strength, or lack of will-power (e.g. how to lose weight), or through temporary or permanent loss of an ability. The aged tennis coach may not be able to play any longer, but he knows how to play and can still instruct others in the skill. One can be said to know how to do something only where there is a means, method or technique that has to be mastered in order to be able to V. To know how to V is to

[19] For elaboration, see M. R. Bennett and P. M. S. Hacker, *The Philosophical Foundations of Neuroscience* (Blackwell, Oxford, 2003), pp. 158–71.

know the way to V.[20] Commonly, someone who knows how to V has mastered the technique of V-ing. To have mastered a complex or difficult technique is to have acquired a skill. Some skills decline and vanish through desuetude (e.g. speaking a foreign language), whereas others are retained despite lack of use (e.g. driving a car or riding a bicycle).

iv. *Innate and acquired abilities*

Human powers, both active and passive, may be innate or acquired. That an ability is innate does not imply that one is born able fully to exercise it. Nor does it imply that it may not be improved through experience or perfected through training. Perceptual abilities are innate, although it may take time before they achieve their optimal condition (newborn children cannot see well). They are innate inasmuch as they depend upon the goodness or weakness of the sense-organs with which we are born. But they can be improved to some degree by training and exercises (and, in a rather different sense, we speak of a 'trained' eye, ear or palate, as the powers of visual, auditory and gustatory discrimination improve). Deficiencies in a human being's perceptual powers may themselves be innate or inflicted. Typically such deficiencies are due to defects in the relevant sense-organs (but they may also be consequences of a brain defect). These may be innate abnormalities, disease-inflicted defects, results of injuries, or deterioration of ageing. Defects in a sense-organ (or relevant parts of the brain) lead to sub-optimality in the exercise of the corresponding sense-faculty. Goodness (absence of deficiencies) in a given sense-organ (e.g. eyes or ears) enables the person to perceive well in the corresponding modality (e.g. see or hear well, possess good eyesight or hearing), and to do those things well which people with a good sense-faculty can do. Goodness of a sense-faculty is normalcy in perceptual achievement. Normalcy is typically judged to be relative to the species – what counts as good eyesight in mankind would be poor eyesight in a bird of prey. Sometimes, however, it is judged relative to human discriminatory abilities, as when we say that rhinoceroses or elephants have poor eyesight and eagles wonderful eyesight.[21]

[20] See White, *Nature of Knowledge*, pp. 14–29.

[21] See G. H. von Wright, *The Varieties of Goodness* (Routledge & Kegan Paul, London, 1963), pp. 51–9.

Motor abilities are likewise innate, although with our species it patently takes a considerable amount of time before most of them unfold. The acquisition of many rudimentary motor abilities involves learning (the child is taught to walk), and it takes years before they reach their normal level in the physically mature individual. The natural endowment differs substantially among different individuals, and hence too does the talent for the various forms of physical activity of which human beings are capable. The development of motor abilities depends upon use (as well as nutrition and general health). The possibility of substantial further development through training and exercise is considerable, and is cultivated by sports and training for warfare. Here too, weakness or deformation of the limbs or impairment of the ability to control their movement may be innate or inflicted, and the latter through poor or weak health in general, or through specific diseases, injuries or ageing.

v. *First- and second-order abilities*

The ability to learn is a second-order ability – that is, an ability to acquire abilities through instruction and experience, through exercise and exercises. To have an innate talent or natural aptitude for a subject (music, mathematics) or mode of activity (dancing, singing) is to have a second-order ability to acquire and develop a corresponding first-order ability with unusual facility or to an unusually high degree. The flowering of talent is skill and excellence in performance. To become and be a V-er (a dancer, singer, philosopher, etc.), one must have mastered the techniques of V-ing. A talented V-er is one who finds it easy to master or has mastered the techniques of V-ing and will be able to or can V well, in comparison both with those who are not V-ers and with other V-ers. A poor V-er is one who can V, but cannot V well.

The ability to learn a language, on which so many of the abilities characteristic of mankind depend, is innate, largely species-specific (although chimpanzees are capable of mastering the rudiments of a non-vocal language), and, with the exception of the mentally subnormal, shared by all human beings. Interestingly, if the ability to learn a language is not exercised by the age of about 10, it is lost (as is evident from documented cases of wolf-children). *Mastery* of a language, however, is subject to large individual variations, as is the ability to master a multiplicity of languages. Other abilities to acquire intellectual abilities are even less equally distributed by nature. Human powers by and large vary between individuals, commonly diminish or increase with circumstantial change, and wax and wane with maturation and senescence.

Learning enhances human potentialities, gives people the ability to do things which, without education, they would not be able to do. This includes both active powers, especially skills, and relatively passive powers, such as the ability to enjoy and take pleasure in experiencing things that demand education – for example, to listen to classical music or to look at paintings with pleasure and understanding, or to be able to follow a lecture or a book with understanding. Education is a good for man, because it enhances human abilities. This, given that opportunities are available, extends human choices and enriches human life. It should not, however, be confused with the enhancement of human freedom. Enlargement and diminution of freedom pertain to opportunities for action and permission to take advantage of them, not to abilities to act.

8. Human powers: further distinctions

i. *Human active and passive powers*

In discussing powers of the inanimate, we noted the distinction between active and passive powers – between the potentialities to do things and to act on other things, on the one hand, and the potentialities to undergo change and to be acted on by other things. A parallel distinction can be applied to human beings and their acts or actions, on the one hand, and to what they may undergo, on the other. But its application is more complicated. Those things we can do at will are the most straightforward cases of the exercise of our active powers. But this includes not only physical action, but also thinking, calculating, reasoning, imagining. These need not be *expressed* in acting on anything, in taking action, or indeed even in acting. And, as noted, they are often not exercised deliberately or at will – thoughts cross our minds unbidden, we jump to conclusions, and our imagination runs riot. So when we classify these powers as being among the active powers of mankind, it is because it makes sense to say of such a power that it is exercised at will, not because it always is so.

The passions. The philosophical tradition has taken the affections to be among the passive powers of mankind – it is not for nothing that they are referred to as 'the passions'. The affections are commonly taken to include agitations (being and feeling surprised, delighted, revolted, disgusted, startled, horrified, thrilled, shocked), emotions (anger, grief, love, hate, jealousy, envy, pride, shame) and moods (feeling cheerful, depressed, contented, irascible). These we think of as occurrent states, or, in certain cases, as dispositional states (see below), and we think of our potentialities to feel them as passive powers (as when we speak of our capacity for feeling surprise or horror, for feeling love or hope, and for being in good cheer). Being passions, they are not voluntarily actualized. One cannot feel astonished on demand, or intend to hope, let alone feel anxious on purpose. But they are not wholly beyond our control. Their manifestations can often be suppressed, and the feelings can be modified, sometimes by reasoning, sometimes by deliberate distraction of attention, sometimes by single-minded attention, for example, to that which is life-enhancing.

The passions are 'dispositional' in two different senses. On the one hand, we commonly speak of the passions as 'dispositional states', as when we say that someone has been in a state of depression for some months – that is, has a tendency to feel depressed during his waking hours – or that someone is angry about the government's educational policy – that is, is prone to express indignant objections to government educational policy when occasion arises. On the other hand, the passions are also construed as traits of character or temperament. To describe someone as irascible, jealous or compassionate by nature is to describe his affective pronenesses and tendencies.

Sensibility. Affective sensitivity is a measure of one's passive powers of responsiveness to objects, situations and people. It is a natural endowment, but one that, on the one hand, can be cultivated (sensitivity to nature, the arts, other human beings) and, on the other hand, can degenerate – for one's sensibility may be numbed through suffering or age. An excess of 'sensibility' (*vide* Jane Austen's novel) is a disposition to over-react – a tendency to become agitated to excess, or indeed to *indulge* in excessive agitations (including the agitations that accompany occurrent emotions). The latter is a lack of self-control, the former a lack of judgement. Sentimentality (not to be confused with sentiment) likewise is a proneness to suffer agitations – agitations that are disproportionate to their object.

Susceptibilities and liabilities of health. The passive powers of humanity (*qua* living creatures) that most resemble the powers of inanimate things are dispositions of health. These are not voluntary powers, although they are subject to varying degrees of indirect control. Dispositions of health are the susceptibilities and liabilities of the organism to disease and malfunction, exhibited in physiological reactions of the body. They are aspects of the physiological nature of the person or animal. Like the dispositional properties of the inanimate, they are called forth by characteristic circumstances, defined by their causes and by what they are dispositions to do or undergo, and hence too by their characteristic manifestations.

A person is in good physical health if his organs are both good (i.e. are not defective) and functioning well (i.e. normally), and if his overall condition is not deficient through disease. Medical susceptibilities are pronenesses, typically due to heightened sensitivity, to infections or injuries of certain kinds. Liabilities to diseases, infections or malfunctioning organs are conditional on circumstances. Those who are especially *susceptible* to a given infection are more likely than others to contract the disease *if* exposed to contagion or to the conditions that produce it. To have a disposition to catch cold is a liability or a tendency. A person has a *liability* to catch cold if, *were* he exposed to infection or draughts, etc., he *would* more often than not catch cold. A person has a *tendency* to catch cold if he catches cold more often than not whenever exposed to infection, draughts, etc., and is so exposed with some frequency. Such a tendency implies a liability, but not vice versa. For what tends to happen must happen reasonably frequently, whereas what is liable to happen may never happen because the conditions for it to happen are not fulfilled.[22] Allergies are likewise physiological tendencies or liabilities of the animate organism, for example, to break out in a rash, to sneeze, to have breathing difficulties in response to stimuli such as pollen, horsehair, pollution, etc.

ii. *The vehicles of human powers*

We noted the distinction between a power and its vehicle in the case of the inanimate. The same distinction can be applied to human powers. The vehicles of many animal powers can be said to be the organ the animal uses in the exercise of that power. So the vehicles of perceptual powers are the sense-organs, and of locomotion the legs. Depending upon the context and one's purposes, one may wish to

---

[22] See White, *Nature of Knowledge*, p. 114.

include in the vehicle the relevant parts of the nervous system that enable the organ to function and make it possible for the animal to use its organs in the exercise of its powers.

It is, however, unclear what should be said about powers that do not involve the use of any organ, such as the powers of thought and understanding. One does not think or understand with or in one's brain as one sees with one's eyes and digests food in one's stomach. One moves one's eyes (shields them from the glare, brings them to the ocular or to the keyhole) to see what one wishes or to see better. But one cannot (and need not) thus move and control one's brain in order to think or to understand something. One can, in principle, watch a human being's stomach digesting food, but one cannot, even in principle, watch one's brain thinking or understanding, not because positron emission tomography is insufficiently advanced as yet, but because the brain neither thinks nor understands anything. It is the animal as a whole, the human being as an organism, that thinks and understands, is thoughtless or fails to understand.[23] The most that can be seen in the brain is what happens there *when* the human being whose brain it is thinks or understands something. One might say that the vehicle of the power is the brain, since without the normal functioning of the brain one would not possess the powers of thought and understanding. But then without the normal functioning of the brain, one would not possess the powers of locomotion either, and no one would wish to say that the brain is the vehicle of our power to walk. It may well be that the fruitfulness of the analogical extension of the distinction between a power and its vehicle from those contexts in which it is plainly useful (e.g. stuffs and their ingredients) peters out here.

iii. *Ability and opportunity*

The powers of inanimate and animate things alike need conditions for their actualization. In the case of an inanimate agent, the satisfaction of the conditions necessary for the actualization of its powers provides the occasion for the agent to manifest its powers. If the conditions for it to V obtain, then it will V. But, as we noted, this is not so for the voluntary and partly voluntary powers of animate

[23] For elaboration, see Bennett and Hacker, *Philosophical Foundations of Neuroscience*, ch. 3.

creatures. The conditions necessary for it to be possible for the creature to *exercise* its powers are *opportunities* for it to do so, of which it may take advantage or refrain from so doing – whether it does so is up to the agent.

The *horizon of action* – the possibilities for action available to an agent – is fixed by the intersection of his abilities, the opportunities that arise, and often also the availability of equipment. The availability of equipment – of a bread knife to cut the bread, of a screwdriver to unscrew the screws, of a taxi to reach the station on time – is intermediate between ability and opportunity. An ability is a generic feature of the agent that persists over time. An opportunity is an individual feature of the situation. Consequently, opportunities are in constant flux, and some opportunities may never recur. Hence Fortuna must be seized by the forelock.

Opportunities are not only occasion-specific, they are also agent-relative, being relative to the degree to which the agent possesses the relevant power. What is an opportunity for a highly skilled V-er may be none at all for a novice, a weakling or an incompetent. One may be unable to take advantage of opportunities despite having the requisite ability because of temporary incapacitation, or because of objective impediments (i.e. those pertaining to the circumstances) or subjective impediments (pertaining to the subject). Temporary incapacitation (one form of subjective impediment) includes physical injury and illness – having broken my leg, I cannot play tennis tomorrow. I still know how to play, and can still play with my customary skill, but not while I am incapacitated. Objective impediments include opportunity costs ('I should like to . . . , but it would mean that I can't . . .'). Subjective impediments may include commitments one has undertaken ('I should like to . . . , but I must . . .').

9. Dispositions

We noted above that the liabilities and susceptibilities of health most resemble the powers of the inanimate in their dispositionality. Liabilities and susceptibilities are not frequency concepts. A fragile object may be liable to break if dropped, but this does not imply that it has a *tendency* to break if dropped (although things *of that kind* do have such a tendency). A person may be liable to succumb to temptation if the opportunity arises, but does not have a tendency to succumb to temptations if there are no temptations.

Tendencies and pronenesses, both animate and inanimate, are linked to frequencies of behaviour. Increases in tendencies and pronenesses are increases in the frequencies of the occasions on which they are realized. Human tendencies and pronenesses, unlike inanimate ones, can sometimes be controlled by their subject, suppressed or eradicated – as when one breaks a habit, controls one's stammer, or overcomes one's shyness.

Tendencies and pronenesses are not, as such, human dispositions. Smokers tend to smoke more when under pressure, are prone to spend too much on cigarettes, and are liable to contract cancer if they do not curb their habit.[24] But smoking is a habit, not a disposition, and the frequencies and liabilities associated with the habit are not dispositions either.[25] Nevertheless, genuine human dispositions *are* linked with tendencies, pronenesses and liabilities. A person of indolent disposition tends not to strain himself, a vain person is prone to boast, and a tactless person is liable to drop clangers. But what is *meant* by the term 'disposition' when associated with human beings undergoes a significant shift by comparison with its application to inanimate things.

Physiological dispositions of health apart, *human* dispositions are dispositions of *temperament* and of *character*. These are very unlike inanimate dispositions. We have already noted that an inanimate substance may have a disposition to V yet never manifest it, since the conditions required for its actualization never arise. By contrast, as noted, a person cannot have a disposition of temperament or character and never exhibit it. Similarly, an inanimate substance may have a disposition to V for only a few minutes (or, indeed, seconds) in the course of its existence – but a human being cannot have a character trait for only a few minutes.

Dispositions of temperament are such traits as dourness, taciturnity, cheerfulness, melancholy, vivacity, stolidity, sensitivity, delicacy,

[24] White, *Nature of Knowledge*, p. 114.

[25] Note that a habit implies a regularity, but not every human regularity implies a habit. One may have a habit of taking a nap in the afternoon, but it is not a habit to sleep at night. Regularities that are natural to human beings and what is customary in a social group are not habits. It was customary for Romans to wear togas and is customary for men in contemporary Western societies to wear trousers. But it was not a habit of Romans to wear a toga, and it is not a habit of ours to wear trousers – although a Scotsman may make it a habit to wear a kilt for parties. Similarly, what is a social or medical requirement, such as regularly brushing one's teeth, is not a habit.

excitability, placidity, irritability and irascibility. As the etymology of 'temper' suggests, these are *aspects of the nature of a person*. Traits of temper are dispositions of attitude and of modes of responsiveness, traits defined by what they are dispositions to be, feel, become or do, by the manner of one's actions and reactions – for example, to be stern or sullen, sensitive, delicate or excitable in one's responses, to become annoyed with but little reason or to lose one's temper. They are manifest in one's facial expression, tone of voice, gestures and demeanour, in the way one reacts to what befalls one.

Traits of personality, such as gentleness, brashness, timidity, pedantry, as well as such sociable characteristics as courteousness, politeness, tactfulness, and perhaps self-evaluative traits such as conceit, vanity, pride, arrogance and humility are also dispositions. They verge upon, and in the case of the latter group, cross the boundary into the sphere of the virtues and vices. Whether the virtues and vices should be deemed dispositions is a disputed matter. Prudence, fortitude, industry, temperance, courage are among the self-regarding virtues. Honesty, generosity, kindness, benevolence, charity, justice are among the other-regarding virtues. We do say such things as 'He is of a prudent (kindly, charitable, benevolent) disposition'. The virtues and vices are character traits, and one may be inclined to consider character traits and traits of temperament alike as human dispositions. Von Wright questioned this on the grounds that no act category[26] or specific activity answers to a virtue or a vice. Almost any act could, in some circumstance or other, be courageous. An act which is courageous in one circumstance and done by A need not be so in the same or different circumstances if done by B. The (logical) results of courageous acts need have no feature in common – what makes them courageous is not their result. Hence virtuous acts cannot be characterized in terms of their results, and the virtues cannot be characterized in terms of their achievements. Rather, the acts that manifest a virtue or a vice are characterized by reference to the virtue or vice they exemplify. This marks a conceptual difference between the virtues and vices, on the one hand, and habits, on the other.

However, dispositions of temperament are similarly not defined by an act category that answers to each trait. Furthermore, habits, as

---

[26] I.e. category of acts named after the generic state of affairs instances of which logically result from the performance of the acts of the kind in question, e.g. opening the door, shutting the window, emptying the kettle.

we have seen, are not classified as dispositions. Unlike characteristic human dispositions, habits are not generally viewed as part of the nature, personality or character of a human being, as both traits of temperament and the virtues and vices are. The habit of taking a walk every afternoon is not a trait or aspect of the temperament, personality or character of a person, although if done with clockwork regularity (as in Kant's case), the habit may exemplify punctuality. One may, like Kant, be of an orderly, reliable disposition, but not of a taking-a-walk-in-the-afternoon disposition. But it is true that concepts of traits of temperament and personality approximate tendency or frequency concepts. Someone who but rarely manifests charm, courtesy or tact in his social intercourse is not a charming, courteous or tactful person, but rather a person who can be charming, courteous or tactful. It seems true of at least some of the virtues and vices that they are less closely tied to tendency and frequency than traits of temperament and personality. A magnanimous or courageous person, by contrast with an irascible man, an alcoholic or a pedant, need not be a person who has a *tendency* to do anything in particular, for the occasions on which magnanimity or courage are called for may be relatively rare in his life. If that is correct, it may be a symptom of a deeper difference: namely, that the exemplification of the virtues and vices is linked with motivation, reasons for action, and judgement (practical wisdom) in a way in which the exemplification of the other traits is not. Whether such differences justify denying that the virtues and vices are dispositions is unclear.

Dispositions of temper and character may be innate or acquired, permanent or impermanent, modifiable or unmodifiable. Even if impermanent and modifiable, they are, at any rate, relatively abiding. Unlike inanimate dispositions, one cannot have a kindly, dour or cheerful disposition for only a few minutes, although one may be cheerful for a few minutes and be disposed to be kind to A for only a few minutes. It is noteworthy that in the case of human beings, having a disposition to V is not the same as being disposed (tempted, inclined) to V. One may indeed be and feel disposed to do something for a few moments, until one learns of good reasons not to do it, but one cannot have, for a few moments, a disposition to do something. Whereas one may be disposed to do a particular act on an occasion – for example, to go to the cinema tonight – one cannot have a disposition to perform a specific act on a given occasion, for dispositions are inherently general.

5

Agency

1. Inanimate agents

'Agency', and its cousins 'act', 'action' and 'to act on a thing', have many related uses, one of which, especially in the hands of philosophers, is as categorial terms. As such, like most of our categorial terms (including 'substance', 'causation' and 'power'), their contour lines are blurred. This is unsurprising, since they signify formal features that characterize the use of a multitude of diverse expressions. But usage is not cast from a mould, and divergences at the boundaries are typical rather than exceptional. The categorial term 'agent' articulates a general pattern in the use of subject-referring terms in sentences ascribing acts, actions or actions on another thing to a subject. There is no reason to suppose that a single, complete pattern is discernible. The indeterminacy is multiplied by the fact that the concepts of act and action are themselves blurred categorials. The grammatical data are, as it were, scattered points on a graph; any attempt to draw a single, unbroken line through them may well distort the conceptual phenomena. We should countenance the possibility that there are different 'centres of variation'. If so, there may be a number of different broken lines connecting different points in different, but related patterns. To attempt to complete these broken lines may well be to falsify the conceptual forms that concern us, not to render their depiction more accurate. It should be borne in mind that we are not introducing special technical terminology, sharpened and regimented for the purposes of a theory that might be tested in experience, the terms of which will be jettisoned if the theory is not confirmed. Our purpose is philosophical, and our judgements must be guided by their power to illuminate some of the very general features of our conceptual scheme. Our objective is to isolate a range or ranges of features which shed light upon our use of a multitude of verbs and their cognates, and so to illuminate the most general features of the ways in which we think about ourselves and what we do, and about the things we encounter in nature and what they do. Illuminating these structural features will clarify forms of our thought about nature and about ourselves of which we are rarely aware. We are rarely aware of them precisely because they *inform* our thought and talk.

The conceptual fields from which the categorial notions of inanimate agency and developed animate agency respectively are abstracted differ importantly. The large network of concepts of two-way powers, of perception and cognition, of voluntariness, desire and intention, of reason, motive, purpose and end, apply (to a degree) to developed sentient animals and (in their full richness) to human beings. The network of internal relations that inanimate agency displays is not merely less rich, but also, as we shall see, different from the comparable pattern of internal relations exhibited by advanced animate and rational agency. It is not surprising that our concept of agency exhibits not one central paradigm, but rather two, the first focused upon the forms of inanimate agency and the second upon the manifold forms of animate, sentient and volitional agency of self-moving creatures. Our various notions of active and passive, blurred as they are, are clustered around these. Furthermore, within each paradigm there are distinct centres of variation.

An agent, in the most general sense of the term, is something that *does something* or *acts*.[1] The term, as used in the ensuing discussion, is, like 'substance' and 'power', a philosophical term of art signifying a very general category. What is pervasive in our ordinary discourse is not the term 'agent', but rather agent-referring expressions by the use of which we refer to things that have the power either to act *simpliciter* or to act on other things.

Not everything a thing *does* exhibits agency. To sleep, to bleed, to sneeze, are things that animate, sentient agents do, but they are not acts they perform. Among the acts a self-moving agent such as a human

---

[1] From the Latin *agere*, to act or do, and the participle *agens*.

being may perform are those movements he makes that are of a kind that he *can* make voluntarily. But not all the acts such an agent performs need be movement-involving. For to hold or hold on to something is no less an act than to catch hold of it or to let it go; sitting for a portrait is no less a voluntary action than sitting down in an armchair. And human beings may voluntarily, intentionally and deliberately listen to or for something, look at, watch or glare at something or someone, as well as attend to and concentrate on what is said or what is visible. It would be arbitrary to insist that these are doings but not acts.

Self-moving animate agents and inanimate agents alike *act on* other things. As we shall see, the notion of *acting on* another thing may be variously construed. Nevertheless, it is clear that agency is exhibited both in acting *simpliciter* and in acting on another thing (no matter how broadly or narrowly these two ideas are construed).

A complementary notion to that of an agent is that of a *patient* – that which is *acted on* or that to which or to whom *something is done*. When the action of an agent on another thing is causally efficacious and brings about or sustains a change, the patient is the thing that is thereby changed. But an agent may also do something that prevents or stops a change that would otherwise occur. In such cases of *preventive* or *suppressive agency*, the patient is prevented from changing or changing further. This may be done by acting on the patient, or by interfering with, or acting on, something else that would otherwise have acted on the patient. Being the agent acting on a patient does not preclude being the patient of reciprocal action.

Individual agents can be divided into two very general classes, inanimate and animate. Inanimate agents are paradigmatically inanimate substances (including artefacts), but also partitions (lumps, nuggets, grains, pools, drops) as well as quantities (milligrams, ounces, pints, litres) of stuff. But we conceive of many kinds of thing as agents of change that are not substances, such as rivers and waves. So, the stone I threw broke a window, this electric kettle has just boiled a quantity of water, a drop of blood stained my handkerchief, and the wave swept away our sandcastle. We also treat as agents insubstantial things that are neither substances nor partitions or quantities of stuff, such as wind, electricity, light, heat and frost. So we say that the light darkened the photographic plate, that the heat melted the wax, or that the frost made the pipes burst. But in the latter two cases, we merely show a preference for the agential form of representation.[2]

It has been suggested that the concept of agency is, or should be, limited to animate intentional agency, since only animate agents act intentionally, and only ascription of action to intentional agents explains actions (conceived as events) in a manner that goes beyond what is explained by the corresponding statement of event causation.[3] But there is no reason for thinking that our concept of an agent is thus constrained, and, as I have argued (see chap. 3), far from event causation being logically prior to agent causation, it is agent causation that enjoys priority. Inanimate agents, no less than animate ones, *act on* other things and are causally responsible for change or prevention of change.

Inanimate agents *do* things. Among the things they do are things they do *to* something or other. We must distinguish, among things done to something, between those the description of which (by means of causative verbs, such as 'break', 'crush', 'bend', 'melt', 'heat', 'freeze', 'dry') entails a change to the patient and those the description of which (by means of non-causative verbs, such as 'hit', 'brush', 'knock', 'pull', 'push', 'lean against', 'shine on') does not. That sentences of the form 'A V's P' in which causative verbs occur describe the action of an agent on a patient is uncontentious – for here the agent's action on the patient *is* to change the patient: for example, to break, crush, bend, melt, heat, freeze or dry it. But it is more contentious to hold that when a non-causative verb occurs in a sentence of the same form it also describes the action of the agent on the patient, even though no change to the patient is entailed by the description. In both cases, the agent *does* something *to* the patient; the only question is whether the latter be deemed a case of *acting on* the patient. Here usage offers no guidance. To subsume such descriptions as 'The stone hit the window' under the formal concept of *acting on a patient* implies loosening the nexus between inanimate agency and causing change. For if we allow 'A hit P' to count as an action of A on P, then we

---

[2] This is comparable to the preference we show for the active causal form of representation, already remarked (above p. 71), when we say that the moon causes the ocean tides *by exerting gravitational force* on the ocean – as if the latter were something that the moon might *do* to the oceans.

[3] E.g. D. Davidson, 'Agency', repr. in his *Essays on Actions and Events* (Clarendon Press, Oxford, 1980), p. 54.

include descriptions that do not imply any change to P – as when an agent may hit, brush, knock against, illuminate, lean against a patient. There is no pressing reason for restriction here, but only for distinction. The answer to the question 'What did A do to P?' is rightly given by 'A hit P' or 'A leaned against P' or 'A illuminated P' – these are cases of an agent doing something to a patient, and it is not obviously illegitimate to view them as cases of acting on the patient. But if we wish to mould the concept of inanimate agency so as to restrict it to action the description of which entails the production, prevention or suppression of change, then the doings of an agent to a patient, the description of which does not have any such entailment, will *not* count as *acting on* the patient.[4]

However that is decided, it is evident that sometimes an agent causes a change to a patient *by doing* something *to* it. This is patent in the case of mechanical action and traction. In such cases, what the agent does to the patient which produces the change in or to the patient may be termed the *mode of operation* of the agent.[5] So, the stone breaks a window *by* hitting it; the sun melts the ice *by* shining on it; and the electric kettle boils the water *by* heating the element immersed in it. If we restrict the concept of action on a patient to what is described by a causative verb in an appropriate context, then we may say that in such cases of mechanical action or manipulation, the agent *acts on* the patient *by doing something*, and we shall have to insist that this 'doing' is not itself *acting on the patient*. But we may more liberally admit as cases of acting on a patient those doings the description of which does not entail (but is consistent with) change. So we shall have to say that the agent *acts on the patient in one way* and thereby *acts on it, productively or preventively, in a further way*.

It is important not to overlook the many kinds of case in which an agent acts on a patient *without any mode of operation*. Examples of these are legion in the domain of chemical action (e.g. the acid in the test tube dissolves the lump of zinc) or thermal action (e.g. simple heat transference).

Both causative and non-causative verbs, applied to an *inanimate* agent, are used to describe things it *does*, but not *acts* it performs.

---

[4] It should be noted again that prevention of change to a patient may be effected not by acting on the patient, but by acting on something else that would otherwise have acted on the patient.

[5] The term 'mode of operation' was introduced by D. G. Brown, *Action* (George Allen & Unwin, London, 1968), pp. 34f.

Inanimate agents may *act on* other things (taken narrowly or broadly), but they do not *take action*.[6] They may *have* an activity (as enzymes do), but they do not *engage* in an activity. One may observe *the action* of a quantity of acid on a metal plate, observe it eating into the plate, and observe the consequent release of gases. But the action of the acid on the metal is not an action it takes, and eating into the metal is not an act it performs or an activity in which it engages. The active, in the case of natural, inanimate substances, may be contrasted not only with the passive, but also with the inactive (as in the case of chemicals) and the dormant (as in the case of volcanoes).

Inanimate substances, in particular mechanisms, may *have an action*. The action of a machine – that is, its movement or manner of operation – may be economical, complicated, slow or fast.[7] It is striking that we do not normally pluralize the noun 'action' when applied to inanimate agents – we may admire the actions of a hero, but the action (not the actions) of a machine. Not every movement of a mechanism counts as its action. The recoil of a rifle is not an action of the rifle, although the recoil of the barrel of a modern artillery piece is an action of the gun; the shaking of the washing machine is not its action, but the agitating rotation of its drum is. It seems that the action of a mechanism is the movement of a part of the mechanism that is intrinsic to the function of the artefact. If the action of a machine is ingenious, elegant or beautiful, as is that of the movement of a Tompion clock, it may be well worth seeing it *in action*. The malfunctioning of a machine may put it *out of action* until it is repaired.

Nevertheless, inanimate agents are not generally said to act or to take action.[8] They cannot be caught in the act of V-ing; nor can they be interrupted in the act. They may take time to do what they do or they may do something in a moment, but they can neither take time to perform the act of V-ing nor perform it in a moment, for they cannot *perform* acts. Similarly, although they do things, they cannot

---

[6] A. R. White (ed.), *The Philosophy of Action* (Oxford University Press, Oxford, 1968), pp. 1f.

[7] See Brown, *Action*, p. 32.

[8] An idiomatic exception is when we say of a drug that it will start to act within an hour; 'to act' here means 'to take effect'. There are a few other marginal exceptions, but we do not generally say of inanimate agents that they act; nor do we speak of the act, let alone of the acts or deeds that they do or perform. That is no coincidence.

be said to do or perform *deeds*. These limitations are neither constraints nor inabilities. Our observations are grammatical remarks
specifying what it makes sense to say. (We should not forget that
we are trying to elucidate the concepts we have and operate with,
and that it is by means of such elucidations that we may illuminate
conceptual puzzles and problems that grow out of our existing concepts and our unclarities about them.) If one extends the concepts
of acting and of taking action, of act and deed, beyond these limits,
one will obscure important distinctions between kinds of agents and
kinds of agential doings to no good purpose.

2. Inanimate needs

Although inanimate beings do not have wants, they can often be said
to *need* things.[9] All needs, of inanimate and animate beings alike,
involve

  (i)   an object of need – that is, what is specified in answer to the
        question '*What* does it need?'
  (ii) an end – that is, what answers the question 'What does it need
        it *for*?'
  (iii) circumstances or conditions – that is, what answers the ques-
        tion 'What *gives rise* to the need?'[10]

The objects of inanimate needs may be (i) things (including partitions and quantities of stuffs), (ii) conditions, (iii) doing things, or
(iv) having things done (to the thing that needs them). What a being
needs, in a certain circumstance or condition, is what is necessary
for it, in that circumstance or condition, for a certain end. Since
inanimate agents do not have ends of their own, the ends for which
they can be said to need things are intrinsically related to the ends
of other beings.

Artefacts commonly need something in order to fulfil, or fulfil optimally, the function for which they are made. An engine needs petrol

---

[9] For a useful discussion of needs, see A. R. White, *Modal Thinking* (Blackwell,
Oxford, 1975), ch. 8.

[10] The interrogative 'Why does A need X?' can be used to ask what the agent needs
the object of need *for*, as well as to ask for the circumstance or condition of the
agent that gives rise to the need for it.

in order to run and lubricants in order not to overheat – without the former, it cannot function at all, and without the latter, it cannot function well. It may need to run once a fortnight in order not to rust, and to have its gaskets replaced periodically in order to function at optimal efficiency. The petrol that is *needed for* the engine cannot be said to be *good for* the engine; but oil is both needed *and* is good for the engine, inasmuch as it prevents damage to it. A knife needs to be sharpened periodically in order to cut better – yet being sharpened would not be said to be 'good for' the knife. But wax is good for furniture: it prevents its surface or veneer from cracking and deteriorating. The beneficial, in respect of artefacts, is therefore a *preventive*, rather than an *augmentive* or *productive*, notion. Clearly, the non-fulfilment of the needs of the inanimate is not deleterious to their lives or detrimental to their welfare, since they have neither. Rather, it is deleterious to their condition and to their powers (and the latter often because of the former).

It is not only artefactual inanimate agents that can be said to need things, but also non-artefactual things that are used by or impinge upon the interests of human beings. So, for example, the soil in a field, given the circumstance that it has been over-used, needs fertilizer to produce good crops next year. A river, given that it has been silting up, may need to be dredged if it is to be navigable (which is something we may want) or if its waters are not to harm our interests by flooding. Given that snowfall in winter is common, a hill or a mountain-side may need to be terraced if snowslides are to be prevented.

Inanimate agents, we have remarked, *do* things and do things *to* other things. The powers of inanimate agents are one-way powers. If the conditions for the actualization of their powers are satisfied, their powers will be actualized. Their needs are what is necessary in the circumstances for the optimal actualization of their powers (or for their suppression) relative to the good or goal of some living being. It makes no sense to ascribe to inanimate agents preferences or choices whether to actualize their powers. There is no such thing as an inanimate agent *refraining* from actualizing its powers on an occasion. As previously noted, such agents do not have an *opportunity* to do what they do, there is only an *occasion* for them to do it. To mark these important categorial differences between inanimate and animate agency, we might say that inanimate agents do not *exercise* their powers at all (only beings that can be said to refrain from taking advantage of an opportunity to act can be said to exercise their power of acting). Rather, when appropriate *conditions* are satisfied, their powers are *actualized* and *exhibited* (made manifest) in what they do. This difference between inanimate and animate agents is pivotal for the concepts of acting and taking action, of act, action and deed, that apply to advanced sentient agents.

3. Animate agents: needs and wants

Animate agents are living substances, ranging through the spectrum of biological taxa from micro-organisms to plants and animals. They can be divided into insentient and sentient ones. Insentient animate agents, such as plants, have neither perceptual nor volitional powers, though they may be responsive to their environment in various ways, exhibiting tropisms or even, as in the case of the Venus fly-trap, reacting instantaneously to stimuli. They may *act on* other things, and effect changes in other things. They *do* things, but they cannot be said either to *act* or to *take action*.

All animate beings have *needs*. The objects of their needs may be *for* a tangible or intangible thing or quantity of stuff or for a circumstance of one kind or another, *to do* something or other, or *to have something done* to them. What insentient animate beings, such as plants, or primitive sentient creatures need are:

(i)   Those things the absence of which is deleterious to their lives and normal development, such as nutriments, water, light or shade, and appropriate climatic conditions.
(ii) Those things that are necessary for them to serve the purposes for which we use them.

In this sense, plants are intermediate between animals and artefacts (gardens, one might say, are living artefacts). On the one hand, plants need water and light, appropriate soil, and insects for pollination, if they are to flourish and reproduce. On the other hand, cultivated plants can be said to need to be pruned (if overgrown) or fertilized (if the soil is poor), in order that they may bear good fruit for us in optimal quantity or grow well and flower for the delectation of our senses.

What plants do (e.g. grow towards the light, produce flowers and fruit), as opposed to what happens to them, is linked to what is needed for the maintenance of their natural life cycle and for their reproduction.

What they are artificially made to do (e.g. grow along trellises or up walls) is linked to the purposes of cultivators. The *organs* of a plant have a purpose or function, which is their contribution to maintaining the normal life and reproductive cycle of the plant. But a plant itself cannot be said to have purposes *of its own* or to *pursue* goals. Nevertheless, what a plant *does* is explained teleologically – that is, as being done for the sake of a goal (to obtain more light or water) or for a certain purpose (e.g. to facilitate pollination). But these goals and purposes are not goals and purposes *of* the plant. The teleological behaviour of plants is *explicable* in non-teleological terms. But this does not mean that teleological explanation of plant behaviour is *reducible* to non-teleological explanation.

Sentient agents have perceptual powers. Primitive sentient agents display behavioural dispositions and tendencies, attraction and aversion, but not wants. The boundary between mere attraction (and aversion) and wanting is blurred. Insects have needs, and likes and dislikes, that are exhibited in their attractive and aversive behaviour. They have primitive preferences in so far as it makes sense to describe them as being more attracted to one kind of flower or substance rather than to another. A rudimentary form of wanting is also attributable to them. The goal-directed behaviour of the bee suffices to warrant describing it as wanting to get at the nectar, the wasp buzzing against the window-pane as wanting to get out, the ant as trying to drag a morsel of food to the ant-nest. But there is little more to such primitive wanting than purposiveness. What little more there is consists in persistence and primitive manifestations of being thwarted – for example, buzzing and fluttering. But what is patently lacking in purposive insect behaviour is a rich range of adaptive responses to circumstances relevant to the attainment of the goal of the behaviour coupled with substantial cognitive powers and their exercise. Instead, there is a dominance of relatively inflexible stereotypical behaviour. The moth cannot control its fatal attraction to the flame, any more than the wasp, buzzing on a window-pane, striving blindly, so to speak, towards the light, can redirect its efforts. Similarly, the concept of pain can *perhaps* get a foothold on insect behaviour,[11] but the concept of pleasure can get little, if any, purchase.

---

[11] 'Look at a wriggling fly and at once . . . pain seems able to get a foothold here' (Wittgenstein, *Philosophical Investigations*, 2nd edn (Blackwell, Oxford, 1958), §284). Note Wittgenstein's cautious phrasing: it *seems to be able* to get a foothold. Can a fly have aching joints? A headache?

More developed sentient agents with a richer behavioural repertoire have two-way volitional powers. I shall call them 'volitional agents'. Volitional agents act in pursuit of goals, persist in the face of obstacles, display a relatively *wide* range of adaptive behaviour in response to the circumstances of their pursuit of their goals, including the exploration of, and choice between, alternative routes to the goal, recognition of the termini of the phases of phased activities, and manifestations of various forms of frustration and distress at failure. Volitional agents also have active and passive *hedonic* powers. They take pleasure in perceiving things, especially in smelling and tasting things, in warmth (when it is cold) and cold (when it is hot), and (among the more evolved animals) in some of their own activities – observe the young of higher mammals exploring objects in their environment, a pod of dolphins at play, or dogs running in a park. They may also take pleasure in being patients – for example, in being groomed, licked, patted or stroked. Consequently, their behavioural powers are exhibited not only in pursuit of their needs, but also for other ends, such as the pleasure of the activity (think of cubs or kittens 'at play') or curiosity.

What an animal that possesses such a rich repertoire of behaviour and response does in pursuit of its goals can commonly be redescribed in terms of its knowing things to be thus-and-so in its environment, of its wanting to attain (its aiming at) a certain goal, and of its acting *because* of what it knows *in order* to attain what it wants (to achieve its goal). Describing the animal as knowing what it knows and as wanting to attain a certain goal is not to be conceived as describing the causes of its behaviour. Such a description is something that can be read off its behaviour in the circumstances, and is sometimes an explanatory (teleological) redescription – but not a *causal* explanation. We shall explore this theme in the sequel.

The link between perceptual (hence cognitive), volitional and hedonic powers is not coincidental but conceptual. So too is the connection between them and the power to act and to take action. A criterion for whether an animal wants a certain thing is that if it perceives that thing and apprehends an appropriate opportunity for obtaining it, then, other things being equal, it takes steps to get it. When it gets what it wants, it is typically pleased, and exhibits its pleasure in its reactive behaviour (cats purr, dogs wag their tails). When what it wants is a tangible object, then if it gets it, it commonly takes pleasure in doing *with* it whatever it wanted it *for*.

Some of the ends for which something is needed are independent of contingent goals and are characteristic of normal members of the species. These are absolute needs. Others are dependent on contingently chosen goals or wants. These are relative needs. In the case of human beings, there are also needs that are conceived to be basic requirements of normal members of a society at a given time. These might be called '(socially) minimal needs'. What we deem absolute needs depends upon our conception of health, and hence upon our conception of the optimal functioning of a normal member of the species.[12] Relative needs are dependent on contingent goals: in order to purchase a house, one needs money; if one wants to read Aristotle in the original, one needs to learn ancient Greek. Socially minimal needs, which are characteristic of cultural beings, depend on historically variable, shared conceptions of the basic requirements of a tolerable social life. What is deemed a necessity today may have been unnecessary in the past, or a luxury rather than a necessity, or altogether unimaginable. Neither absolute nor minimal needs are simply statistical notions, but rather partly normative ones, the former being dependent upon the axiological conception of health, the latter upon the conception of the requirements of a tolerable human life. Failure to satisfy the absolute needs of a sentient creature is detrimental to its welfare (see fig. 5.1).

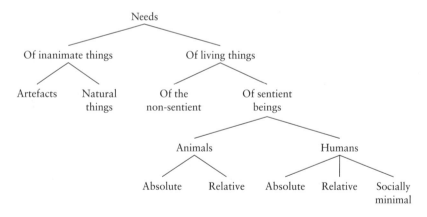

Figure 5.1. *Needs*

---

[12] Needs can also be created by addictions. Here, satisfaction of the needs does not necessarily contribute to the long-term welfare of the addict.

It should also be noted that the organs and faculties of living creatures need things. What they need is what is essential for their normal functioning and exercise, or what will improve their functioning, if the organs are innately defective, diseased or damaged through injury or age, and ameliorate the exercise of the faculties, if the faculties are poor or weak. What is thus needed is said to be good for the relevant organ or faculty. Instead of ascribing the need to the organ or faculty, we can also ascribe it to the animal, who needs it *for* its organ or faculty in order that it (the animal) be able to function normally (or, at least, better).

The satisfaction of the non-relative needs of developed animals is a condition for the possibility of their flourishing. Flourishing is doing well in a form of life (which, with us, but not with other animals, is a socio-historical, cultural, form of life), in the activities characteristic of the form of life (and, with us, the activities of the agent that contribute to his good), and faring well in the circumstances of life. What is good for developed sentient beings is primarily that which promotes or protects those perceptual, cognitive and physical faculties, affective dispositions, and skills that normal members of the species need in order successfully to pursue their goals and, in the case of humans, their projects.[13] Living beings have *a good*. What befalls them, what they do, and how they act may not only be good for them, as things may be good for machines or for the environment, but may serve *their good* and so contribute, productively or protectively, to their flourishing.[14]

What we have called 'volitional agents' are developed sentient creatures that can be said to want things and to act or take action to get what they want. The term 'want' has a wide and flexible use. It includes:

(i)   Mere wishing or hoping (as in 'I want the Blues to win')
(ii) Felt desire (ranging from appetites and cravings to urges and obsessive preoccupation with the lack of something and

---

[13] See Thomas Schwartz, 'Von Wright's Theory of Human Welfare: A Critique', in P. A. Schilpp and L. E. Hahn (eds), *The Philosophy of Georg Henrik von Wright* (Open Court, La Salle, Ill., 1989), pp. 217–32.

[14] See G. H. von Wright, *The Varieties of Goodness* (Routledge & Kegan Paul, London, 1963), ch. 3, for an illuminating discussion of welfare and the category of the beneficial, and his reply to his critics in Schilpp and Hahn (eds), *Philosophy of Georg Henrik von Wright*, pp. 777f.

reflection on the means of attaining it and the pleasure of
possessing it)
(iii) Inclination ('I just wanted to – I felt like it')
(iv) Endeavour and purpose
(v) Reasoned purpose

Note that these are not exclusive. A want that is a reasoned purpose
may also be the object of obsessive preoccupation, and hence felt as
a ubiquitous and perhaps tormenting presence. Apart from the first
kind of case, wanting is essentially linked with acting (and trying).
The concept of wanting something and acting *because* it is wanted
gets a grip when an animal possesses the power to V or refrain from
V-ing, and V's (or tries to V) either for its own sake (*that* is what it
wanted, because it is, e.g., enjoyable) or in order to attain something
it is aware of lacking and cares about sufficiently to take action.

Only what an animal can do or refrain from doing can it do because
it wants to do it. (Hence, one role of 'because I wanted to' is to earmark behaviour as action.) Apart from the second kind of case of
felt desire, wanting is misconstrued as a mental state, *a fortiori* as a
mental state that is a cause or part of a cause of acting. The causal
construal of wanting has some (remote) plausibility in the case of
felt desires and urges, but none in the primary invocation of wants in
explanation of animal behaviour and human action. We shall examine
the matter in chapter 7.

There are both similarities and differences between what is needed
and what is wanted. What is wanted, like what is needed, may be
something that does not exist, as when one wants (and needs) a drug
the supply of which has been exhausted (or even a drug that has not
yet been discovered). The object of a want, like that of a need, is
commonly generic, rather than particular: one may want (as one may
need) a drink – not specifically *this* drink, or food – not *this* particular piece of bread. However, to do something because one needs to,
like doing something because one is obliged to, implies a constraint
– need being a form of practical necessitation. To do something
simply because one wants to is the opposite of constraint.[15] Indeed,
doing something simply because one wants to defines liberty of spon-
taneity. Moreover, the restrictions on what can be wanted differ from

[15] But pathological wants may *become* needs. One who is subject to such wants
is a slave to his irrational desires.

the restrictions on what can be needed by an agent. If an agent wants something or to do or undergo something, the agent must be able to recognize its having or attaining, doing or undergoing, what it wanted. But an agent may need, need to do or to undergo, something without being able to recognize if the need has been satisfied. This reflects a deeper point concerning the relation of the needs and wants to a human being's beliefs. What a person needs is independent of his beliefs. But what he wants, if the want is not an appetite, mere inclination or urge, is normally a function of his beliefs about the means to his ends or about the desirability characteristics of the objects of his wants – that is, characteristics the specification of which precludes the further question of 'Why do you want things satisfying that description?' That is why the ascription of needs to animals is unproblematic, whereas the ascription of wants is as blurred as the ascription to them of beliefs.

If something is needed, then it is needed *for an end*. But if something is wanted, it need not be wanted for any purpose – one may just want (to have) a so-and-so (in one's possession). Similarly, one may just want to do such-and-such, without wanting to do it for any *further* purpose: one just feels like doing it. But one cannot just need something, or need something just because one feels like it. It may be that what one wants is wanted for its desirability characteristics (because it is enjoyable to do, or beautiful to look at). But one does not need things for their desirability characteristics. Rather, the reason an agent needs something consists in the agent's condition or in the obtaining of circumstances giving rise to the need or in the end for the sake of which the thing is needed. There can *be* a reason both for wanting and for needing something. One may *have* a reason for wanting something or to do something, but a person cannot *have* a reason for needing, by contrast with having a reason for wanting, something. There must *be* a reason why he needs X, but that is not *his* reason for needing it, although the fact that he needs it may be his reason for wanting X. His reasons for wanting Y may be good reasons, poor or even bad reasons, but he cannot *have* good, poor or bad reasons for needing X. That is why what a person wants or wants to do reflects on his character, whereas what he needs or needs to do reflects on his circumstances or condition.

Developed animals, we have observed, have wants no less than humans, but their wants are limited relative to ours.[16] Lacking a

---

[16] For a helpful discussion of animal wants and the relation between animal and human wants, see Bede Rundle, *Mind in Action* (Clarendon Press, Oxford, 1997), chs 3, 5 and 6.

language, they can express wants only by means of non-linguistic behaviour. So one can ascribe wants to them only on the grounds of their non-linguistic behaviour. Can they not have wants which they cannot express? May we not be unavoidably ignorant of the range of their wants? The issue is not an epistemological one. An animal can want something and not exhibit the fact that it does. It may feel thirsty or hungry, but not display its appetites because of fear (if it is being threatened) or be unable to display them because it is paralysed. But it only *makes sense* to ascribe to it wants that it *can* (logically) exhibit in its behaviour. For the wanting of a non-language-using animal is a *preparedness to act*, given an opportunity. This may, but need not be, a felt appetite. Hunger, thirst, animal lust, fear and aggressive anger are felt. The desire to play is not – unlike felt appetites, it is exhibited primarily not in taking steps to get . . . , but in the voluntary activity of playing. In both cases, there must be something in the behavioural repertoire of the animal that would *count* as manifesting a given want. *This*, we must be able to say, is what a creature that wants such-and-such a goal and perceives such an opportunity *does*. Otherwise we cannot render intelligible the thought that the animal *has* the want in question. The horizon of animal wants is limited to what animals can do or try to do, as exhibited in their preparations for action, in their endeavours, and in their acting. Human beings, by contrast, can also want, want to do, to be or become what they can describe. The grounds for ascribing wants to them are not only what they prepare to do, try to do, and do, but also what they *say*. Human beings can *now* want something at some *future* date, precisely because they can express such wants by means of future-referring expressions in their language. Animals can have only immediate wants for the present or the immediate future.[17] For there is nothing in their behavioural repertoire that would make it possible for them to express a want now for something or to engage in an activity *in the remote future*.

4. Volitional agency: preliminaries

Sentient agents, as we have noted, have perceptual powers and are self-moving. These two kinds of power of sentient beings are

---

[17] Including desires to commence an activity that may have a considerable temporal trajectory, as in the case of the beaver starting to fell trees for a dam. But it cannot now want to construct a new dam next autumn.

conceptually intimately connected. For the criteria for whether an
agent perceives something in its environment consist in how it behaves
(looks, listens, smells, moves or stops moving) in response to objects
and events around it, and the criteria for whether an organ is a sense-
organ of a certain kind consist in how the animal employs the organ
in question (orientates it) in the acquisition of knowledge about its
environment. For a sense-organ is an organ subservient to a sense-
faculty, and the sense-faculties are cognitive faculties. They are
capacities by the exercise of which the animal can achieve or receive
information about its surroundings. The exercise of a sense-faculty
involves the use of the correlative sense-organ. An animal uses its
eyes to see, turns its head to look, brings its head closer to the object
scrutinized in order to see it more clearly; it uses its nose to smell,
brings its nose closer to the object it is smelling in order to smell it
better. Touch is anomalous relative to the other senses, since animals
can feel tactile qualities with most parts of their bodies, and the behaviour characteristic of apprehending and exploring tactile qualities
is very varied and species-, as well as circumstance-, dependent. The
exercise of the sense-faculties, as noted above, is a source of pleasure,
revulsion and sometimes pain.[18]

Being self-moving, having perceptual, recognitional and cognitive
powers as well as hedonic susceptibilities and preferences, it makes
sense to say of volitional agents that they *act* in pursuit of their wants
and needs, that they adopt goals and *take action* in order to attain
what they want and to avoid what they apprehend as harmful, dangerous, unpleasant or repellent. So they can be said to have goals
and purposes *of their own*. These may be the satisfaction of their
natural or acquired appetites,[19] the attainment of their needs, or the
fulfilment of their contingent ends. They can adjust their behaviour
in response to what they perceive, in order to get what they want
or avoid what they apprehend to be threatening them. They can perceive alternative things that attract or threaten them, and pursue, attack
or flee from one rather than another, as well as apprehend and take
alternative courses of action in order to achieve their purpose. So

---

[18] It is curious that English, unlike German (*Lust* and *Unlust*) has no term that
is the strict contrary of pleasure. Pleasure, unlike pain, is not a sensation, although
there are pleasurable sensations, and pain is certainly unpleasant. Displeasure is the
contrary of the pleasing rather than of the pleasant and pleasurable, although the
pleasant and pleasurable are normally pleasing.

[19] Addictions are acquired appetites.

volitional agents can be said to do or refrain from doing things that are within their power. Having two-way powers is constitutive of being able to act. Not all the acts of a volitional agent are voluntary acts. For such an agent can also act involuntarily or non-voluntarily (under duress or because obliged by circumstances or in ignorance). But behaviour is deemed an act only if it is of a *kind* that can be done voluntarily. In the case of rational agents, it is generally behaviour of a kind that *can* be done intentionally, *can* be done for reasons, *can* be decided on. The horizon of action of rational agents coincides with the range of their will.

So, only volitional agents can be said to act and to take action. It would be mistaken to suppose that whenever an agent acts, it takes action. To take action is to act voluntarily in response to a circumstance (e.g. a threat or perceived danger) or in pursuit of a goal, given perception of an opportunity. It involves purposive movement in pursuit of a goal or in avoidance of a perceived danger (we would not deem 'freezing' at the perception of a threat as *taking action*). But only a being that *can* take action can act. For a creature that can be said to take action is a creature that can do or refrain from doing something *voluntarily*, that can have and seize an opportunity (as well as forgo one), that can *opt for* or *choose* one course of action over another. The boundary between mere animal behaviour – in the case of insects or fish – and the voluntary actions of more developed creatures is broad and blurred.

The boundary between act and action is likewise blurred. These terms are sometimes intersubstitutable. We say that actions speak louder than words, by which we mean that the acts a person performs, his deeds, are better tokens of his intent or character than his words (i.e. than what he says). We weigh the actions of people and judge them accordingly: that is, we judge their deeds. Nevertheless, there are differences. We contrast action with *inaction*, acting or taking action with *doing nothing*. Differently, we contrast action with *reaction*, the latter, in the case of volitional agency, being a response to the action or deed of another or to some event that has occurred or condition that obtains and has been apprehended. We make ready for action, are galvanized into action, or put out of action. We compare the man of action with the thinker, the doer with the mere talker. One may be caught in the act, but not in the action; there are acts, but not actions, of mercy, compassion, folly or desperation.

Conceptions of the active are diversified and extended in the domain of human volitional agency. For human beings are conceived to be active not only when they act on another thing and bring about change, but also when they act (without necessarily being characterized as acting *on* anything) by contrast with being contemplative. Differently, being active is associated with taking action, as opposed to doing nothing – another form of being passive (as when one passively watches things happening rather than interfering). The latter, of course, may be perfectly voluntary. Yet another contrast is that between doing something willingly as opposed to being forced to do something against one's will – when one is a passive victim forced to do the will of another.[20] Finally, one can be conceived to be active in thought, feeling and action when one fully identifies with what one thinks, feels and does, by contrast with being passive in one's beliefs, feelings or deeds – when one feels them to be not fully one's own.

Although non-human animals are volitional agents and can be said to take action to avoid danger or to catch a prey, we speak more readily of *animal behaviour* than of the *acts* animals perform.[21] This may be a consequence of the fact that we invoke the formal concept of an act largely in contexts when intentional and rational adjectival and adverbial modifications of what was done by an agent are in question. So, having been informed that someone V'd, we may query whether his *act* was intentional or unintentional, deliberate, reasonable, spontaneous, benevolent or malicious, or negligent, and so forth – through a wide range of epithets that have little or no application to non-language-using agents.

5. Doings, acts and actions

Statements about inanimate agents come in many different forms. One is produced by attaching a verb to the relevant agent-designating term. The resultant statement need not specify something the inanimate agent does. To say that the stone is lying in the road or that the litre of water fills the bottle is not to state what the stone or litre of water is doing. The resultant statement may specify what the inanimate agent does or is doing, without describing any action. For a description of

---

[20] Of course, non-human animals too may be forced to do things against their will, i.e. to do something that they do not want to do. But, in another sense of 'will', non-language-users no more have a will than they have an intellect.

[21] Other than in a circus.

a mere motion or change of the inanimate agent itself is not a description of inanimate action. Stones can be described as rolling downhill, the sun as shining, rivers as flowing, coals as glowing, wheels as rotating, puddles as growing larger, waves as breaking – all of which statements describe things done by the inanimate agent in question, but do not describe an action. To describe instances of action of a natural inanimate agent is to describe its *doing something to* a patient, most commonly to describe the production or effecting of a change *in* or *to* another thing *by* the agent's operating *on* it. Inanimate suppression or prevention of change, as when a doorstop keeps the door open by holding it in position or a wad of cloth prevents water from flowing through a pipe by blocking it, may also be considered a form of agency, since, although the agent does not produce a change, it prevents a change by its action (see fig. 5.2). Preventive and suppressive agency will not be discussed here, but the remarks that follow can readily be adjusted to budget for such cases.

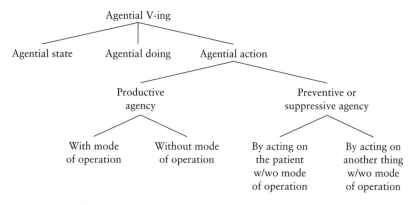

Figure 5.2. *Varieties of inanimate agential V-ing*

We have already distinguished two different kinds of description of an agent's doing something to a patient: those that entail a corresponding change in the patient and those that do not. In the first kind of case, corresponding to the transitive use of the causative verb in a sentence of the form 'A V's P' is its intransitive occurrence in correlative sentences of the form 'P V's'. For example, if a stone breaks a window, then the window breaks; if the sun melts the wax, the wax melts; and if the wind shakes the tree, then the tree shakes. There are also cases in which a change is logically implied by the agent's action, but it is not signified by an intransitive form of the same action verb. So, for example, the falling stone may kill a mouse, and if it does, then it follows that the mouse is dead. Such (logically) *effective inanimate agency* is manifest in acting *on* something and *causing* something to happen to it. So it is to *produce* or *effect* a change in the patient, the description of which is entailed by the act description.

As noted, verbs that signify action of an agent on a patient but do not entail any change to the patient are to be distinguished from the class of logically effective act descriptions. Where a verb of action of the latter kind is in question, one may, following von Wright, call the *logical upshot* of an agent's action on a patient 'the *result* of A's action'.[22] Taken thus as a term of art, the result of A's action is entailed by the action's occurring: if A breaks P, it follows that P is broken; if A opens P, then P is open; if A kills P, then P is dead. The result, thus understood, can be conceived as the *end state* of the change that logically results from A's action (e.g. that the patient is broken, open or dead). Here we have one paradigm of agent causation. The agent *causes* or *brings about* the end state *by acting on the patient*. Corresponding to the causative verb of action, we sometimes have an intransitive verb applicable to the patient – if A breaks P, we can describe P as breaking; if A opens P, P opens; if A kills P, P dies. These can also be called 'the results' of agential action on a patient. We can describe the 'transaction' from an agential perspective or from that of the patient. The availability of these two *forms of description* is a source of confusion.

Note that the result of preventive or suppressive agency is the non-occurrence of an event that otherwise would have occurred, the non-commencement or termination of a process that would otherwise have commenced or continued, and the failure of a state to obtain that otherwise would have obtained.

The action of A upon P produces a state of affairs that is a logical upshot of the action (its production defines the action). The transaction between A and P can be described actively (what the agent does to the patient) or passively (what the patient is made to do, or how the patient is transformed, by the agent). The event signified by the latter description may itself cause further events. So a stone may break a window by hitting it, and the room may consequently cool down. The window's being broken is a (logical) result of the stone's breaking it; the cooling of the room is a (non-logical) *consequence* of the stone's action on the window. Whereas the relation between an action and its result is internal (logical), the relation between an action and its consequence is external.

When an inanimate object acts on a patient, and the result of its action has further consequences, we do not *typically* ascribe to the inanimate agent the action corresponding to that consequence. So, for example, if the stone breaks a window and, as a consequence, the room cools down, we should not say that the stone cooled the room by breaking the window. Similarly, if the sun melts some butter on the table cloth, as a consequence of which the table cloth is stained, we should not say that the sun stained the table cloth by melting the butter. By contrast, if a human agent opens the door and as a consequence the room cools down, then we *may*, in certain cases, say that the person, intentionally or inadvertently, cooled the room by opening the door. Similarly, if a person melted some butter by heating it, and the butter dripped on to the table cloth, thereby staining it, we should say that he stained the table cloth by dripping butter on it. It has been suggested by Donald Davidson that this 'accordion effect'[23] is the true mark of agency, which precludes conceiving of inanimate things as agents, since it does not apply to the description of inanimate action on patients.[24] Furthermore, he claimed, the 'accordion effect' applies only where *something* is being done intentionally, and a human being is the agent of an act only if what he does can be described under some aspect that makes it *intentional*. Hence an act can be involuntary under one description only if it is intentional under another. But this seems wrong. One can start in alarm, or cry out involuntarily because stung by a wasp, without doing anything intentional. If Tyrrel was alarmed by a sudden shout in his ear, and, as he started in alarm, he inadvertently loosed the arrow in his bow, which hit the king and killed him, then Tyrrel involuntarily started in alarm, inadvertently loosed the shaft, and unintentionally killed the king. So it is not true that the mark of action is that it is intentional under some description. Furthermore, even in

---

[23] As Joel Feinberg termed this possibility of expanding or contracting descriptions of action; see 'Action and Responsibility', in M. Black (ed.), *Philosophy in America* (Cornell University Press, Ithaca, NY, 1965), p. 146.

[24] Davidson, 'Agency', p. 54.

this scenario, it is true to say that Tyrrel killed the king by loos-
ing the arrow – so the 'accordion effect' may apply even though
nothing was done intentionally. Finally, although it may be true that
we do not normally extend 'accordion' descriptions of this kind
to inanimate objects, it is not true that we never do so. If a man
takes a drug, and the drug gives him a heart attack, from which he
dies, then the drug killed the man by giving him a heart attack.[25]
There is no good reason for claiming that inanimate things are
not agents of change and that they do not bring about changes in
patients by acting on them.

6. Human agency and action

We have noted that inanimate movement as such is not an act of the
inanimate agent. When we describe a wheel as rotating, a ball as rolling
downhill, a river as flowing, a pendulum as swinging back and forth,
a ship as steaming ahead, we are not describing them either as *acting* or as *acting on* anything.[26] We are merely describing what they
are *doing*. Animate behaviour of self-moving creatures, and hence too
of human beings, is different. The following discussion of agency and
voluntary action is restricted to human action.

Human beings are creatures that have a will – that is, a capacity
for *reasoned* wants, goals and purposes, for deliberation and action
for reasons. Because we possess cognitive and volitional powers,
because we are self-moving agents with the power to foresee the effects
of our behaviour, we naturally conceive of our action on other
things as interfering 'in the course of nature', bringing about, sustaining or preventing changes in the world around us. We knowingly
make things happen, *prevent* things from happening that otherwise
would take place, and *keep things going on* that, but for our intervention, might cease. We can thus intervene 'in the course of nature'
intentionally, deliberately, with a further purpose. Since we can do
so intentionally, we can also do so involuntarily or not voluntarily
(e.g. under duress), unintentionally, inadvertently, by accident or by

---

[25] I am grateful to Maria Alvarez and John Hyman for pointing out this kind of
exception to Davidson's claim.

[26] Of course, this does not mean that they are *not* acting on another thing. But
our description does not characterize them as so acting.

mistake. The concept of human action and its conceptual environment is therefore distinctly and importantly different from that of inanimate things.

Human beings move. They move from place to place; they turn around or turn over, jump up and down, without moving to another place; they move their limbs and sense-organs; they move the features of their faces. They slip, fall, trip over things; they start in alarm, tremble with excitement, scream in terror; they cough, sneeze, vomit, yawn, breathe in and out; they blink, smile, laugh, frown; they nod or shake their heads, wave or point, walk or run, jump and climb. Not all of these verbs signify acts or actions of human beings. Some signify things that *happen to* a human being, such as slipping or falling. Other verbs signify things that human beings *do*, but are not acts they *perform*. Some of these are *reactions* that cannot be initiated at will, but some cases of which, sometimes, can be inhibited at will: one cannot sneeze or yawn at will, but sometimes one can stifle a sneeze and inhibit a yawn. Some are reactions that can voluntarily be brought about – as when one induces a sneeze by taking snuff. However, many of these verbs do signify acts that human beings perform. What is noteworthy about them is that they do not imply *acting on* another thing and, as in the cases of effective action, thereby bringing about (or preventing) a change in or to it. Unlike inanimate doings that are mere motion or change, when human beings (or other animals) do such things, they *act*. When we describe a human being as raising his arm, wiggling his finger, rising to his feet or sitting down, walking or jumping, we are not thereby describing him as acting *on* another thing – but we are describing him as *acting* (and in some cases, in appropriate circumstances, he may be said to be *taking action*).

To be sure, a human being may move as a non-self-moving substance may move – for example, when he slips or trips and falls, or is blown over in a gale. So too a human being's limbs may move without him moving them, as when someone or something else moves them, or as when they are made to move as in a 'reflex action' (which is not an action of the person, but a reaction), such as the knee-jerk reaction when the knee is struck below the patella. Nevertheless, characteristic human movements are actions of which it makes *sense* to say that they are voluntary, intentional, made or done deliberately or on purpose, for a reason or out of a motive. Characterizing the nature of human action, distinguishing human action from the mere movements of a human being or of their limbs that are not themselves actions, has much preoccupied philosophers. There is no consensus

on the matter, and widely divergent accounts of the conceptual structures involved are still current.

The problem can be nicely crystallized in the question: What
distinguishes the rising of one's arm from the raising of one's arm?
One may raise one's arm voluntarily with no specific intention, or one
may raise it intentionally; one may raise one's arm with the further
intention of waving to someone across the road or of taking a book
off the top shelf of a bookcase. But one's arm may rise without one's
raising it at all: someone else may raise it; or it may be raised by an
exercising machine; or one may raise it oneself with one's other hand
(perhaps because it is 'asleep', broken or paralysed). Or, although one
does not raise it, one lets it rise 'of its own accord' – as when one
presses it against a wall for a minute and then steps back, letting the
deltoid muscles contract. Raising one's arm is an action. What differentiates it from one's arm's rising without one's raising it?

7. A historical overview

Various answers to the last question have been essayed over the past
four centuries. By far the most common has been the idea that when
one moves, or moves a limb, one's movement is caused by a mental
phenomenon of willing. But there was extensive disagreement over
how to conceive of willing. Here we can distinguish two broad categories of answer.

(i) Most typically (e.g. by Descartes, Locke, Hume, Bentham, Austin,
Mill and Prichard), the mental phenomenon was held to be an act
of volition. But there were considerable differences as to how such
acts are to be construed. Locke held that to will is to exercise the
power of thought to initiate bodily movement. This act of thought
was evidently neither merely thinking of an act or movement, nor
desiring to move, since we can think of or want to do things we do
not do. He concluded that acts of will are *sui generis*, indefinable
because simple, but known by introspection. Hume (like Augustine)
conceived of acts of will directed at movements of the body as com-
mands addressed to the body. Austin (the jurist) identified acts
of volition with wishes or desires. And Prichard held that they are
mental acts of trying.

(ii) A second alternative that was pursued was to take willing
to be the occurrence of an idea or image of the desired movement
or of a memory image of the kinaesthetic sensations that allegedly

accompany the desired movement, coupled with the knowledge that such a movement is within one's power (James, Russell; and also Hume[27]). Accordingly, willing is not something one does, but something that happens to one. James's ideo-motor theory held that the occurrence of a mere idea of the appropriate kinaesthetic sensations was all that was necessary to initiate motion. The innervation theory, propounded by Wundt, Bain, Helmholtz and Mach, held that in addition to images of kinaesthetic sensations a feeling of innervation, of impulse or volitional energy directed at the appropriate muscles, was required.

So, the received empiricist view was that some mental occurrence constitutes willing (which is either a mental act or a mental phenomenon), and that the willing causes the movement of the body. A human action was therefore considered to be a human movement caused by willing, and acting was causing the movement by willing.[28] Explanations of human behaviour as caused by willing I shall call 'volitionist' (see fig. 5.3).

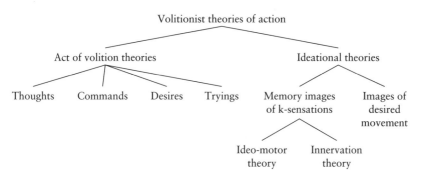

Figure 5.3. *Volitionist theories of action*

These traditional analyses of human actions were plagued by a fundamental unclarity. The protagonists of the volitionist accounts did not clearly distinguish between a philosophical account of the conceptual articulations of our vocabulary of act descriptions and

[27] Hume, *Enquiry Concerning Human Understanding* §52.

[28] Some philosophers, such as Reid, held that the action itself (e.g. the raising of the arm), as opposed to the bodily movement (e.g. the rising of the arm), was caused by the act of will.

the adjectival and adverbial modifiers which they may take, on the one hand, and the empirical explanation of the mechanisms of human movement, on the other. The conflation of empirical and conceptual issues, already patent in Descartes and Hume, had become glaring as neurology was beginning to achieve maturity as a science at the end of the nineteenth century. Innervationist and ideo-motor theories of action indiscriminately wove together speculative neuroscience with conceptual analysis, to the detriment of both. The empirical pre-suppositions of the accounts were the result not of careful observation, but were rather dogmatic assumptions motivated by the demands of a preconceived picture of how human actions *must* eventuate. The a priori data for the theories were that human beings act volun-tarily, can be and are typically perfectly aware of what they are doing and do not mistake what they do voluntarily for what merely happens to them (including the mere movements – twitches and jerks – that are not their actions at all). The empirical data are that movements of the body that are not generated by external causes involve muscular contractions that are typically generated by neural activity in the motor centres of the brain that is then transmitted along efferent nerves to the relevant muscles. The a priori data seemed to be explained if a voluntary human action is a movement caused by a mental act or event, on the assumption that such acts or events are transparent to their agent: that is, if the phenomenon of willing occurs, the subject is aware of its occurring, or if the subject performs an act of willing, he knows that he is doing so. The empirical data seemed to be explained if the mental act or phenomenon of willing causes the neural phenomena, or if it is contingently identical with their incep-tion in the brain.

Substantial difficulties and incoherences were identified by Ryle, Wittgenstein and others, in the volitionist account of action.

(1) It presupposed that every voluntary human movement constituting an action is preceded by an act or occurrence of willing. But there is no empirical reason for supposing this to be true. We are not aware of performing an act of will (let alone of an effort of will or an inner act of trying) or of the occurrence of a volition (a mental image or a representation of a kinaesthetic sensation) antecedently to everything we do voluntarily. When one utters a sentence, every word is spoken voluntarily, but it would be ridiculous to claim that one consciously performs successive acts of will, one for each word (or phoneme?) an instant before utterance. And it would defeat the purpose of the

account to suggest that one performs this manifold, but without being conscious of doing so – for part of the point of the account is precisely to explain, by reference to the transparency of each mental act or occurrence of willing, how it is that we can distinguish, without evidence, between what we voluntarily do and what happens to us.

This empirical qualm gives rise to deeper conceptual worries.

(2) As noted, there was considerable disagreement over exactly what willing is, some holding it to be a sensation, impression or idea, others taking it to be a mental act. The dilemma is acute, for if willing is a mental act, then presumably it is itself either voluntary or involuntary. If it is a voluntary act, then presumably it must be preceded by another act of will, for just as what transforms a physical movement into a voluntary act is the causing of it by an act of will, so too what makes a mental occurrence a voluntary mental act (as when one voluntarily thinks something over, imagines something or tries to remember something) as opposed to something that merely happens to one, is (presumably) the causing of *it* by an act of will. But, first, this threatens a regress. Secondly, it is not evident that there is any such thing as willing to will. There is such a thing as willing (or wanting) *to bring it about* that one wills (or wants) to V. But this does not make willing to V voluntary – it makes the bringing about voluntary, if one brings it about. However, if willing is not voluntary, it is difficult to see why we are held responsible for its consequences (i.e. for the movement that is partly constitutive of our overt action that is held to be voluntary). For the causal consequences of a non-voluntary act are themselves not voluntary. Moreover, willing was surely intended to be a *doing*, something of which the agent is the active subject, and not merely something that happens to one.

In truth, however, willing (wanting, the voluntariness involved in our actions) is neither a mental act one performs nor something that happens to one; it is neither voluntary nor involuntary, neither action nor passion.[29]

There are, to be sure, such things as acts of will, but they are (ordinary) acts performed with great effort to overcome one's reluctance

---

[29] This is argued, with great depth, but also formidable obscurity, by Wittgenstein in the *Investigations*, §§611–28. For explanation of his remarks, see P. M. S. Hacker, *Wittgenstein: Mind and Will* (Blackwell, Oxford, 1996), Exegesis §§611–28, and for discussion of his account, see the essay 'Willing and the Nature of Voluntary Action', ibid. I have drawn here upon some of the arguments in that essay.

or difficulties in acting, typically in adverse circumstances.[30] They are not mental acts called 'willing', which cause bodily movements. There is such a thing as will-power, but it is not the mental equivalent of muscle power. Rather, it is determination in pursuit of one's goals. There is such a thing as strength of will, but it is not a matter of causally efficacious mental acts of willing, but rather of tenacity in sticking to one's purpose.

(3) One strand in the traditional account actually undermines the very distinctions that it aimed to elucidate. If willing is conceived to be a mental event, the occurrence of a felt desire or wish, or of a mental image of a desired movement or of a mnemonic image of associated kinaesthetic sensations, then the distinction between action and reaction, between voluntary and involuntary acts, is in effect undermined. For there is all the difference in the world between a sensory state or a mental occurrence that causes a bodily movement and moving because one wants to. A bodily movement triggered by a sensory state (e.g. sneezing or coughing caused by a tickle in the nose or throat) is the paradigm of a *bodily reaction*, not of a voluntary action of which one is the agent. So too is a bodily movement caused by a mental occurrence. Certain thoughts that cross one's mind may cause one to move in certain ways, as the thought of something fearful may cause one to shudder or flinch, the thought of something comic may cause one to smile, and the occurrence of erotic thoughts or desires may cause bodily *reactions*. But these, far from being typical human actions, are not things we do at will, although if we know of these regular responses, we may *bring them about* at will by thinking the appropriate thoughts.

(4) If volition is conceived to be an experience, something that happens to us, the concept of rational, volitional agency is distorted, if not abolished. We are agents responsible for our voluntary actions. But if our actions are mere bodily movements caused by desires, wishes or impressions that occur to us, then, it seems, the agent, the 'willing self', drops out of the account. But we surely wish to distinguish between acts of which we are the agent and those things that are caused by sensory or mental events (e.g. as when a pain makes us

---

[30] The assault on the myth of volitions was opened by G. Ryle, *The Concept of Mind* (Hutchinson, London, 1949), ch. 3.

flinch or limp). In these cases, the cause of our movements is indeed 'within us', but the resultant movements are not voluntary. We do not conceive of our voluntary actions as movements that were caused or made to happen by our own inner states, even if those inner states are held to be our desires (e.g. a desire to sneeze). Of the movements that are constitutive of our own voluntary actions, we do not say that they were caused or made to happen by our wants. Nor do we say that *we* were caused to make them by our wants. Rather, we say that we moved, or made a movement, *of our own volition*. We do not say that we brought them about by doing something else: namely, *an act of volition*.

(5) By focusing upon voluntary action, the traditional volitionist account fails altogether to budget for *involuntary* actions of which we are the agent. For the account analyses voluntary action as movement caused by willing (which may be an act or a mental occurrence). In the absence of willing, it would seem, there is only a bare bodily movement. But we must distinguish between one's arm's rising because someone or something raises it, and raising one's arm involuntarily (in alarm or astonishment, e.g.) – in both cases one's arm moves. In neither case does one move it voluntarily. But in one case one moves it involuntarily, and in the other one does not move it at all.

It was clear that the major flaw in volitionist accounts was to conceive of the relation between willing and movement as a causal relation between two occurrences. This either bypassed agency altogether (if the willing was conceived to be merely an experience, e.g. the occurrence of a mental image), or pushed agency too far back (as if all that voluntary agents *really* do is to perform acts of will – then everything else follows causally). But willing, if it is causally implicated at all, must be *direct* – not an inner act the *consequences* of which are the movements of one's body. The willing must not be conceived as doing something, the doing of which then causes the movement of one's body. That would be a case of *bringing about* the movement of one's body by doing something else. Rather, the willing would have to be an 'immediate causing'. We shall examine this further in a moment.

An obscure alternative to the empiricist volitionist accounts that was sensitive to precisely these points was that proposed by Schopenhauer and adopted by the young Wittgenstein. According to this analysis, wishing and wanting (conceived as a felt desire) are experiences (hence representations), but the act of will is not an experience. Schopenhauer insisted against the prevailing tradition that 'we certainly do not recognize the real immediate act of will as something different from the action of the body, and the two as connected by a bond of causality; but both are one and indivisible'.[31] 'Thus actual willing', he insisted, 'is inseparable from doing, and, in the narrowest sense, that alone is an act of will which is stamped as such by the deed.'[32] One cannot will without acting, Wittgenstein similarly insisted in 1916: 'The act of will is not the cause of the action but is the action itself' – it is raising one's arm or moving one's leg, getting up or sitting down'; 'The fact that I will an action consists in my performing the action, not in my doing something else which causes the action.'[33] Willing cannot be a 'representation' – an experience. When one exercises one's will, one *does* something, one acts – one is not a mere spectator, but the *agent* of one's actions. Willing must not fall short of the action itself.

But although this attempts correctly to remedy the flaws in Cartesian and empiricist accounts, it is, Wittgenstein argued in the *Investigations*, still inadequate. For any account of voluntary action must allow for the fact that we often want to act and fail – try as we may, we cannot raise our arm. So 'willing' – if it is anything – must be *capable* of falling short of acting. Furthermore, in so far as willing does *not* thus fall short, then it does not fall short of acting *in the ordinary sense of the word* – that is, it not only does not fall short of one's bodily movements, it does not fall short of one's speaking and writing, going to London, or giving a lecture. Nor does it fall short of imagining, thinking or remembering – which one may do voluntarily – or indeed of trying, attempting or making an effort.[34] In so far as this conception intended to capture the difference obliterated by the empiricists between will and representation, it overlooked, as they did, an important point. One can *act* involuntarily

[31] A. Schopenhauer, *The World as Will and Idea*, tr. R. B. Haldane and J. Kemp (Routledge & Kegan Paul, London, 1883), vol. 2, p. 206.

[32] Schopenhauer, *The World as Will and Representation*, tr. E. F. J. Payne (Dover, New York, 1958), vol. 2, p. 248.

[33] L. Wittgenstein, *Notebooks 1914–16*, ed. G. H. von Wright and G. E. M. Anscombe (Blackwell, Oxford, 1961), pp. 87–9.

[34] L. Wittgenstein, *Philosophical Investigations*, §615.

as well as voluntarily. Many of the things we do involuntarily (e.g. because we are not aware of doing them) are still actions of ours, for some of which we may be held responsible (e.g. negligent acts). But it would be peculiar to identify the will also with the involuntary actions that we perform. Finally, it is unclear what we are to make of this artificial verb 'to will' – what work is left for it to do here at all? It seems no more than 'an active principle', as it were, with no volume of experience at all.

8. Human action as agential causation of movement

A rather different analysis of action has also been suggested, one that bypasses the volitionist predicaments. If 'V' is a causative verb, then if an agent V's a patient, the patient V's (intransitively). So we can often paraphrase 'A V's P' by 'A causes P to V'; for example, if A breaks P, then A causes P to break, and if A kills P, then A causes P to die. We have noted that over a wide range of the actions of an inanimate agent on a patient, we can observe the *mode of operation* whereby the agent caused the result in the patient: the red billiard ball caused the white billiard ball to move *by hitting it*, the tree caused the destruction of the house *by falling on it*, the river caused the bridge to collapse *by washing away its foundations*. But, as noted above, this is not uniformly so. A bath of acid may dissolve a lump of zinc: it causes the lump of zinc to dissolve. But there is nothing observable that it *does* to the lump of zinc whereby it brings it about that it dissolves, and it needs chemical theory to explain how and why the dissolution occurs. A magnet attracts iron filings: it causes them to move towards it. But there is nothing it does to them to make them move. Taking the behaviour of causative verbs of action as a clue, it has been argued that *basic human actions* (i.e. actions that involve bodily movement, which we perform but not *by* performing some other action) are *the causing of a movement by the agent*. For, it is argued, to move something *is* to cause it to move. So, for an agent to move his arm is for him *to cause* his arm to move; to raise one's arm is *to cause* one's arm to rise; and to nod or shake one's head is *to cause* one's head to nod or shake.[35] The power to cause

---

[35] This has been argued by Maria Alvarez and John Hyman in 'Agents and their Actions', *Philosophy*, 73 (1998), pp. 219–45. See also White (ed.), *Philosophy of Action*, Introduction, p. 2.

one's body to move is an original power, exercised *without doing any-thing else*. Here, as in the inanimate cases of the action of an acid on a metal, of magnetism or gravitational attraction, there is *no* mode of operation whereby one brings about the effect. The ability to do so, it is held, is constitutive of being a self-moving creature with volitional powers.

It is striking that in his fragmentary remarks on voluntary move-ments, Wittgenstein sketched in a similar idea that anticipated this conception:

> One imagines the willing subject here as something without any mass (without any inertia); as a motor which has no inertia in itself to over-come. And so it is only mover, not moved. . . .
>   *Doing* itself seems not to have any volume of experience. It seems like an extensionless point, the point of a needle. This point seems to be the real agent. And the phenomenal happenings only to be con-sequences of this acting. 'I do . . .' seems to have a definite sense, separate from all experience.[36]

This has formal affinities with the view that raising one's arm is *causing one's arm to rise* – the causing *is* the acting. For *causing* one's arm to rise *is* (allegedly) raising one's arm – and the causing itself is not of the action but of the movement. Here too, the agent, the causing subject, 'seems to have no mass' – he causes a movement of the limbs *directly* (he does not *bring it about*). This *causing* is, as it were, *pure* doing ('will' rather than 'idea', with no phenomenal content). Just as *doing*, in Wittgenstein's tale, 'seems not to have any volume of experience' (seems like an extensionless point), so too does *causing* here. Here the concept of human agential *causing* (which is something one *does*), like the concept of human *willing* as misused by certain philosophers, has been removed from the language-games in which it is at home and embedded in language-games in which it has no genuine role to play.

(1) We know what it is to raise one's arm. We know what it is to make one's arm rise by raising it with one's other hand or with an exercise machine. But it is altogether obscure what is meant by *caus-ing* one's arm to move *without doing anything to make it move*. In general, for a volitional agent to cause something to move is to spin

---

[36] L. Wittgenstein, *Philosophical Investigations*, §§618, 620.

or rotate it, to push, pull or throw it, as a consequence of which *it* moves.[37] It is indeed to *make* it move (wobble, rotate, rise or fall, roll or slide, etc.) by acting on it. To make *another thing* move is *to bring it about* that it moves. But when we move our eyes, grimace (smile or scowl), move our limbs, rotate our body, nod or shake our head, wiggle our toes or fingers, when we turn over or turn round, when we walk or run, when we talk or laugh, we do not *cause* our limbs, features, or ourselves to move. We do not *make* them or ourselves move. Nor do we *bring it about* that our limbs move, or that we move.

If someone were to tell us that he had seen A across the street, we might ask him what he then did. Were he to reply, 'I caused my arm to wave', we would not know what he was driving at. If he told us that A had asked whether he would lunch with him, we might ask how he responded. Were he to reply, 'I caused my head to nod' (let alone 'I caused my head to shake'), we would wonder what was wrong with him. To smile is not to cause one's lips to move in a certain way; to walk is not to make one's legs move – although one might use such a phrase when one forces oneself, in spite of one's total exhaustion, to walk on.

(2) To move one's leg is not to bring it about that one's leg moves – that is done by giving oneself an electric shock in the appropriate place or hitting one's knee below the patella. When I nod my head in assent, I don't make my head nod or bring it about that my head nods – that I do when I seize it in my hands and move it up and down.[38] When I move, or move my limbs, voluntarily, I don't *act on* myself or on my limbs – I don't do something *to* myself. My body, the body I *have* (see ch. 9), is not the reflexive patient on which I act. I *am* a body, a living spatio-temporal continuant of a certain kind; but when I move, I don't *move myself*, I just move.

---

[37] Note that to pick something up and put it down elsewhere, to carry something from one place to another, is not to *make it* move, but merely to move it – to bring about a change in its location. To hit a billiard ball with a cue, on the other hand, will make the ball move (cause it to move).

[38] If I raise my head, does my head rise? If I raise a patient's head from the pillow, does his head rise? No – it is raised. If I shake your hand, your hand cannot be said to shake, but rather to be shaken. Your hand shakes if you have Parkinson's or are trembling. I may shake my hands as athletes do before a race, but then my hands do not shake, they are shaken. The pattern that mesmerizes us is only a fragment – which we mistake for a whole.

Consider cases in which one moves, rather than those in which one moves a limb. 'To rise to one's feet' does not mean or imply 'to cause oneself to rise'. 'To make oneself rise to one's feet' indicates exertion of effort (an 'act of will') in the context of difficulty or reluctance. 'To cause one's body to rise to one's feet' is gibberish, and it is barely improved by 'to cause one's body to rise to its feet'. Of course, another person may make someone else stand (by threats), may bring a paralytic to his feet by hauling him upright, and a good party orator may bring his audience to their feet – but none of these are what *we* do to ourselves or cause ourselves when we rise from a semi-incumbent position to our feet.

(3) If raising my arm is causing my arm to rise, what is the causing? It is not an experience. It has no 'phenomenological content'. It seems to be a 'pure doing' – an extensionless point. My *causing* my arm to rise seems to 'have a definite sense, separate from all experience'. *Causing*, in this account is precisely parallel to *willing*, conceived (or better, misconceived) as a *direct* bringing about of a movement by the will. But there is no such thing as a human being directly *bringing about* a movement. It is a misuse of the phrase 'to bring about' to say that when one raises one's arm one brings it about that one's arm rises. For the application of the phrase to human behaviour is restricted to *indirect* causation: to bring it about that one's arm rises is to raise it by some means – for example, with one's other hand, or with a pulley, or by pushing it against the wall and then stepping back and letting the deltoid muscles contract.

(4) It is unclear how to characterize involuntary movements of which we are the agent – as when we involuntarily withdraw our hand from a slimy surface. This is not something that happens to us, but something we do. So presumably here too we cause our hand to move. But if so, our causing is involuntary. So causing the movement of our limb, in this sense, can itself be voluntary or involuntary – which is problematic. For just as willing seemed both to have to be an act and also could not be an act, so too causing – when one allegedly causes one's arm to rise in raising it – seems both to have to be an act and also could not possibly be one.

(5) We have granted that there are manifold cases of substance causation, and of the description of substance causation, that involve

no mode of operation (e.g. magnetism, gravitation, chemical action). But we establish that there is such a causal relation by noting that the presence of a magnet in the vicinity of iron filings makes the iron filings move, that the presence of a large mass (the sun) in the vicinity of a smaller moving mass (a comet) makes the smaller body fall towards the larger. There is no comparable method for ascertaining that when a human being moves his arm, he causes it to move (makes it move). Both in the case of a magnet attracting filings and of a human being moving his arm, there is no 'mode of operation'. But absence of a mode of operation is not a ground for assuming the presence of substance causation, and the analogy with substance causation without a mode of operation limps.

It is ill-advised, in trying to elucidate the categorial character of human action, to allow oneself to be mesmerized by the movements we make, and thereby to exclude consideration of human acts and actions that do not involve movement. To hold something open that would otherwise close, or to hold something closed that would otherwise open, is to act no less than to open or close something – and that need involve no movement or tensing of muscles by the agent. So too is to hold a piece of paper in place by keeping one's hand or foot on it. To hold tight to something that is already tightly held in one's hand is as much an action as to let it go, and to hold something still is no less an action than to move it. None of these can be construed as causation of movement. But they are voluntary (or involuntary or non-voluntary) acts of ours.

The distinction between the moving of self-moving animate creatures and that of inanimate objects is important to us. It is sharply marked in our conceptual scheme and has ramified conceptual consequences. It is noteworthy that the *OED* distinguishes, among the transitive senses of 'to move', between (1a) 'To change the place or position of; to take from one place or situation to another; to shift, remove; *occas.* to dislodge or displace (something fixed)'; (2a) 'To put or keep in motion; to shake, stir or disturb (an object which would otherwise be at rest)'; and (3a) 'Of a living being or its powers: to change the position or posture of (its body or any member)'. Among the intransitive senses, it distinguishes (17a), 'Of living beings: to change position or posture, to exhibit motion or physical activity (in respect of the whole body or of a member)', from (18a), 'Of inanimate objects: To suffer change of position or posture (as a whole or in respect of its parts); to be stirred'. And this, it seems, is correct. Moreover, it is not a coincidence that the authors of the *OED* drew such a distinction, for the distinction reaches deep.

Description of inanimate agent causation involves attribution of causal responsibility for a change (an event) or for prevention of a change (the non-occurrence of an event) to an inanimate agent. Animate agency, in particular human agency, displays conceptual forms that are similar and conceptual forms that are different. When we describe our (causative) actions on patients, and represent ourselves as *interfering in the course of nature*, then the logical structure of action is similar to that of inanimate agency in so far as the agent acts on the patient and thereby brings about a change to the patient (or suppresses a change that would otherwise have occurred). This, in *our* case, but not in the case of inanimate agents, may be voluntary, involuntary or non-voluntary, intentional or unintentional, deliberate or spontaneous. But the descriptions of animate movement, no matter whether voluntary or involuntary, are importantly *unlike* descriptions of inanimate motion. As we noted, stones move, wheels turn, rivers run – these are things that the inanimate agents *do*, but not acts or actions of theirs. But when a human being moves, turns, runs – he acts. In so doing, however, he does not act *on* himself, cause himself to move, or bring it about that his limbs move.

Human beings, like other sentient animals with wants, have the power to move, to act, at will. 'To act' in this context does not signify *causing a movement*, but *making* one. We acknowledge a special role for such so-called basic actions, not because they are the causing of a movement that may be the first link in a causal chain, but because they are the *first act*, the first thing for which a purposive or intentionalist explanation may be apt.[39] To say that a human being moved his limb is to subsume behaviour under the category of action. It earmarks behaviour as being of a kind that is in general under voluntary control, as something of a kind which a sentient agent can choose to do or not to do, and hence indicates the propriety of asking whether there is an intentionalist explanation of the deed. The attribution of the movement to the agent is not causal. But it is an action, and therefore is of a kind that falls within the ambit of the variety of teleological explanations appropriate for human action. The agent may have moved his hand *in order to . . .* , or *because he wanted*

---

[39] See Rundle, *Mind in Action*, p. 175.

to . . . , or *because he thought that . . .* , or *out of fear . . .* , and so forth. A's movement is to be understood to be liable to the range of explanations of the exercise of two-way powers by a rational agent. It does not imply that there *is* a purposive or intentionalist explanation (maybe A moved unawares, involuntarily, voluntarily but not intentionally), but only that the question of why he moved, where the question 'Why?' asks for such an explanation, can be raised. What it does imply is that the behaviour was of a kind that is typically under the control of the agent and for which he might be held responsible, that it is something such an agent can normally do or refrain from doing at will, and may have a reason for doing.

It is striking that the intelligibility of a request for an intentionalist explanation is precisely what is absent from the description of the results of agential movements, where these are characterized not as resultant states of affairs, but as movements. 'His arm rose', 'His leg moved', 'His head nodded' are all perfectly compatible with absence of any action whatsoever. Someone else may have raised his arm, the leg of the drowned man may have moved in the waves, and a person's head may have nodded in his sleep. That is why it is misleading to say that when someone raises their arm, their arm rises. For the act description invites intentionalist questions, whereas the result description excludes them. We sometimes use the result description for rhetorical purposes: 'When the teacher asked the question, ten hands shot up' – here it is obvious that ten hands were raised. 'His head nodded gravely', we may say – and it is clear from the adverbial modifier that the person nodded his head. But unless the context makes it clear that a rhetorical device is being used, it would be wholly misleading to invoke the result description. Were someone to say to another, 'Your head nodded', it would normally be taken to be an accusation that he had fallen asleep. To invoke both act description and result description 'in the same logical breath' would be to mix up two quite different language-games.

The conception of human action as 'interfering in the course of nature', as bringing about or preventing the coming about of a given state of affairs, is *one* prototype of human action. It is *one* centre of variation of our ramified concept of action. The further away one moves from this prototype, the more strained and inappropriate it becomes. This is patent when one converges on polymorphous acts such as hurrying, practising or working, and equally evident with respect to such acts as winning a battle, losing an argument or composing a symphony. It has no grip when considering numerous other

things we do voluntarily, non-voluntarily or involuntarily, intentionally or unintentionally, such as deciding, reflecting, deliberating,
recollecting, imagining or turning one's mind to something, on the
one hand, or perceptual acts such as watching, gazing, looking, star-
ing, scanning, observing, or listening to or for something, on the other.
It is out of place when considering facial expressions that we voluntarily or involuntarily assume, such as smiling, grinning, pouting,
frowning, scowling or glowering. It is similarly out of place for
primitive vocal acts such as giggling, simpering, cackling, guffaw-
ing, sniggering, crowing, tittering, growling, groaning, whimpering,
sobbing, moaning, grunting or crying out, as it is for the huge range
of sophisticated speech-acts we perform. So too, it is inappropriate
to stretch it in the attempt to incorporate a human being's exercise
of his powers of self-movement. For to move, move one's limbs or
head, smile or laugh, is not to *interfere in the course of nature*, it is
not to *make* oneself move or to *cause* one's limbs, head or face to
move, and it is not to *bring about* their movement. These concepts
are located within the ambit of a quite different centre of variation.

6

Teleology and Teleological Explanation

1. Teleology and purpose

Our discourse and thought about the living world around us, about ourselves, our bodies and our activities, and about the things we make is run through with description and explanation in terms of goals, purposes and functions. We characterize things, such as organs and artefacts, and also social institutions, in terms of their essential functions and their efficacy in fulfilling them. We explain animal morphology in terms of the purposes served by their shape, limbs and features. This is not a causal explanation (although it is perfectly consistent with, and indeed calls out for, one), since we explain what the organ or feature is *for* – not *how it came about* and not *how* (by what causal processes) it fulfils its function. We describe what it enables the animal to do, and how it affects the good of the animal or its offspring. We commonly explain why certain substances, both animate and inanimate (artefactual), or constituent parts of substances (organs of living things or components of artefacts) *do* what they do by describing what they do it for. We often render animal behaviour (both generic and specific) intelligible by citing the purpose that it serves. We explain and justify human action, including our own, by specifying the rationale of the prospective or antecedently performed action, and we often account for the behaviour of social institutions likewise. These kinds of description are called 'teleological descriptions', and these kinds of answer to the question 'Why?' 'teleological explanations' – explanations by reference to an end or purpose (*telos*).

Explanation may be *idiographic* (concerned with understanding something particular) or *nomothetic* (concerned with disclosing the general laws of recurrent phenomena).[1] When a nomothetic explanation is couched in terms of purposes, as in the case of functional explanations of morphogenesis, physiological explanations of organ functions, or explanations of stereotypical animal behaviour and reflexes, it may be termed *teleonomic*.[2] Teleological explanations of human action by reference to reasons and intentions are generally not teleonomic, but idiographic. They explain why a particular agent, on a specific occasion, performed a particular act. They render the act intelligible, but not by relating it to a regularity or law.

It is sometimes supposed that by contrast with causal explanation, which is held to explain a phenomenon by reference to a past event or condition, teleological explanation always explains by specifying the future event or state of affairs at which the agent 'aims', and that future event or state explains the phenomenon. But this is mistaken. For teleological explanation *need not* be 'forward-looking' in *that* sense.[3] So, for example, to explain animal behaviour as done in order to *avoid* a specific danger or perceived evil is to describe what the animal is 'moving away from', not the indeterminate future state of affairs of being out of danger that it is 'moving towards'. In these cases, it is the current danger or evil that bears the explanatory burden of the teleological explanation. A rather different kind of case is to be found in motive explanations. We may explain why a person V'd by saying that he acted out of such-and-such a motive – for example, jealousy, love, revenge, ambition, greed, patriotism, fear. Here reference to a *pattern* of reasoning that essentially involves backward-looking reasons (as well as forward-looking ones) is invoked to explain the behaviour. To act out of revenge, for example, is to endeavour

---

[1] The terminology and distinction originate in the works of Wilhelm Windelband, *Geschichte und Naturwissenschaft: Rede zum Antritt der Rektorats der Kaiser-Wilhelms-Universität Strassburg* (Heitz, Strassburg, 1904), and Heinrich Rickert, *Die Grenzen der naturwissenschaftlichen Begriffsbildung: eine logische Einleitung in die historischen Wissenschaften* (Mohr, Tübingen, 1902).

[2] By 'teleonomic' I mean no more than that *regularities* are explicable in terms of purpose.

[3] See A. J. P. Kenny, 'Cosmological Explanation and Understanding', in L. Hertzberg and Juhani Pietarinen (eds), *Perspectives on Human Conduct* (Brill, Leiden, 1988), pp. 72–87. I have found this the single most illuminating paper on the topic.

to harm someone *because* of the harm he has inflicted upon one in the past. That the pattern involves a backward-looking component does not prevent it from being teleological. The backward-looking component renders the *purpose* of the action perspicuous. The key to teleology, as Aristotle taught, is that it explains by reference to *that for the sake of which* something exists, occurs or is done – that is, by reference to a *purpose*.

Anthony Kenny nicely distinguished two ways in which things may have a purpose: (1) they may *act for a purpose*, or (2) they may *exist for a purpose*. Things that exist for a purpose, for the most part, have that purpose as their *function*.[4]

(1) The purpose of the behaviour of a subject is *that for the sake of which it does what it does*.[5] This may be the end of the behaviour of an inanimate being: for example, of the behaviour of an artefact or component of an artefact. So, for example, we ask of a machine or machine part, 'What is it doing that for?', and the answer to our question specifies the purpose of the behaviour. It may also be the end of the behaviour of an organ of an animate being, for we may ask of the heart of a living being, for example, why it beats, meaning: what does it beat *for*? And it may be the end of the behaviour of an animate being itself. For the behaviour of animate beings, both plants and animals, is likewise often characterized as having a purpose. But when we do something for its own sake, it is not done for a purpose. One may do something for the purpose of doing *something else*, but not for the purpose of doing the thing itself.

Animals that act for a purpose are said to *have*, and, in the case of developed animals, may be said to *adopt*, purposes *of their own*. Their purposes are the ends or goals they pursue. The behaviour of

---

[4] The qualification 'for the most part' is required for the sake of works of art (see sect. 2 (v) below). To be sure, there are other uses of 'function', e.g. 'The Rawlinson dinner is a major College function', 'I can't function in the morning without a cup of coffee', 'The log in the river functions as a stepping stone'. One must be careful not to conflate the teleological use of 'function' that is our concern here with a causal one, as when we say that the trees function to hold the topsoil, thus preventing landslides.

[5] I shall use the term 'behaviour' quasi-technically to signify anything that an agent, animate or inanimate, can be said to *do*. Thus used, it has a much broader extension than 'act', 'action' and 'action on (another thing)'. Artefacts and organs of animate beings *do* things, but they do not *act* (see ch. 5, sect. 1), though they may *have an action* or characteristic *activity*, and they may *act on* other things.

human beings that we are most commonly concerned to explain is one form of purposive behaviour. It is behaviour characteristic of language-using animals that can act for reasons.

Teleological explanation of *human* action is typically an explanation in terms of reasons, motives and intended goals. This is patent in our innumerable quotidian explanations and justifications of our behaviour, in which we recount what we were, are, or are going to be up to by specifying our purpose. Such forms of description and explanation permeate narrative, both fictional and factual. More generally, they are characteristic of the study of mankind in autobiography, biography, history, psychology and the social sciences. In the hermeneutic tradition of Droysen and Dilthey, such explanation is contrasted with causal, mechanistic explanation characteristic of the physical sciences, and is said to yield *understanding* (*Verstehen*) in a distinctive form, by contrast with *explanation* (*Erklärung*) in terms of causal law that is the mark of the natural sciences.[6] This distinction and this contrast earmark fundamentally different ways of rendering phenomena intelligible, and it is an important philosophical task to illuminate the conceptual differences. It has been characteristic of the dominant forms of the analytical philosophical tradition to try to reduce teleological forms of description, explanation and understanding to mechanistic ones. This trend traces its ancestry back to Descartes and the success of mechanistic science in the seventeenth century (see sect. 5 below). The analytical-hermeneutic tradition, a subordinate trend within analytic philosophy that was led by Wittgenstein and developed by his followers (e.g. Anscombe, Kenny, von Wright, Winch), opposed the methodological monism characteristic of the Vienna Circle and their heirs.

(2) We also attribute purposes to artefacts, organs and institutions. Such things are said to exist *for a purpose*. That *for the sake of which* such a thing exists is its *function*. The function of a thing is specified by a positive answer to the question 'What is this for?' This question we ask typically of artefacts, of parts and components of artefacts, of organs and parts of organs of living things, of features of both artefacts and organs, and of social institutions. The answer

---

[6] For an overview of the two forms of explanation and their histories, see G. H. von Wright, *Explanation and Understanding* (Routledge & Kegan Paul, London, 1971). Note that it is not denied that causal explanations of natural phenomena yield understanding. On the contrary; but the understanding is of a different kind.

may list a variety of ends served, for such a thing may have a plurality of functions. To say of an object that it exists in order to V or to enable the whole of which it is a part to V is *not* to explain *how it came about* that the object exists. A functional description or explanation is not a covert causal description or explanation. It explains, to repeat, what the thing is *for*: it is for V-ing, or to enable the thing of which it is a part to V, and the V-ing serves the good of a being.

This account goes against a tendency among philosophers of biology and theorists of evolution to think that specifying a function of a feature of a living thing explains 'why it exists' *in a causal*, rather than a *teleological* sense.[7] 'Functional attributions', it has been suggested, 'have clear explanatory work to do. They indicate the lines along which we should account for the presence of the entities to which functions are ascribed. To say that the function of X is F is to propose that a complete explanation of the presence of X . . . should be sought in terms of selection for F.'[8] Specifying the function of a thing explains how the thing 'got there' – it came to be there *because it does such-and-such* (the 'because' being aetiological).[9] The function of a given organ in animals of a certain kind is that effect of its presence which explains its existence in the species by reference to natural selection.

But this is misconceived. (i) Functional characterizations of things are indeed explanatory, but the explanation involved is teleological, not aetiological. They explain what end is served by a thing. To say that knives are for cutting, and clocks for telling the time, to say that eyes are for seeing and legs for walking, is to specify the ends or purposes served by artefacts and organs, not the causes of things of a kind having certain features. (ii) The aetiological reduction of teleological explanation of organs conflates two quite distinct questions: 'What is this organ in animals of this kind *for*?' (What does it do, or enable the animal to do, that serves the good or the goals of the

[7] 'In biology, the function of a feature of an organism is frequently defined as that role it displays which has been responsible for its genetic success and evolution' (Simon Blackburn, *Oxford Dictionary of Philosophy* (Oxford University Press, Oxford, 1996), pp. 149f.).

[8] Philip Kitcher, 'Function and Design', *Midwest Studies in Philosophy*, 18 (1993), p. 390.

[9] L. Wright, 'Functions', *Philosophical Review*, 82 (1973), p. 161. See C. Boorse, 'Wright on Functions', *Philosophical Review*, 85 (1976), pp. 70–86 for useful criticisms.

animal (or, in certain kinds of case, of its offspring)?') and 'How did it come about that animals of this kind have organs of this type?' One can say, for example, that the function of the stomach is to digest food. That accounts for its 'being there' *only* in the sense that it specifies *what it is for*. But there is an evolutionary phylogenetic explanation of why creatures with stomachs evolved,[10] as well as an ontogenetic explanation of how a fertilized egg of an animal of this kind develops so as to produce an animal with a stomach. It is important to keep these three explanations separate, and not to roll the first into the second. (iii) The function of an organ may well be understood long before there is any explanation of *how it came about* that it is present in the kind of animal concerned. Indeed, the function of an organ may be *discovered* quite independently of any understanding of natural selection and without ascribing the function to design, as in the case of Harvey's discovery of the function of the heart in the circulatory system. (iv) It is mistaken to suppose, as many philosophers of biology do, that there can be no coherent attribution of function to a thing that does not allude either to design or to natural selection. Aristotle's investigations of biological functions alluded to neither. Our common and correct understanding that eyes are for seeing and legs for locomotion commits us neither to theology nor to the theory of evolution, but only to such natural axiological notions as the good of a being, good and ill health, normal capacities and activities of a member of a given species.

That a thing typically V's in certain circumstances does not show that V-ing is its function. Volcanoes erupt, but that is not their function – volcanoes have no function. Inanimate nature exists *without*

---

[10] Wright analyses 'the function of A is to V' as '(i) A is there *because* it V's (that explains its presence), and (ii) the V-ing is a consequence of A's being there' ('Functions', p. 161). To this it can further be objected that (a) 'A is there because it has function V' (V-ing is what it is for) has significant content, but 'A is there because it has a consequence because of which it is there' has little or none. (b) It fails to exclude such absurdities as the claim that since obese people do not exercise because they are obese, the function of their obesity is to stop them exercising. (c) The evolutionary (causal) explanation of why flightless cormorants have wings does not explain their function, since they (now) have none. (d) Among the functions of the forelegs of sea turtles is to dig nests in sand, but that does not explain what they were selected for, since turtles had forelegs long before they came to lay eggs in sand.

In short, to say that an organ in a kind of creature is an evolutionary adaptation for a given task is to give a phylogenetic, not an ontogenetic, explanation. Nor is it, as such, an explanation of the function (purpose) of the organ in an animal now. For the task that was 'selected for' need not be the current function.

purpose, and the behaviour of natural inanimate objects is purpose-
less. Much in animate nature too lacks purpose. Cancerous growths
do not have the function of killing their host, although that is what
they do; residual limbs, bones or organs no longer have the function
that their ancestral forms once had, and may have none at all (the
coccyx or appendix in man).

That A's doing such-and-such is a necessary condition of the
possibility of B's doing so-and-so does not show that the function of
A is to do such-and-such. A's behaviour may indeed make B's behaviour possible, but it need not be there for that purpose. Homeostatic
mechanisms, both in artefacts (e.g. thermostats) and in organisms (e.g.
the operation of sweat glands), exemplify such causal relations, but
that is not the reason they are deemed purposive. Thermostats have
a function in virtue of *design* that aims at a good (the purpose for
the sake of which the artefact exists), and homeostatic mechanisms
in nature have a purpose because of their role in the maintenance
of some feature that is necessary for the life of, is protective of, or
beneficial for, the organism of the type in question.

The concept of function *here*, in the sense that concerns us, gets
a grip only where *the benefit of a being* is appropriately involved.[11]
A thing (organ or artefact) has a function only if it exists for the
sake of a good. In the case of organs, their function is related, in
one way or another, to *what is beneficial for*, serves the good of, the
animal (or of its offspring, e.g., in the case of marsupial pouches or
mammalian mammary glands) or *contributes to the animal's successful
engagement in activities characteristic of its kind*.[12] In the case of

---

[11] This Aristotelian insight is prominent in Darwin's *The Origin of Species*. Thus,
e.g., 'if any slight innate change of habit or structure *benefited* an individual wolf,
it would have the best chance of surviving and of leaving offspring' (p. 139), 'Only
those variations which are in some way *profitable* will be preserved or naturally selected.
And here the importance of *the principle of benefit* being derived from divergence
of character comes in' (pp. 161f.); 'it would be a most extraordinary fact if no
variation had ever occurred *useful to each being's own welfare*. . . . But if variations
useful to any organic being do occur, assuredly individuals thus characterised will
have the best chance of being preserved in the struggle for life; and . . . they will tend
to produce offspring similarly characterised' (pp. 169f.). (My emphases.)

[12] Must sexually selected features (e.g. the peacock's tail) have a function? *Ex hypothesi*, they contribute to its reproductive success. The production of offspring,
however, is no benefit to the animal or to its mate. But such features improve the
animal's ability to engage successfully in the reproductive activities characteristic of
its kind. Animals, by nature, seek to mate. Sexually selected features facilitate the
animal's pursuit of this natural goal, and, in that sense, benefit it (see pp. 177f.).

artefacts, their function is related to their *usefulness* when employed for the purpose or purposes for which they were made.

Some of the features of artefacts may be said to have a purpose the fulfilment of which does not contribute causally to the functioning of the artefact or to its usefulness. They may make it attractive, or singular. Of course, one may extend the concept of function and say that their function is (merely) to adorn the artefact (or confer prestige on the owner).

Note that a thing may V, and its V-ing may be beneficial for something, yet it does not follow that its function is to V. Rain clouds precipitate rain, and the rain benefits crops. But, as Aristotle pointed out, rain does not fall in order to make crops grow (*Physics* 198^{b}17–20). It should also be noted that a thing that does have a function may have beneficial effects that are not part of its function. The heart produces a variety of sounds that are *useful* for diagnostic purposes. But producing sounds is not one of the functions of the heart, and being useful for diagnosticians is not the same as serving the good of the being that has the heart.

Specification of the function or functions of a thing explains what it is for: it exists in order to perform or fulfil that function or those functions. The function of a thing is an aspect of its *nature*. It is no coincidence that as the functions of the inner organs of the body were gradually clarified, the organs were duly *redefined* in terms of their functions: the heart is the organ for circulating the blood by pumping, the kidney the organ for filtering metabolic waste products from the blood and maintaining water balance. Of course, the function of a certain organ in a given species may change through evolutionary pressures – what was an arm may become a wing or a flipper. But then the organ, although homologous with its ancestral organ, as it were, has changed its nature (and a new species may have emerged too).

An individual thing of a certain kind may be *used* to *fulfil* a function, as when one uses a pen to block a hole or one's nose to support one's spectacles, but the function the thing then performs is not *its* function. We may call this a 'heteronomous' function, and contrast it with the 'autonomous' (essential) functions of things. The heteronomous function of a thing is not what things of its kind are *for* and is not part of its *nature*.

An individual thing of a certain kind may have a function, yet never perform it. Some artefacts are never used, and some 'fail-safe' organs or artefactual devices may be called into action only in the event of other organs or components of the artefact being overworked, damaged or malfunctioning, which may never occur.

2. What things have a purpose?

'Absence of haphazard and conduciveness of everything to an end are to be found in nature's works in the highest degree, and the end for which those works are put together and produced is a form of the beautiful,' remarked one of the greatest of biologists when discussing zoological research.[13] Only living beings and things related in *various* ways to living beings have a purpose. Teleology is accordingly at home in the sciences of life, in the study of living beings and their forms of life, and in the study of man and his works. It is fruitful to examine more closely the range of things that can be said to have a purpose.

(1) Animals can be said to have purposes *of their own*, which are the goals they pursue. Living beings, as such, however, do not have *a function*. They may have been created for a purpose, by parents, animal breeders or botanists. But if so, that purpose is not their purpose. A plant may be created, by cross-breeding or genetic engineering, in order to have an appealing scent, shape and colouring – but that is not the function of the plant nor yet its purpose, even though it was created for that purpose and is used by us for a corresponding function. For living things do not exist for the sake of anything in the sense in which their organs exist for the sake of the end that is their function.[14] To be sure, we commonly say such things as 'Bramleys are for cooking (not for eating)', this being what we use them for and why this variety was produced. This specifies their use, but not their function, for they are not artefacts. ('Shoulder of lamb', the butcher may say, 'is for roasting', but that is not what lambs have shoulders for.)

---

[13] Aristotle, *Parts of Animals* 645ª23–5.

[14] An interesting exception is perhaps to be found among 'social' insects. It is at best misleading to say, as some biologists do, that the hive or colony is a 'super-organism'. But one might well say that the queen bee exists for the sake of laying eggs, or that the workers exist for the sake of collecting food for the hive.

(2) The goal-directed activities of animals have a purpose, which is the end for the sake of which they are done. We may distinguish between conscious and non-conscious purposive behaviour. Purposive behaviour that is non-conscious is varied. The reflex behaviour of animals, such as the flexor reflex of the limbs, the lacrimal and pupillary light reflexes of the eyes, cough and sneeze reflexes all have patent purposes essentially related to the good of the animal. Similarly, the non-conscious instinctive activities of an animal are commonly purposive. Such activity may be in response to circumstances (seasonal change, threats, presence of prey), it may involve migratory patterns, or the construction of artefacts (spiders' webs, birds' nests) or patterns of social interactive behaviour with its own kind (mating displays, reaction to alpha males or females). Much of such behaviour is stereotypical and geared to recurrent situations. To that extent, and especially where the behaviour is beyond the control of the animal, it may be deemed teleonomic.

The group activities of animals commonly have a purpose. This may be collective purposive activity, with relatively little co-ordination – as in migratory patterns of herd animals or birds. Or it may be highly co-ordinated collective activity, especially marked in social insects (ants, bees) and animals, as in the allocation and fulfilment of roles among animals that hunt in groups (e.g. wolves, African wild dogs, pelicans or dolphins) or in the watching and guarding behaviour of members of groups (as among baboons or meerkats).

Conscious purposive behaviour of animals, both individual and co-ordinated-collective, may be plastic and adaptive to changing circumstances. It may also, in a primitive sense, be planned. Human conscious purposive behaviour is characteristically intended. Such intended behaviour may be planned well in advance of acting, critically evaluated and reconsidered in the light of circumstances. So we can and do relate our plans in advance, and ask, of others' planned behaviour, what its purpose is.

The activities of plants, such as growth, flowering, the production of fruit and seed, is purposive, but not consciously so. The purposes that can explain the behaviour of plants, their tropisms, pattern of growth and flowering, etc. are not the purposes of the plant. Plants do not have autonomous purposes.

(3) The organs of animals (like those of a plant) have a purpose, which is, as noted, their function. The normal activity of a given internal organ is typically *needed* for the health of the animal. The

goodness of any organ lies in its performing its function properly (non-defectively), as is appropriate for an organ of that type in an animal of that kind. Proper performance of the function of an organ is typically performance that directly or indirectly enables the animal to engage optimally in the characteristic activities of an animal of that kind in its natural environment. Some organs, e.g. the gall-bladder in man, may have a primarily protective or 'fail-safe' function. They are, as Aristotle noted, not absolutely necessary, but it is good that they are there.[15]

The functions of organs are innate rather than acquired. This does not mean that at birth the organ is already fulfilling its function. Some organs are immature at birth and either do not function at all or function poorly. Nor does it mean that the functioning of an organ, even in a mature animal, cannot be improved by exercise or training. What it means is that if an organ needs to mature before it can fulfil its function, its natural growth will be such as to ensure, in the case of the normal animal, that when it is mature it will be able to fulfil the function for which it exists (the function it *should* fulfil) by nature. Note that the notions of *normality* and of *characteristic activity* are not statistical but normative, determined by a proper specimen of the animal kind in its natural environment.[16]

The internal organs of an animal are, for the most part, not under the voluntary control of the animal. They are *needed* by, not *used* by, the animal. The external organs are, for the most part, used by the animal in pursuit of its goals. They are needed for the natural motor, sensory and reproductive activities of the animal. Their normal functioning is a condition for the animal's possessing and being able to exercise its faculties optimally. A use to which an organ is put (e.g. the human nose) *need not* be part of its function.

The purpose of an organ is its function or functions. The function of organs is typically a characteristic activity. This characteristic activity can also be said to have a purpose. The heart pumps blood – that it is its function; but it pumps blood *in order to* circulate it. The lungs

[15] Aristotle, *Parts of Animals* 640ª34f., quoted below, p. 186.

[16] Sometimes natural environment is insufficient for optimality. A so-called *specimen tree* that is used as a paradigm of health and normality for its kind is a tree that grows without being shaded by other trees. So it displays the full potentialities of the species, which are *not* normally achieved in its natural environment in a forest.

inhale and exhale air – that is what they are *for*; but the inhalation
has as *its* purpose the obtaining of fresh oxygen, and exhaling the
purpose of evacuating carbon dioxide.

It is noteworthy that we also talk of features and constituents of
living things that are not organs as having a function: for example,
colouring and markings, hair or whiskers, the various fluids that are
secreted for a purpose, both internally (digestive fluids) and externally
(tears), blood and lymphatic fluids. These too typically serve the good
of the animal, and are needed by the animal.

(4) The morphogenesis of an organism and its parts is teleonomic.
An organism grows from its seed in a fixed pattern and order. This
can be said to be for the sake of producing an organism of the given
type, the order of normal development being such as to enable
growth of the appropriate kind to occur in the right place and at the
right time in the evolving creature (e.g. seedling or foetus). Deviation
from the appropriate order is a malfunction. It generates defective
organs and subnormal organisms. As Aristotle remarked, it can generate 'monstrosities' as a result of defective seed (*Physics* 199[b]1–7).

(5) Artefacts have purposes. These are the purposes for which they
were designed or manufactured. They may, therefore, be deemed *extrinsic* (imposed by design). The function of most artefacts is the use for
which they are made. Like organs, artefacts with a use have both
morphological and functional features. They are typically *defined* by
their functions. The goodness of such an individual artefact is goodness of its kind: a good knife is a knife that serves well the purposes
for which knives exist. This form of goodness von Wright has called
'instrumental goodness'.[17]

Works of art are artefacts, but their purpose *need not* be a function.
For works of art are not necessarily made to be useful, and the form
of goodness of works of art is not their utility. (It was, however, characteristic of twentieth-century totalitarian regimes to constrain the
arts within the limits of socio-ideological function.) The purpose of
some works of art may be nothing other than to delight the eye or ear
of the beholder or listener, or to glorify God, or to express the joys
and sorrows of human life or of the artist. But these cannot *illuminatingly* be assimilated to functions. The goodness of works of art is

[17] G. H. von Wright, *Varieties of Goodness* (Routledge & Kegan Paul, London,
1963), pp. 19–32.

neither the goodness of instruments nor that of organs; it is neither the useful nor the beneficial. A work of art need be neither useful nor beneficial, although it can be both. But architecture (a paradigmatically practical art) may be beautiful as well as useful and beneficial; and good design may make the useful aesthetically as well as instrumentally excellent.

Artefacts may be designed or not designed. Design is purpose derived from a conception of an end. Things are designed when made to a plan. Actions performed according to a plan are intended. So intention is to action what design is to artefact.[18] Human artefacts are designed. Most non-human artefacts are not. As Aristotle observed, artefacts of animals such as spiders and ants are made 'neither by art [craft] nor after inquiry or deliberation', but 'it is both by nature and for an end that the swallow makes its nest and the spider its web . . . [so] it is plain that this kind of *aition* [cause, explanation] is operative in things that come to be and are by nature' (*Physics* 199ª20ff.). The spider's spinning and the bird's nestmaking are purposive activities (*this* is done in order to . . .), but there is no *conscious* purpose. For one cannot say that the animal knows the purpose of its activities or intends the purpose of its actions. Neither the insect nor the bird is guided by a conception of the artefact it is making or by a conception of the good that it will serve. The behaviour pattern is innate rather than learnt, triggered by circumstance rather than 'after inquiry or deliberation'.[19]

Artefacts are used for a purpose. Typically they are used for the purpose for which they were designed and made – that is what they are for. But, like organs, they can be used for purposes other than what they are for too – a knife with a heavy handle may be used to knock a nail into the wall, but that does not make it a hammer. Artefacts other than machines, despite having a purpose, typically have no characteristic behaviour. For it need not be part of their function that they should *do* anything. Chairs and tables have functions, but no characteristic activity that fulfils their function. Their function is to be patient, not agent.

(6) Social institutions, organizations and offices have functions. Unlike human beings, they typically exist to serve an end or ends.

---

[18] See Kenny, 'Cosmological Explanation', p. 79.

[19] But the rudimentary tools of the great apes and their use perhaps involve elementary design and primitive conscious purpose.

This may be the result of intentional design (e.g. written constitutions, courts of law, governmental agencies, and the specified roles of officials within such institutions), or it may have evolved independently of design by nature (as in the case of the family or natural socially organized groups of animals). Like human beings, institutions may have purposes of their own. They can be said to have purposes 'in a derivative sense'. For their purposes may be distinct from those of the human beings that belong to them. The will and purpose of parliament, for example, may be quite different from that of its members, or even of a majority of its members (see fig. 6.1).

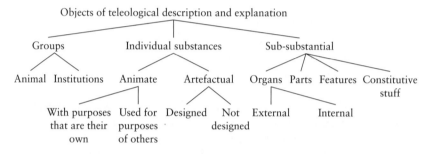

Figure 6.1. *Schema of the domain of teleology*

Functionalist doctrines in sociology (Durkheim, Merton) and social anthropology (Malinowski, Evans-Pritchard) in the twentieth century held that the existence of social practices and belief systems is to be explained in functional terms – if not by reference to patent function, then to latent one (the Freudian analogy here is not coincidental). So the existence of irrational social practices (e.g. witch hunting) may be explained in terms of their function in maintaining social stability. Behind the patent purposes of social institutions, it was argued, lie latent functions that provide the true explanations of why they exist. So although the overt purpose of universities, for example, is to educate and to foster learning, their 'true' function, it might be said, is to keep large numbers of the young off the labour market. Although the patent function of transfer payments (unemployment benefits, child allowances, etc.) is to alleviate the lot of the poor, the latent function, a Marxist sociologist may hold, is to preserve the power of the ruling classes. In so far as the so-called latent function is not a conscious purpose of those maintaining the institution in question or an overtly determined purpose of the institution, it seems doubtful whether the notion of function here invoked is genuinely teleological, even in those cases where the causal explanation of the persistence of the practice is plausible and where the society actually benefits from its persistence. Rather, an *analogy* with biological function is being improperly exploited. It masks what is actually no more than a causal explanation.

3. Purpose and axiology

Purpose, we have suggested, is essentially linked to life. Only living things and what is appropriately related to living things can have a purpose. That is because living creatures are the primary things that *have a good*. For living things can thrive and flourish, decline and decay. They can be healthy or ill, can be injured and maimed. They have a life cycle (natural phases of life), and they are doomed to die. They have needs, and advanced sentient animals have wants and purposes of their own.

The notion of the good of a being is biologically rooted. It has various aspects. It is linked to that of the welfare of the creature; hence to the satisfaction of its absolute needs. Failure to satisfy these is detrimental to the health of a being and hence, in the case of an animal, detrimental to its capacity to exercise its abilities optimally. The notion of the good of a being is also linked to that of its flourishing (thriving): that is, to the non-privative aspects of its health, on the one hand, and to its successful engagement in its characteristic life activities, on the other.

The good of man is also a biologically rooted notion, but it is not only biological.[20] Human welfare is associated with the satisfaction not only of absolute needs, but also of socially minimal needs that are a prerequisite for the successful pursuit of any normal projects that human beings adopt in the course of their lives, and hence are normally required for a tolerable life.[21] These include the cultivation of human faculties and the acquisition of skills. The notions of normalcy and

---

[20] The concept of the good of man was made prominent in von Wright's highly Aristotelian account in *Varieties of Goodness*. It was criticized by T. Schwartz and K. Baier in P. A. Schilpp and L. E. Hahn (eds), *The Philosophy of Georg Henrik von Wright* (Open Court, La Salle, Ill., 1989) and subsequently modified by von Wright in his response 'A Reply to My Critics', ibid., pp. 773–789.

[21] T. Schwartz, 'Von Wright's Theory of Human Welfare: A Critique', ibid., p. 223.

of socially minimal needs are both socio-historically relative and normative. In a society such as ours, education (the formation of character, the training in skills, acquisition of knowledge, the development
of intellectual powers, and the cultivation of sensibility) is a constituent
element of the welfare of members of society. It is needed if it is to be
possible for a normal person to form, and pursue with reasonable
chance of success, worthy life plans and projects.

Welfare is part of the good of man, but it is the lesser part. It is
both a normative and a variable notion, dependent upon the state
of a society and the conception of the requirements of a tolerable
human life and life opportunities in it. Beyond it is the flourishing,
thriving and prospering that nature, endeavour and fortune bestow.
These are related to the degree of fulfilment of a person's projects –
if they are wisely, or at any rate not foolishly, chosen, and to the
personal and social relationships enjoyed. The *beneficial* favourably
affects the good of a being; the *advantageous* augments the possibilities available or enhances the abilities to take advantage of them.
Among the characteristics that serve the good of a human being who
has them are certain character traits that can and should be cultivated
by education and training. These are the self-regarding virtues, such
as prudence, fortitude, tenacity, courage and industry. They can be
exercised not *only* for the benefit of their possessor but also for the
good of others. They are, like the other-regarding virtues, not only
beneficial, but also of intrinsic value – they are needed for the good
of man, but are also partly constitutive of the good man.

A human being, however, may thrive and flourish without being
happy. Happiness, Aristotle emphasized, is the *summum bonum*
of mankind. G. H. von Wright, invoking a broad conception of
welfare, characterized happiness as 'the flowering of welfare'.[22] It is
noteworthy that nothing corresponds in the life of non-language-
using animals to happiness, conceived as the *summum bonum*. Only
creatures endowed with reason can be blessed with happiness.

Social groups, societies and institutions can also be said to have a
good – in a 'derivative sense', since they are not living creatures, and
can be said to have a life only metaphorically speaking. But it is significant that the metaphor of the life and death, the rise and fall, of
institutions and societies is so natural and widely used. The relationship
between the good of individuals and the good of social groups is much

---

[22] Von Wright, *Varieties of Goodness*, p. 62.

debated. It would be foolish to say, as a recent British Prime Minister did, that there is no such thing as society, there are only individuals. For it is a mistake to suppose that the good of a society or nation-state is *reducible* to the good of its members. The good of such social groups *is* logically related to the good of their constituent members. But the relationship is not simple.

The concept of purpose is interwoven not only with that of the good of a being, but also with that of the *nature* and *essence* of a being. That is evident in the case of the purpose (function) of organs and artefacts, which are commonly *defined* by their function. Animals and human beings, on the other hand, are not. Aristotle asserted that human beings (and animals in general) have a function (*ergon*) (*Nicomachean Ethics* 1097^b–1098^b). This is sometimes taken literally, and if this were warranted, the claim would surely be misconceived. But arguably Aristotle meant only that human beings and other animals have a characteristic activity or operation – a species-specific manner of function*ing*. It is indeed part of the nature of human beings, of creatures that are persons, that they can engage in characteristic activities that 'follow or imply a rational principle' (ibid.), and the exercise of this distinctive ability to follow reason is pertinent to their good and a *sine qua non* of their *summum bonum*. But human beings do not, *qua* human beings, have a function (but only *qua* doctors, policemen or plumbers). They may be used, by other human beings, for a purpose. But they cannot be said to 'exist for a purpose' – unless they adopt one as the purpose of their life.

Organs of plants and animals alike have functions related to the welfare, flourishing and reproduction of their possessor. Reproductive organs, in both plants and animals, enable the creature to reproduce. That is their function – that is what they are *for*. But offspring in general do *not* contribute to the good of the being (vegetal or animal). Nevertheless, sexual reproduction is one of the natural activities of all but the lowliest of life forms. We are inclined to conceive of reproductive activities throughout nature in teleological terms, but we must take care neither to anthropomorphize nor to conflate causal sequence with function. That the sexual organs have a purpose – namely, to enable the creature to reproduce – is patent. They enable the creature to engage in reproductive activity that is natural to all species. But if we ask, for example, what the reproductive activity of a being is for, things become more problematic. Plants and lowly organisms are not even conscious creatures, so their modes of reproduction involve neither conscious purpose nor non-conscious purpose that benefits them or their offspring. The higher animals, other than human beings, have no notion of the conception that results from their copulatory activity and certainly no desire to produce offspring. Copulation in the mating season is simply a natural appetite of animals. It is not done for any further purpose. Nor can its outcome be said to serve the good of the animal. Only human beings can be said to engage in sexual activity in order to produce, or for the further purpose of producing, offspring. Similarly with plants: their reproductive organs can be described in teleological terms – they are *for* the production of seed. But if we query what the plant produces seed for, and we want to answer, 'in order to reproduce', we sever function from the good of the being. Similarly, if we say that the purpose of copulation among animals is reproduction (rather than the mere satisfaction of appetite), we have detached the concept of the purpose of action from that of a good. This, to be sure, we may do – but then the concept is duly attenuated. Some may wish to link it to the good of the species. But the onus is upon them to render that notion perspicuous. For a species is not a super-individual, and the notion of *its* welfare is problematic. Reproduction, one might say, is the price paid to evolution for the blind selection in a species of those features which each living creature possesses that serve its good or enable it to pursue the goals characteristic of its kind (including copulation).

Healthy organs are *beneficial* to the creature that has them, directly or indirectly enabling them to engage optimally in the activities characteristic of their form of life. Malfunctioning (diseased, damaged or defective) organs are *bad for* their possessor, being detrimental to the creature's welfare.[23] Defective organs are organs that hinder or prevent an animal from engaging optimally in the characteristic activities of its kind. They do not fulfil, or do not fulfil adequately, their purpose. Organs may be deficient innately, through injury or disease, or through the deterioration of age. An organ may be morphologically or functionally deficient. Typically, morphological deficiency implies functional deficiency. A malfunctioning organ renders the animal ill or causes it pain and deleteriously affects the natural abilities of the

---

[23] It would be mildly perverse to say that having eyes or legs is *useful* to a human being. This is perhaps because lacking an organ or healthy organ is *detrimental* to a creature as well as disadvantageous, whereas lacking a useful artefact *may* be disadvantageous to a person (if it is needed for a purpose) rather than detrimental (though it may be to the detriment of his project). But properly functioning organs are *needed* for a creature to lead a normal life.

animal and their optimal exercise. The animal is then relatively incapacitated. If its motor organs are permanently affected, it is said to be crippled. If its sensory organs are affected, the organ is characterized as weak or subnormal, relative to the norm for the species, or non-functional, in which case the animal is, for example, blind or deaf. If a sensory organ is subnormal, the corresponding sense-faculty is poor, and the animal can be said to have poor eyesight, hearing or sense of smell.[24]

Artefacts, on the other hand, are useful, rather than beneficial. They are useful inasmuch as they causally facilitate the attainment of some end. They are used to serve the purposes of their users, and are good of their kind if they serve well the purposes for which they were designed.

The description of the causal mechanisms that enable the organs of an animal to fulfil their function, and indeed the description of the causal interrelationships between the various organs of an animal, do not in general suffice to explain or predict what the animal does or will do. Rather, they explain how it is that the animal has the powers it has and explain the internal mechanisms that are brought into play when the animal does whatever it does. But *one* way of explaining why an animal does what it does is by reference to its purpose in acting.

The purposive activities of animals and man alike are aimed at a good, subjectively conceived. Those activities that are aimed at satisfying the absolute needs of an agent are subservient to the welfare of the agent. Those that are aimed at satisfying the wants of an agent are rendered intelligible, directly or indirectly, by reference to desirability characteristics. Among the purposive activities of animals are those that are done for the sake of other animals, for example for the benefit and protection of their young, or, among social animals, for the benefit of the social group. In the case of human beings, who engage in practical reasoning, desirability characteristics can be cited in specifying reasons for acting that themselves require no reason and can therefore be termini of chains of practical reasoning.

The connection between purpose and axiology has a further aspect. When something V's for a purpose, no matter whether that thing is a living being or a part of a living being or an artefact or functional part of an artefact made by a living being, it may V well

---

[24] For an illuminating discussion of medical goodness, i.e. the goodness of organs and faculties, see von Wright, *Varieties of Goodness*, ch. 3.

or poorly. So too, if a thing has a function, it may (in general) fulfil that function well or poorly. So the goodness of organs and artefacts that have a function is determined by the extent to which they fulfil well or poorly the function for which they exist. In the case of living beings that act for a purpose, then in those cases in which their actions involve skill, they are adjudged good or poor V-ers according to the excellence of their standard performances of V-ing – that is, whether they are *good at* V-ing. But to be a good human being is not to be good at an activity. One who acts in accordance with the requirements of practical reason and morality is not thereby skilful at any characteristic activity. To lead a good, praiseworthy, life is not to be good at living.

4. The beneficial

Since a living being has a good, things can be *beneficial* for it – that is, may be *good for it* and *do good to it*. Things that can thus be benefited are *beneficiaries*. Other things too may be beneficiaries, including inanimate things. But whatever can be said to be a beneficiary is either a living being that has a good or something causally or intrinsically related to a living being. Living beings may be benefited by the circumstances of their lives, the environment in which they live and things in it, the accidents of fate and fortune, the deeds of and relationships with others, and their own activities. They may also be harmed by such things.

What is beneficial is what favourably affects the conditions in which a being lives, or the condition of the being. The conditions in which a being lives may be causally effective in benefiting it. They may be hedonically effective: that is, both the cause and the object of enjoyment. They may offer it opportunities for growth or action advantageous for it. The beneficial affects the condition of a being if it preserves or improves its health, powers or faculties. It may affect the condition of a being causally, as medicine may be good for the ill and exercise for the healthy. But it may affect the good of a being constitutively, as a good education may mould the mind and character of the young. The beneficial may be *protective*, preventing deterioration in health, power or condition; *curative*, making the bad better; or *promotive*, augmenting the good of the being. What is beneficially preventive or curative is related to the needs of a creature. What is beneficially promotive may be related both to the welfare and to the flourishing of the being.

Organs of a living being are also beneficiaries. It is because organs have functions that things can be good or bad for them, as exercise is good for the heart and alcohol is bad for the liver. What is good or bad for an organ is what causally promotes or impedes its functioning. That in turn is good or bad for the creature whose organs they are. Normal organs are organs that function in the way that is needed by a creature if it is to lead a normal life for a creature of its kind. For it is they that thereby endow it with the powers that characterize its kind. Bad (defective, subnormal) organs are detrimental to the creature since they do not fulfil their function adequately (and may cause pain to the animal), thereby preventing or impeding its performance of the activities characteristic of its kind. Subnormal performance of the organs involves relative incapacitation of their possessor. Note that it is not only the animal and its organs that are spoken of as beneficiaries, but also the animal's faculties. We speak of things being good for one's eyesight, one's memory or one's intellect.

Both artefacts and environments can be beneficiaries in a derivative sense. Things are beneficial (or harmful) for the land or the seas, for the atmosphere or stratosphere in so far as these environments are themselves beneficial (or harmful) for the living beings that inhabit them or are affected by them. Artefacts no more have a good than do environments. But things can be good or harmful for artefacts. As already noted, what is beneficial for an artefact is what prevents its deterioration, so that it continues to serve its purpose well (or at least as well as possible given its condition). Improvements to an artefact (e.g. a machine) are not good for the artefact, although making the improvements may benefit the user or owner of the artefact and will make the artefact a better one of its kind.

Social institutions are beneficiaries. Though not living beings, and though not literally capable of being healthy or ill, they can flourish or decay. Something may be done *for the good of* the State, the Church or the Army. Circumstances, policies and actions may be *good for*, or *damaging to*, social institutions. They cannot, however, *do good to them*, since they are not sentient beings.

5. A historical digression: teleology and causality

The philosopher who above all others gave teleological explanation a central role in his account of the natural world and in his reflections on our descriptions and explanations of natural phenomena, including ourselves and our activities, was Aristotle. He viewed the whole of the natural world as pervaded by teleonomy. He held that inanimate objects have natural tendencies to behave purposively, to be 'directed at an end'. Bodies that consist primarily of 'earth' (a dry, cold element) fall, in order to reach their natural place in the ordered cosmos. Those that consist primarily of 'fire' (a dry, hot element) rise, because it is part of their nature to 'strive' upwards. The elements tend to 'seek' their natural place – to move upwards or downwards (if not interfered with) according to their nature. The fixed stars, made of a different element from anything sublunary, rotate eternally on their spheres because that is their nature and is what is proper for them.

We do not share the Aristotelian teleonomic conception of physics. Indeed, we find it profoundly alien. It is a vision of the nature of the world that we cannot recapture. Moreover, it is a conception that proved to be explanatorily unfruitful. We would, of course, grant natural *tendencies* of agential action on, and reaction to, things in inanimate nature (though not perhaps natural *places* for things to be).[25] But there is no natural *purpose* in inanimate nature as we understand it. Nor do we conceive of inanimate nature as aimed at an end or at a good for a being. We conceive of the cosmos as nomic, but not as teleonomic. The universe, according to our world picture, is not *governed* by laws, but is *described* by laws. It is nomic (regular), but not normative (rule-governed).

Although we cannot accept this Greek vision of the cosmic order, it is evident that the domains of biology and of human action and artefact are fruitful fields of application for teleological and teleonomic description and explanation. This Aristotle saw clearly. He did not link purpose essentially to design, but to the good or beneficial. The purposes of organs are *intrinsic* (rather than imposed by design (*extrinsic*)), and they are part of their *nature*. They are to be understood in terms of the benefit they yield to the animal (or its offspring). (Of course, he did not deny that the purpose of an *artefact* is linked to the design of its maker. But even here, he was aware that animal artefacts such as spiders' webs exemplify purpose 'neither by art nor after inquiry or deliberation' (see p. 173 above).) This conception is profoundly different from the later Christian one. Purpose *without*

---

[25] Indeed, Newton characterized centripetal force (and hence too gravity) as that by which bodies are drawn or impelled, or in any way tend, towards a point as to a centre.

design is something Aristotle takes as given – a fundamental feature of nature, for which no further explanation is either necessary or possible. It was not until Darwin's theory of natural selection that the beginning of an adequate explanation of the existence of biological teleonomy was produced.

Aristotle distinguished four ways in which the term *aition* is used (*Physics* 195ª3). *Aition* is traditionally translated as 'cause', and Aristotle is commonly said to have distinguished four kinds of cause: formal, material , efficient and final cause. But it is misleading to translate his observation about the use of *aition* as 'four ways in which the term "cause" is used'. The concept of efficient causation dominates our causal thought (although not, as noted in ch. 3, exclusively; see pp. 57f.), and, as we shall see, articulating Aristotle's insights in terms of *forms of causation* is a source of misunderstanding and confusion. One might, less misleadingly, say that Aristotle distinguished between four different 'becauses'; or, less clumsily, that he distinguished between four different kinds of explanation. The number of the ways in which *aition* is used, Aristotle wrote, 'is the same as that of the things comprehended under the question "why"' (198ª14–15). 'Things are called "*aitia*" in many ways' (195ª4): the form, the mover (that which brings about the change, the agent), that for the sake of which (the purpose), and the matter.

> The ultimate answer to a 'why' may take us, in the case of unchanging things like mathematics, to the 'what' (to the definition of straight, or commensurable, or the like); or it may take us to the originating change (why did they go to war? Because there had been a raid), or to the purpose (so as to come into power) or, in the case of things that come into being, to the matter. (*Physics* 198ª14–21)[26]

Aristotle's distinctions are not a conclusion of elaborate argument, but an ordered datum – a datum concerning how we answer certain kinds of why-questions about phenomena. He is systematizing different ways of rendering phenomena intelligible: that is, different kinds of answers to questions of why things or events (including activities) are as they are or occur as they occur. He rightly notes that one answer to the question of why a thing is as it is or why an activity occurs

---

[26] I have used Kenny's translation here in his *Ancient Philosophy* (Clarendon Press, Oxford, 2004), p. 190.

as it occurs specifies *that for the sake of which* it exists or occurs – that is, the *purpose* of the thing or activity. He did not think that the four kinds of explanation he enumerates are mutually exclusive or reducible one to another. On the contrary, one and the same phenomenon will typically have complementary explanations:

> We must explain the 'why' in all the senses of the term, namely that from this that will necessarily result (either without qualification or for the most part); that this must be so if that is to be so; that this was the essence of the thing; and because it is better thus (not without qualification, but with reference to the substance in each case). (*Physics* 198^{b}5–9)

So, for example, the matter of a knife is metal; its form is its having both a handle to grip and a blade to cut, it originates (has its efficient cause) in (the activity of) its maker, and its purpose is to cut. That things are made of the substance (stuff) of which they are made renders a variety of their properties intelligible: we make knife blades of steel – that is why they are sharp and do not blunt quickly, why they sink in water rather than float, why they rust if exposed to the elements for a length of time. The form of a thing explains its essential nature ('a knife without a handle that has no blade' is a joke). The activity of its maker explains how it came about that this knife exists at all. The purpose of a knife is to cut – that is what it enables its users to do (see table 6.1).

In some cases, one kind of explanation enjoys a certain priority over others. Hence Aristotle observes:

> The causes concerned in natural generation are, as we see, more than one. There is the cause for the sake of which, and the cause whence the beginning of motion [origin of change] comes. Now we must decide which of these two causes comes first, which second. Plainly, however, that cause is the first which we call that for the sake of which [the purpose]. For this is the account of the thing, and the account forms the starting point, alike in the works of art [craft] and in the works of nature. (*Parts of Animals* 639^{b}12–16)

In art (craft, technology) and biology alike, specification of the function of the thing is the most fruitful starting point of the investigation of how it works. Once we know what A *is for*, and what the goal of the functioning of A is, we are guided in our search for the

Type of 'cause'	How it explains	Examples
efficient	explains why something exists, occurs or is so by reference to the originator – agent or event	A child exists because his parents begat him. The bridge exists because the engineer built it. The window broke because of the impact of the stone.
formal	explains why something is so by reference to the nature or essence of the thing as expressed in its definition	It has a folding blade because it is a pocket knife. The sum of its angles is 180° because it is a triangle.
final	explains why something is so, happened or was done, by reference to its purpose	It is sharp because it is for cutting. He did it for her sake. He went to town in order to shop.
material	explains why something is so, or occurred, by reference to the material constitution of a thing	It does not bend because it is made of steel. It cuts glass because its tip is diamond.

Table 6.1   *The four Aristotelian causes or 'becauses'*

appropriate structures and operations that will causally explain how that function is effected.[27]

> Of the method itself the following is an example. In dealing with respiration, we must show that it takes place for such and such a final object; and we must also show that this and that part of the process is necessitated by this and that other stage of it. By necessity we shall sometimes mean that the requisite antecedents must be there, if the final end is to be reached; and sometimes that things are thus and so by nature. (*Parts of Animals* 642ᵃ31–5)

[27] Of course, we are not always blessed with such knowledge. Discovering what the heart is for and discovering how it fulfils its function were complementary in Harvey's brilliant investigations. Note, however, that Aristotle's principle is not only or merely heuristic, since he thinks that purpose is part of the essential nature of all things.

In craft, it is the conception of the end for which the artefact is being produced that guides the order and methods of production. The end or purpose of a thing may, and typically does, presuppose certain kinds of efficient or material cause. The purpose of a saw is to cut, but it would not serve that purpose were it not made of hard metal. Animals develop in fixed ways in order to attain their mature state. Morphogenetic description is patently teleonomic. But this is perfectly compatible with the fact that the efficient cause of the embryo is generation from parental seed and ovum.

Aristotle linked purpose to the *nature* or *essence* of the thing that is to be explained. So, in trying to understand the parts of animals and of man, the most appropriate method is: 'to say, a man has such and such parts, because the essence of man is such and such, and they are necessary conditions of his existence; or, if we cannot quite say this, then . . . at any rate it is good [beneficial] that they should be there' (ibid., 640³34–5). Essence may include characteristic parts and shapes, functions and bodily activities, the way of life of an animal, including its feeding habits, and its characteristic behavioural dispositions.

Teleonomic physics dominated medieval science. But the medievals did not countenance naked purpose, as Aristotle had done. Aquinas synthesized the Aristotelian world view with the Judaeo-Christian one. Natural phenomena, so eloquently described in the Book of Job (Job 38), were conceived to be the purposive products of benevolent divine creation. Aquinas accepted Aristotle's conception of the teleonomy of inanimate nature exhibited in the natural tendencies of objects to move towards their 'natural place'. But he did not accept Aristotle's conception of naked purpose. In the Fifth Way Aquinas argued that 'We observe that some things which lack awareness, namely natural bodies, act for the sake of an end. . . . Now things which lack awareness do not tend towards a goal unless directed by something with awareness and intelligence, like an arrow by an archer. Therefore there is some intelligent being by whom everything in nature is directed to a goal, and this we call "God".'[28] Purpose was accordingly associated with design. If things had a natural *telos*, that was because this is how their Maker had designed them. The beneficial purposes of

[28] Aquinas, *Summa Theologiae* I, 2, 3, tr. and cited by A. J. P. Kenny, *The Five Ways* (Routledge & Kegan Paul, London, 1969), p. 97.

animal (and human) organs, for example, proclaimed the benevolence and foresight of the Almighty.

The grip of teleonomic *physics* was decisively broken by the scientific revolution of the seventeenth century.[29] Galileian dynamics and cosmology definitively established the explanatory adequacy of efficient causal explanation in nomic terms for cosmology and for physics in general. Kepler's conception of cause was a cousin of the Aristotelian formal cause inasmuch as he thought that the causes of things lie in hidden mathematical harmonies: for example, the cause of there being only six planets, he had supposed (prior to the sad discovery that the orbits are elliptical), is that the five perfect Platonic solids can be inserted between the spheres of the six planets. Galileo, by contrast, being concerned with dynamics and accelerated motions, held that these always presuppose some force or forces as cause. Primary causes are such forces as gravity, secondary or immediate causes are specific motions. In the latter sense, 'that and no other is in the proper sense to be called cause, at whose presence the effect always follows, and at whose removal the effect disappears',[30] and any change in the effect is due to an alteration in the motions constituting the cause. Far from eliminating design, however, both scientists celebrated it, seeing their discoveries as confirmation of design. The cosmos was not imbued with *intrinsic* purpose at all. But it evidenced *design* (*extrinsic, imposed* purpose) everywhere – it was the clockwork of God.[31]

---

[29] But not yet wholly eliminated. Galileo thought that motion in a circle was 'natural', that it is impossible that anything should by nature move in a straight line, since straight motion is by nature infinite, and such an object would then move towards a place at which it is impossible to arrive. But that would be contrary to nature. (*Dialogue on the Great World Systems*, 1st Day)

[30] Galileo Galilei, *Opere Complete*, vol. 4 (Florence, 1842), p. 216, quoted in E. A. Burtt, *The Metaphysical Foundations of Modern Science* (Routledge & Kegan Paul, London, 1932), p. 92.

[31] A corollary of this conception was a deist tendency to equivocate regarding the laws of nature. Seventeenth-century scientists (and philosophers) conceived of nature not only as *describable* by laws, but as *subject* to laws. Thus Galileo asserted: 'Nature acts through immutable laws which she never transgresses' (*Letter to Duchess Cristina*, 1615), quoted by Burtt, *Metaphysical Foundations*, p. 64), Descartes wrote of the laws of dynamics 'which God has so established in nature . . . [that] we cannot doubt they are exactly observed in everything which exists or occurs in the world' (*Discourse on Method*, Part V, in Ch. Adam and P. Tannery (eds), *Oeuvres de*

Kepler held that 'The chief aim of all investigations of the external world should be to discover the rational order and harmony which has been imposed upon it by God and which He revealed to us in the language of mathematics.' He viewed the cosmos as the artefact of the Great Geometer, and his astronomical investigations into the planetary orbits were driven by the hope that they would reveal a geometrical design, and so manifest the wisdom and benevolence of the Designer. Galileo held that although the only laws to be sought in physics are laws of efficient causality, the cosmos is the handiwork of God created according to a mathematical design: 'Philosophy [natural philosophy] is written in that great book which for ever lies before our eyes – I mean the universe – but we cannot understand it if we do not first learn the language and grasp the symbols in which it is written. The book is written in the mathematical language . . . without whose help it is impossible to comprehend a single word of it.'[32]

The two great philosophical spokesmen for the scientific revolution, Bacon and Descartes, excluded all teleology from natural science. Bacon wrote: 'Inquiry into final causes is sterile, and, like a virgin consecrated to God, produces nothing.'[33] Descartes was equally adamant: 'I consider the customary search for final causes to be totally useless in physics; there is considerable rashness in thinking myself capable of investigating the impenetrable purposes of God.'[34] In conversation with Burman he elaborated: 'This rule – that we must never argue from ends – should be carefully heeded. For, firstly, the knowledge of a thing's purpose never leads us to the knowledge of the thing itself; its nature remains just as obscure to us. Indeed, this constant practice of arguing from ends is Aristotle's greatest fault.'[35] Gassendi objected. However, it is striking that the grounds of his

Descartes, rev. edn (Vrin/C.N.R.S., Paris, 1964–70), vol. VI, p. 41 (subsequent references abbreviated 'AT')(AT VI, 41)); and Boyle spoke of 'the laws of motion prescribed by the Author of things' (*The Works of the Honourable Robert Boyle*, ed. Thomas Eirch (London, 1672), vol. 5, p. 177).

[32] Galilei, *Opere*, vol. 4, p. 171. It is noteworthy that the Neoplatonism that had progressively displaced Aristotelian philosophy in the Renaissance involved a reversion to Pythagoreanism that proved crucial to the development of physics.

[33] Francis Bacon, *De Augmentis Scientarum* (1623), III, ch. 5.

[34] René Descartes, *Fourth Meditation* (AT VII, 55; *The Philosophical Writings of Descartes*, trs. S. Cottingham, R. Stoothoff and D. Murdoch (Cambridge University Press, Cambridge, 1985), vol. II, p. 39 (subsequent references 'CSM')).

[35] Descartes, *Conversation with Burman*, 16 Apr., 1648 (AT V, 158; CSM III, 341).

objections are not that teleology offers a distinctive form of explanation, but rather that it affords the best evidence for a Designer:

> [T]here is obviously a danger that you may be abandoning the principal argument for establishing by the natural light the wisdom, providence and power of God, and indeed his existence. Leaving aside the entire world, the heavens and its other main parts, how or where will you be able to get any better evidence for the existence of such a God than from the function of the various parts in plants, animals, man and yourself (or your body), seeing that you bear a likeness of God? We know that certain great thinkers have been led by a study of anatomy not just to achieve a knowledge of God but also to sing thankful hymns to him for having organized all the parts and harmonized their functions in such a way as to deserve the highest praise for his care and providence.[36]

Descartes replied: 'The points you make to defend the notion of final cause should be applied to efficient causation. The function of the various parts of plants and animals etc. makes it appropriate to admire God as their efficient cause – to recognize and glorify the craftsman through examining his works; but we cannot guess from this what purpose God has in creating any given thing.'[37] This is a *non sequitur*, since although we may not be able to guess the purpose of God in creating a given animal species, it does not follow that we cannot know the purpose of, for example, the elephant's trunk or the wings of the eagle, or investigate and discover the purposes that the internal organs of an animal and their proper functioning have in serving the good of the animal as it engages in its characteristic activities.

Descartes explained the method that he practised:

> When dealing with natural things we will, then, never derive any explanations from the purposes which God or nature may have had in view when creating them and we shall entirely banish from our philosophy the search for final causes. For we should not be so arrogant as to suppose that we can share in God's plans. We should, instead, consider him as the efficient cause of all things . . . and see what conclusions should be drawn concerning those effects which are apparent to our senses.[38]

[36] Gassendi, in the *Fifth Set of Objections* to Descartes's *Meditations* (AT VII, 309; CSM II, 215).

[37] Descartes, *Fifth Set of Replies* (AT VII, 375; CSM II, 258).

[38] Descartes, *The Principles of Philosophy*, I, 28; this stands in striking contrast to the teleological remarks in Meditation 6 (AT VII, 83).

He further elaborated:[39]

> In this book I have deduced the causes . . . of these and many other
> phenomena from principles which are known to all and admitted by
> all, namely the shape, size, position and motion of particles of mat-
> ter. . . . there is nothing in the whole of nature (nothing, that is, which
> should be referred to purely corporeal causes, i.e. those devoid of thought
> and mind) which is incapable of being deductively explained on the
> basis of these selfsame principles.
>
> . . . Up till now I have described this earth and indeed the whole
> visible universe as if it were a machine: I have considered only the
> various shapes and movements of its parts.
>
> . . . all the knowledge which men have of the natural world must
> necessarily be derived from notions of shapes, sizes and motions, and
> the rules in accordance with which these three things can be modified
> by each other – rules which are the principles of geometry and
> mechanics . . . I do not recognize any difference between artefacts and
> natural bodies except that the operations of artefacts are for the most
> part performed by mechanisms which are large enough to be easily
> perceived by the senses . . . The effects produced in nature, by contrast,
> almost always depend on structures which are so minute that they com-
> pletely elude our senses.[40]

It is striking that the young Leibniz, castigating Campanella,
Marcus Marci, Agrippa and Scaliger, wrote: 'they ascribe to [sub-
stantial forms] appetite or a natural instinct . . . The result is such

---

[39] Descartes, *Principles*, IV, 187, 188 and 203.

[40] This was held to apply to the biological sciences too. For Descartes held that
physiology requires nothing more than mechanical principles, and conceived of
animals as mere biological machines. The human body too is a machine, but unlike
animal machines, it is controlled by a mind. For human voluntary action consists in
the mind's bringing about muscular contractions by immediately affecting the pineal
gland, and hence mediately affecting the animal spirits.

The thought that an organism is a machine, as Descartes held, and indeed that we are
mere machines, as he denied but La Mettrie affirmed, proved powerful. So, among our
contemporaries, C. Blakemore remarks: 'We are machines, but machines so wonder-
fully designed that no one should count it an insult to be called such a machine'
(*The Mind Machine* (BBC Publications, London, 1988), p. 270), and R. Dawkins
says: 'What about our own bodies? Each one of us is a machine, like an airliner only
much more complicated' (*The Blind Watchmaker* (Longman, Scientific and Technical,
Harlow, 1986), p. 3).

Are animals and their parts *machines*? Machines are designed, animals are not.
Machines do not have a good, animals do. Machines have controls, animals do not

axioms as these: nature does nothing in vain; everything avoids its own destruction; nature strives for continuity; like enjoys like; matter desires a nobler form; and others of this kind, though there is in fact no wisdom in nature and no appetite; yet a beautiful order arises in it because it is the timepiece of God.'[41] Nor is it to be supposed that the Almighty is so poor a craftsman as to need 'to wind up his watch' periodically (as Newton held) – it is a perfect machine which needs no tinkering to keep it going (when God works miracles, he does so in order to supply not the wants of nature, but those of grace).

Kant dedicated the whole of Part 2 of the *Critique of the Power of Judgment* to an examination of teleological explanation of nature. His investigations were, however, vitiated by the assumption that teleology is a special kind of causality, and that the fundamental idea of purpose in nature is restricted to design. '. . . we have no basis at all for presuming a priori that ends that are not our own, and which also cannot pertain to nature (which we cannot assume as an intelligent being), nevertheless can or should constitute a special kind of causality, or at least an entirely unique lawlikeness thereof.'[42] Kant was mistaken to suppose that there cannot be natural purposes (e.g. of organs) that are not a corollary of design. He was confused in thinking that an explanation of what something is for must be a kind of causal explanation of why it exists. This confusion stemmed from the Christian transformation of Aristotelian teleology in living things into the purposiveness of divine design. The upshot was Kant's claim that the purposiveness of nature amounts to no more than a regulative principle. We are, he held, driven to view

---

(even though they may be controlled in certain ways) – indeed, human beings are self-controlled, autonomous. The purpose of machines is the purpose for which they were designed; animals do not exist for a purpose. But animals have purposes, which are whatever ends they may pursue, whereas machines have no purposes of their own. Animals are alive, have a characteristic life cycle, can be healthy, prosper and flourish, or fall ill and die. It ill becomes a biologist to overlook or obscure the distinctive logical forms that characterize our concepts and descriptions of living beings.

'Mechanism' in biology may be understood to mean the quest for explanation in causal terms. It has indeed proved fruitful. But it does not exclude teleological explanation and description. Nor does its success imply that animals are machines.

[41] G. W. Leibniz, *Letter to Jacob Thomasius*, 20/30 Apr. 1669, in *Philosophical Papers and Letters*, ed. L. E. Loemker, vol. I (University of Chicago Press, Chicago, 1956), p. 158.

[42] Kant, *Critique of the Power of Judgment*, 5: 359–60.

nature in general *as if* it were created by design (intelligent purpose). Teleology has no genuine explanatory role, but at best provides a heuristic analogy: 'teleological judging is rightly drawn into our research into nature, at least problematically, but only in order to bring it under principles of observation and research in *analogy* with causality according to ends, without presuming thereby to *explain* it' (ibid.).

One may be sceptical about any heuristic value to teleology *conceived as design* in physics even in Kant's day, let alone ours. But it is striking that the argument from purpose to design in biology remained prominent until Darwin. Like Gassendi and indeed Newton, William Paley, archdeacon of Carlisle in the late eighteenth century and a highly influential theologian, found the exquisite adaptiveness of forms of life so impressive that it provided, he thought, an overwhelming argument in favour of design. While one might countenance the intelligibility of absence of design in inanimate nature, he held, one could not do so when confronted by complex artefacts, such as a watch. But, he wrote, 'every indication of contrivance, every manifestation of design, which existed in the watch, exists in the works of nature; with the difference, on the side of nature, of being greater and more, and that in a degree which exceeds all computation.' So, he argued, 'there is precisely the same proof that the eye was made for vision, as there is that the telescope was made for assisting it.'[43]

This conception, from purpose to design to Designer, was shattered by Darwin, who showed that natural selection explains how purpose can evolve in life forms *without design*.[44] Having been greatly influenced by Paley in his youth, Darwin was insistent that it *must* be shown 'how the innumerable species inhabiting this world have been modified, so as to acquire that perfection of structure and co-adaptation

[43] W. Paley, *Natural Theology, or Evidences of the Existence and Attributes of the Deity Collected from the Appearances of Nature*, 12th edn (J. Faulder, London, 1809), p. 18. Newton had likewise been impressed by the eye: 'Was the Eye contrived without Skill in Opticks, . . . does it not appear from Phaenomena that there is a Being incorporeal, living, intelligent, omnipresent . . . ?' (*Opticks*, 4th edn (William Innys, London, 1730), pp. 344ff.)

[44] Kitcher mistakenly argues that 'one of Darwin's important discoveries is that we can think of design without a designer' ('Function and Design', p. 380). It should be noted that pattern does not imply design and hence Designer either. There is plenty of pattern in nature (e.g. in crystals), but that does not entail a Patterner.

which most justly excites our admiration'.[45] Strikingly, Darwin is commonly thought to have eliminated teleology from nature and natural science. But that is quite mistaken. He gave a definitive explanation of how there can be purpose in nature even though there is *no design*. That is possible through the process of natural selection that favours advantageous adaptation.[46]

Although Darwin did not eliminate teleology from biology, teleological explanation fell into disfavour among scientists and philosophers throughout the twentieth century. The dissociation of purpose from design proved difficult to grasp. Broad, writing in the 1925 held that what he called 'a teleological system' is one 'composed of such parts arranged in such ways as might have been expected *if* it had been constructed by an intelligent being to fulfil a certain purpose which he had in mind' and such that 'if we were to use this hypothesis as a clue to more minute investigation, we continue to find that the system is constructed as if the hypothesis were true'.[47] This was in effect to recapitulate Kant's view that attribution of teleology to nature and natural phenomena is at best heuristic (and at worst, misguided projection). Behaviourists were more radical. They viewed ascription of purpose to animal behaviour as inexcusable anthropomorphism, and purpose in human behaviour as suspiciously mental (allegedly discoverable only by introspection) and therefore on the Index. They dismissed teleological explanation with contempt, holding that ' "the idea of end" is totally inefficacious causally, *for*

---

[45] C. Darwin, *Origin of Species* (Penguin, Harmondsworth, 1968), p. 66. It is striking how frequently Darwin was responding to Paley, sometimes explicitly (see p. 229), sometimes implicitly, e.g. in his detailed discussions of the formation of the eye (p. 217), which Paley, like Newton, had thought could be explained only by design.

[46] Andrew Woodfield remarks that although Darwin's theory looks as if it vindicates Aristotelian teleology, 'Upon further reflection it hardly amounts to a ringing endorsement since Darwin's theory can be stated without employing the term "function" or any teleological language at all' ('Teleology', in *The Routledge Encyclopaedia of Philosophy* (Routledge, London, 1998). One can recount the theory of evolution without mentioning the beneficial, describing evolutionarily relevant changes only as conducive to successful reproduction. But one would then have omitted a crucial construction line, and screened out the essential link between adaptation and the good of the animal. It is neither an oversight nor an error that Darwin did not do this. (One can describe triangles without mentioning that the sum of their internal angles add up to 180°.)

[47] C. D. Broad, *The Mind and its Place in Nature* (Kegan Paul, Trench, Trubner & Co., London, 1925), p. 82.

more often than not it is merely an *idée fixe*'.[48] They associated teleology with vitalism, which they repudiated, insisting on the universal
validity of causal explanation in the physical sciences. The latter
sentiment dominated the logical positivists' account of explanation
in science.

The Manifesto of the Vienna Circle explicitly identified vitalism as
one of the residues of past metaphysics which they aimed to extirp-
ate. The concepts of *dominants* invoked by Reinke and of *entelechies*
invoked by Driesch are not reducible to 'the given', and are therefore to be rejected as metaphysical. Once these have been (rightly)
brushed aside,[49] what remains of vitalism is the thesis that the processes of organic nature proceed according to laws that cannot be
reduced to physical laws. But that, the authors of the Manifesto
proclaimed, amounts to the (preposterous) thesis that biology is not
subject to uniform and pervasive regularities.[50] 'Naturalism' became
the battle-cry of logical positivists. But this was narrowly construed,
for 'naturalism' was restricted to what is necessary for the purposes
of physics. This misguided limitation was an aspect of the Vienna
Circle's reductionist doctrine of the unity of science. It also involved
the further misunderstanding that since science should be 'value-free',
it may not employ any axiological terms in its explanations. Applied
to the understanding and explanation of living beings and their organs,
their functioning and malfunctioning, this was sorely confused.[51] That
science should be dedicated to discovering the truth, and should not
be biased by political, moral or ideological considerations does not
mean that axiological notions invoked in the biological sciences

[48] Edwin B. Holt, 'Response and Cognition', *Journal of Philosophy, Psychology
and Scientific Methods*, 12 (1915), p. 406.

[49] They were indeed no more than illicit surrogates for design.

[50] *The Scientific Conception of the World: The Vienna Circle* (Reidel, Dordrecht,
1973), p. 16. This was published in 1929 without any authorial attribution. It was
written by Neurath together with Hahn and Carnap.

[51] A similar misunderstanding is evident in Woodfield's remark on Aristotelian teleology: 'Aristotle's doctrine was naturalistic in the sense that it did not postulate a
supernatural designer, but it was not wholly naturalistic, since it employed the notion
of benefiting' (*Routledge Encyclopaedia of Philosophy*, 'Teleology', §2). It is misconceived to suppose that a naturalistic biology may not invoke, as Darwin's did,
the notions of what is beneficial for an organism, of the welfare, good or ill health
of an organ or organism. If Aristotle's doctrine was illicitly 'non-naturalistic' in this
respect, it is in the good company of physiology, pathology and medicine in general.

(especially, but not only, in medical science) are illicit. Similarly, the fact that physics is, in a readily explicable sense, *the* fundamental science does not imply that the vocabulary of physics is adequate for the sciences of life or that its forms of explanation constrain those that are to be used in biological sciences. Indeed, it is only to be expected that the conceptual framework for description and explanation of living beings and their behaviour should differ from that of inanimate matter.

The most comprehensive investigation of teleological (functional) explanation in biology by a logical empiricist is to be found in chapter 12 of Ernest Nagel's monumental treatise *The Structure of Science* (1961). He argued that teleological (functional) explanations in biology can always be reformulated in non-teleological terms without loss of content.[52] 'A teleological explanation in biology indicates the *consequences* for a given biological system [i.e. an organ or organism] of a constituent part or process; the equivalent non-teleological formulation of this explanation . . . states some of the *conditions* . . . under which the system [i.e. the creature or its organs] persists in its characteristic organization and activities.'[53] Consequently, Nagel concluded, 'The difference between a teleological explanation and its equivalent non-teleological formulation is thus comparable to the difference between saying that Y is an effect of X and saying

[52] The function of chlorophyll, he wrote, is to enable plants to photosynthesize. But that, he claimed, is equivalent to saying that a necessary condition of photosynthesis in plants is the presence of chlorophyll. This does not make it clear that photosynthesis is necessary for the *welfare*, indeed survival, of *the living plant*. But it is such true axiological statements that give substance to the assertion that what X (e.g. chlorophyll) is *for* is to V or to enable the organism to V (the plant to photosynthesize water and oxygen). Furthermore, by taking as an example the presence of certain *materials* (e.g. chlorophyll) in organs of an organism (leaves of a plant), Nagel neglects the distinctive forms of teleology involved in characterizing *organs* and their activities.

[53] E. Nagel, *The Structure of Science* (Routledge & Kegan Paul, London, 1961), p. 405. It is a very striking fact that twentieth-century writers (scientists and philosophers alike) on biology and psychology, from the behaviourists onwards, persist in using forms of words that obscure their subject matter from their sight. The use of the term 'system' is supposed to exemplify the admirably detached and value-free character of objective scientific research, but it contributes significantly to numbing our linguistic sensibility and reducing our awareness of the fact that we are dealing with living things. This serves to screen out the conceptual commitments involved in discourse about what is alive as opposed to inanimate matter and artefacts.

that X is a cause or condition of Y. In brief, the difference is one of selective attention, rather than of asserted content.'[54] This is, I think, mistaken.

A functional explanation of the activity of an organ O may take the general form: O V's *in order to bring it about that* E (the end or goal). So we rightly say that the heart pumps blood in order to circulate it, that the lungs inhale and exhale in order that the blood be oxygenated, that the stomach secretes hydrochloric acid in order to break down the foodstuffs in it. We may grant that if an organ V's in order to bring it about that E, then, other things being equal, it will not be the case that E unless the organ V's. The organ is teleologically explained by specifying what it is for, and the activity of the organ is explained by citing the state of affairs that it is to bring about. It brings it about as a result of its causal powers. But the teleological explanation is *not* equivalent to the causal explanation that O's V-ing is causally necessary for E. For it further explains both *what the organ is for* and *what the purpose of the organ's activity is* by reference to an outcome, and it links both organ and its activity, explicitly or implicitly, to the good of a living being. Moreover, as already remarked, our knowledge of a teleological explanation (e.g. of sweat glands) is commonly quite independent of our knowledge of the causal mechanisms that make it possible. The difference between a teleological explanation and a corresponding causal one is not merely one of 'selective attention', since the teleological explanation attends to factors that the mere causal explanation disregards: namely, the characteristic form of life and activity of the organism.

By mid-twentieth century, scientists and philosophers of science had, to a remarkable degree, lost any clear grasp of the logical character of teleological description and explanation. C. L. Hull, a behaviourist psychologist, held that 'In its extreme form teleology is the name of the belief that the *terminal* stage of certain environmental organismic cycles somehow is at the same time one of the antecedent determining conditions which bring the behaviour cycle about.'[55] In much the same vein, J. L. Mackie argued that if there were such a thing as backward causation,

[54] Ibid.

[55] C. L. Hull, *Principles of Behaviour* (Appleton-Century, New York, 1943), p. 26.

this would be, in a very clear sense, a case of teleology or final causation: the 'end' would indeed be responsible for the coming about of
the 'means', and any explanation of these earlier occurring items would
have to refer to this end. . . . it would be radically and intrinsically different from ordinary, forward, efficient causation, and it might well
be described as the purest and simplest kind of teleology.[56]

These remarks exhibit misunderstanding, and they make clear how
the translation of Aristotelian terminology as 'final causation' can mis-
lead the blinkered eye. 'Final causes' are not deviant efficient causes
that succeed their effects. The charge that teleological explanation
tries to explain a present event *causally* by reference to a later one
displays incomprehension and misunderstanding. That for the sake
of which something occurs or is done is not a kind of efficient cause,
but a purpose. Citing it explains, not by identifying a cause, but by
pointing out an end.

It was symptomatic of the Cartesian heritage that the characteristic twentieth-century analytic accounts of explanation of human action
reduced teleological explanation in terms of human reasons and purposes to a form of causal explanation. Although human behaviour
is characteristically explained by reference to its purpose – that
for the sake of which it is done – the prejudice against any form of
explanation of empirical phenomena other than causal has inclined
modern thinkers to suppose that although explanation of action
by reference to purposes *looks* teleological, it is not. It is actually
an explanation of action in terms of the human agent's *having* that
purpose – which causes the appropriate behaviour. So apparent ends
for the sake of which an agent acts are transformed into *antecedent
causes* of his behaviour, apparent goals at which his action is aimed
are transformed into *causally efficacious mental states*: namely,
desires and beliefs. Those mental states, it seems, must be identical
with brain states, and they must cause the muscle contractions that
are constitutive of the behaviour that is to be explained. Teleological
explanation, which seems bewildering, is traded for the identity
of mental states with brain states, which seems scientific. But this
is neither scientific nor even true. The contingent identity thesis is
a blank cheque on a non-existent bank. Beliefs, as we shall see, are

---

[56] J. L. Mackie, *The Cement of the Universe* (Clarendon Press, Oxford, 1974),
pp. 274f.

not mental states. For the most part, neither are desires. And no one has ever given us criteria of identity for a brain state that might be a candidate for being contingently identical with believing or wanting something. Explanation of behaviour in terms of agential reasons will be the theme of the next chapter.

7

Reasons and Explanation of Human Action

1. Rationality and reasonableness

Human beings are rational animals. To be a rational creature is to possess the faculty of reason. The faculty of reason is exercised in reasoning and in discerning reasons *why* and *for*. It is exhibited in reasoned discourse and action, and in giving reasons *why* and *for*. To lack that faculty is not to be an irrational but a non-rational creature. To possess the faculty of reason implies that, from occasion to occasion, one may, in one's thought, feeling and action, be *either* rational *or* irrational (completely or to a greater or lesser degree). Reason*ing* is drawing conclusions from grounds. A reason is an explanatory or justificatory step in actual or warranted (or purportedly warranted) reasoning. It may, in a given circumstance, be a decisive, or a weighty, a good, or a not very good reason. From reasons, conclusions are drawn. Such transitions from grounds to conclusions are principled operations. Principles of deductive reasoning determine what counts as *valid* reasoning. The study of logic is the endeavour to identify such constitutive principles. But not all reasoning is deductive.

The power of reason may be possessed to a greater or lesser degree, some people being better at reasoning, or at reasoning in some distinctive domain (e.g. mathematics), than others. It may be exercised, from occasion to occasion, with greater or lesser competence. Incompetent reasoning need not be irrational, nor need it show the irrationality of its agent. It may simply be an error, or a manifestation of lack of understanding. It exhibits irrationality only when it violates fundamental canons of reasoning, or when the agent is impervious to correction. Good reasoning is exhibited when the conclusions are warranted by the grounds from which they are derived or by reference to which the agent justifies them. Poor or bad reasoning is manifest when the conclusions drawn are not thus warranted, when the conclusions that are warranted are not drawn, or where no conclusion is drawn where one is warranted.

Rationality, therefore, is not only an attribute of thinking beings, but also a property of the exercise of their rational faculty and of the results of its exercise. So arguments and reasonings, as well as their conclusions in thought and will, and their manifestation in utterance and action, are also said to be rational (or irrational). Rationality and reasonableness (of which more in a moment) are exhibited not only in reasoning and its conclusions, but also in sensitivity to reasons, in responsiveness in thought, will and feeling (and corresponding action) to relevant considerations. This requires some elaboration.

Much of our knowledge and most of our beliefs are not acquired through reasoning. Much of our noetic or doxastic framework is picked up as part of the general human, or local cultural, inheritance transmitted to us as the unquestioned presuppositions or assumptions of our thought and talk. Much of what we know or believe, we have acquired through hearsay and education. Much we have learnt ourselves by the use of our cognitive faculties – our perceptual powers and our correlative cognitive receptivity (i.e. our abilities to recognize or to notice things, to become conscious or aware of things and of how things are). And some things we learn through our power of reasoning. Reason is exhibited not only in our reasoning our way to new truths that are consequences of what we already know or believe, but in our responsiveness, in respect of our existing beliefs, to fresh information. Believing is not an action; it is not even something we do. Nevertheless, it is responsive to reason. If our reason for believing that p is that q, and we discover that it is not the case that q, then we normally cease believing that p. Believing (expecting, suspecting, fearing) that p is *unreasonable* if, on learning that the evidence for p was false, we nevertheless continue to believe (expect, suspect or fear) as before. But we are *irrational* if, on learning that q, which we know to be incompatible with p, we nevertheless still *think* (rather than believe) or *imagine*, expect, suspect or fear that p. Knowing that q and that if it is the case that q, it cannot be the case that p, we sometimes nevertheless 'cannot help' *thinking* or *imagining* that p. When reason falters thus, such irrational thoughts, suspicions, hopes and fears invade us, and we are in the grip of delusion.[1]

Similarly, we manifest reason in our deliberations on the *ends* to pursue and the *means* whereby to achieve them, and hence in our reasoned decisions and formation of plans and intentions. The rationality or reasonableness of our desires and wants is exhibited not only in our reflective choices and the reasons we give for them but also in the responsiveness of our desires to relevant information that we obtain and to shifts in our values and valuations. Our wanting G is irrational to the extent that, on learning that G lacks the desirability characteristics that were our reason for wanting it, we nevertheless continue to want it. Cravings, urges, obsessive desires are relatively or absolutely insensitive to reason.

Our feelings (emotions and attitudes) likewise commonly rest on reasons, by reference to which we justify or rationalize them. Though we cannot choose our emotions and attitudes, many are warranted by features of their objects, either *tout court* or in degree. Good fortune is a reason for feeling pleased, great good fortune a reason for joy; offensive behaviour is a reason for indignation, very offensive behaviour a reason for anger. Our feelings are rational to the extent that they are warranted by and sensitive to reason – that is, that they change appropriately if the beliefs about their objects are found to be false or exaggerated. Phobias, irrational attitudes and passions are immune to reason, either in respect of their object or in degree. (For an overview, see fig. 7.1.)

It is therefore unsurprising that reason has traditionally been thought to be not only a guiding faculty but also a regulating one – Plato's charioteer controlling the steeds of passion and appetite. For it is exercised not only in rational deliberation and choice, and corresponding thought and action, but also in controlling belief, appetite, passion and action through reflection, and in responsiveness to reasons.

---

[1] It is striking that if one recognizes that it cannot be the case that p, one cannot go on to say sincerely that one nevertheless continues to *believe* that p. For to declare a belief (i.e. that one believes things to be thus-and-so) is to subscribe to that belief (i.e. to what is believed), and one cannot sincerely subscribe to what one recognizes cannot be so. But the obsessive *thought* that p may impose itself upon one; the suspicion, fear or wish that p may continue to haunt one. There is a striking asymmetry here with irrational desires. For to declare a desire is not to endorse it. So desires, cravings and passions may indeed persist and sincerely be declared to persist in the face of reason. (See S. Hampshire, *Freedom of the Individual* (Chatto & Windus, London, 1965), pp. 70ff.)

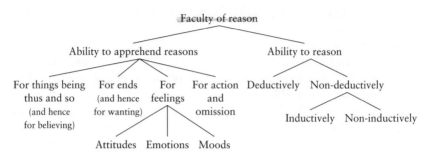

Figure 7.1. *Aspects of the powers of reason*

We distinguish between the rational and the reasonable, although the distinction is not everywhere sharp or clear. Anything reasonable is also rational, but not everything rational is reasonable ('rational economic man' in pursuit of profit maximization is not a model of reasonableness). A person is rational to the extent that his reasoning in pursuit of his goals is not swayed by passion and prejudice. But one may be rational in pursuit of foolish, unreasonable or evil goals, if one chooses means appropriate to their attainment. Rationality is closely tied to instrumentality – the choice of efficient means to ends – and to formal correctness in reasoning. Like reasonableness, rationality is also tied to freedom from the distorting effects of bias and emotion on thinking. But reasonableness, unlike rationality, is more closely linked to the appreciation of values and their multiplicity, and to awareness of the legitimate concerns of others and hence too to the ability to find appropriate 'balance' between conflicting demands of situations and people. One is reasonable if one does not go beyond the limits assigned by reason: if one is undogmatic and therefore open to countervailing considerations, if one is not insensitive to the interests of others, not extravagant or immoderate in one's expectations, and not excessive in one's demands and aims. There is, therefore, a privative aspect to reasonableness (as there is to rationality): one is reasonable if one is free from the various forms of *unreasonableness* to which human beings are subject. But it would be mistaken to conceive of reasonableness as no more than a privative attribute.[2]

---

[2] A suggestion mooted by Paul Grice, *Aspects of Reason* (Clarendon Press, Oxford, 2001), pp. 23–5.

2. Reason, reasoning and reasons

Descartes declared that reason 'is the only thing that makes us men and distinguishes us from the beast'.[3] In fact, mankind possesses a multitude of powers distinguishing us from other animals (e.g. self-consciousness; a sense of history and tradition; knowledge of, and hence capacity for, good and evil; a sense of beauty and the power of imagination; as well as destructiveness and savagery unparalleled among animals). But it is true that we are the only rational animals. *Pace* Sophocles, reason is not 'the choicest gift bestowed by heaven'[4] – it is bestowed only by the very same blind workings of chance that made us language-using animals. Our rationality, our limited responsiveness to reasons, and our fallible ability to reason are corollaries of our being language-users. For only language-users can *engage in reasoning*; and only language-users can *deliberate* and *give reasons* for what they think and do. Only creatures that can deliberate (weigh reasons) and form their beliefs or resolve to act on the basis of *the balance of reasons* can be said to *have reasons* for thought and deed. Non-language-using animals (including small children) can have purposes. But animals cannot reason their way to the adoption of a purpose; they cannot weigh the reasons for and against what they do or what they aim at, or give reasons justifying or explaining their behaviour to themselves or others. No doubt we can apply an attenuated notion of reason to them; but there is no need to.[5] If we do, then we sever the concept of a reason and acting for a reason from the abilities to deliberate, to reason, to consider different reasons for and against thought and action, to weigh conflicting reasons and to make reasoned choices both in thought (what to believe) and in action (what to do).[6]

---

[3] Descartes, *Discourse on the Method* (AT VI, 2) – surprisingly, since his official position was that it is thought or consciousness that distinguishes us from other animals.

[4] Sophocles, *Antigone* l. 683.

[5] Aquinas nicely remarks that the higher animals exhibit 'a semblance of reason', and that they share in 'natural prudence'. Aristotle too had noted that some animals have *phronēsis*, 'namely those which are found to have a power of foresight with regard to their own life' (*Nicomachean Ethics* 1141ª28). Neither of these careful observations warrants ascribing to animals reasons for doing what they do.

[6] Alasdair MacIntyre argues that 'non-human animals in some sense have reasons for acting as they do', for although we have the power to reflect on our reasons,

Rationality is essentially connected with the ability to understand and to offer answers to the questions 'Why?' and 'What is to be done?'. To learn the ways in which one can answer and justify the answers to such questions is to learn to give reasons. To learn to give reasons is internally related to learning to reason. Sound theoretical reasoning aims to derive a truth from true premises in accordance with principles of reasoning. Throughout the long history of the debate on its nature, practical reasoning has been variously conceived. To reason practically is to make a transition from premises, at least one of which must specify a desideratum (differently conceived as given by reference to a need, a want, a purpose, a norm or a value), to an action (on some accounts), or (on others) to the formation of an intention, or (on yet others) to a prescription. According to some philosophers it is essentially first-personal, its conclusions being the action, or decision and intention formation, of the agent. Whether the principles of practical reasoning are or are not the same as those of deductive reasoning has been, and still is, much debated. Some, who conceive of them as different, emphasize that practical reasoning (like inductive reasoning, at least on some accounts) is essentially *defeasible*, being purpose-relative and context-sensitive in a way in which deductive reasoning is not.[7] Accordingly, deductive reasoning is *truth-preserving*, but practical reasoning, on such an account, preserves *satisfactoriness* relative to a given goal or purpose. The addition of further true premises to a piece of deductive reasoning cannot change the validity of the inference to the conclusion; that is, the same conclusion still follows from the larger set of premises. But adding premises concerning facts (including opportunities and opportunity costs), goals (including the good and the right) or negative goals (including

---

which other animals lack, nevertheless, 'any exercise of the power to reflect on our reasons for action presupposes that we already have such reasons about which we can reflect . . . the kinds of reason that we share with dolphins and chimpanzees. Did we not share such reasons with [them] we would not have arrived at that starting point and a denial that we have such reasons would render the transition to specifically human rationality unintelligible' (*Dependent Rational Animals* (Duckworth, London, 1999), p. 56). I agree with the premiss but deny the conclusion. A child must be taught to give reasons before it can learn to evaluate them, weigh them, and make reasoned choices on the balance of reasons. But until it has mastered a language, it cannot give reasons, either to itself or to others. Until it has learnt what the question 'Why?' ('For what reason?') means, it cannot engage in justification either *ex post* or *ex ante actu*. Only when it has learnt to answer can it be answerable.

[7] See A. J. P. Kenny, *Will, Freedom and Power* (Blackwell, Oxford, 1976), ch. 5.

the bad and the wrong) to a piece of practical reasoning may invalidate the conclusion; that is, the conclusion may not be satisfactory relative to the end, given the additional facts and objectives; or the end may no longer be warranted, given further values at stake. Both theoretical and practical reasoning are purposive, deliberative activities. One may engage in reasoning, and rehearse one's reasons, aloud or *in foro interno*, but the latter only on the condition of the ability to do the former. As we shall see, one may V or have V'd for a reason, even though one did not reason to the conclusion to V.

Putting aside the use of 'reason' to signify the faculty, the noun can occur either as a count noun ('a reason', 'three different reasons') or as a mass noun ('there is some reason for hope'). Its most general use is to introduce explanations, as when we say that the reason *why* such-and-such is so-and-so. A narrower use is *attributive*, as when we say that something is a reason *for someone* to think or act. A third use is the familiar form of rational explanation of thought, feeling or action: A's reason for V-ing was. . . .[8] We shall briefly examine these (there are other uses).

We may ask ourselves, or be asked, why *p*, and we may answer that the reason why *p* is that *q*. Here *that q* explains (or partially explains) why it is the case that *p*. The explanation may be of different kinds, including the varieties of formal, material, causal and teleological explanation that Aristotle characterized as *aitia*. The general forms 'The reason why *p* is that *q*' and 'That *q* is the reason why *p*' are doubly factive in the following sense: the explanandum must be factive (i.e. it must be the case that *p*), otherwise there is nothing to explain, and the explanans must be factive (i.e. it must be the case that *q*), otherwise there is no explanation. 'The reason why' cannot be said to be good or bad. Human beings learn to give explanatory reasons in the course of learning to answer why-questions. That ability presupposes the ability to employ the forms of description that are required for explananda and explanans and grasp of the forms of explanatory nexus signified by 'because'.

The concept of *a reason* is invoked, and reasoning is involved, not only in explaining why things are so, but also in providing a justification *for* thought, feeling and action. This may be prospective or retrospective. It may concern one's own beliefs, feelings and actions

---

[8] See Grice, *Aspects of Reason*, pp. 37–44 to which I am indebted in the following account.

or those of others. The characteristic form of such justifications is person-relative: 'that *p* is (or was) a reason *for A* to V' or 'there is (or was) a reason *for A* to V, namely that *p*' (or a generalization thereof, e.g. 'that *p* is a reason *for anyone* in such a situation to V'). Typically the reason cited, namely that *p*, is held to justify, to provide a rationale for, thinking or believing something, for one's feelings or attitudes, or for one's actions. Such a reason applies to a particular person or persons – is a reason *for* him or them to think, feel or act. That something is a reason for A to V does *not* imply that it must also be a reason for anyone in a like situation to V – B may have different purposes, tastes and preferences from A (that *The Marriage of Figaro* is on at the opera tonight may be a very good reason for A to buy a ticket, but none for B, given that he dislikes opera). It only implies that if it is not a reason for B to V, there must be a difference in virtue of which it is not. The operative notion of *justification* here is not moral, although moral reasons are one form of justification. The reason specification is factive, but specification of what it is a reason for (which may be judging things to be so, feeling thus-and-so, or doing such-and-such) does not imply its occurrence or performance. That there was a reason for A to V does not imply that he V'd. He may not have known that *p*; he may have known that *p*, but not have realized that it was a reason for him to V; or he may have known that it was a reason for him to V, yet not have V'd through weakness of will, or through forgetfulness, or because prevented, or because the reason that *p* was outweighed by countervailing reasons. Not only is the act specification not factive in this sense, but further, even if A did V, and *that p* was a reason for him to V, and he knew that it was, it does not follow that his reason for V-ing was *that p* – he may have V'd for some other reason, or may have V'd without any reason.

If *that p* is a reason for A to V, then reasoning from the premiss that *p*, in the context of other premisses pertinent to A's situation and goals, may support the conclusion to V. But that warrant is defeasible by reference to additional data, including countervailing reasons. Justification may be a matter of degree – one may have complete justification, or only some justification. Reasons may be cumulative; they may conflict and have to be 'weighed' one against another. Because there are degrees (quantities) of justification, the justificative use of 'reason', unlike its explanatory use, allows occurrence as a mass noun, as when we speak of there *being reason* to think, *some reason* to feel, *little reason* to do.

The explanatory and justificative uses of 'reason' come together in what are the most distinctive forms of teleological explanation of human action: 'A's reason for V-ing was that p' and 'A's reason for V-ing was to W'. 'Reason', thus employed, is always *attributive* (since it is the action of a person, or artificial person, such as a company, college, or government, that is to be explained) and is never a mass noun. Specification of what A did – his V-ing – is factive (otherwise there is nothing to explain). Specification of A's reason in the form 'that p' is likewise factive. Less so is specification of a person's reason in the form 'to W', 'in order to W', or 'in order to attain G'. 'A's reason for V-ing was to attain goal G' explains why he V'd, gives his reason for V-ing, even if V-ing did not, as it happened, lead to the attainment of the goal. So, for example, 'His reason for investing in Crooks Electrics was *to make a quick fortune*' requires no qualification if he lost his investment next day when Crooks went bankrupt. But 'His reason for investing in Crooks Electrics was *that he would make a fortune by doing so*' demands a parenthetical addendum if he made no fortune. An appropriate insertion (*mutatis mutandis*) of 'as far as he knew' or 'to the best of his knowledge' in a sentence of the form 'His reason for V-ing was that p' cancels the factivity of the that-clause). In this sense, the factivity of 'A's reason was that p' can be said to be *defeasible*. In such cases, we explain A's V-ing by reference to *his* reasoning, to his *mistaken* apprehension of his situation or his *mistaken* belief.

Note that where factivity is thus cancelled, it is still *what the agent believed*, and not his believing it, that explains his V-ing. What he believed was false, but his reasoning was from what he believed, namely that p, to the conclusion to V – that was how he reasoned, and that he reasoned thus explains why he did what he did. Commonly, rather than cancelling the factivity of 'his reason was that p' by insertion of a parenthetical 'as far as he knew' or 'to the best of his knowledge', we may avoid the implication of truth by other means: we may say 'he V'd because he *believed* that p' or 'because he *thought* he had a reason, namely that p'. For if it is false that p, then *the fact* that p cannot have been a reason for him to V, since it is not a fact that p. It would, however, be mistaken to suppose that this form of explanation adverts to his believing whatever he believes and explains his acting by reference to his believing (conceived as a mental state that caused him to act) rather than by reference to what he falsely believed. Cancellation of factivity apart, if there was a reason for A to V, namely that p, and A knew that p and knew that p's being the case was a reason for him to V, and he V'd *because p* (or *in order* to W), then A's reason for V-ing was that *p* (or to W). We shall investigate below how the 'because' is to be understood.

The general form 'A's reason for V-ing was that *p*' also applies to cases where V-ing is, for example, believing, expecting, fearing, hoping, suspecting, assuming, supposing, etc., that *q*. These are not actions, although they may be rational and reasonable or irrational and unreasonable, depending upon the reasons A has that warrant or seem to warrant them, and the reasons for which he actually V'd. Our focus, however, will be upon 'rational' explanation of *acting* or *refraining from action*. It should be noted that explanations of A's V-ing by reference to his reasons for V-ing can be incorporated in explanations of the form 'the reason why *p* (e.g. why A V'd) is that *q*' (where *q* is A's reason for V-ing). Here factivity is not cancellable, so if it is not the case that *q*, we explain why A V'd by reference to his believing that *q*.

Philosophers have sometimes raised the 'ontological' question of what reasons are. To the question 'What are causes?', philosophers have commonly answered (wrongly, as we have seen): 'Events, and only events, are causes.' One may ask, in the same ontological frame of mind, 'What are reasons?' One answer is that reasons are *facts*, facts that can be cited in giving reasons, and the statement of which can occur as premises in reasoning. This is, or can be, misleading inasmuch as it suggests an ontological insight that identifies what kinds of entities reasons are. But facts are not any kind of *entity*. Against the ontological claim are the following considerations:

(i) The factivity of reason specifications of the form 'A's reason was that *p*' is, as we have seen, defeasible or cancellable. When undefeated, one can indeed say that what was A's reason, namely that *p*, is a fact; that is, that it is the case that *p*. To say that reasons are facts amounts to no more than the broadly correct observation that specification of reasons in the form of nominal clauses is factive: that is, that if A's reason for V-ing was that *p*, then *p*. It is not an 'ontological classification' of reasons.

(ii) The supposition that anything that can serve as a reason for a person's V-ing is a fact misleadingly stretches the use of the term 'fact' to include a priori truths (e.g. that $25^2 = 625$, or that red is darker than pink) that are certainly not *matters of fact*, as well as ethical norms (e.g. that it is wrong to kill or right to be fair) that are not usefully classifiable as *facts*, and the assertion of which is not a *statement of fact*. But they can occur as premises in reasoning, can be proposed as reasons, and can be cited as a person's reasons for thinking or not thinking, doing or not doing, something.

(iii) It delimits, without warrant, the forms of words that can be adduced in giving a person's reason for thinking, feeling, resolving or doing something. We have noted that in addition to the nominal form 'A's reason for V-ing was *that p*', we also specify an agent's reason by means of an infinitive clause, as in 'His reason for going to London was *to see the Queen*', 'His reason for going abroad was *to get rich*', or 'His reason for castling was *to avoid being put in check*'. Any implied factivity here is patently weak – to attain G may well have been A's reason for V-ing even if he failed to attain G despite V-ing. One might claim that the infinitive forms can always be paraphrased by the factive nominal form. This is doubtful, but even if true, it is not obvious why the possibility of such paraphrasis shows that reasons are facts. We certainly learn to respond to 'Why are you V-ing?' with answers that specify the purpose of our action – namely, 'In order to W' or 'In order to get G' – long before we learn to array them in the regimented lines of the nominal forms of a practical syllogism. So we should surely admit that reasons can be given in *various* forms, even if they can always be arrayed in nominal clauses.

The question 'What (kinds of entities) are reasons?' is as misleading and fruitless as the question 'What (kinds of entities) are beliefs?'[9] The only appropriate answer is: they are not any kinds of entities. It is better to ask how we use the term 'reason' (or 'belief') and what needs the concept meets.

---

[9] What is believed, not the believing of it. It is sometimes held that since beliefs (i.e. believings) are 'propositional attitudes', what one believes when one believes that *p* is the proposition that *p*. But that is mistaken. One *can* believe propositions, as one can believe statements, announcements, stories and rumours. But to believe that *p* is not the same as believing the proposition that *p*. If it were, then what A believes to be so could not be the same as what B suspects and C fears to be so, since one surely cannot suspect or fear propositions. The Russellian term 'propositional attitude' exemplified Russell's confusions, and its current widespread adoption perpetuates them. Most of the psychological verbs that can take nominal clauses as objects do not or need not signify attitudes towards propositions, and commonly do not even signify attitudes. Strikingly, verbs that can often be construed as signifying attitudes towards propositions and their kin, such as 'ridicule', 'endorse', 'dismiss', 'repudiate', typically *exclude* the construction with a that-clause: one may ridicule, endorse or dismiss a claim, proposition or rumour that *p*, but one cannot ridicule, endorse or dismiss that *p* (see B. Rundle, 'Objects and Attitudes', *Language and Communication*, 21 (2001), p. 147).

A may have *a* reason for V-ing. This reason may be *decisive* or not decisive. If it is decisive, then it would be irrational or at any rate unreasonable for A not to V in the circumstances. If it is not decisive, then there is some reason for A to V, but failure to V is not irrational or unreasonable. What one chooses to do when one's reasons for action are not decisive reveals one's preferences and tastes, and so too one's temperament and character. There may be *multiple reasons* for A to V. These may conjunctively support or decisively determine the conclusion to V. But some of the reasons may individually provide decisive reason to V, and therefore conjunctively overdetermine the conclusion to V. If A then V's, the question of what his reason for V-ing was may arise: did he V for the reason that *p*, or did he V for the reason that *q*? The answer to this question is often crucial for the evaluation of his act and his character. We shall revert to this matter below.

There may be reason for A to V and also reason not to V. Obligations may conflict, duty and inclination may clash, passion may war with prudence, and self-interest with the welfare of others. The agent, aware of such *conflicting* reasons, must 'weigh' them against each other and decide where the 'balance of reasons' lies. There may not always be an answer to this question. Sometimes the conflicting reasons may be *incommensurable*. Then the choice that must be made cannot be made 'on the balance of reasons'. It does not follow that deciding what to do is arbitrary – it would be grossly inappropriate to toss a coin when deciding whether to join the Free French in Britain or remain in occupied France to take care of one's aged mother.[10] Nor does it follow that it is universalizable. One may conclude that doing what one painfully chooses is 'the only thing one can do', while recognizing that another person, in a like situation, might, with equal justice, decide differently for himself. In making such 'existential choices', one also *determines* one's nature.

3. Explaining human behaviour

Human behaviour is varied in type, reflecting both the manifold abilities of mankind and the complexity of social forms of life and associated institutions. The vocabulary of act descriptions is correspondingly rich and variegated. We need, and often want, to under-

---

[10] The example is Sartre's, but I am putting it to a different use.

stand our fellow human beings – for we are social creatures, living in close contact with, and in various forms of co-operative and competitive relationships with others. So, when their behaviour is not transparent, or when a tale of their behaviour is opaque, we ask for explanation. Correspondingly, we give others an account of our own behaviour. We strive, sometimes, to make ourselves intelligible to others. We tell others fragments of our autobiography – for amusement, to elicit sympathy or induce interest, to vindicate or exculpate, as example or counterexample. In the course of so doing, we explain our behaviour (as well as our thoughts and feelings) in a variety of kinds of ways, of which explanation in terms of agential reasons is but one. *What* we thus explain can be variously characterized in terms of control, intellect and will, on the one hand, and in terms of a variety of forms of context-sensitive descriptions on the other. These constrain in various ways the kinds of explanations that are possible and delimit the scope of explanation in terms of reasons. So, before we examine the categories of explanation of behaviour, we must first sketch the various ways of characterizing the explananda.

(1) *Behaviour: control, intellect and will.* As already noted (pp. 123f., 145f.), human behaviour can be mere doing that falls short of action. We may slip, stumble, choke – these are not actions we perform voluntarily, not voluntarily or involuntarily. Some of the things we do are unchosen *reactions*, such as blushing, weeping, laughing, sneezing, trembling. Some of these, although not such as can be initiated at will, can often be stopped or partially suppressed at will. To that extent they verge upon the voluntary. The category of human action is the category of the kinds of things human beings can do or refrain from doing at will.[11] Accordingly, acts can be chosen, attempted and intended. One can deliberate whether to V,

---

[11] So, as previously intimated (p. 109) perceiving in its various generic modes is not action, although watching, looking, gazing and peeking, and listening to, as well as listening for, are. Similarly, deciding, changing one's mind, and in some cases, thinking and imagining are exercises of two-way powers and can be done at will (voluntarily, intentionally, on purpose). But we would not count them as forms of *behaviour*, and *in some contexts* not even as acts or action.

It is noteworthy that certain kinds of success-descriptions, e.g. 'win', 'solve', 'discover', do not signify actions but only things done. Accordingly, one can ask for the reason why A won, but one cannot ask for A's reason for winning, solving or discovering (see A. R. White (ed.), *The Philosophy of Action* (Oxford University Press, Oxford, 1968),'Introduction', p. 3).

decide to V, be asked or ordered to V. Depending upon the disposition of one's will and intellect, one can V impulsively, intentionally, deliberately, willingly or reluctantly, thoughtfully or thoughtlessly.

Action can be voluntary without being intentional:

(i)   if it is an inhibitable response which one has not inhibited, such as a yawn or sneeze – which might be deemed *partly* voluntary;

(ii) if it is done knowingly but neither because one wanted to do it nor for a further reason, as when one whistles while one works or gestures while one speaks (and knows one is so doing);

(iii) if it is knowingly done as an unwanted (or not wanted) consequence or by-product of intentional action, as when one crushes the grass beneath one's feet while walking across the lawn or wakes one's wife when putting the cat out at night.

Intending belongs to a family of concepts that includes *being about to*, *meaning to*, *having it in mind to*, *proposing to* and *planning to*. The objects of intending are varied: one may intend to V; one may intend another to V if one has a form of authority over them; one may intend, or intend another, to be or become a so-and-so; and one may intend a certain state of affairs to obtain if one has appropriate control over whether it comes about or is maintained. Intentional actions, like fully voluntary actions, are an exercise of two-way powers. An intentional action need not be voluntary (action done under duress is not), but it cannot be involuntary. One may form an intention in advance of acting and then act on it (or fail to, because, e.g., one is prevented, one forgets or changes one's mind). Such intention formation may be the upshot of deliberation and decision. But one may act intentionally without any antecedent deliberation or decision. If an agent V's intentionally, he must know that he is V-ing and must be doing so either because he simply wants to, feels inclined to or feels like it, or because he has a reason or further reason for V-ing.

An agent may V with a further intention of X-ing. The further intention in the act may be merely concurrent (as when one goes to the cinema with the intention of having a drink afterwards), or V-ing may be a means to X-ing (as when one climbs up a ladder in order to change a light bulb). In the latter case, but not necessarily in the former, *to X* is A's reason for V-ing, and 'X-ing' (or, in some cases, 'trying to X') is a further description of what A is doing. To say that A's V-ing is intentional is not to give A's reason for V-ing; but to say that A V'd *in order to X* is. Here, to X is A's purpose *in* V-ing *and* his reason for it. One may also V with the intention of doing X, without V-ing intentionally, if one V's accidentally or by mistake – as Tyrrel accidentally killed the king, intending to kill a stag.

Clearly, one may V intentionally, *on* purpose, without V-ing *for* a purpose, as when one V's with the intention of V-ing, as opposed to V-ing unintentionally (unknowingly, by accident or by mistake) or not intentionally (knowing that one is V-ing but not wanting to V, as when one wakes up one's wife while letting the cat out). That one V's with the *further* intention of X-ing does not imply that one's purpose in V-ing is to X. When one goes to the cinema with the intention of catching the 10.30 bus home, one's purpose in going to the cinema is not to catch the bus home. So specifying a further intention with which one V's *need not* give one's reason for V-ing. Specifying one's purpose *in* V-ing, however, does. For one cannot V with the purpose of V-ing, but only V with the purpose of doing something else. To specify the purpose for which one did something is to *explain* why one did it.[12]

Is every intentional act done for a reason? That depends on whether one takes V-ing 'just because one feels like it', or 'because one feels inclined to', as V-ing for a reason. If so, then all intentional action is done for reasons. If not, then one must distinguish between knowingly doing something just because one felt like it, 'for no particular reason' as we sometimes say, from acting intentionally for a reason. Certainly to feel a sudden urge or impulse to V is not necessarily to have a reason for V-ing, and to V because one feels an urge or impulse to is not necessarily to act for a reason. The urge, impulse or craving may be 'quite mad' – that is, completely irrational.

The consequences of our intentional actions may themselves be intentional, unintentional (if not foreseen) or not intentional (e.g. if foreseen but not part of the agent's purpose) and the agent's action may accordingly be redescribed in terms of its consequences. For example, if the agent opened the door, as a consequence of which the room cooled down, then he either intentionally, unintentionally or not intentionally cooled the room down by opening the door. The act, thus described, obviously admits of various kinds of explanation, depending on whether it is intentional or not, and, if not intentional, whether done knowingly or unknowingly, voluntarily or not voluntarily, by accident or by mistake, and so forth.

---

[12] See A. R. White, *Grounds of Liability: An Introduction to the Philosophy of Law* (Clarendon Press, Oxford, 1985), pp. 73–5.

The cognitive and volitional character of the behaviour under consideration can often restrict the range or even determine the character of the explanation that might be offered for it. One cannot have a reason for doing something involuntarily or a motive for doing something inadvertently, and one cannot ask for the point of someone's doing something unknowingly. One can ask for the purpose of an intentional action, but not of an unintentional one.

(2) *Behaviour: alternative descriptions.* Human behaviour can be described in a large variety of ways. Often it can be described in terms of physical movements. Whether the movements are merely the movements of the agent's limbs and body ('his knee jerked') or whether they are movements the agent *makes* ('he moved his leg') constrains the kinds of explanation appropriate. But there are many things human beings do, and for which we may want an explanation, which are not movement-involving, such as thinking of a solution or planning a move; looking at a painting, watching a scene, listening to or for a noise; waiting for a bus; keeping the door open, holding tight, gripping firmly; concentrating on a problem, a lecture or on what one is looking at; omitting, abstaining or refraining from doing something.

Whether or not behaviour is movement-involving, it can be described or redescribed in many different ways, by reference to its antecedents (as is patent in such verbs as *to reply, repeat, re-enter, requite*), its consequences (e.g. such causative verbs as *to break, mend, dry, wet, open, close, pacify, irritate, console*), or its circumstances. The varieties of ways in which acts can be described or redescribed in terms of their circumstances is large, and can be variously classified. Describing an act in terms of its circumstances specifies it, often as a species of a larger genus of a given kind of act. Commonly, act descriptions can be analysed in terms of a simpler act and the specifying circumstance, as *perjury*, for example, is telling a lie in the circumstance that one is under oath, or *bigamy* getting married in the circumstance of already being married. The circumstances of an act can be construed narrowly, so as to exclude such subjective factors as voluntariness, knowledge and intention (and their negations), or it can be stretched to include these. Many moral and legal act descriptions incorporate such factors: *to steal* is to take something, knowing one has no title to it; *to lie* is to tell an untruth with intent to deceive. Acts can also be described in terms of the manner of their performance (e.g. *mumble one's thanks, hurry to school*), or in relation to the identity or some feature of the patient affected by their performance (*suicide* determines the identity of the patient with the agent, *rape* requires the unwillingness of the patient). A multitude of acts, as is evident from the foregoing examples, are described by reference to social, moral or legal norms that prohibit them (e.g. *murder*, *trespass*), require them (*pay taxes, obtain a license*), or make them possible (*marry, make a will, score a goal, checkmate one's opponent*).

The character of the description of behaviour that requires explanation commonly excludes certain kinds of explanation. Acts that by their nature can be performed only once (such as suicide) cannot be explained in tendency or frequency terms, such as habit and custom (a suicidal tendency is not a tendency to commit suicide, but a standing temptation to do so). Acts that by definition or description are mistakes or accidents cannot be explained in terms of reasons, purposes or motives; nor can involuntary acts or doings that are not acts (such as slipping or stumbling). Acts that can be performed only intentionally, such as *cheating, lying, forging*, exclude explanation in terms of inadvertence and inattention. Certain kinds of omissions can be explained by reference to lack of legal power or right. But possession of legal (or other normative) power does not explain why an agent exercised it on an occasion, it explains only that it was possible for him to do so.

(3) *The varieties of explanation.* Citing an agent's reasons for thinking, feeling or doing something explains why he thought, felt or did what he did. It is *one* form, perhaps the most distinctive and important form, of explaining human thought, feeling and action. But it is not the only form, and before we examine its conceptual character in further detail, we should bring to mind the variety of explanations of human behaviour.

'Why did A V?' is the most general form of a request for an explanation of A's doing what he did, and it can accordingly elicit any form of explanation of human behaviour, depending only upon the constraints imposed by the description of what the agent did. The kinds of answers that can be offered to explain behaviour are delimited not only by the description of the act, but also by the kind of question. For commonly the speaker phrases his question in a manner that restricts the possible answers. 'What did A V *for*?' is a request for the point and purpose of an act, and it presupposes its intentionality. It precludes various forms of efficient-causal explanation, as well as explanations in terms of ignorance and inadvertence. 'What made A V?' can be asked if V-ing was not an act of A, but something he did (such as stumble, slip, or choke), or if it was an act, but one which was distinctly uninviting, unreasonable or irrational – something which A would not have done but for the explanatory factor. In the first kind of case, the question invites a causal explanation: A slipped because the pavement was icy; he fell because he was pushed; he choked because a piece of bread got stuck in his throat. In the second kind of case, an explanation in terms of an obliging factor is invited: he divulged the secret because he was threatened; he took the slow road because the motorway was closed. But a causal explanation is also possible in some such cases: for example, he acted as a result of post-hypnotic suggestion.

We can distinguish (non-exhaustively) the following forms of explanation of behaviour:[13]

(i) *Explanations in terms of constitutive redescription.* We are sometimes puzzled by certain kinds of ritualized, semi-ritualized or otherwise rule-governed activities. Why are these people gathered together and behaving thus? They are engaged in a political demonstration, a trade union dispute, or are celebrating a victory, commemorating an event, attending a wedding, a funeral or a memorial service, playing a game, and so forth. Here the explanation consists in redescribing the behaviour in its broader social setting and with reference to social norms. In *this setting*, behaving thus *counts as* doing so-and-so. Understanding what they are doing in these terms often resolves our puzzlement, for we may need no further explanation of why they are doing what they are doing *thus* described.

(ii) *Explanation by polymorphous redescription.* A quite different kind of explanation by redescription is explaining a specific activity in terms of its polymorph, as when we explain someone's shutting the door as obeying an order, someone's singing as practising for a recital, someone's visiting as his keeping his promise.

(iii) *Regularity explanations.* We commonly explain behaviour as an instance of a regularity. Why is Emma going for a walk? – It is a *habit* of hers to go for a walk every afternoon. Why is Mr Darcy changing his clothes? – It is *customary* to dress for dinner at Pemberley.

---

[13] For illuminating discussions of hermeneutics, see A. J. P. Kenny, *Action, Emotion and the Will* (Routledge & Kegan Paul, London, 1963) and *Will, Freedom and Power* (Blackwell, Oxford, 1975); B. Rundle, *Mind in Action* (Clarendon Press, Oxford, 1997); G. H. von Wright, *Explanation and Understanding* (Routledge & Kegan Paul, London, 1971) and *Practical Reason* (Blackwell, Oxford, 1983), essays 1–5; and A. R. White, *Philosophy of Mind* (Random House, New York, 1967), ch. 6.

Why did Fanny Price hesitate to ask Sir Thomas? – Because she is timid (a *disposition* and *character trait*). It is noteworthy that these different kinds of regularity explanations are not causal, and the explanation is not subsumption-theoretic despite the fact that the behaviour is explained as instantiating a regularity. They do not exclude explanations in terms of agential reasons, but they indicate that the behaviour is not exceptional. In many cases, no further explanation is required.

(iv) *Inclination explanations.* We often explain behaviour as exemplifying a preference (that may be without reason) or liking either for the specific thing or activity in question, or for things or activities of the kind in question, or a dislike for some thing or activity. The inclination explanation, in the cases of likings and dislikings, may also refer to a regularity. Sometimes we explain behaviour by reference to feelings that involve inclinations, as when we attribute A's outburst to his feeling indignant (hence feeling inclined to protest) or greedy (hence feeling inclined to take a second helping of pudding). Occurrently felt emotions and attitudes such as anxiety, fear, tenderness, pity, amusement, curiosity are all associated with inclinations to behave, and conduct is commonly explained by reference to such a felt inclination. Hence someone may be trembling *out of* fear, laughing *with* amusement, their tears may be tears *of* tenderness or pity. The behaviour that we explain thus is not caused by the emotion but is an expression of it.

(v) *Causal explanations.* Causal explanations obviously play a significant role in rendering human behaviour intelligible – but not the ubiquitous role that philosophers who conceive of reasons as causes suppose. We explain doings that are not actions, such as stumbling, slipping or blushing, in terms of causes. We explain many involuntary or only partially voluntary actions causally: he laughed because he was being tickled, cried out because he was hit, sneezed because he had taken snuff. Whether, in what sense and to what extent, intentional action can be explained causally will be examined in section 5 below.

(vi) *Explanations in terms of reasons.* Intentional action is the primary object of explanation of behaviour in terms of agential reasons. Saying 'I just intended to V', unlike saying 'I just wanted to', does not explain one's V-ing. But specifying one's purpose (which is *one* kind of 'intention with which') does. However, there are many other kinds of factor that can be an agent's reason for acting. We can classify them in numerous different ways: facts and values, norms and obligations, backward- and forward-looking reasons (past facts, prospective consequences, purposes and goals). It is a moot point whether desires, wants and preferences, on the one hand, and beliefs (the believing, not what is believed), on the other, should be regarded as reasons for doing anything. Some philosophers have argued that *all* reasons are desires and beliefs, or combinations thereof. Others insist that desires are not reasons at all – it is the reason for wanting to V that is a reason for V-ing; and believing is rarely a reason for acting – it is what is believed that is normally a reason. We shall examine this below.

(vii) *Motive explanations.* Motive explanations are more specialized than explanations in terms of reasons.[14] To give A's motive for V-ing (e.g. revenge) need not be the same as giving his reason (e.g. that B killed his father). Acting out of a given motive is not the same as exemplifying a disposition – A may act out of revenge on a single occasion without being of a vengeful disposition. To act out of irritability, timidity or conceit is not to act from any particular motive. Motives are not feelings, even though a person's behaviour can be explained by reference to the motive of pity or love. One may feel pity or love, overflow with compassion or affection – but one cannot feel one's motives or overflow with them. To say that someone acted out of anger is not to explain his behaviour by reference to a motive, but by reference to an emotion. Motives, unlike feelings and emotions, cannot be pleasant or unpleasant, do not wax and wane, and do not occur at a given time or place. They are not kinds of mental event or state, but kinds of explanation. One salient type of motive explanation specifies a *pattern* of backward- and forward-looking reasons. To say that A V'd B out of gratitude is to explain A's V-ing by reference to B's having intentionally benefited A (a form of backward-looking reason), and A's V-ing in order to requite B's generosity. But A's specific reason – for example, that A provided him with a generous loan when he needed one – is not mentioned. Similarly, to explain A's V-ing B as done out of revenge is to explain the action in terms of B's having harmed A or an interest of his, and A's acting in order to harm B in return. But A's specific reason for V-ing B – for example, that B killed his father – is not specified. In

[14] See Kenny, *Action, Emotion and the Will*, ch. 4, and White, *Philosophy of Mind*, ch. 6. Note that motive explanations must not be confused with motive attributions, which typically specify forward-looking reasons, as when we say that A had a motive for the crime: viz. that he stood to inherit the victim's estate. *Having a motive*, in this sense, amounts to there being a reason for the agent to V, and unlike *acting for a reason*, does not imply that the agent performed the deed at all.

many cases, the pattern is of a remedy-demanding antecedent circumstance that provides a backward-looking reason for acting, an action with a certain intention, and a prospective consequence that is thought to remedy the prior condition – thus providing a forward-looking reason. Differences between motives (e.g. between ambition, greed, patriotism, vindictiveness, gratitude) are then evident in the kinds of antecedent remedy-demanding condition and the kinds of prospective values or advantages aimed at. Some motives, such as revenge, friendship or gratitude, involve not merely acts done with an intention *that exemplifies* a pattern, but acts that can be done with the intention *of exemplifying* a pattern. Here one can speak of acting *in order* to wreak vengeance or *to show* friendship or gratitude (for an overview, see fig. 7.2).

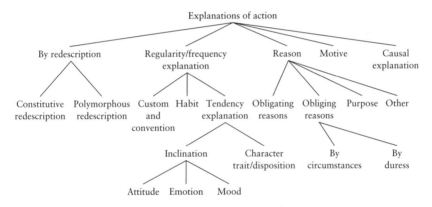

Figure 7.2. *Schema of types of explanation of action*

To these forms of explanation of action we may add further forms of explanation distinctive of *inaction*:

(i)   inability, physical, technical (skill) or intellectual
(ii)   prevention, natural or human
(iii)   lack of equipment
(iv)   lack of opportunity
(v)   ignorance of opportunity
(vi)   forgetting one's intention
(vii)   lack of normative power

The question of why A did not V may be just as pressing as the question of why he did.

It should be noted that some factors can be cited when offering one kind of explanation which may be logically excluded from another. So anger may be a factor in an explanation in terms of a passion, and timidity a factor in a regularity explanation, but neither can occur in a motive explanation. Values (fairness, filial piety, friendship) and norms (obligation, duty, rightness) may be cited as factors in explanations in terms of reasons, but not as factors in causal explanations.

4. Explanation in terms of agential reasons

We noted that a person's reason for V-ing can be given by means of a nominal clause 'that p' or by means of infinitive clauses 'in order to W' or 'to attain G' ('His reason for going to London was to see the Queen', 'To attain fame was Hume's reason for writing the book', 'He went to Egypt for no other reason than to see the Great Pyramid'). We commonly use the infinitive clause when we explain why A V'd by specifying his reason in the form of his goal or purpose (that for the sake of which he acted). But we also explain A's behaviour in terms of his *reasoning* (actual or counterfactual). Here we give his reason in the form of a nominal clause that can appear, denominalized, as a premiss in reasoning that supports the conclusion to V. So the infinitive clause that was used in explaining that he V'd in order to attain G will find its correlate in a premiss citing a goal or desire for an end.

A's reason for V-ing can be *that p* or *in order to* W or *to attain* G only if A knows or believes that p or that V-ing is a way of W-ing, or a means to W, or necessary to attain G.[15] A reason, specified in sentential form, is a step in reasoning. If *that R* is A's reason for V-ing, then *that R*, in conjunction with other premisses, must support, or be thought by A to support, the conclusion to V. But it would be mistaken to suppose that whenever A V's for the reason that R, he goes through a process of reasoning 'in his head', let alone aloud. Often what is to be done is too obvious to require, or too pressing

---

[15] In certain cases, *that p* may be A's reason for V-ing even though it makes no sense for A to know (or not to know) or believe (or not to believe) that p: e.g. if his reason is *that he is in pain*. For examination of these kinds of cases, see P. M. S. Hacker, 'Of Knowledge and of Knowing that Someone is in Pain', in A. Pichler and S. Säätelä (eds), *Wittgenstein: The Philosopher and his Works* (Wittgenstein Archives of the University of Bergen, Bergen, 2005), pp. 203–35.

to allow, any deliberation, yet one can give reasons for one's action. Often what is done is spontaneous – but not therefore without reason. To give one's reasons for V-ing is not the same as reporting on one's reasoning.

There are various criteria for something's being A's reason for V-ing. Typically, they consist in the antecedents and context of his action. Often a person's reason for doing what he does is patent – seeing that it is raining, he puts up his umbrella; having been told that a ticket costs a pound, he hands over a pound coin; wanting a drink, he says to the bartender 'May I have a scotch'. There is nothing mysterious about our ability to discern immediately the reasons for much of our fellow human beings' behaviour. We see the actions of other human beings, in the contexts in which they are embedded, as intentional, purposive and commonly conventional – that is, governed by constitutive rules that define the act and its meaning. We do not see them as mere 'bodily movements' (similarly, we see the world around us as consisting of relatively persistent coloured material substances in objective space and time, and not as expanses of colour, here, now, in one's 'subjective' visual field).[16] But sometimes it is *not* obvious what another person is doing, or it is opaque what his reasons are for doing what he is doing. So we may ask him. If he sincerely says that his reason for V-ing is that R, then, normally, that R *is* his reason for V-ing. Looked at askew, this can seem mysterious. If the agent's answer is not a report on the reasoning he has just gone through, on what he said aloud or to himself, what exactly is it? How does he know what his reason is or was? Is it a hypothesis of his that his reason was that R? Why should his word be accepted? What sort of *authority* (if any) does his word have, and whence does it derive?

One way to approach these questions is 'analytic-genetic': that is, to reflect on how we might conceive of the roots of the language-game of giving reasons for our actions. A human child, like other young mammals, finds a multitude of things in his environment attractive or repulsive, sources of pleasure or of fear and dislike, and objects of curiosity with regard to his 'interference' in the course of things. He learns to act in pursuit of what he wants, and, as his rudimentary linguistic skills develop, he learns to supplement his frustrated strivings and screamings to get with a 'Want!', and subsequently to substitute

---

[16] In both cases, what is presented by philosophers as a foundation is actually an abstraction.

for them an 'I want' and, later still, 'I want the (or a) so-and-so' (such utterances, it should be noted, are not reports on his mental state). As his motor skills develop, he learns to manipulate objects in his environment, and learns what happens when he acts on (pokes, pushes, pulls, throws) them. Rapidly, he, like any other young mammal, learns to bring about such-and-such by doing so-and-so. But, unlike other young mammals, he is learning to speak. Once he has mastered the rudiments of speech, the child may be asked *what* he is doing or trying to do, *why* he wants to do what he is trying to do, *what* his purpose is in doing what he is doing. He learns to describe his actions. Later he learns a new language-game: the practice of announcing an action: 'I'm going to V' – for which he must learn that when one says 'I'm going to V', one must go on to V. Here lie the primitive roots of intention formation in advance of action, of our non-inductive knowledge of our own future actions, and of the relative predictability of the action of others on the basis of announced intention. (If announced intentions for the immediate future were not typically followed by the intended action, the very concept of intention would lose its point.)

Once this language-game is in place, there is room for further questions: namely, 'Why are you going to V?', and for answers of the form 'In order to W', 'To get X', and 'Because I want X' – that is, specification of one kind of reason – namely, the purpose of V-ing, that for the sake of which the V-ing is to be done. The answer 'Because I want X' invites the question: 'Why do you want X?', and the child learns to specify what it is about X that is attractive or appealing – he learns to give a further kind of reason: namely, to specify a desirability characteristic. And the child also learns to specify what it wants X *for* – for example, to eat it, or to play with it, or as a means to a further end. Here we have the beginnings of reasoning and of giving reasons. It is noteworthy (and not contingent) that reasoning marches hand in hand with intention formation. The transition from voluntary and purposive action that lies within the competence of mere animals to intended and deliberative action is an aspect of the emergence of rationality. The child's emergent rationality is his growing ability to reason from given data to conclusions. A criterion for his reasoning thus is his answering such questions. To learn to answer such questions, to learn what *counts* as an adequate answer, is itself to learn to reason.

In sincerely saying that his reason for V-ing is that R, the agent need not be recounting the reasoning he has just gone through – he may not have gone through any. So what makes it his reason for V-ing? *He* makes it his reason. For although one cannot choose to *have* a reason to V, one can, reflecting on the reasons one has, choose or decide to V, *for* such-and-such a reason (rather than from another reason (that one has)). It is *this* reason, not *that* one, that one takes to be decisive, or that one takes to justify, one's V-ing. It by reference to *this* factor, not *that* one, that one would justify one's decision and that one would subsequently cite to explain why one did what one did. It is not that he decides to-V-for-the-reason-that-R, but rather for the reason that R (and not for the reason that S) he decides to V. If A is told to leave the room by B, he may say, 'I am leaving the room because you told me to', or he may say 'I am leaving the room, but *not* because you told me to'.[17] What his reason is for leaving the room is a matter of his *reasoning* – he decides to V *for that reason*, and his avowal of his reason characterizes his action. Each reply, in different scenarios, may indicate very different things. The first may indicate A's compliance and willingness to obey; or it may signify resentment (since he would not have left the room otherwise); or it may be meant to shift responsibility for A's absence on to B. The second reply may signify A's indignation at something that preceded the order to leave; or outrage at B's impertinence; or to notify B that A was going to leave anyway; or to remonstrate that despite appearances, A would not dream of taking orders from B.

In sincerely giving his reason, A provides *others* with an interpretation of his behaviour – a particular way of understanding it; but *he* does not interpret it. The way of understanding he thus provides them with is *his* way of understanding his own behaviour – the way *he* conceives it. In *saying* that he is V-ing because it is the case that R, A is not merely citing the fact that R as a reason for him to V; he is *declaring* it to be his reason for V-ing, *endorsing* a particular teleological explanation of his V-ing, and taking responsibility for it under the description 'V-ing, for the reason that R'.[18] Patently, his reason for V-ing is not something he discovers to be such, nor is it a hypothesis of his – although he may lie to others and may deceive himself. What is sometimes denominated 'first-person authority' in

---

[17] The example is Wittgenstein's; see *Philosophical Investigations*, §487.

[18] An account of this kind was intimated by Wittgenstein, *Philosophical Investigations*, §§487–9, and developed by G. H. von Wright, 'Of Human Freedom', repr. in his *In the Shadow of Descartes* (Kluwer, Dordrecht, 1998), pp. 20–7.

these contexts is mischaracterized thus. The agent is not 'an authority' on his own reasons for acting, as he might be an authority on Sanskrit literature. His sincere word is *a criterion* for his reason's being that R, but not because he *infers* this from evidence he has which others lack.

This hermeneutic account illuminates cases of an agent's giving his reasons for V-ing *ex post actu* where he went through no reasoning, and where his giving his reasons is neither recounting his reasoning nor reporting an explicit decision to V for the reason that R. Here, one might think, the agent's ability to explain or justify his action by citing his reason *is* mysterious. For if there is nothing for him to remember by way of reasoning, how can he *now* say what his reason for V-ing *was*? One might suggest that in declaring the fact that R to have been his reason, he is averring that he *would have* cited the fact that R as his reason had he been asked. This can be misleading. Although it may be true that had he been asked, he would have given the fact that R as his reason, this counterfactual is not a hypothesis based on past experience. After all, the normal form of thus giving one's reasons for a past action is not 'I think my reason was that R', or 'Judging by my reason for V-ing last time, it is probable that my reason was that R'. Indeed, were someone to respond thus in standard cases, we would doubt his sanity. Nor is saying that his reason was that R a matter of 'inner observation' – as if he were, so to speak, reporting a causal connection 'seen from the inside'. For there is no such thing as *introspectively observing* his reason 'at work', so to speak, since introspection is not a form of observation, and reasons don't 'work' – they are neither causal agents nor mental events.

The ability to give one's reasons *ex post actu* should be compared with the ability a speaker has to say what he meant by an utterance (e.g. 'He is by the bank') or whom or what he meant by a demonstrative or indexical in his utterance (e.g. 'He'll be there then'). The question of how the speaker *knows* what his reasons are or were, *in the standard case*, should be rejected as being as misconceived as the question of how a person knows what he means or meant.

The agent's avowal of a reason *ex post actu* must render intelligible the intention in the act. For it must present the reasoning that he holds to warrant the act, even though, *ex hypothesi*, he went through no reasoning. It must provide his rationale for having performed it. So the reason he gives must cohere with the context of his action, the motivational background and his subsequent behaviour. (Failure so to cohere, and, in some cases, failure to cohere with his general behavioural dispositions, may cast doubt on his sincerity or on his self-understanding and self-knowledge.) The agent, we assume, knows now what he then knew or was aware of (which others, trying to understand why he acted as he did, may not know), and he knows now what he then believed (otherwise he may say that he cannot recollect why he V'd). He also knew what he was doing (otherwise he was not acting intentionally) and still knows , and knows whether he succeeded or failed to do what he was aiming to do (so he can, in appropriate cases, say what he was trying to do). So citing his purpose as the reason why he V'd is little more than being able to elaborate what his intention in the action was. Citing backward-looking reasons for his V-ing (e.g. that he was responding to B's X-ing and not to C's Y-ing), none of which he stated (either overtly or *sotto voce*) at the time, since he acted purposefully without reflection or deliberation, is not to *interpret* his action. That is something others may do, or he may do under very special circumstances of self-doubt. Rather, it is to *determine* its character. In saying that his reason for V-ing was that R, he is making a connection between what he knew or believed to be so and his action (or his action and re-collected purpose). In making that connection, he is endorsing a certain kind of description of his behaviour, and taking responsibility for it under that description.

Where an agent has (or had) multiple reasons for V-ing and avows that he is V-ing (or V'd) for one reason rather than another (because it would help Jack, not because Jill was looking; because it was right, not because it was also profitable), doubts may arise. He may be lying. He may be deceiving himself with regard to his own motivation. Or his motivation may be intrinsically, not epistemically, opaque. Here is an aspect of human behaviour and its understanding that can be constitutionally indeterminate. A may insist, in all sincerity, that he V'd for the reason that p, but B may repudiate A's explanation, insisting that he V'd for the rather less reputable reason that q. A may persuade B of the correctness of his explanation (it never even occurred to him that q). Alternatively, B may convert A to seeing his own behaviour differently, perhaps in the light of facts about his character or facts about his past that he had not brought to mind. Or their disagreement may remain unresolved. Sometimes the failure of resolution may not be epistemic. The facts of the case may all be known, yet lend themselves to more than one perfectly plausible story. In such cases, the disagreement may, sometimes tragically, be unresolvable.

5. Causal mythologies

We have displayed human action for reasons as a form of teleological behaviour, even though it often incorporates backward-looking reasons. But even when an agent acts for backward-looking reasons – for example, thanks B because B did him a favour, or benefits B because B acted meritoriously – A does so *in order* to express gratitude or reward desert – that is his purpose. We have emphasized the role of reasons in *reasoning*, either in advance of acting or after the event. An agent's citation of his reason for V-ing presents a warrant for his behaviour. But the most popular philosophical account of acting for reasons is causal (i.e. in terms of efficient causation). Reasons are held to be causes, and explanation in terms of reasons is argued to be a form of causal explanation.[19] This conception needs to be confronted.

It is bizarre to suppose that reasons are causes, since in reflecting on the reasons for and against doing something or other, one is surely not reflecting on what will *cause* one to do what reason dictates, but rather trying to decide *what* reason dictates. And in recounting, after the act, for what reason one V'd, one is not describing or explaining what *caused* one to V, but what one's *rationale* for V-ing was. Moreover, if one's reason for acting were a cause of one's behaviour, it would be puzzling how it is that one normally *knows* this cause (save in cases of 'mixed motives', self-deception or forms of pathology). For although one can know immediately what startled one (the sudden explosion *made* one jump) or what caused one to slip (the banana skin *made* one slip), it is far from obvious that knowing that

---

[19] The *locus classicus* for the causal conception is D. Davidson's 'Actions, Reasons and Causes' of 1963, repr. in his *Essays on Actions and Events* (Clarendon Press, Oxford, 1980). He held that 'failing a satisfactory alternative, the best argument for a [causal] scheme . . . is that it alone promises to give an account of the "mysterious connection" between reasons and actions' (ibid., p. 11). He did not consider the hermeneutical account I have proposed, but only the so-called logical connection argument. His paper reinstated the Vienna Circle's methodological monism and the Cartesian-empiricist account of action for reasons as movement caused by a mental act, event or state. The promise of an adequate causal account, however, was never fulfilled. For Davidson 'despaired', as he put it, of distinguishing V-ing for the reason that R from V-ing because R (i.e. the right from the wrong causal chain), as when one's desire to bring it about that *p* causes one to tremble, which brings it about that *p*. So 'the best argument' for a causal account of acting for a reason turned out to be no argument at all.

one's reason for going to London is to see the Turner exhibition (but nothing made one go) or knowing that one's reason for staying home is that one promised to do so (but nothing made one stay at home), is comparable.

The causal theorist cannot argue that when one cites one's reason for V-ing, either in advance of, or after, acting, the reason is the cause of one's acting. For it is clear that reasons are not causes. One's reason for going to London may be in order to see the exhibition, but *in order to see the exhibition* cannot be a cause of one's going; one's reason for taking an umbrella may be that it is going to rain, but *that it is going to rain* cannot be the cause of one's now taking an umbrella; one's reason for writing '25' in the questionnaire may be that $\sqrt{625} = 25$, but *that $\sqrt{625} = 25$* cannot cause one to write '25'. We *attribute* reasons to an agent: a person can be said to have reasons for V-ing or for refraining from V-ing – but cannot be said to *have a cause for V-ing*. The reasons a person has may be good or poor, selfless or selfish, moral or immoral– but causes cannot be any such thing. Reasons justify or purport to justify the action for which they are a reason, causes do not even purport to do so. Accordingly, reasons may be convincing, defensible, weighty, compelling, persuasive, weak or barely acceptable. But causes can be none of these. The fact that p may not have been A's reason for V-ing, yet it may be *a* reason for V-ing for all that; but one cannot say that if event e_1 was not the cause of e_2, it was a cause for e_2 for all that.

The causal theorist may shift ground and argue not that reasons are causes, but that explanation in terms of reasons is a form of causal explanation. His claim would then be that if an agent wanted goal G and believed that V-ing was a way to attain G and V'd for this reason, then his wants and beliefs conjunctively caused the agent to V. 'If the connection between desire and action is not some kind of causal connection, what kind of connection can it be?', the causal theorist may exclaim; 'Perhaps the adoption of the causal framework is not a mistaken choice, not because it is the correct choice, but because it is inevitable.'[20] It is inevitable, so it is claimed, because no *non-causal* analysis of acting for a reason can explain the difference between

[20] D. Pears, 'Sketch for a Causal Theory of Wanting and Doing', repr. in his *Questions in the Philosophy of Mind* (Duckworth, London, 1975), p. 98.

(i)   A's having a reason (construed as a combination of belief and desire) for V-ing and V-ing, but not V-ing for that reason

and

(ii)   A's having a reason for V-ing and V-ing *for* that very reason.

Only a causal account of acting for a reason can make the relationship between an agent's reason for V-ing and his V-ing for that reason intelligible.[21] But, as should now be clear, that is wrong – the choice is not inevitable, only mistaken. The causal account, as its main defender admitted, cannot explain the relationship. But the hermeneutic account can.

The causal theorist's claim is that reasons are combinations of beliefs and desires. But that is mistaken. That I believe that *p can* be a reason for me to V: for example, if someone says, 'Would everyone here who believes that *p* please raise their hand', then *that I so believe* may be a reason for me to raise my hand. But normally it is not *my believing that p* that is my reason for acting; it is what I believe – namely, *that p*. Indeed, normally the kinds of factors I might cite as my reasons are not even what I *believe* but what I *know* (and it is debatable – though will not be debated here – whether, if I know that *p*, it follows that I believe that *p*). Nor is it obviously true that my wanting to V, as such, is a reason for me to V. If I want to V, then my reason for V-ing is arguably whatever reasons I may have for wanting to V.

The causal theorist may claim that beliefs and desires are mental states, and it is they, or their 'onset' that cause an agent to act when he acts for a reason. But to believe something is not to be in a mental state. Felt desire (feeling thirsty, hungry, lustful) may qualify as a mental state, but *the feeling* is not itself a reason at all, although that one has it may be. And wanting to attain a certain goal is not a feeling. Mental states are paradigmatically moods, occurrent emotions,

---

[21] Davidson held that 'cause and effect form the sort of pattern that explains the effect, in a sense of "explain" that we understand as well as any. If reason and action illustrate a different pattern of explanation, that pattern must be identified' ('Actions, Reasons, and Causes', p. 10). But, as is evident from ch. 3, the causal explanation is surely not generally understood (by philosophers) 'as well as any', and the pattern of explanation in terms of reasons is no *more* problematic. It is no easier to gain an overview of the conceptual field of causes than to attain an overview of that of reasons.

agitations, being in pain, concentrating on something. They obtain when one is awake and lapse with loss of consciousness. They have degrees of intensity, and may wax and wane. They can be interrupted by distraction of attention and later resumed. But if one believes that the battle of Hastings was fought in 1066, one does not cease to believe this when one falls asleep; there are no degrees of believing that the battle of Hastings was fought in 1066 (I can't believe *more* than you, only be more or less *convinced* than you), and one's belief cannot be interrupted by distraction of attention and later resumed.[22] If believing that *p* were a mental state, then it would make sense to say, 'I believe that *p* (thus describing my own mental state B), but it is not the case that *p*'. It would similarly make sense to say, 'I believe that *p* (am in mental state B), but as to whether it is the case that *p*, that, as far as I am concerned, is an open question (or, that is a matter on which I take no stand)'. But these make no sense. For to assert that one believes that *p* is normally to take a stand on whether it is the case that *p*.[23] So to believe something (*a fortiori* to know something) is not to be in any kind of *mental state*.

The contemporary causal theorist may hold that the efficient causes of action are neurophysiological states and events that allegedly are (contingently token-identical with) mental states of believing and wanting. But believing that *p could not be* a neural state, since a neural state could not have the consequences of believing. Asserting that one is in a given neural state S is compatible with going on to deny that *p*, or withholding judgement on whether it is the case that *p*. But asserting that one believes that *p* is not. The only thing that such neurophysiological states and events *could* explain are movements consequent upon muscular contractions, not actions. A neurophysiological explanation of what somatic events were necessary for one to move one's fingers may be available, but it is not an explanation of why one was playing the piano or of why one was playing the *Hammerklavier*, let alone one that renders one's playing intelligible in terms of polymorphous redescription – for example, that one is practising for tomorrow's Beethoven concert or keeping a promise.

---

[22] For detailed defence of the claim that believing that *p* is not a mental state, see P. M. S. Hacker, 'Of the Ontology of Belief', in Mark Siebel and Mark Textor (eds), *Semantik und Ontologie* (Ontos Verlag, Frankfurt, 2004), pp. 194–202.

[23] See A. W. Collins, *The Nature of Mental Things* (University of Notre Dame Press, Notre Dame, Ind. 1987), chs 1–3.

A mere muscular contraction is typically insufficient to determine what act was performed, and its neurophysiological explanation cannot explain whatever act was performed in or by moving voluntarily or intentionally.

Reasons, by contrast, explain acts and omissions. It is true that the agent's wanting to W or to attain G is commonly a factor in explaining his V-ing. But this explains the agent's action, not its constitutive movements. If we are puzzled by a chess-player's gambit, we want an explanation of his move, not of his movement. Neural events in the brain may explain how it is that the chess-player is able to move his hand. If they did not occur as normal, he would not be able to move or control the movements of his hand. But neural events cannot explain his move – only those principles of chess strategy that he was aware of can do that. Nor can they warrant the redescription of his action in terms of its normative consequences – for example, that he checked his opponent.

We have already noted the multivalency of the blurred notion of wanting (pp. 134f.). 'I want/He wants' can be employed to signify the agent's wish, inclination, felt desire (which may be an appetite, a drive, a craving, an urge), endeavour or purpose. The explanatory role of reference to what the agent wants or wanted can be correspondingly various. Sometimes 'I did it because I wanted to' serves merely to exclude other explanations, in particular causal ones. It excludes the possibility of my V-ing's being an involuntary start, a nervous twitch, or an electrical innervation. It identifies what I did as a voluntary *action*, therefore as something for which it *makes sense* to ask for my reason for doing it. It is no more a causal explanation of what I did than 'I did it on purpose'. With such addenda as 'but not because you told me to', it both identifies the action as voluntary and *excludes* one kind of reason.

Often, 'I V'd because I wanted to V' or 'He is V-ing because he wants to' *intimates*, in its context, that the agent finds V-ing in one way or another attractive or appealing, that he likes or enjoys V-ing. These desirability characteristics *are* reasons for wanting to V. So, if he V'd because he wanted to, his V-ing was not instrumental – he was not V-ing with any *further* intent or purpose. His *reason* for V-ing is whatever reason he had for wanting to V. In such cases, normally, V-ing successfully yields satisfaction or gratification. In this use of 'want', a criterion for someone's V-ing because he wants to V is that he is pleased to be V-ing or to have V'd. (Sadly, it sometimes happens that we want to V and do so, only to find it disappointing. Here one's want is satisfied, but that gives one no satisfaction at all.)

'I V'd because I wanted to attain G' *does* explain the speaker's V-ing by giving his reason. But the reason given is his *purpose*: that is, to attain G. 'He V'd because he wanted to attain G' describes the aim of his act, not its psychological cause – one could just as well say 'He V'd *in order to* attain G'. And to say that he V'd in order to attain G is not to specify a cause of anything. It characterizes his act of V-ing as a means (or supposed means) to a goal. It does not signify that the agent V'd out of a desire to V. Here one can say, 'I didn't want to V at all, I did it only in order to attain G.' Did he not 'want the means' (to V), given that he wanted the end (to attain G)? That would be misleading. Certainly the agent's V-ing was an action of his, something he could have refrained from doing – but if it was done under duress, it was not voluntary at all (though not involuntary either). The victim did not *want* to hand over his money to the gunman – he *chose* to, in order to save his life. But there is no reason to assimilate *choice* to *want*. We often choose to do things we don't want to do at all (and in the 'thin' sense in which a philosopher may insist that we want to do whatever we intentionally do, we may want *not to do it* much more than we 'want' to do it – judging by any normal criteria for strength of want).

So, when an agent V's for a further reason, that does *not* mean that he V's because he wants to V. As just noted, he may V under duress – his reason being to avoid the evil consequences of refusing to V. He may V because he has to (it is part of his job), because he promised to, because he was ordered to, or because it is right. He may find V-ing odious, tiresome, and may much prefer to do other things. But the reason for V-ing may outweigh all other considerations. He is not acting because he wants to V but because it is his duty. Does he not *want* to do his duty? No doubt; but that is not his reason for V-ing – which is rather that it *is* his duty to V.

Wanting *can* be a mental state, as when one is gripped by desire, overcome by appetite, beset by a craving. But then *it is not a reason for acting*, although to give quietus to one's craving or appetite may be. More commonly, wanting is not a mental state at all – both when reference to it is merely indicative of purpose (in which case the verb can often be replaced by 'in order to'), and when reference to it is indicative of liking or favouring. To explain an act by reference to wanting to do it, or wanting a further end, is neither to give a causal (nomological) explanation, nor to intimate that there is one. To explain that a person V'd because he wanted to attain G – that is, that he V'd in order to attain G – is not to explain his reason for aiming to attain G. That is explained by the desirability characteristics of G.

The incoherence of the causal tale is made manifest by an argument of Wittgenstein's.[24] Suppose I form the decision to pull the bell rope at five o'clock (I want to call the butler and believe that by pulling the bell rope I shall do so). The clock strikes five. Should I now wait patiently for my arm to go up? If my wants and beliefs can be causes of my behaviour, then I should be able to sit back and let them bring about the movement of my arm. Should I, bearing in mind my antecedent decision, describe what happens with the words 'And see! My arm goes up when the clock strikes five'? No; the upshot is not that my arm rises, but that *I raise it* – if I act in order to get what I want. Were the causal story true, I should, at least until the novelty has worn off, *be surprised* that when I have such-and-such wants and beliefs, such-and-such movements eventuate. Were the causal story true, how would an agent know whether he was acting voluntarily or moving involuntarily? For, as we have seen, one might have all the relevant beliefs and desires (the 'primary reason') and the appropriate movement might ensue, yet the question of whether I moved my limb would still be open. The causal story cannot distinguish between an agent's limb's moving *because* he has a certain reason and his moving his limb *for* a reason. But that is precisely what is explained by the altogether unmysterious rational-teleological account of human action in terms of reasons.

Explanation of action in terms of agential reasons is a form of teleological explanation or an adjunct thereof. It enables us to *understand* the agent's behaviour idiographically rather than nomothetically. Knowing his reasons for doing what he did, we may come to know what kinds of things weigh with him in his deliberations, and what kinds of considerations move him to act. We can see the extent of his rationality and the degree of his reasonableness, as well as the values for the sake of which he is prone to take action. Such explanations enable us not only to judge the agent and evaluate what he did, but also to judge his character. It enables us to understand our fellow human beings *as persons*.

---

[24] See Wittgenstein, *Philosophical Investigations*, §627.

8

The Mind

1. *Homo loquens*

That an entire mythology is laid down in our language is nowhere
better exemplified than in the words, phrases and idioms we invoke
in speaking about ourselves, our nature and our identity.[1] We human
beings are *persons*. We *have a mind*, which may be sharp, lively or
dull. We *have a body*, with which we may feel comfortable or ill at
ease. We are also said to possess – and sometimes to lose – *a soul*.
We speak of *having a self*, to which we are instructed to be true.
And it seems entirely natural – even though mistaken – to suppose
that it is *a self*, *an I*, or *an ego* to which we refer when we employ
the first-person pronoun. These expressions 'human being', 'person',
'mind', 'body', 'I' and 'soul' are used quite unproblematically in the
daily stream of life. But they typically slip out of focus as soon as
we subject them to philosophical scrutiny. The more closely we look
at them, it seems, the more blurred they become.

Is the person distinct from the human being? Locke supposed that
one and the same person can be now a prince and later find himself,
with all his memories, 'inhabiting the body' of a different human being

---

[1] See Wittgenstein, *The Big Typescript*, p. 434, where he ascribes the insight to
Paul Ernst. See also Nietzsche, *The Wanderer and his Shadow*, §11: 'There is a
philosophical mythology concealed in *language*.' The mythology lies in the *forms*
of representation: we represent the mind as an *entity*, the body as something we
possess, knowledge as an *acquisition*, memory as a *store*, understanding as an *act* or
activity.

– that of a cobbler.[2] Since all the memories a person has are dependent on the human brain, is the real person perhaps just the brain, with all the memories stored in it, that is locked within his skull? A human being has a body. Is he then distinct from his body, as Socrates supposed,[3] or is he identical with his body, as Sartre boldly asserted.[4] A human being, like all living creatures, is a material body, a spatio-temporal continuant consisting of matter (i.e. of stuffs of various kinds). But is the body one *is* identical with the body one *has?* How can one be identical with something one has? Or, since one can apparently doubt the existence of one's body but not of one's mind, is one, as Descartes held, identical with one's mind?[5] But a mind too is something one has, and if it is what one *is*, *who* has it? The grounds of language on which we walk are treacherous.

How is the mind related to the body? Descartes conceived of the mind as the controller of the conduits of animal spirits flowing from the ventricles to the muscles: 'When a *rational soul* is present in this machine [the body] it will have its principal seat in the brain, and reside there like the fountain-keeper who must be stationed at the tank to which the fountain's pipes return if he wants to produce, or prevent, or change their movements in some way.'[6] In the first half of the twentieth century, the mind was compared to a telephone operator in a central telephone exchange. Today it is compared to the software of a computer. (We find it irresistible to conceive of ourselves on the model of our latest technology.)

How is the person related to his soul? Plotinus held that he was identical with his soul; Aquinas insisted that he was distinct from it.[7] What is a self? Is it the soul? Is it the same as, or quite distinct from, the mind? Is it what speakers refer to when they speak of themselves, or only when they speak of their selves? Many threads cross here;

---

[2] Locke, *Essay Concerning Human Understanding*, II. xxvii. 15. He thereby commits himself to the questionable idea of the relativity of identity, since accordingly A may be the same person as B but a different human being.

[3] Plato, *Phaedo* 114d-116a, quoted above, ch. 1, n. 11.

[4] J. P. Sartre, *L'Etre et le Néant*, III. ii. 3.

[5] Descartes, *Meditations*, II.

[6] Descartes, *Treatise on Man* (AT XI, 131), in *Philosophical Writings*, ed. and trs. J. Cottingham, R. Stoothoff and D. Murdoch (Cambridge University Press, Cambridge, 1985), vol. 1, p. 101.

[7] 'Anima mea non est ego' – see above, ch. 1, n. 14.

the task is to trace them without becoming entangled in the web of words. The aim of the final three chapters of this book is to bring these philosophically contentious concepts into sharp focus. To anticipate: I shall argue that to have a mind is to have a distinctive array of rational powers, and that our peculiar talk of having a body is to be construed in a manner analogous to our talk of having a mind. In both cases the distinctive possessive form is misleading. Our talk of *having* a body is a way of speaking of a limited and distinctive array of corporeal *characteristics* of human beings. Consequently, one may darkly say, the body I am is not the body I have. Light will be shed on this dark saying as the tale unfolds.

Let me first briefly recapitulate. Human beings are substances of a certain type (the concept of a human being is a substance concept) – an evolutionary offshoot of the anthropoid apes, whose upright posture and consequent laryngeal changes made articulate vocalization possible. The human species has not only a distinctive appearance and anatomy, posture and mode of locomotion, but also a unique form of life. Our rational powers endow us with a horizon of possibilities of action, thought, and feeling vastly more extensive than anything accessible to other animals. Our ability to reason enlarges the possibility of knowledge and enables us to strive for theoretical understanding. It has made possible the benefits and evils of science and technology. Our ability to act for reasons makes us uniquely answerable for our deeds. We alone in the animal kingdom have knowledge of good and evil, have a conscience, and are susceptible to feelings of guilt, shame and remorse for our wrongdoing. It is no coincidence that only human beings can be said to have a soul, for to the soul belong the moral sensibility, the commitment to righteousness and moral goodness, as well as the darkness that besets those who have lost their way.

All but the lowliest forms of animal life are conscious. It was a far-reaching Cartesian confusion to identify the human mind with the domain of consciousness.[8] Animals undergo periods of sleep or

---

[8] 'Cartesian', i.e. a Galtonian portrait, since it would be unfair to ascribe this mistake to Descartes himself without qualification. 'Consciousness' was a novel term on the stage of European thought, and its early use differed from ours, being associated with knowledge to which one is privy. (For the history of the word, see C. S. Lewis, *Studies in Words* (Cambridge University Press, Cambridge, 1960), ch. 8.) Descartes's error was not so much that he did not distinguish intransitive consciousness (being awake as opposed to asleep or unconscious) from transitive consciousness (being conscious of something or other) as we do, or that he did not realize (as we should)

unconsciousness, and duly awaken and regain consciousness. Their attention is caught and held by objects and events in their environment, and it is of these that they become, and then are, conscious. They enjoy or suffer various states of consciousness, such as feeling contentment, hunger, thirst and pain. But only human beings are *self-conscious*. We can reflect on what we are doing or undergoing, on our reasons for acting, thinking or feeling, on our motives and motivations, on our likes and dislikes, on our character traits and relations to our fellow human beings. Being able to reflect on these, we can often come to understand them better, and in some cases to modify them in the light of our evaluations. We can take into account, in our reasoning and behaviour, facts about ourselves, about our experiences, past and prospective, and about our own character traits and dispositions. For we can not merely feel cheerful or depressed, we can also wonder why we are so feeling, and be pleased or disturbed that we are. We can be aware that we are ignorant or well-informed about something, that we have certain beliefs or doubts, that we have done and undergone various things in the past. Such facts about ourselves may weigh with us in our deliberations and occupy us in our reflections; they may be our reasons for acting, feeling or thinking thus-and-so here and now. This is partly constitutive of our being self-conscious creatures.

Other animals have cognitive abilities – they see their prey moving to the left, hear a mouse in the undergrowth, smell a female in heat. They know their young, recognize their call, they know how to do innumerable things, know the way to water-holes, remember where salt is to be found, and so forth.[9] They can think things to be thus-and-so, and be right or wrong, even though it makes no sense to say of them that they think something to be true or false.

---

that the objects of transitive consciousness – what one can be conscious of – extend well beyond the confines of one's own psychological attributes. It was his identification of the mind with consciousness (narrowly construed and misunderstood), his association of consciousness with the private, and his conception of the private as a domain to which the subject has privileged and infallible access resulting in indubitable knowledge.

[9] There has been much debate in recent years on whether mere animals can believe things. But this is to get hold of the wrong end of the stick. We should start by reflecting on whether they can be said to know things. Then the question of whether they can be said to believe thus-and-so or, better, to *think* things to be thus-and-so, can be handled far more easily.

When they are wrong, they can sometimes recognize and rectify their error.[10] But the horizon of their thinking is determined by the limits of their behavioural repertoire. They can intelligibly (truly *or* falsely) be said to think only what they *can* express in their behaviour. The horizon of human thought is vastly wider. We can think of specifically dated events, of the distant past and remote future. We can think general thoughts, discover and reflect on sempiternal laws of nature, and understand and come to know the timeless truths of arithmetic, geometry and logic. We are blessed, and cursed, with the ability to think of how things might have been, and with the ability to imagine countless possibilities – an ability that lies at the heart of our story-telling, and more generally, of art. For, again, we are unique in nature in possessing an imagination, which also makes possible artistic creativity and aesthetic appreciation.[11] Only human beings create works of art, and can be awestruck by the sublime, moved to tears by works of the imagination. Only creatures with imagination can have a sense of humour. We can apprehend the incongruous with laughter, be amused at jokes, and rise above our suffering with irony.

Non-human animals live in the perpetual present. Human beings live in time in a quite different sense. Other animals too have a memory; but only human beings have a past. Human beings have, and can know, a history. In this sense, they can be said to have, and to be able to tell, an 'autobiography'. They can dwell lovingly, proudly

---

[10] Rectifying their error is not the same as *correcting* their belief, even though when they rectify their error they no longer believe or think what they previously believed or thought. Davidson argued that only a creature that 'understands the possibility of being mistaken' can believe something, and that this requires a grasp of the difference between true and false belief, which in turn requires possession of the concept of belief ('Thought and Talk', repr. in *Truth and Interpretation* (Clarendon Press, Oxford, 1984), p. 170). This confuses the power to correct error, as manifest in behaviour, with the power to reconsider and correct belief. Adjusting one's behaviour to one's perceptions may involve rectification of misperception and/or rectification of error, e.g. in thinking that the cat is still in the tree into which it sprang. It does not, in the case of the dog, involve reflectively correcting its *belief*, but its *behaviour*. Its corrected behaviour is a criterion for its no longer believing or thinking what it previously believed or thought (for a different view, see J. R. Searle, 'Animal Minds', *Midwest Studies in Philosophy*, 19 (1994)).

[11] 'A spider conducts operations that resemble those of a weaver, and a bee puts to shame many an architect in the construction of her cells. But what distinguishes the worst architect from the best of bees is this, that the architect raises his structure in imagination before he erects it in reality' (Karl Marx, *Das Kapital*, ch. 7, sect. 1).

or guiltily upon their lives. Many other animals are social creatures, but humans are also socio-historical beings, conscious of themselves as belonging to a social group *with* a history. Our sense of identity and cultural form of life is bound up with such a history, both actual and mythical. Similarly, only human beings can dwell on, and in, the future and the possibilities it holds. Animal life is full of fear; human life is also full of hope. Only human beings are aware of their mortality, can be occupied or preoccupied with their death and the dead. We are unique among animals in being able to strive to understand our lives and the place of death in life. So we are uniquely God-creating, myth-generating creatures – making the gods in our image, initially to explain the phenomena of nature and appease the forces of nature, later to try to make moral sense of our lives and fortunes by holding out vain hopes (and unwarranted threats) of a life after death.

Whence these unique powers? Alone among animals (with the possible, marginal, exception of chimpanzees), human beings have a crucial, highly specific, innate capacity (a second-order ability to acquire an ability): it is part of our nature to be born with the ability to learn to speak a language. From this, from our animal nature coupled to mastery of a language, all else flows. We are language-using animals – *homo loquens*, not *homo sapiens*. Stripped of language, we are but killer apes. All the distinctive powers cited are either constitutive of or corollaries of our mastery of a developed language. The horizon of possible thought is determined by the limits of the expression of thought; but with us, unlike other animals, those limits are set by the *linguistic* expression of thought. If one has mastered the use of tenses and of temporal referring expressions, one can think of the past and the future. One can remember not only *where* – as exhibited in an animal's seeking or homing behaviour – but also *when*. Non-human animals may *prepare* for the future – bury food for later consumption, build dams or dig burrows, but only man can *plan* for the future.

If a creature has mastered a language with logical connectives and quantifiers, then and only then is it possible for it to conceive of general truths, to think both of how things are and how they are *not*, to think both of what exists and of what does not exist, to think conditional thoughts, and with the aid of tensed verbs and modal expressions, counterfactual thoughts. It is striking, although it may be a contingent nexus, that with our powers of linguistic representation go also our powers of pictorial representation – no other animal can make an image.[12] Only a language-using creature can apprehend the 'eternal truths' of mathematics. That is because such truths are essentially norms of representation that find their ultimate rationale in rules for the transformation of empirical *sentences* concerning magnitudes.[13]

Our linguistic skills not only extend the limits of thought, they also shift the horizons of desire and will and introduce the 'if only-s' that haunt us with regrets and remorse, and gild our wishes and longings. Non-language-using animals may now want food or drink, but cannot now want food or drink next Wednesday. Animals have purposes, pursue goals, and opt for different ways of attaining them. But the trajectory of their desires reaches no further than their behavioural repertoire can express, and the objects of their desires are constrained by their limited non-linguistic recognitional abilities. They can opt for one or another alternative, but not deliberate. There are reasons why an animal acts as it does, but, as we have seen, only in the most tenuous of senses can we say that they have reasons for acting as they do. Only a language-using creature can reason and deliberate, weigh the conflicting claims of the facts it knows in the light of its desires, goals and values, and come to a decision or make a choice in the light of reasons. In so far as non-human animals can be said to decide at all, such animal decision is not a matter of calling a halt to a process of reasoning, of weighing the pros and cons of a course of action and coming to a reasoned conclusion. It is only a matter of terminating a state of indecision.

What applies to the will applies equally to attitudes and affections. Non-human animals can like and dislike things, take pleasure in activities, feel fear and rage. But a wide range of emotions, which are infused with thought, belief and concept-laden cognition,[14] are beyond the powers of such animals, either in their nature (e.g. remorse, guilt)

[12] Indeed, not all animals can recognize an image. Few animals can recognize an image as an image – if a cat paws at a picture of a mouse, it is not trying to deface an image.

[13] For elaboration of this Wittgensteinian conception of the role and status of mathematics, see G. P. Baker and P. M. S. Hacker, *Wittgenstein – Rules, Grammar and Necessity* (Blackwell, Oxford, 1985), pp. 263–348.

[14] Many philosophers are inclined to ascribe concepts (or 'proto-concepts') to animals. This is ill-advised. Of course, animals possess recognitional abilities and discriminatory powers of a high order. That is not sufficient for possession of any concept, and not even necessary for some concepts. It is necessary for possession of the concept of red. But a being to whom possession of this concept may be ascribed must grasp

or in their objects (e.g. fear of war, anger at injustice) or both. Only with a language-user can there be a deliberate gap between emotion felt and emotion expressed.

A creature that has mastered a language with demonstrative and indexical devices, including the personal pronouns, can acquire the self-reflexive cognitive and cogitative abilities that constitute self-consciousness. To have grasped the meanings of typical psychological verbs requires both knowledge of the grounds for third-person ascriptions and mastery of the groundless first-person use. Only if a speaker has mastered the Janus-faced use of pivotal psychological verbs is he in a position to reflect on his own sensations, attitudes and feelings, on his thoughts, plans and projects. Only if he has learnt to give reasons can he be in a position to reflect on the reasons he has. Only if he can reflect on his reasons and probe his motives can he strive for that self-knowledge that is attainable by self-conscious creatures. Hence too, only human beings can wrap themselves in the tattered cloak of self-deception.

2. The Cartesian mind

It was remarked in chapter 1 that in the modern era it has been Cartesian dualism that provided the framework of thought about human beings, their minds and their bodies. Human beings were conceived to be material bodies conjoined to mental substances (minds). Relations of two-way causation were held to obtain between these two categorially distinct things. Mental attributes were conceived to characterize the mind, physical attributes to characterize the body. A driving force behind Descartes's metaphysics was the determination of the scope of the new physics – the science of matter in motion –

---

that red is a colour; that it applies to extended objects, but not to sounds or smells; that if something is red all over, it cannot simultaneously be green all over; that red is darker than pink, and more similar to orange than to yellow, and so on. In short, he must grasp the logical articulations of the concept, i.e. the rule-governed use of a word that expresses it. To be sure, concept possession is a complex ability, which admits of degrees. Is mere recognitional ability sufficient to ascribe a minimal mastery of the concept? That is a matter of decision, but there is little to be said for deciding in favour of the proposal. It would detach the concept of concept possession from the cluster of abilities with which it is normally and usefully associated, and detach the concept of a concept from its connection with the concepts of application and misapplication, use, misuse and abuse, subsumption, extension, replacement and substitution.

and its laws. Convinced of the unity of the natural sciences and the reducibility of biology to physics, Descartes treated living organisms as machines. He drastically redrew the boundaries of the mind. The Aristotelian scholastics characterized the mind in terms of the powers of the intellect and rational will – that is, of the Aristotelian rational *psuchē*. Descartes, by contrast, included within the mind the powers of the sensitive *psuchē* that he denied to mere animals.[15] For sensation and perception, imagination (*fantasia*) and desire, no less than thought and reasoning, deliberation and rational decision, are, he held, *modes of consciousness* – and the domain of the Cartesian mind is the domain of consciousness, or, as our contemporaries put it, of conscious experience. The limits of physics, Descartes held, lie at the portals of the human mind.

List 8.1 The Cartesian conception of the mind

A substance

Immaterial

Identical with the person or self

Distinct from the body a person has

A part of a human being

The subject of mental (psychological) predicates

An agent

In two-way causal interaction with the body

Defined by consciousness of mental attributes

The essence of the mind is thought, which includes seeming to perceive, having sensations as if in the body, mental images, emotions and desires, as well as knowing, believing, thinking and judging.

Transparent to the subject

The contents of the mind are privately 'owned' and epistemically private

The contents of one's mind are indubitable

---

[15] See A. J. P. Kenny, *The Metaphysics of Mind* (Clarendon Press, Oxford, 1989), chs 1–2.

The essence of the mind, Descartes argued, is thought (see List 8.1); but he extended the concept of thought to include sensations felt (as if in parts of the body), perceptions (understood as seeming to see, hear, smell, etc.), mental images, cognitive and cogitative functions such as thinking (as normally understood), understanding, judging and believing (which he conceived of as acts of the will, not of the intellect), as well as feeling emotions and desire. Thought included 'everything which we are aware of as happening within us, in so far as we have awareness of it. Hence *thinking* is to be identified here not merely with understanding, willing, imagining, but also with sensory awareness.'[16] Thought was, therefore, defined in terms of consciousness, and consciousness was assimilated to self-consciousness misconceived – that is, as that of which we are immediately aware within us. The mind was alleged to be transparent. Thoughts were held to be luminous objects of private indubitable knowledge: if a person has a certain thought (feels pain, seems to perceive, imagines, thinks, judges, understands, feels passions, wills), he apprehends immediately, indubitably and infallibly that he does. There can be nothing in the mind that is not illuminated by the light of consciousness. The light of the Cartesian mind casts no shadows. But other people cannot be immediately aware of what passes in one's mind. They can observe only externalities – bodily movements – and infer probabilistically or analogically what thoughts are occurring to the mind whose body they observe.

This conception of consciousness is like a virus. It is with us today in *mutated* forms, infecting current 'consciousness studies' that bedevil the thought of philosophers, psychologists and cognitive neuroscientists. It survives in the doctrines of those who most eagerly repudiate dualism, and identify the mind with the brain. For the mind that is identified with the brain is, with some qualifications, the Cartesian mind materialized (list 8.2). This conception of consciousness is the source of the idea that consciousness is the last great mystery in the universe.[17] It is the root of the thought that consciousness is uniquely private, that each person has privileged access to his own domain of consciousness, that what he observes there *in foro interno* has a unique,

---

[16] Descartes, *Principles of Philosophy*, I, 9.

[17] It is sometimes held that our ignorance about consciousness may be 'the largest outstanding obstacle [to] a scientific understanding of the universe' (see D. Chalmers, *The Conscious Mind* (Oxford University Press, Oxford, 1996), p. xi).

ineffable, qualitative character. When in the grip of this picture, we are inclined to agree with T. H. Huxley, 'How it is that anything so remarkable as a state of consciousness comes about as a result of irritating nervous tissue, is just as unaccountable as the appearance of Djin when Aladdin rubbed his lamp.'[18] But consciousness correctly conceived is no more of a mystery than attention, of which perceptual transitive consciousness is a form. It is at root a biological phenomenon, and corollary, of sentient life.[19]

List 8.2   Brain–body dualism: the crypto-Cartesian mind of cognitive neuroscience

An organ – the brain

Material

Identical with the person   *like Ǫ*

Distinct from the (rest of the) body a person has

A part of a human being   *(like Descartes)*

The subject of mental predicates (the brain believes, thinks, calculates, wants, intends, perceives, etc.)

An agent

In two-way causal interaction with the body   *mind-body Ǫ*

Defined by consciousness of mental attributes

The essence of the material mind is the qualitative character of experiences (qualia) of which the subject is conscious.

The qualia are privately 'owned' and epistemically private

---

[18] T. H. Huxley, *Lessons in Elementary Physiology* (1866), p. 193. It is striking and significant that this confused observation continues to be sympathetically quoted to this day by philosophers, psychologists and neuroscientists. For commentary on it, see M. R. Bennett and P. M. S. Hacker, *Philosophical Foundations of Neuroscience* (Blackwell, Oxford, 2003), pp. 302–7.

[19] For detailed discussion of consciousness, see Bennett and Hacker, *Philosophical Foundations of Neuroscience*, chs 9–12. The mystery currently associated with consciousness is the product of conceptual entanglement.

The Cartesian-empiricist conception of the mind that so plagues us involves a misconstrual of consciousness, a misrepresentation of self-consciousness, a misunderstanding of introspection and a distortion of self-knowledge.

Consciousness is misconstrued in so far as it is identified with self-consciousness misrepresented – misrepresented as a state of awareness of acts and states of the mind, rather than as a power of reflexive reflection. Consciousness is taken both too narrowly and too broadly.

It is taken too narrowly inasmuch as the objects of consciousness are wrongly confined to 'everything which we are aware of as happening within us'. But one can be conscious of the ticking of the clock no less than of one's anxiety about the time, of someone looking at one no less than of one's embarrassment, of the immanent danger of war no less than of one's fear of its outbreak, of one's own socially superior or inferior origins no less than of one's pride or chip-on-one's-shoulder. The objects of possible consciousness encompass much more than what is currently 'in' or 'passing before' one's mind. They include whatever may catch and hold one's attention, but also anything (past, present or future) that may occupy one's thoughts and weigh with one in one's deliberations.

Consciousness is taken too broadly inasmuch as the objects of actual consciousness encompass much less than the range of Cartesian thoughts (or empiricist ideas and impressions). One is not conscious of everything that one perceives or of all one's perceivings, but only of those objects of perception that catch and hold one's attention, and only of those perceivings that strike one or that one reflects on.[20] One is not conscious of everything that one thinks (which includes all the presuppositions and assumptions one takes for granted), but only of those thoughts that occupy one's mind and on which one dwells. One is not even normally conscious of one's thinking, unless, for example, the very fact that one is sunk in thought occurs to one and is itself the object of further reflection. One may be in the grip of an emotion, such as jealousy, without being conscious of it – as

[20] I disregard here the complications produced by the Cartesian limitation of perceptual 'thoughts' to *seeming* to perceive. That is a further confusion, and one which has gained currency in recent philosophy through the Grice – Strawson revival of the causal theory of perception. Seeming to perceive is no more a necessary constituent of perceiving than trying to V is a necessary constituent of V-ing, or seeming to recollect of recollecting.

when one becomes annoyed at Jill's flirting with Jack; and one may prejudge things without even being aware of having done so.

The doctrine of the transparent mind is equally misconceived. There is much that can be said to be 'in the mind' of which we are not conscious. Subliminal perception is now widely recognized. In a post-Freudian era, we should not need to be reminded of the ubiquity of unconscious thoughts, beliefs, wishes, desires and emotions – although we should be warned against the Freudian misconception of the unconscious as a hidden domain, just like the conscious mind, only unconscious. It is mistaken to suppose that whenever we take ourselves to know, understand, want or believe something, we know indubitably that we do so. We commonly think that we know, understand or want things that we do not actually know (but only believe), do not really understand (but misunderstand), and do not really want at all. We commonly wonder whether we really believe something, and often deceive ourselves about what we really believe. Even in cases where doubt *is* patently excluded, as when one is in pain or as when one thinks that it is a beautiful day, it is far from obvious that one *knows* that one is in pain or *knows* that one is thinking that it is a beautiful day. For ignorance here is excluded – but not because the requirements of knowledge are satisfied. Doubt too is excluded – but not because the conditions of certainty have been met. Rather, both are precluded by *grammar*, by the meaning-constituting rules for the use of words. It makes no *sense* to doubt whether one is in pain or whether one is thinking such-and-such.[21]

Cartesian consciousness was bound up with *awareness* of how things are with one. This was reinforced by the Lockean conception of introspection as *inner perception*: 'it is impossible for anyone to perceive without perceiving that he does perceive. When we see, hear, smell, taste, feel, meditate or will anything, we know that we do so.'[22]

---

[21] This is a radical Wittgensteinian account (see *Philosophical Investigations*, §246). I have defended it against criticisms in 'Of Knowledge and of Knowing that Someone is in Pain', in A. Pichler and S. Säätelä (eds), *Wittgenstein: The Philosopher and his Works* (The Wittgenstein Archives at the University of Bergen, Bergen, 2005), pp. 123–56.

[22] Locke, *Essay Concerning Human Understanding*, II. xxvii. 9. See also W. James: 'The word introspection need hardly be defined – it means, of course, the looking into one's own mind and reporting what we there discover. *Everyone agrees that we there discover states of consciousness*' (*Principles of Psychology*, vol. 1, p. 185).

Introspection was explicitly compared to looking into a *camera obscura*.[23] But this too is mistaken. There is no such thing as my seeing that I see something or perceiving that I hear, smell, taste or feel. I can no more *look into* my own mind than I can look into another's, and we often have more insight into the mind of another than into our own. The perceptual metaphor bound up with 'introspection' is misleading, and is a poor model in terms of which to comprehend the logical character of consciousness of what passes in our mind. We confuse the ability to *say* how things are with us with the ability to *see* how things are with us.

To be able to say how things are with one (subjectively speaking) is not to have *access* to anything, it is to be able to *give expression* to something. When one says that one has a headache, what one has is a pain, not access to a pain. It is true that others can ascribe psychological attributes to a person only on the basis of what he says and does, whereas the person himself can avow how things are with him without observing his own behaviour. Of course, one can report one's pains and confess one's thoughts – but that is not because one has observed something *in foro interno*. To say what one thinks is not to describe one's thoughts, and a description of one's pains does not rest on observation. We wrongly suppose that our sincere word has a privileged status because it rests on privileged *access*. Its authoritative status is not derived from its describing observations of a private peepshow. The subject's sincere word is an expression or manifestation of his thought or experience. Its special status is grammatical, not epistemic – the agent is not *an authority* on his pains and thoughts as he might be an authority on something which only he has seen and studied. Rather, his utterances are logical (non-inductive) *criteria* for how things are with him, and his sincerity, in cases where self-deception can be excluded, guarantees truth.

Introspection is not a form of *inner perception*. It is not a faculty by means of which we discern what is allegedly not detectable by

---

[23] 'That external and internal Sensation, are the only passages I can find, of Knowledge, to the Understanding. These alone, as far as I can discover, are the Windows by which light is let into this *dark Room*. For, methinks, the *Understanding* is not much unlike a Closet wholly shut from light, with only some little openings left to let in external visible Resemblances, or *Ideas* of things without; would the Pictures coming into such a dark Room but stay there, and lie so orderly as to be found upon occasion, it would very much resemble the Understanding of a Man, in reference to all Objects of sight, and the *Ideas* of them' (Locke, Essay, II. xi. 17).

others: namely, that which is in our mind. We see things *in* our mind's eye, not *with* our mind's eye. In one sense, introspection is a form of *reflection*, not a form of observation. The introspective person is one who reflects upon himself, on his emotions and motives, on his attitudes and moods. Introspection is a form of self-reflexive thought. It is a route to self-knowledge and self-understanding. In another sense, introspection is a matter of *attention* to one's moods and emotions, sensations and feelings. One may attend to one's pains in the course of the day, and note them down for medical purposes. One may be aware of the waning of one's passion for Daisy – one is no longer so excited at the prospect of her coming, and less entranced by her chatter. So one may register one's feelings in one's diary – but one does not *perceive* one's pain or passion.

There is such a thing as self-knowledge. But to say that I have a headache, that I am thinking of this or that, that the noise is irritating me and I want a drink, is not exhibiting it. The inscription on the Temple of Apollo was not instructing Socrates to pay attention to his stream of consciousness. The child who acquires and begins to exercise the linguistic skills that enable him to give expression to and report on how things are with him is not yet learning to know himself. Self-knowledge involves knowing one's character traits, dispositions and skills, strengths and weaknesses, knowing what moves one and why, what one's most fundamental commitments are, what one's attitudes are and why one holds them. All of these one may come to know in various ways: for example, by being told by others, by realizing the character of one's past behaviour, by reflecting on what reasons one had on various occasions, and seeing the patterns into which they fall, by noting the degree of self-control one is able to attain. Some of the sources of self-knowledge may not be available to others – for example, one's memory of what one was going to say but didn't, of what one felt but did not show, of what one thought but kept to oneself. But, first, it is precisely here that one is fallible and open to self-deception; and secondly, there is nothing intrinsically private about such data – if one tells others, they too will know.

The Cartesian mind is an aberration. It was offered as a more correct representation of human nature and the principles that guide explanations of human thought, feeling and action than the Aristotelian conceptions that it displaced. In fact, it is not. And it has foisted on us a wholly inadequate framework for the representation of human nature.

3. The nature of the mind

We are trying to understand the structure of a fragment of our conceptual scheme. That we speak of ourselves as having a mind is a crucial aspect of our discourse about human beings. English idiom is rich in phrases incorporating the word 'mind'.[24] These are far from universal (many languages, even closely related languages such as German, do not have a word that corresponds precisely to 'mind'). But our idioms are the flowers that the genius of English has naturally grown, and they cover the terrain that we are trying to survey. There is much to be learnt about it from them.

One advantage of so doing is that it will enable us to resist, at least *pro tempore*, the temptation to answer the philosophical question 'What is the mind?' by giving a definition. 'The mind' being a nominal, 'What is the mind?' is commonly construed as 'What sort of *entity* is the mind?'. Philosophers then debate whether it is an immaterial substance in causal interaction with the brain, or a bundle of perceptions causally connected with a human body, or whether it is in fact the brain, or a bundle of mnemonically connected impressions severally identical with states of the brain. But 'What sort of entity is the mind?' is as pernicious a question as 'What sort of entity is a number?'. It raises the wrong kind of expectations, and sends us along the wrong paths before we have had a chance to get our bearings. So the *first* step to take is to examine the use of the noun 'mind'.[25]

---

[24] In the following paragraphs I have made free use of earlier writings of mine. See P. M. S. Hacker, *Wittgenstein: Meaning and Mind* (Blackwell, Oxford, 1990), Pt 1: *The Essays*, ch. IV: 'Men, Minds and Machines', and Bennett and Hacker, *Philosophical Foundations of Neuroscience*, ch. 3, sect. 3.10. See also J. M. F. Hunter, 'The Concept "Mind"', *Philosophy*, 61 (1986), pp. 439–51; A. J. P. Kenny, 'The Geography of Mind', repr. in his *Essays on the Aristotelian Tradition* (Clarendon Press, Oxford, 2001); B. Rundle, *Mind in Action* (Clarendon Press, Oxford, 1997), ch. 2, sect. 1; R. Squires, 'On One's Mind', *Philosophical Quarterly*, 20 (1970), pp. 347–56.

[25] Is this not depressingly parochial? No more so than our questions about the nature of the mind – which are importantly different from questions about the nature of the soul, *Geist or Seele*, or of the *psuchē*, or of *nephesh* (*ruach* or *neshama*). These questions are to be answered by conceptual investigations, and the sole way to examine concepts is to investigate the uses of the words and phrases that express those concepts. Of course, the one investigation (e.g. of *nephesh*) may often shed light on the other (e.g. of *mind*), both by way of similarity and by way of difference.

The English word 'mind' is etymologically derived from expressions in Indo-Germanic languages: *mynd* (ME), *gimunt* (OHG), *gamunds* (Oteut), *manun* (OE), that were associated primarily with memory, thought, opinion and intention. Contemporary usage, as so often, has not cut itself free of its origins.

(i) *Memory*. To hold something in mind is to retain it in memory; to keep something in mind ensures that one will not overlook it. To bear something in mind is to remember it, so that one can take it into account. To call or to bring something to mind is to recollect it. For something to be, go, pass or slip out of mind is for it to be forgotten. To cast one's mind back to an incident is to try to remember something about it. Someone who is absent-minded is forgetful or inattentive.

(ii) *Thought*. To have a thought cross one's mind is for something to have occurred to one. Ideas come to mind, flash through one's mind ('the lightning speed of thought'), or lurk, just out of reach, at the back of one's mind – as one tries to think of something. To turn one's mind to something is to begin to think about it. To have something on one's mind is to be thinking about it or to be pre-occupied with it. To have a load taken off one's mind is to be relieved of anxiously thinking about it. One's mind is in turmoil if one does not know what to think or do. One's mind wanders when one cannot concentrate. One's mind goes blank when one finds oneself at a loss and does not know what to say. A person is said to have an original cast of mind if he displays originality in thought, discourse and action.

(iii) *Opinion*. To know one's mind is to have formed one's opinion, and to tell one's mind is to express it. To be of one mind with another is to agree in opinion or in judgement. To speak one's mind or to let someone know one's mind, is to tell what one opines. To give someone a piece of one's mind is to tell him, harshly, what one thinks of him.

(iv) *Intention*. To be minded or to have it in mind to do something is to be inclined or to intend to do it. To have half a mind to do something is to be tempted to do it, and to be in two minds is to waver between alternatives. To make up one's mind is to decide, and to change one's mind is to reverse one's decision or judgement. To have a mind of one's own is to be independent in judgement and will.

English idiom ramifies in further directions. At the most general level, the mind is associated with intellectual faculties: a person is said to have a powerful, agile, subtle or devious mind if he is skilful, quick and ingenious at problem solving, or if his solutions, plans and projects display subtlety and cunning. Hence too, it is connected with appropriate intellectual virtues and vices: a person has a tenacious, idle, vigorous, judicious or indecisive mind according to the manner in which he grapples with problems requiring reflection and according to the typical upshot of his reflections. A person is of sound mind if he retains his rational faculties, and out of his mind if he thinks, proposes or does things that are irrational. He is not in his right mind if he is distraught, and he has lost his mind if he is bereft of his rational faculties. Other uses fade off in other directions: we speak of people being broad- or narrow-minded, small- or petty-minded, having a dirty mind or a mind like a razor, displaying presence of mind or lacking peace of mind. It is striking that we do *not* say that a person has a *wise* mind (and perhaps not an *intelligent* or *clever* mind either) – we reserve this for the person himself. It is he, not his mind, that is wise.

The *second* step is to derive some morals from these reminders of linguistic idiom. First, each such use, as is evident from the above examples, is readily paraphrasable without the word 'mind'. All that is needed is a corresponding psychological predicate applicable to the human being. In this sense, reference to the mind is eliminable without loss. Talk of the mind, one might say, is merely a convenient *façon de parler*, an oblique way of speaking about human faculties and their exercise. Of course, this does not mean that the mind is a fiction. It does not mean that human beings do not have minds of their own – which would be true only if they were pathologically indecisive. Nor does it mean that people are mindless – which would be true only if they were stupid and thoughtless. It would be quite wrong to suggest that 'minds should be written off as an intellectual loss'.[26] What is true (and perhaps what was intended) is that the *philosophical construal* of the mind as an immaterial substance is incoherent. It is similarly mistaken to suggest that our minds 'are pretend entities', that the agency of the mind 'is not a real agency . . . but an agency we pretend exists, and the qualities of which we pretend explain the behaviour'.[27] It is true that the mind is no agent (of which more in a moment), but we no more *pretend* that our mind is an agent than

[26] Squires, 'On One's Mind', p. 355.

[27] Hunter, 'The Concept "Mind"', pp. 442, 444.

we pretend that our character is an agent; and we no more *pretend* that our mind is an entity than we pretend that our abilities are entities. Rather, in superficial reflection on the mind, we are easily misled by our language into thinking that the mind is a part of a human being, that it is an immaterial substance – the person or self, and we are prone to ascribe agency to the mind thus conceived. That *is* a conceptual confusion. But our rich and elaborate talk of the mind is not at all like our talk (and pretence) of Father Christmas. To repeat, to say that our ordinary talk of the mind is a mere *façon de parler*, or that it is a *logical construction*, is not to say that there are no minds. On the contrary, it is to say that there are, only that they are not kinds of things. The mind, it might be said (adapting a phrase from Wittgenstein), is not a *nothing*, but it is not a *something* either. It should be noted, however, that the proposition that human beings have minds is at best a mere grammatical one: that is, a rule for the use of words in the misleading guise of a description of how things are. What it amounts to is that if A is a human being, then it *makes sense* to ask what sort of mind he has (subtle or crude, judicious or frivolous), whether he has anything on his mind or whether he has made up his mind, and so forth.

Secondly, it is obvious that in the various idioms one is not speaking of one and the same thing, called 'the mind'. When we say that someone changed his mind, that he has a dirty mind, and that he has turned his mind to a certain question, we do not imply that there is one thing: a mind, which has changed, is dirty and has been turned.[28] We are indeed speaking of the very same thing – *namely, the human being* – and from case to case, and phrase to phrase, we are saying different things *of* the human being.

Thirdly, it is evident that the question of whether the mind is identical with the brain, under one interpretation, becomes transparently absurd, since the mind is not a kind of entity that might be identical with anything. The question is accordingly transformed into a different one: can psychological attributes be identified with neural states, processes or events in the brain. I shall not discuss this question here in the detail it merits. But it is appropriate to note a few general points.

(i) Neural, cortical, states are states of the brain; mental states are states of the human being; but the identity of a state is logically

---

[28] Rundle, *Mind in Actions*, p. 26.

dependent upon the identity of the entity that is in that state. So a state of a human being cannot be identical with a state of a human being's brain. The brain may be in a sclerotic state – but the human being cannot be. The human being may be in a cheerful state, but his brain cannot be.

(ii) Being in a neural state cannot have the consequences that possession of certain mental attributes has. If someone believes something to be so, then he is either right or wrong; but his being in such-and-such a neural state cannot be either right or wrong. One cannot say 'I believe that p, but it is not the case that p'. But if believing that p were a state of the brain, then it would be perfectly in order to say 'I believe that p (that is, my brain is in such-and-such a state), but not p', or 'I believe that p, but whether it is or is not the case that p is, for me, an open question'. If intending to V were a brain state, then one could intelligibly say, 'I intend to V, but the possibility of V-ing is foreclosed.' But one cannot.

(iii) The notion of a brain state is left wholly opaque. The human neo-cortex alone contains tens of billions of neurons, each with up to 10,000 synapses, in constant dynamic interaction and change. No one knows what is to count as a proper description of a brain state, let alone of a brain state that is identical with the person's having a given mental attribute. No one has laid down criteria of identity for such brain states. Indeed, the concept of a description of a brain state as deployed by contemporary philosophers is reminiscent of the notion of a state description of the universe invoked with similar enthusiasm and comparable vacuity by members of the Vienna Circle in the 1930s.

(iv) Identifying types of brain states (assuming that we have been given criteria of identity for them) with types of mental states is excluded, both because of significant individual differences, and also because of neural differences between species. But so-called token identity is merely an unverifiable hypothesis of dubious intelligibility.

Fourthly, the very distinctive range of idioms appertaining to the mind suggests that it is not because we have minds that psychological predicates apply to us, but rather because a fairly specific subset of psychological predicates apply to us that we can be said to have minds. That fish can see and hear, that birds can be frightened of a cat, that cats can want to catch a bird – all of which Descartes denied – does not show that he was wrong to deny that they have minds.

Fifthly, if we say that a human being has an F mind, it does not in general follow that he is F – one needs to examine each predicate in its own right. If someone has a judicious mind, then he is judicious. If he has a decisive mind, then he is decisive. But if he has an idle mind, it does not follow that he is idle; if he has an agile mind, it does not follow that he is agile.

Sixthly, although we speak of someone's having a quick, agile, original mind, or a slow, idle and dull one, it is a categorial mistake to suppose, as Reid (and others) did, that the mind is 'that in [man] which thinks, imagines, reasons, wills'.[29] We ascribe agile, devious, imaginative minds to human beings, but do not, on the whole, speak of the mind as if it were an agent, although we do sometimes speak of it as if it were a patient. It is not my mind that thinks, imagines, reasons or wills, it is I. On the other hand, my mind may go blank, be in turmoil, or wander – but these are neither acts nor activities of the mind. It is not my mind that makes up its mind or decides, that changes its mind or reverses its decision, that has half a mind, or is inclined, to do something – it is I, a human being. It is not the mind that feels pain, perceives, knows, is conscious of this or that, feels happy or upset, desires this or intends that. It was a Cartesian confusion to ascribe the whole range of psychological attributes to the mind. That incoherence is multiplied by present-day materialists' identifying the mind with the brain, and ascribing the same range of predicates to the brain.

What, then, is the mind? If a definition is meant to provide a rule for the current use of a word, then there is no useful definition of 'the mind', although from idiom to idiom we can explain what is meant. But if we cannot fruitfully define 'mind' in *this* sense of 'definition', we can ask what must be true of a creature for it to be said to have a mind. It is evident that it is above all human beings that are the subjects of this array of idioms. We do sometimes extend the odd idiom to an animal, as when we say of a horse or a dog that will not do what we want it to do that it has a mind of its own, and describe an animal that dithered when confronted with alternatives as having finally made up its mind. But this, although it need not be crude anthropomorphizing, is just a natural extension of language

---

[29] Thomas Reid, *Essays on the Intellectual Powers of Man* (Edinburgh University Press, Edinburgh, 2002), p. 20 (cp. Mill, who held that the mind is 'the mysterious something which thinks and feels'). But there is no more 'something' within us, no part of a human being, that thinks and feels than there is a part of an aeroplane that flies.

from our own case – an idiomatic way of saying of the animal that it is stubborn or that it opted for A rather than B. What, then, is it about human beings that inclines us to invoke the whole panoply of the language of the mind? Surveying the range of characteristic English idioms yields interesting results. They are, as we have seen, clustered around forms of thought, opinion, recollection and will that are possible only for language-users. For the vast majority of idioms of the mind are concerned with the intellect and the will, their exercise, and the traits and dispositions that exemplify these faculties.

Once this is clear, it becomes evident that the domain of the idiom of mind coincides roughly not with that of the Cartesian mind, but with that of the Aristotelian rational *psuchē* (see list 8.3). Aristotle's profound account of *psuchē* was concerned with demarcating the animate from the inanimate, with the classification of the animate into (very general) categories according to the classes of powers that characterize living beings, and hence with the forms of explanation of behaviour distinctive of them. The *psuchē* is 'the actuality of a body that has life'.[30] The actualities (*entelechiai*) of a substance are those things it is or is doing at a given time. Among its actualities are its active and passive powers. The unexercised powers (both dispositional powers, *hexeis*, and abilities, *dunameis*) of a living thing are first actualities. These distinctive powers of the organism are exercised in its vital operations, the exercise being the second actuality (*energeia*). So the *psuchē* can also be said to be 'the first actuality of a natural body which has organs' (*DA* 412^{b}4–6). For the organs of an organism confer upon it the possibility of exercising the functions of life appropriate to the kind of living being it is. The question of whether the *psuchē* and the body are one thing or two, Aristotle taught, is as meaningless as the question of whether the wax and the impression made upon it are one thing or two (*DA* 412^{b}6–7). The *psuchē* is no more a *part* of a living being than the power of sight is a part of an eye. Nor is the *psuchē* an 'inner agent', an immaterial substance that is the subject of experience and originator of action, animating the body but independent of it, as is the Cartesian mind. To have a *psuchē* is not to possess something or to be related to something – it is to be able to do a certain range of things characteristic of living beings. Hence too, Aristotle, unlike Descartes, did not attribute to the

---

[30] Aristotle, *De Anima* 412^{a}20; other references in the text flagged *DA* are to this work.

psuchē the exercise of the distinctive powers of the being whose *psuchē* it is: 'to say that the *psuchē* is angry is as if one were to say that the *psuchē* weaves or builds. For it is surely better not to say that the *psuchē* pities, learns or thinks, but that the man does these things with his *psuchē*' (*DA* 408ᵇ12–15) – doing something with one's *psuchē* being akin to doing something with one's talents. The *psuchē* does not have parts as the body has organs, but only as one ability, one faculty, can be distinguished from another. We distinguish abilities by their exercise or manifestation. Reason is distinguished from imagination inasmuch as drawing inferences is distinct from thinking up novel possibilities. Sight is distinguished from smell inasmuch as discerning colours is distinct from discerning scents.

List 8.3 **An Aristotelian conception of the mind**

Not a substance

Neither identical with the human body, nor distinct from the human body; i.e. the questions of sameness and difference make no sense

Not a part of a human being

Informs the living organism, but is not 'embodied' in it

To possess a mind is to have an array of powers of intellect and will.

The distinctive powers of the mind are all linked to responsiveness to reasons.

Excludes sensation, perception, fantasia and appetite

Not an agent

Does not stand in a causal relationship to the body

Not a subject of psychological attributes, acts or activities

Not essentially private

Not essentially transparent

The intellect and the will, and their actualization in thought and action, are not essentially indubitable to the subject.

Our concepts and conceptions of living things are altogether different from our concepts and conceptions of the inanimate.

Our explanations of the characteristic activities of living things are altogether different from our explanations of the activities of the inanimate. All living things have a characteristic life cycle. Vegetal forms of life possess the power of growth, deriving from their environment the nourishment they metabolize to sustain their life. So the matter of which they consist is constantly changing and being replaced, and their identity is independent of the identity of their constitutive matter. They possess powers of reproduction. Like all forms of life, they are liable to disease, injury, decay and death. Given appropriate conditions, they may flourish. They possess the array of distinctive powers that Aristotle characterized as vegetative *psuchē*. (A residue of this classification is still evident in our talk of a person being reduced by illness or injury to a 'vegetative state'.) Animals, in addition to having a vegetative *psuchē*, have a *sensitive* one. They possess powers of sensation and perception, and locomotion – they are self-moving.[31] The most universal and fundamental power of perception that is essential to animal life is touch, and thereafter taste. Whatever has developed powers of sensation and perception also feels pain and pleasure, and may take pleasure or suffer pain in perceiving. Feeling pain and pleasure is also exhibited in the manifestations of desire and aversion (which are also the roots of the passions). So to have a sensitive *psuchē* is to be able to perceive, feel, want and move – which are systematically interwoven and interdependent powers. What is distinctive of humanity is the rational *psuchē* – the ability to reason and to act for reasons. To have a mind is to have an intellect and a rational will. It is to be able to reason, to apprehend things as affording reasons for thinking, feeling and acting. It is to be able to deliberate, decide or choose what to do or believe, and to modify one's feelings and attitudes, in the light of reasons. These far-reaching and complex powers are corollaries or consequences of being language-users.

---

[31] Of course, plants may turn towards the sun, wrap their tendrils around anything up which they can grow. Whether this is to count as a manifestation of the power of self-movement is unclear. But be that as it may, the Aristotelian classification is meant only to give a general overview.

9

The Self and the Body

1. The emergence of the philosophers' self

The word 'self' is recorded as far back as the tenth century, and, as we shall see, has had a multitude of respectable uses. But it is only in the late seventeenth century that it acquires the specific philosophical use as the name of a private entity within each human being. The first such use the *OED* registers is the poet Thomas Traherne's in 1674: 'A secret self I had enclos'd within, / That was not bounded with my clothes or skin.' In 1690, Locke gave this notion a wider stage on which to perform:

> every one is to himself that which he calls *self*. . . . For . . . conscious-ness always accompanies thinking, and 'tis that, that makes everyone to be, what he calls *self*; and thereby distinguishes himself from all other thinking beings. . . . it is by the consciousness it has of its pre-sent Thoughts and Actions, that it is *self* to it *self* now, and so will be the same *self* as far as the same consciousness can extend to actions past or to come.[1]

Unlike Descartes, Locke did not think that he was a thinking *sub-stance*, but only that the self with which he is identical is *annexed* to a substance, which may change without the self changing. For if I 'have the same consciousness' that I did such-and-such in the past as that I am writing now, 'I could no more doubt that I . . . was the

---

[1] Locke, *Essay Concerning Human Understanding*, II. xxvii. 9f.

same self, place that *self* in what Substance you please, than that I that
write this am the same *my self* now whilst I write (whether I consist
of all the same substance, material or immaterial, or no) that I was
Yesterday.'[2] The self, thus understood, seems to be what one refers
to by means of the first-person pronoun. By 1711, the first-person pronoun has sprouted a definite article,[3] and Shaftesbury rightly worries
about the criteria of identity of its alleged referent: 'The Question is,
"What constitutes the 'we' or 'I'?" and 'Whether the *I* of this instant
be the same with that of any instant preceding or to come.'[4] The
reductio ad absurdum was reached when Hume noted that this
innermost *subject* of experience is not even an *object* of experience.
'When I enter most intimately into what I call *myself*, I always stumble
on some particular perception or other . . . I can never catch *myself* at
any time without a perception, and can never observe anything but
a perception.'[5] He denied that we are 'every moment intimately
conscious of what we call our SELF'. The only *object* that would
satisfy the required specification, he argued, would be a constant
invariable *impression* which would give rise to the idea of the self.
But there is none such.[6] Hence he concluded that what is called 'the
self' is 'nothing but a bundle or collection of different perceptions
which succeed each other with inconceivable rapidity, and are in perpetual flux and movement'. The unity of this bundle consists in no
more than mnemonic and causal connectedness.

Hume's account earmarks the stalemate between rationalism and
empiricism, as is evident in Reid's reaction to Hume's 'bundle
theory'. 'Whatever this self may be, it is something which thinks,
and deliberates, and resolves, and acts and suffers. I am not thought,
I am not action, I am not feeling; I am something that thinks, and
acts, and suffers.'[7] But, constrained by the misconceived framework

[2] Ibid., II. xxvii. 16.

[3] An indefinite article, as in 'an other I' (i.e. a second self, a good friend), is first
recorded in 1579. Use with the definite article is recorded in 1599, but apparently
did not become common until eighteenth-century philosophical corruption.

[4] Shaftesbury, *Characteristics of Men, Manners, Opinions, Times* (Cambridge
University Press, Cambridge, 1999), p. 420.

[5] Hume, *Treatise of Human Nature*, I. iv. 6.

[6] He was obviously unacquainted with tinnitus. But sufferers from the disease are
not thereby blessed with first-hand acquaintance with a self.

[7] T. Reid, *Essays on the Intellectual Powers of Man*, Essay III, ch. iv.

of the debate, his objections falter. For the only alternative to Hume's subjectless bundle seemed to be a vague Cartesianism: 'My thoughts, and actions, and feelings, change every moment – they have no continued, but a successive existence; but that *self* or *I*, to which they belong is permanent, and has the same relation to all succeeding thoughts, actions and feelings, which I call mine' (ibid.). That the subject of experience is not the set of the modes of experience is true. What is hopelessly confused is the supposition that the subject of experience is an entity *within* a human being.

Kant went one step further. Rational psychology, he argued, confused the unity of experience with the experience of a unity. Cartesians mistook the absence of reference to a complex object – a manifold subsumable under the category of substance – for the presence of reference to a simple object, the Cartesian ego. Kant did not abandon the perceptual model of inner sense, but he saw that within these constraints the self-ascribability of representations is a purely formal feature of conceptualized experience. It makes no sense to *look* in inner sense, as Hume purported to do, for a subject of experience. Rather, any representation of which one is aware must be such as one can attribute to oneself – the 'I think' must be *capable* of accompanying all my representations.[8] But the first-person pronoun *here*, Kant argued, is purely formal and does not refer to an inner, mental substance that might be an object of acquaintance. Nevertheless, Kant did not deny that there is an empirical self. This empirical self, he claimed, is merely myself as I appear to myself, not myself as I am in myself. The latter is supposedly a noumenal entity, that must be both unknowable (since it is noumenal) and also the known subject of the moral law, the possessor of the will that is good or evil. The mysteries of transcendental idealism wrought havoc among the post-Kantian German Idealists, leading to such excesses as: '*What* was I before I came to self-consciousness? . . . I did not exist at all, for I was not an I. The I exists only insofar as it is conscious of itself . . . *The self posits itself*, and by virtue of this mere self-assertion, it exists.'[9]

---

[8] The level of generality at which Kant operates masks from the eye the questionable character of the reasoning. If having a pain is a representation, it *cannot* be accompanied by an 'I think', although we ascribe the pain to ourselves.

[9] J. G. Fichte, *The Science of Knowledge* (Cambridge University Press, Cambridge, 1982), pp. 97f. (originally published in 1794/5).

The conception of the self or 'the I' that emerged from the Cartesian and Lockean tradition has proved to be enticingly mysterious. Despite the Humean absurdities and the Kantian obscurities to which it led, it still has profound appeal. A recent philosopher writes that the sense of the self

> comes to every normal human being, in some form, in childhood. The early realization of the fact that one's thoughts are unobservable by others, the experience of the profound sense in which one is alone in one's head – these are among the very deepest facts about the character of human life, and found the sense of the mental self. It is perhaps most often vivid when one is alone and thinking, but it can be equally vivid in a room full of people. It connects with a feeling that nearly everyone has had intensely at some time – the feeling that one's body is just a vehicle or vessel for the mental thing that is what one really or most essentially is.[10]

This sense of self, we are told in strikingly Reidian terms, is the sense 'that people have of themselves as being, specifically, a mental presence; a mental someone; a single mental thing that is a conscious subject of experience, that has a certain character or personality, and that is in some sense distinct from all its particular experiences, thoughts and so on' (ibid.).

The self as understood within the tradition, has many facets. Logically speaking, it is the subject of successive states of consciousness and conscious experiences. Epistemically understood, the self is an intrinsically *private* entity – something *within* the human being, that each one of us *has*, to which only he has access and with which only he is truly acquainted. Self-consciousness is then conceived to be consciousness of that self and its states. Confusingly, the self is also supposed to be what each person *is*, or at any rate what he *essentially* or *ultimately* is. Thus understood, the self is what is *most fundamental* about a human being. It is at this point that the self parts company with the mind. For the Cartesian mind was not the purported heart and core of the personality – not the heart of the onion that Peer Gynt looked for in metaphorical search for his true self. It is here too that the admirable ideal of *sincerity*, of absence of dissimulation, feigning, pretence and deceit:

---

[10] Galen Strawson, 'The Self', repr. in R. Martin and J. Barresi (eds), *Personal Identity* (Blackwell, Oxford, 2003), p. 338.

to thine own self be true
And it doth follow, as the night the day,
Thou canst not then be false to any man

becomes confused with the quite different ideal of *authenticity*: of being true, not to oneself, but to one's hidden self:

Go through the sad probation all again,
To see if we will now at last be true
To our only true, deep buried selves
Being one with which we are one with the whole world.[11]

As we shall see, these various facets do not cohere. That is unsurprising, for the philosophical notion of the self is incoherent. It is the product of philosophers' entrapment within the web of grammar, of misconceptions of logic and ontology, misunderstandings of the epistemology of self-consciousness and self-knowledge.

2. The illusion of the philosophers' self

That something is awry should be evident. A person cannot both *be* and *have* a self. For one cannot be something that one has, no matter whether it is a mind, a body or an identity. If the self is something – or better, some thing – *within* a human being, then he cannot be identical with his self, since the human being cannot be identical with one of his constituent parts. We speak of the human being as a person, and as having a mind, as having a soul, and as having a self, in addition to having a body. One should worry that the vessel is getting overcrowded, or that there is some double counting on the manifest.[12]

The word 'self' originates as a *pronoun and pronominal adjective*, akin to the Latin *ipse*, the function of which was to emphasize the identity of the associated nominal. In Old English 'se selfa man þe' means 'the *very* man who' or 'the *same* man who'. The use to emphasize a nominal persisted until the nineteenth century (as in 'Thys is

---

[11] Matthew Arnold, 'Empedocles on Etna'.

[12] For an illuminating discussion of these matters, see A. J. P. Kenny, *The Self*, Aquinas Lecture 1988 (Marquette University Press, Milwaukee, 1988).

the thing selfe that is in debate' (Sir Thomas More, 1532); 'If a man do perform any praiseworthy Action, the self deed will sufficiently commend him' (J. Guilim, 1610); and 'I confess to a satisfaction in the self art of preaching' (Lowell, 1848)), gradually becoming superseded by the emphatic pronoun 'itself'. Related to this was the use of 'self' with a personal pronoun in the nominative as in 'Ic sylf', 'he sylfa' (1000) that is recorded as late as the seventeenth century (for example, 'Self did I see a swain not long ago' (P. Fletcher, 1633)) but was replaced by the reflexive pronouns 'myself', 'himself', 'herself', etc. When occurring with a possessive genitive, it meant 'own', as in 'her self visage' (Thomas Cromwell, 1539). As an *adjective*, 'self' has an equally venerable use, which persisted until the early seventeenth century, to signify 'same', as in 'he was that self knyght that the kiss had taken of her' (Caxton, 1489) or 'Of this selfe blood that first gaue life to you' (Shakespeare, 1588). 'One self', from the fifteenth to the seventeenth century had a use to mean 'one and the same', as in 'good and beautiful be after a sorte one selfe thing' (T. Hoby, 1561). This still survives in the phrase 'the selfsame so-and-so'. The use of 'self' as a *noun* originated in early Middle English, when 'self', preceded by a possessive pronoun as in 'þi self', 'his self', 'oure awn self', began to be taken as a neuter noun governing the preceding genitive, rather than a pronominal adjective in concord with it. From this evolved such uses as 'your dear self' and 'her sweet self', and by extension 'my other self'.

Thus far we have surveyed those uses of this seemingly inoffensive four-letter word that signify identity, function to emphasize identity, or to indicate pronominal reflexivity, noting its natural drift towards an independent nominal and towards signifying 'person'. A rather different facet of its development is relatively late. By the eighteenth century one can see the full emergence of a use of 'self' to signify what a person is at a particular time, hence one's nature, character, physical constitution or appearance, considered as different at different times. So we speak of *our former self*, of *one's later self*, of being or looking *one's old self* again after illness. Concurrently with the emergence of this diachronic use, the term was extended to signify a set of *synchronic* characteristics that can be conceived as constituting one of various conflicting personalities within a human being: for example, 'The noblest Digladiation is in the Theater of our selves' (Sir Thomas Browne, 1682); 'Every man may, yea, ought to love himself: not his sinful self, but his natural self: especially his spiritual self, the new nature within him' (Burkitt, 1703); or 'Whatever your lowest self, and not your best self, may like' (MacDonald, 1866). From this it is but a step to distinguish the notion of one's self, understood as one's concern for one's interests, hence that 'within' oneself that is selfish and self-interested, as in 'But self will still predominate' (F. Burney, 1782) or 'She's better than I am — there's less o' self in her, and pride' (G. Eliot, 1859). It is then a co-ordinate step to speak of a person's true self, which may be what is *best*, or alternatively, *most fundamental* in oneself. These, unfortunately, are not at all the same (see table 9.1 for an overview of the evolution of 'self').

We noted that we owe primarily to Locke the philosophers' special use of 'self' to indicate an entity within a human being — the true subject of psychological attributes or the collection of co-conscious thoughts that inhere in a substance, or the bundle of subjectless perceptions connected by causation and memory that constitute the real person. This is a misconception of the *mind*, on the one hand, and of the *person*, on the other, that requires eradication.

It is perfectly true that a thoughtful child may not only realize but be bemused by the fact that others cannot perceive his thoughts — but he is unlikely, unless precocious, to realize that he cannot perceive his thoughts either — he *has* them, but does not perceive them, and he can share them with others if he pleases. He may also come to think that he is therefore 'alone in his head' — but this, far from being an experience of a profound truth is a manifestation of a profound confusion.[13] For a human being is not 'alone in his head', since he is not in his head, and he is not alone, although he can be lonely.

---

[13] That intelligent children are subject to philosophical wonder, and are prone to ask philosophical questions, is familiar. They are also prone, as one might expect, to profound philosophical confusion, which they normally do not resolve, but, with the passing of time, forget. Tolstoy relates how, as a boy, 'I imagined that besides myself nobody and nothing existed in the universe, that objects were not objects at all, but images which appeared only when I paid attention to them, and that as soon as I left off thinking of them, these images immediately disappeared. . . . There were moments when, under the influence if this *idée fixe*, I reached such a state of insanity that I sometimes looked rapidly round to one side, hoping to catch nothingness unawares where I was not' (*Childhood, Boyhood and Youth* (Oxford University Press, London, 1930), p. 197). Far from insight into eternal verity, this, like the idea of being alone in one's head, exhibits susceptibility to perennial fallacy.

Part of speech	Use/example	Evolves into/example
pronoun and pronominal adjective	akin to *ipse*, as in 'se selfa man þe'; 'the thing selfe', emphasizing a noun	'itself', 'the thing itself','the very . . .', 'the same . . .'
with personal pronoun	'Ic sylf', 'he sylfa', 'self did I'	reflexive pronouns: 'myself', 'himself', 'herself'
with possessive genitive	'her self visage'	'own'
adjective	'the self knyght that', 'this self blood that'	'same'
	'One self thing'	'the self same thing'
noun preceded by possessive pronoun	'þi self', 'his self', 'oure awnself'	'your dear self', 'her sweet self', 'my other self'
noun preceded by temporal adjective	to signify a person's nature, character, appearance, considered diachronically	'my former self', 'one's later self', 'his old self'
noun preceded by adjective such as 'higher', 'lower', 'sinful', 'spiritual' or quantifier	to signify synchronic characteristics represented as homunculi standing for aspects of personality	'the higher self', 'the natural self', 'the best self', 'many selves'
noun preceded by adjective 'true'	to signify traits of character most essential or fundamental or best about a person	'his true self'
noun with definite article or quantifier	one's concern for oneself or one's interests, the self-interested aspects of the personality	'the self predominates', 'there is too much self in his writings'
as a pseudo-sortal noun	philosophical use to indicate the allegedly real bearer of psychological attributes within a person that remains identical over time	'the same self', 'the self', 'my self'; also 'the I' and its Latin cousin, 'the Ego'.

Table 9.1 *The evolution of 'self'*

(Would it alleviate his feeling of solitude if he felt that there was someone else in his head too?) What is true is that he may think, and suffer psychological torment, without telling another what he thinks or sharing his suffering. This is indeed a fact of human life, but it 'founds the sense of mental self' only if it is misconstrued. Again, it is true that in rather special circumstances we are prone to invoke the picture of one's body as a vehicle or vessel for oneself – we then speak of 'forcing our body onwards', of our body 'letting us down', or of 'letting our body find its rhythm'. One can have attitudes towards one's body, attitudes of considerable complexity, ranging from love and pride, to contempt, shame, disdain or detachment. But the conclusion that one's body is merely a vehicle for 'the mental thing that is what one *really* or most *essentially* is' is a radical misconception (see sections 3–4 below). For a human being is not *really* a mental thing, but most *essentially* an animate spatio-temporal continuant of a certain kind – even though he may keep his thoughts to himself, and even though he may live his life with an unsatisfiable craving for love and a pervasive sense of solitude.

The Lockean self was introduced as an improvement over Cartesian doctrine. Locke avoided the Cartesian identification of the mind, and hence of the referent of the 'I' in 'I think', with a spiritual substance, and he proposed, as Descartes had not, a criterion of diachronic identity for the mind or self. But, far from achieving greater clarity, this merely muddied already murky waters. The Cartesian mind was construed as essentially private, directly accessible only to the person himself. The Lockean mind and the aberrant conception of a self that it engendered retained this association with essential privacy. But the mind, *properly construed*, is not essentially private. There is nothing essentially private about the rational powers of human beings, even though the exercise of some of them, sometimes, may not be manifest, and, in some cases, can be concealed. One need not always show that one is thinking, but it is often evident that one is – for one may be thinking aloud, or one may visibly be sunk in thought. One need not always reveal what one is thinking, but there is nothing *essentially* private about thoughts one does not express. For one *can* express them – and if one does, they will then be shared with others. Similarly, one does not always display one's feelings, and one sometimes intentionally suppresses them. But one *can* show, and often *cannot help* showing, one's suppressed love, fear or anger. If what goes on in our minds were so essentially private, we would not need to take such pains to conceal it from others when we do not want them to know what we think or feel.

The association of the self with the essentially private is quite distinct from the association of the self with what is essential about a human being. We do speak of a person's true self as that which is most truly him – his most essential character traits and most fundamental commitments. This is perfectly licit, as long as it is kept separate from the previous notions, and is not reified. There is, of course, nothing epistemically private about one's true self thus conceived. Knowledge of what one's most fundamental traits and commitments are is the fruit of painful striving for self-knowledge. But others may know more about one's true self than one does oneself. This conception of the self is distinct from, although analogous to, yet another. One's true self is sometimes understood to be one's *better* self, those traits of character and commitments that display one at one's best. This too is a perfectly legitimate notion, as long as it is neither reified nor confused or conflated with its rivals.

The philosophers' notion of a self as an 'inner' subject of experience, as accessible only to oneself, as the referent of the first-person pronoun and as what one speaks of when one speaks about oneself is an aberration. *One* source of the confusion stems from inserting an illicit space in the reflexive pronouns 'myself', 'yourself', 'ourselves' to yield the expressions 'my self', 'your self' and 'our selves', and taking the word 'self' as a noun designating an entity. Then, it seems, we must investigate what kind of thing a self is. But the question is senseless. It is as if, noting that we can do things for Jack's sake or for Jill's sake and can ask others to do things for our sake, we were to go on to ask 'What is a sake?'. That is patently absurd, even though the space between the possessive nominal or pronoun and the word 'sake' *is* licit. To speak of myself is not to speak of a self that I have, but simply to speak of the human being that I am. To say that I was thinking of myself is not to say that I was thinking of my *self*, but that I was thinking of me, *this* human being familiar to my family and friends.

A second source of confusion is the Cartesian supposition that one can doubt the existence of one's body, but not of that which thinks and doubts. It then seems as if the first-person pronoun 'I' in 'I think' names, or refers to, that entity – the I or Ego, which is the mind or self. The pronoun 'I' is then construed as a referring expression that refers not to the human being using it, but to something within him, his mind or self. On some accounts, 'I' is held to have a double use, sometimes to refer to the body (as in 'I am 6 feet tall') and sometimes to the mind or self.[14] But the first-person pronoun is unequivocal. It is a degenerate referring expression (as a point is a degenerate case of a conic section or a tautology a degenerate case of a proposition with a sense). Just as a tautology is a senseless proposition, so too 'I', in the mouth of its user, has (and needs) no cognitive content ('Who do I mean by "I"? – I mean me, myself'). Its immunity to referential failure and to misidentification (save in cases of identifying oneself in a photograph) are not marks of its being a super-referring expression, but of its being a limiting case of an ordinary one.[15] Far from being a magic arrow that always hits its target, it is more like an arrow stuck in the wall around which one can always draw a bull's-eye. It is more akin to 'here' and 'now' than to 'there' or 'then', and very unlike 'he' or 'she'. It might be said to be akin to the point of origin of the deictic system, and to that extent unlike the points on a graph. Its primary role is to index an utterance. One commonly uses it to speak about oneself, but one does not identify oneself – rather, using it enables the audience to identify the subject of predication. Unlike 'he' or 'she', 'this' or 'that', 'here' or 'there', it has no anaphoric use. In so far as it can be said to be used in order to refer, it certainly does not refer to a self. The fact that it can be used in silent soliloquy should not persuade us that it then refers to a self, only that one is then thinking about oneself.

A third source of misunderstanding is the Lockean misconception of introspection and self-consciousness. For if one thinks of

---

[14] Much is also made of a distinction Wittgenstein drew in the Blue Book between the use of 'I' as subject (as in 'I have a pain') and its use as object (as in 'I have broken my arm'), the latter allegedly involving recognition of a person and being subject to misidentification. But the distinction is wrong (and Wittgenstein never mentions it again). I may be mistaken about whether my arm or your arm is broken, or, in exceptional circumstances, whether *this* arm is mine or yours. But even in such cases, when I say 'I have broken my arm', I do not *misidentify* myself or *mistake* myself for you. Rather, I mistake my arm for yours, mistakenly attribute to myself something attributable to you.

[15] See G. E. M. Anscombe, 'The First Person', in S. Guttenplan (ed.), *Mind and Language* (Oxford University Press, Oxford, 1975), and A. J. P. Kenny, 'The First Person', repr. in his *The Legacy of Wittgenstein* (Blackwell, Oxford, 1984). For a survey of Wittgenstein's ideas on this theme, see P. M. S. Hacker, 'I and Myself', in *Wittgenstein – Meaning and Mind* (Blackwell, Oxford, 1990), and for further elaboration, see H.-J. Glock and P. M. S. Hacker, 'Reference and the First-Person Pronoun', *Language and Communication*, 16 (1996).

introspection as inner perception, then it seems as if what one is conscious of are the attributes of the inner subject of consciousness –
the self. Self-consciousness then appears to be consciousness of the
self and its states, rather than consciousness of – that is, *reflection
and deliberation on* – the attributes, character traits, tendencies and
history *of oneself*.

A fourth source of the illusion is intimately related to this. There
is an asymmetry between first- and third-person ascriptions of many
psychological attributes. To find out whether another is in pain, is
pleased or sad, is thinking, is intending to act, one must look to see.
Other-ascription rests on behavioural criteria consisting in what the
other person does and says. But in one's own case, one does not observe
one's own behaviour in order to find out that one is in pain, and
one does not have to see what one says before one can say what one
thinks. This engenders the illusion that the real subject of psychological predicates is not the observable human being, but some other
entity – a self – within him, that one observes indirectly in the case
of others, and to which one has privileged introspective access in one's
own case.

3. The body

The nature of the mind has been obsessively discussed since Descartes,
and examined in great detail by analytic philosophers of the twentieth century. It is, however, surprising to find how little attention has
been given, in the analytic tradition, to the ways in which we think
and speak about our own bodies.[16] It has, with a few noteworthy
exceptions, been assumed that the concept of the human body is
itself quite unproblematic.[17] Philosophers, deceived by the Cartesian

---

[16] Continental philosophers have not overlooked the human body: e.g. Max
Scheler, *Zur Phänomenologie und Theorie der Sympathiegefühle und von Liebe und
Hass* (Niemeyer, Halle, 1913); Jean-Paul Sartre, *Being and Nothingness* (Methuen,
London, 1957), Pt 3; and Maurice Merleau-Ponty, *The Phenomenology of Perception*
(Routledge & Kegan Paul, London, 1962).

[17] The most helpful exceptions that I have noted are D. C. Long, 'The Philosoph-
ical Concept of the Human Body', *Philosophical Review*, 73 (1964), and 'The
Bodies of Persons', *Journal of Philosophy*, 71 (1974); J. Cooke, 'Human Beings', in
P. Winch (ed.), *Studies in the Philosophy of Wittgenstein* (Routledge & Kegan Paul,
London, 1969).

conception of the mind, found it difficult to see how to fit their mind (understood as the domain of consciousness) into their overall scientific conception (or misconception) of nature. But they found nothing in the least problematic about their body. It is, they supposed, just one physical object among others. This thought lies within the long shadow cast by Descartes:

> the first thought to come to mind was that I had a face, hands, arms, and the whole mechanical structure of limbs which can be seen in a corpse, and which I called the body. . . . by a body I understand whatever has determinable shape and definable location and can occupy a space in such a way as to exclude any other body; it can be perceived by touch, sight, hearing, taste or smell, and can be moved in various ways, not by itself but by whatever comes into contact with it. For, according to my judgement, the power of self movement, like the power of sensation or thought, was quite foreign to the nature of a body.[18]

As already remarked, Descartes, unlike Aristotle, thought about the body as a physicist, rather than as a biologist. Life, in his view, is not categorially different from inanimate nature, merely more complex, and the principles of explanation applicable to living beings (except man), are no different from the explanatory principles needed to explain mere matter. Few passages could, under a veneer of the obvious, be more misleading than the one just quoted. The 'mechanical structure' – the anatomy of the human body – can indeed be seen in a corpse, but not the physiology, not the frenetic activity of the billions of living cells that maintain the dynamic equilibrium between the organism and its environment, nor the ceaseless action of the internal organs that enable the living animal to function and to engage in its characteristic forms of behaviour. The power of self-movement is denied to bodies, and hence, according to Descartes, to animals – whose apparent self-movement, he held, is no less 'mechanical' than the growth of plants or movements of the planets. Real self-movement, he thought, is to be found only in man and is, as it were, a form of telekinesis – being the causation of the movements of the body by the mind. But when *we* contrast mind and matter, when we admire the triumph of mind over matter, we are not speaking of a power of the mind to move matter. We are concerned with a human

[18] Descartes, *Meditations*, 2 (AT VII, 26).

being's heroic resistance to exhaustion and to pain (which we allocate to the *body*) – the triumph of the will over *physical* suffering.

I *have* such-and-such a body, just as I have such-and-such a mind.
Am I my body? Surely no more than I am my mind. Am I then a
third thing? Is the body of a living human being the same as the body
he leaves behind when he dies, that he leaves to science or wishes to
be cremated? – Same *what*? It is not the same *corpse*, since the body
of a living human being is not a corpse. It is not the same *living body*,
since the living body is not to be cremated. Same body? – That depends
on what exactly is meant by 'body' and on whether 'a person's body'
is a covering sortal for such statements of identity.

NN has a head, two arms and two legs. Does his body have a
head, two arms and two legs? 'Of course!', we are inclined to say.
But perhaps we should take things slowly. If NN went to war, and
lost his left leg on the Normandy beaches, it can be said of him, 'Poor
fellow, he lost his left leg in the War.' Can it be said, 'Poor fellow,
his body lost *its* left leg in the War'? If NN dies, we may say to the
undertaker: 'His body has only one leg, *he* lost his left leg on the
Normandy beaches (not: '*it* lost its left leg on the Normandy
beaches'). I can have my mother's eyes and my father's nose. Can
I have my body's nose? Does my body *have* a nose? Presumably only
if it has a face? Can we speak of my body's face? – Well, it is certainly not *false* that it has a face; but it is not *obviously* true either.
(And if it is indeterminate what we should say, *that too is an important datum*.) NN had a quick mind and a noble soul. Did his body
have a quick mind and a noble soul? What would a person's body
do with a mind? or a soul? The thickets through which we must find
a pathway are dense. Let us first generalize the puzzlement.

What is it to *have* a body? What has to be true of a being for it
to be said of it that it *has a body*? – after all, trees and plants certainly do not have bodies. My body cannot think, or speak, and it
cannot walk or run; so, what attributes *can* the body of a living human
being have? We have two arms and two legs. These are *parts* of the
human being, of the human organism. By extension, they are also said
to be parts of the body a human being is said to have. We speak of
ourselves as having a body, and are prone to think, by analogy with
having arms and legs, that the body we have is likewise a part of
ourselves – the material part, the other part being the mind. That is
a natural movement of thought. But in philosophy what is natural
is to err. So we must investigate how the mind that a human being
has is related to the body that he has.

We are trying to understand a small, but important, segment of our conceptual scheme. It is important primarily because it is the source of so much, and of such important, confusion. We are dealing with ancient ways of thinking and speaking that are deeply embedded in our language.[19] They can be illuminated only by a careful examination of the familiar uses of 'A's body', 'my body' and related phrases, and by scrutiny of the peculiar idiom of *having* a body and limbs that runs parallel to *having* a mind. The idiom is a quagmire in the jungle of grammar into which many a philosopher has sunk.

The word 'body' in English has many different uses (see fig. 9.1). At its most general, a body is simply a spatio-temporal material continuant. Differentiating solid, movable bodies from such things as a body of cold air, a large body of land, and a body of water, 'a body' signifies a material object (as in Newton's law: 'a body continues its state of rest or steady motion, . . .'). In this sense, human beings *are* bodies, as are plants and other animals. They are differentiated from inanimate (mere) material bodies in virtue of being alive. This marks a qualitative difference (as Aristotle emphasized, and Descartes denied), which has left its mark on our conceptual scheme – not because our remote ancestors were so sapient, but because the primitive human reactions to what is alive as opposed to what is dead, and to what is alive as opposed to what is inanimate, are so profoundly different.

The animate body that a human being is, is the human organism. Clearly, a human being does not *have* the organism that he *is*. So the body – the organism – that he is, is not the body that he has. The human organism has parts: head, torso and limbs, which are parts of the human being.

It should be noted that we also use the term 'body' to refer to the trunk or main bulk of a living thing.[20] This use derives its significance from one or other of three different contrasts: (i) with the

---

[19] There are numerous word pictures that survive in English, related to the body, that are even older and that characterize numerous different languages, modern and ancient. Such phrases as 'it made my blood boil', 'in the marrow of my bones', 'on my head be it', 'my face burned with shame', 'to get it off one's chest', 'not to breathe a word', date back into the mists of pre-history. See R. B. Onians, *The Origins of European Thought* (Cambridge University Press, Cambridge, 1951).

[20] Also, of course, to the main part of inanimate things, as when we refer to the body (nave) of a church in contrast to the aisles or transepts, or to the body of a document, in contrast to the preamble or appendices.

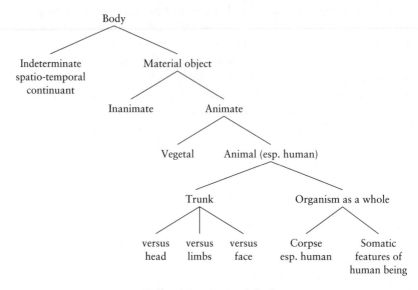

Figure 9.1.   *Uses of 'body'*

appendages, members, limbs; (ii) with the head, as when we speak
of someone having a small head on a stocky body, or when someone is condemned to have his head struck from his body; (iii) with
the face or features, as when we remark that Daisy has an indifferent
face but a beautiful body.

A quite different use is to refer to a corpse, as when we say that
the dead monarch's body is lying in state, that NN's body is in the
next room, or that the battlefield was strewn with bodies of dead
soldiers. A number of interesting features attend this use. First, it is
noteworthy that in ancient Hebrew and in Homeric Greek alike, the
term for body (*guf* (then undifferentiated from *gufa*) and *soma*) was
restricted to what we now call 'the corpse',[21] and no word was used
to speak of the body a living man has. Secondly, it is striking that
not all modern languages employ the same word to refer both to the
body a person has and to the body he leaves behind. German, for

---

[21] Strikingly, 'corpse' ('cors', 'corps'), like the Latin *corpus*, originally could
mean either the living body or the lifeless remains ('dede corps' (1385) was not
pleonastic).

example, uses *Leib* (a cognate of *Leben*) or *Körper* (derived from *corpus*) to signify the living body, and *Leiche* to signify the corpse. Thirdly, it is unclear what creatures can be said to leave a corpse when they die. Certainly a dead tree or plant is not the corpse or body of a tree or plant. The sardines we buy at the fishmongers are not *corpses* of sardines. A dead horse or cow may be a carcass, but perhaps not a corpse (again, if usage here is indeterminate, that too is an important datum.) Fourthly, it is the human being – the mortal man – that dies, not his body. Leonidas died fighting valiantly at Thermopylae. It was he, not his body, that was killed. What was left upon the stricken field was his corpse – his *remains*.[22] Cleopatra killed *herself*, but it is doubtful whether one can cogently say that the beautiful body she had then *became* a corpse. Nor can one say that the alluring body she *had* is dead – she is dead, and what is left is her corpse (and one would not say of it that it is the body she had). Fifthly, we are inclined to assent to such assertions as 'When I die, I shall no longer exist, but my body will persist for a while', and perhaps even to 'When I die, my body will cease to be me, and I will no longer exist'.[23] But the body I have when I am alive cannot, as we shall see, be said to be me, and the body I leave behind – that is, my corpse, is not the living body (the animate spatio-temporal continuant) that

---

[22] Do we not say, of the barge that bears the coffin of Winston Churchill that it 'is taking Sir Winston Churchill on his last journey'? Do we not write of the Norman cortège wending its way through the mists of Normandy bearing the stinking corpse of Henry I back to England, 'Henry of England was coming home'? Do we not say 'Nelson is buried in St Paul's'? – Yes, we do; the moot question is what is meant thereby. Churchill had already made his last journey, and Henry would never come home again – that is presupposed as understood. But the pathos added by these forms of words is patent. What are buried in St Paul's are the bodies – corpses – of the great and glorious dead. They themselves no longer exist. Is a dead animal not an animal? Surely we can say that the rabbit you are now eating is one and the same animal as the rabbit you saw and shot yesterday; is that not an identity statement? Can we also say that the venison you are now eating is one and the same animal as the deer you saw and shot yesterday? 'Dead (animal)' is not a phase sortal. 'Infancy', 'childhood', 'youth', 'adulthood', 'senescence' are phases through which any human being must by nature pass if they live long enough. Being dead is not a phase in human life, but its terminus. When I die, I do not become a corpse – I cease to exist, leaving my corpse – my remains – behind. The adjective 'dead' functions in certain respects like 'fake' or 'counterfeit'. A dead horse is not a horse, any more than a fake Picasso is a Picasso.

[23] Kenny, *The Self*, p. 24.

I am. A living body is not the same *anything* as a corpse – no common
sortal subsumes both. Of course, they can be said to be the same
'spatio-temporal continuant' – but that is no sortal. The corpse is
the dead human being, and a dead human being is no more a human
being than a counterfeit five-pound note is a five-pound note.[24]

The most common use, and the one most pertinent to our concerns,
signifies the physique or figure of a human being, the appearance,
condition of health and fitness. Commonly 'body', thus used, goes
with a modifying adjective, as in 'a supple / healthy / frail / crippled /
athletic / powerful / muscular / beautiful / attractive / sexy / sensual /
body'. Often it is used to draw a contrast with the person's mind,
as when we say, 'His body is frail, but his mind is as active as ever'
(i.e. he is physically frail but mentally alert) or as when young males,
ogling at an alluring young woman on the beach, say, 'Look at her
body!' (i.e. look at her figure), and as when we observe, 'He has a
powerful body' (i.e. a powerful physique). It is this use that we need
to examine. (There are many others, but they are not pertinent to our
present concern.)

What ranges of things can be attributed to *my* body or *NN's* body?
– What can a person's body *be*? It can be sun-tanned all over, be
white through lack of exposure to the sun or red from excessive exposure. It may be painted blue (like the bodies of the ancient Britons),
gleam with oil (like the bodies of the ancient Greeks in the palaestra),
or be covered with dust, mud or blood. It may be badly lacerated
or covered with mosquito bites. It may be tense or relaxed, strong or
weak, fit or out of condition, muscular and hard or fat and flabby.
It may be paralysed or shaking uncontrollably in shock. And it may
be beautiful or ugly, graceful or ungainly, gangly or dumpy. And it
may be covered up, exposed or flaunted.

If a person's body is sun-tanned all over, then that person is sun-
tanned all over. If someone has a powerful, badly scarred body,
then he is physically powerful and badly scarred. And if someone's
body is out of condition, then the person is out of condition. It is
tempting to conclude that anything true of a person's body is also true
of the person. This is generally true, but we should note exceptions.
If Daisy's body is beautiful (if she has a beautiful body), it does not

---

[24] To be sure, there is sufficient flexibility in our form of representation to provide *some* licence to refer to the corpse – the dead body – as a human person, especially immediately after death – as when one discovers the dead body of a comrade
on the battlefield and exclaims, 'Oh no! It's N. He's been shot.'

follow that she is beautiful – for we may continue: 'but she has an ugly face' (see p. 272 above). One may admire her body without admiring her (she may be a dreadful person). A man may say, 'I am interested in her body, not in her mind.' But the civilized alternative to being interested in her body is not being interested in her mind, but being interested in her.

It is noteworthy that our form of discourse about our body licenses describing it, as well as our parts (limbs, head and torso) as *sensitive*. My leg may itch, my swollen hand may throb, and my body may ache all over. It was a grievous error of Descartes to suppose that the human body is an insensate biological 'machine'. It was a mistake to draw the boundary of mind and body between sensibility (and other forms of Cartesian thought) and insensate matter. We, being sapiently more Aristotelian, allocate sensation to the body a human being has no less than to the human being – it is an aspect of the sensitive *psuchē*. Localized sensations such as itches, pains and tickles are located in the body, although not in the manner in which pins or bones are (whereas heartbreaks and heartaches are only metaphorically so). We specify their bodily location when identifying such sensations, and we point to the place of an ache, tickle or itch when asked where it aches, tickles or itches. We assuage the sensation, rub or nurse the part of the body that hurts, scratch the part that itches or tickles. Bodily sensations typically have a physical cause. Its locus is typically, but not necessarily, the place of the sensation. Hence we rightly contrast *physical* pains with the pains of grief, distress and other forms of mental suffering that have no somatic location.[25]

Sensations, then, are in the body. What is the relationship between the sensitivities of my body and the sensations I have? If my body aches all over, I ache all over; if my back aches, then I have a backache, and if my hand hurts, then I have a pain in my hand. But my back does not *have* a backache, and my hand does not *have* a pain,

---

[25] It is noteworthy that when body and soul are contrasted, then further liabilities and susceptibilities other than to mere sensation are commonly allocated to the body – to the flesh. For lust, greed and gluttony, cravings and addictions – the 'lower passions' or appetites – are often (especially in Christian cultures) associated with the body in the divide between body and soul. Consequently, when the soul is contrasted with the body or the flesh, a quite different distinction is being drawn than that between the mind and the body, no matter whether the latter distinction is construed in Cartesian terms or along the lines described in this book.

let alone a pain *in it*. If I have hurt my hand, then I have hurt myself
– but my hand has not hurt *itself*. My body may be racked with pain,
and I may bite my lips to stop myself from crying out – but it is not
my body that cries out, even if I cry out inadvertently.

What else *cannot* be said of a living person's body? A person's
body is not the subject of voluntary and intentional predicates. My
body may tremble or be paralysed, but it does not move itself, it
does not walk, jump or run. Nor is it the subject of perceptual,
cognitive, cogitative or affective predicates. A human being's body
does not see or hear, know, believe or think, feel cheerful or angry.
It may drip with sweat, but it cannot weep. It may be unfit, but it
cannot take exercise. Since a person's body is logically excluded
from being the subject of these distinctive attributes, we are inclined
to think that something *other* than, and *distinct from*, the body
must be their subject; namely, the mind. But it is *the human being*
that is the subject of experience and the agent of action. What,
then, *is* the relationship between a human being and the human
being's body?

4. The relationship between human beings and their bodies

It has been suggested that a human person is *constituted* by his body.
One version of this conception is a more or less self-conscious transformation of Aristotelian hylomorphism (the *psuchē* being the form
of the living body).[26] The human person, it is suggested, stands to
the flesh and blood of which he is constituted as the *psuchē* to the
living body. Admittedly, the human person seems to be competing
with the living body (the organism) for the same constitutive matter
(the flesh and blood), and surely two different things cannot be in
the same place at the same time. This objection is dismissed on the

[26] See David Wiggins, *Identity and Spatio-Temporal Continuity* (Blackwell, Oxford,
1967), pp. 47–9, where such a constitutive Aristotelian view is advanced. A variant
view was propounded in *Sameness and Substance* (Blackwell, Oxford, 1980), p. 164.
There he characterized a person's body as that which *realizes* the person while he
is alive and will be left over when he dies. Both conceptions were abandoned in
Sameness and Substance Renewed (Cambridge University Press, Cambridge, 2001).
Wiggins's heroic odyssey is highly instructive.

grounds that although two things of the *same kind* cannot occupy the same space, things of *different kinds*, such as the human person and the human body, can.

This is out of focus. The human organism consists of flesh and blood (i.e. has an organic constitution variously describable in terms of parts, or in terms of stuffs, the stuffs in turn being describable at various levels of analysis). But the human organism – the individual animal of the species *homo sapiens* – *is* the human being. The human being – the human person (of which more in ch. 10) – is not the form of the human body in *this* sense, he *is* this organism that has the distinctive powers constitutive of being a person. Furthermore, the Aristotelian *psuchē* stands to the living body as the powers of an animate substance stand to the substance. But that is not how the human being or person stands to the organism he is, let alone to the body he has.[27]

A different constitutive account has been essayed. The relation between a human being and his body, it is suggested, is the same as that between a statue, such as Michelangelo's *David*, and the piece

---

[27] It is noteworthy that one can readily generate paradoxes if one asserts *both* that one is made of flesh and blood *and* that one's body is made of flesh and blood. For whereas I *am* the living organism that is made of flesh and blood, I don't *have* it. But it is easy to see how one can unreflectively slide down this slope. The clash can be avoided by restricting ascription of organic constitution to oneself – the living organism.

Similarly, we (especially philosophers) are prone to say such things as 'My body weighs *n* stone' and 'My body is *n* feet tall'. This is normally unobjectionable, since it means neither more nor less than 'I weight *n* stone' and 'I am *n* feet tall'. But it too can be used to generate paradoxes. If I am *n* feet tall and weigh *n* stone, and my body is also *n* feet tall and weighs *n* stone, are there two physical objects here occupying the same space? – The question is surely awry. 'My body', we have suggested, is no more than a *façon de parler* – a way of speaking of my corporeal characteristics, not a way of referring to a physical entity I inhabit. One might compare it, in certain respects, with 'my sake'. If you V for my sake, you V for me. Do you then V for one thing or for two? Here the question is patently awry. What then are we to make of the phrase 'the body I have'? Is *the body I have* as heavy, tall, fat, etc. as the body I am? Does it occupy the same space as the body I am? The phrase 'the body I have' might illuminatingly be compared with the misbegotten phrase 'the sake I have'. If you do something for my sake, but do not do the same thing for A's sake, is that because the sake I have is more worthy than the sake A has? The phrase 'the sake I have' is patent nonsense. The phrase 'the body I have' is not; but if misconstrued, it can lead one into nonsense.

of marble that constitutes it.[28] But a statue is neither constituted by *a piece of marble*, nor is it *a piece* of marble, any more than a cake is constituted by a piece of cake or is a piece of cake, or a car is constituted by a piece of metal or is a piece of metal. 'Piece' is one of the most general non-typical partitives. It applies both to abstract and to concrete non-count nouns (as in 'a piece of news' and 'a piece of bread'), by contrast with such typical (type-specific) partitives as 'grain', 'bar', 'drop', 'loaf', 'lump', 'sheet', 'slice', 'sliver', 'strip'. A desk is not a piece of wood, although it may consist of pieces of wood and also may have been made out of pieces of wood. The *David* was *made out of* a large piece of marble already worked and then abandoned by Agostino di Duccio. It is *made of*, consists of, *marble* (more than a ton of it), but it does not consist of *a piece of marble*. Nor is it constituted by a piece of marble, any more than Rodin's *Balzac* is constituted by *a chunk* of bronze or Leonardo's Sforza monument was constituted by *a lump* of clay. A human person does not consist of a *piece* of flesh. He is made of flesh and blood, but not made out of flesh and blood. And he is not *constituted* by his body.

A quite different conception is vehicular. One might be tempted to claim that 'my body is the vehicle of my agency in the world'.[29] It is tempting to say that my body is the body the arms of which rise when I raise my arms, the legs of which move when I walk, and that it is the body with the eyes of which I see when I open my eyes.[30] The temptation should be resisted, for two reasons. First, my relation to my body is not that of a driver to his car (my car is indeed

---

[28] L. R. Baker, *Persons and Bodies – A Constitution View* (Cambridge University Press, Cambridge, 2000). See also S. Shoemaker, *Personal Identity: A Materialist's Account* (Blackwell, Oxford, 1984), p. 113, who holds that a bronze statue consists of a 'hunk of bronze', and that the *quantity* of bronze of which it is composed is an *entity*. That is mistaken. 'A hunk' is a *particular* designating partitive (like 'grain', 'nugget', 'slice', 'sliver'), and artefacts do not *consist* of the particulate partitions of the stuff from which they were made. So, for example, my gold ring does not consist of three little nuggets, four slivers and five grains of gold, even though these may well have been melted down in order to yield the *n* grams of gold of which my ring does consist. Artefacts can indeed typically be said to consist of constitutive stuff identified by *quantity* designating partitives, such as 'a gram (of spice)', 'a pint (of water)', 'a handful (of rice)'. But these are not things or 'entities', but quantities.

[29] R. G. Swinburne, *Personal Identity* (Blackwell, Oxford, 1984), p. 22.

[30] See e.g. P. M. S. Hacker, 'Strawson's Concept of a Person', *Proceedings of the Aristotelian Society*, 102 (2001), pp. 30f., where I succumbed to this temptation.

the car the front wheels of which turn left or right when I turn the steering wheel). When the driver turns the steering wheel, he makes it go round; but when he raises his arm, he does not make it rise, or cause it to rise (see ch. 7). When he turns the steering wheel with his hands, he brings it about that the car changes course; but when he raises his arm, he does not bring it about that his arm rises. A person may control his body in certain respects, but not as a driver controls his car. Nor is he *in* his body as a driver is in his car – but not because he is 'more closely intermingled with it'.

Secondly, while it is true that I see with my eyes and walk with my legs, it is far from obvious whether we can speak of my seeing *with my body's eyes* and walking *with my body's legs*. My head, torso and limbs are parts of me – of the human being I am. I have a body, and my limbs are parts of my body. But my body does not *have* a body. Does it *have* a head, limbs and torso? Although the mereology of the human being is homologous to that of the body he has, it is the human being that *has* arms and legs – that is, we do not, by and large, extend this very peculiar *possessive form of representation* from the human being to the living body that is his. My leg may be bruised, but we would not say that my body's leg is bruised. I may suffer from meningitis, but we would not say that my body's brain suffers from meningitis. These are forms of words that *have been given no use* – and it is best left that way. Could we use them? Of course – if we changed a great deal of the surrounding grammar. But then the words would no longer mean the same.

One might try to clarify the relationship between a human being and his body by reference to the dependence of perceptual experience upon facts about the body. Whether one sees anything at all depends on whether one's eyes are open. What is visible to one, it is said, depends on where one's body is located, on the direction in which one's head is turned and on how one's eyeballs are oriented. Such facts of experience dependence might be thought to explain why the 'possession' of a particular body should be ascribed to the *same* thing as states of consciousness. They might be thought 'to explain why a particular body should be spoken of as standing in some special relation – called "being possessed by" – to that thing', that human person. They are said to explain

> why a subject of experience should have a very special regard for just one body, why he should think of it as unique and perhaps more important than any other. . . . they might even be said to explain why, granted

that I am going to speak of one body as *mine*, I should speak of *this* body as mine.[31]

This passage is subtly mistaken. We may grant (with deliberate rephrasing) that the visual experiences a human being has depend on where that human being is, on the state of his eyes and on the direction in which he is looking. But such truths do *not* explain why 'a particular body' should be spoken of 'as standing in some special relation – called "being possessed by"' – to that human being. The body a human being *has* is not a body he literally *possesses*, any more than the birthday, the wife, and the mind he has, are things he *possesses*. One may have a house, a ticket to the opera or a copyright. These one can sell or give away – and once sold or given away, they are no longer one's own, but belong to another. One can sell one's body – but to do so will not leave one bodiless. (Similarly, when Faust sells his soul to the devil, he is not left soulless.) To sell one's body is to sell sexual services; it leaves one bereft of certain freedoms, not of a body. Is not having a body logically akin to having two arms or legs? No; for I can lose an arm or a leg, but I cannot lose my body. (Of course, someone may find my body – but then he needn't return it. And if I lose my mind, there is no point looking for it in the lost property office.) Could one not say that the relationship between a human being and his body is one of ownership, but that unlike humdrum relations of ownership, the possession of a body is *inalienable*? No; something can be inalienably possessed only if it *makes sense* for it to be alienated.

It is mistaken to suggest that the various forms of the experience dependence of a human being on his location, orientation and the condition of his sense-organs 'explain why a subject of experience should pick out one body from among others, give it, perhaps, an honoured name and ascribe to it whatever characteristics it has' (ibid.). For, to be sure, a subject of (conceptualized) experience does *not* 'pick out one body from among others' and call it his own. One has no choice, and *could have* no choice, in what to speak of as 'my body'. Furthermore, nothing could explain 'why, granted that I am going to speak of one body as *mine*, I should speak of *this* body as mine'. As an English speaker, I am going to use the English *phrase* 'my body'; I speak of my body as aching, showing its age, fit or out of condition.

[31] P. F. Strawson, *Individuals* (Methuen, London, 1959), p. 93.

But I do not speak of 'one body among others' as mine. If I say, 'My body is aching all over', no one could ask 'Which body is yours?'. It is tempting to claim that 'that which one calls one's body is, at least, a body, a material body. It can be picked out from others, identified by ordinary physical criteria and described in ordinary physical terms.'[32] But this is misleading. 'Which body is my body?' has little use. Far-fetched cases apart, its only use is grammatical: that is, to ask what 'my body' means. 'This 🖐 (pointing reflexively) is my body' has *no* use in *picking my body out from others*, although it might be used to explain the phrase 'my body'.[33] The material body, the animate spatio-temporal continuant made of flesh and blood, that *can* be picked out (by others), identified and described in 'physical terms', *is me*. But I don't call that which *I am* 'my body'. I *am* a body; but I don't *have myself*, don't *have* the body I am. We sometimes speak of ourselves as being *embodied*, but mistakenly so. It is but one step from this figure of speech to think of ourselves as *residing* in our body. It would be far less misleading to think of ourselves, with Aristotle, not as embodied but as *ensouled* (*empsuchos*) – endowed with the powers that characterize humanity.

We have seen that the mind is not a kind of entity, that our customary talk of the mind is no more than an abstraction from our talk of human beings, of their intellectual, mnemonic and volitional abilities and their exercise. It should by now be evident that our parallel talk of our body is in a like manner largely derivative from our talk of human beings. We have and exercise an array of cognitive, cogitative and volitional powers that we exhibit in our behaviour. As agents of this kind, we are said *to have a mind*. We likewise have a variety of corporeal determinables[34] – a *physique*, a *figure*, physical *appearance*, susceptibility to *sensation*, degrees of *fitness* (ability to engage in *physical activity*) and *health*. As such agents, with a mind that is manifest in corporeal activities and reactions, we are also said *to have a body*, and can be described as having *such-and-such* a body (powerful, muscular, lithe, graceful). We describe ourselves thus when

---

[32] Ibid., p. 89.

[33] It might also be used rhetorically in charged circumstances, e.g. sexual, or to declare one's freedom to do as one pleases in a certain respect, e.g. to get oneself tattooed.

[34] Not *physical* determinables (if by 'physical' we mean: pertaining to physics) – that is the Cartesian road to nowhere.

we wish to focus upon such attributes, and to manifest our *attitudes* to them. For we may be proud of our body (if it is fit and beautiful) or ashamed of it (if it is fat, flabby and ugly), admire the beautiful bodies of the young and be shocked by the mutilated bodies of the injured. We may be comfortable with our body, or ill at ease with it (e.g. if we are pathologically obsessed with our physical appearance and condition). Being self-conscious creatures, much preoccupied with sexual attraction and commonly given to degrees of hypochondria, it is hardly surprising that we should think a great deal about our physique, aesthetic appearance, attractiveness, our physical condition.

In the sense in which 'a body' is a material spatio-temporal continuant, then, of course, human beings are bodies – although this is a quasi-technical use of 'body', and not something that can be said unmisleadingly or inoffensively in extra-philosophical discourse. Material spatio-temporal continuants may be inanimate or animate. Those that are animate are organisms of varying degrees of biological complexity. Human beings are highly complex organisms, and in this sense too are bodies. Being a body in this sense, being an organism, implies being a body in the most general sense. We further speak of ourselves as *having* a healthy, ageing, weak or strong body. To be sure, only a creature that is a body in the previous sense can thus be said to *have* a body. The moot question is: What has to be true of a creature that is an animate spatio-temporal continuant for it to be said to have such-and-such a body? The most coherent answer is: only if it can also be said to have such-and-such a mind. No doubt we sometimes extend the idiom to other animals, by analogy with ourselves. We may well say of an injured horse that its poor body was terribly lacerated, just as we may say of a stubborn horse that refused to do what we want it to do that it has a mind of its own. Such uses are harmless extensions, but they show little about the rich web of connections in the paradigmatic case. One might also say that the idiom of *having a body* is a formal mark of advanced sentient life that also leaves a corpse on death. It is no coincidence that human attitudes towards their dead are distinctive, and that the treatment of the corpse is informed by ritual.

So, talk of our body is no less derivative from, or parasitic on, talk of the human being as a whole than is talk of our mind. We say of another: 'She has a beautiful (athletic, clumsy, elegant, dumpy) body, sweet (sour, attractive, expressive, poker) face, lively (dull, inquisitive, quick, slow) mind and kind (soft, hard, broken) heart.' Until we stop to think about it, it would not occur to anyone that we are doing anything other than talking about a single human being – specifying a variety of different modes that our complex species may exemplify in a variety of complex ways. But, like Augustine, once someone asks us, once we stop to think, we become entangled in the web of words.

What, then, is the relationship between the mind and the body? The mind–body problem *is* insoluble. For it is a hopelessly confused residue of the Platonic/Augustinian/Cartesian tradition. It cannot be solved; but it can be *dissolved*. The mind is not an entity that could stand in a *relationship* to anything. As we have seen, all talk of the mind that a human being has and of its characteristics is talk of the intellectual and volitional powers that he has, and of their exercise. The body that a human being *is*, the living organism, has and exercises those distinctive intellectual and volitional abilities that we speak of when we speak of people's minds. But the body that a human being is said to *have*, when we speak of human beings as having beautiful or athletic bodies, is not the kind of thing that could be said to possess intellectual and volitional abilities. For we speak of a human being's body thus when we focus upon corporeal characteristics that the human being in question has. These characteristics, the very distinctive range of corporeal features of a human being that we assign to the body he has, are not the kinds of thing that could make up their minds, call things to mind, or change their minds.

The mind a human being has and the body he has are not the kinds of things that could stand in *any* relationship to each other in the sense in which Jack and Jill (or London and Paris, or a man and his property) may stand in various relationships to each other. The apparent relationship is comparable to the 'relationship' between the meaning of a word and the phonemes into which the word can be analysed – both being abstractions from the meaningful word in use. The English word 'cat' *has* a meaning (it means the carnivorous quadruped *Felix domesticus*), but does not stand in *a relationship* to its meaning, any more than I stand in a *relationship* to my mind. The phoneme *kæt* neither has a meaning nor stands in a relationship to a meaning – it is a phonologists' abstraction from the meaningful English word. Again, one might compare the question of how my mind is related to my body with the question of how the value of a £5 note is related to its colour. For here too one might explain that a £5 note is green and has a value of five pounds, but the colour green does not stand in any *relationship* to the value of five pounds.

Green does not *have* a (monetary) value, the value of five pounds has no colour, and the £5 note itself does not stand in any *relationship* either to its value or to its colour. So too, my body does not have a mind (what would my body do with a mind?). Moreover, it does not stand in a relationship to my mind either, *I* have a mind – and a body, but 'having' here does not signify a relationship.

10

The Person

1. The emergence of the concept

The concept of a person is central to our thought about ourselves, our nature, and our moral and legal relations. That human beings are persons is not a trivial tautology, but a fundamental claim about our moral status and our singularity in the order of nature. 'A *person*', Kant wrote, 'is a subject whose actions can be imputed to him. *Moral* personality is therefore nothing other than the freedom of a rational being under moral laws.' 'Whereas', he added, 'psychological personality is merely the ability to be conscious of one's identity in different conditions of one's existence.'[1] Self-consciousness and awareness of one's diachronic identity, in his view, are preconditions of being a person, but they are not sufficient conditions. In the system of nature, he averred,

> a human being is a being of slight importance and shares with the rest of animals, as offspring of the earth, an ordinary value. Although a human being has, in his understanding, something more than they and can set himself ends, even this gives him only an *extrinsic* value for his usefulness . . . But a human being regarded as a *person*, that is as

[1] Kant, *The Metaphysics of Morals*, 6. 224. His addendum may be directed against Christian Wolff, who, in Lockean spirit, wrote: 'Since we designate as person, a thing that is conscious of having been the same thing previously in this or that state, animals are not persons. On the other hand, since human beings are conscious of having been the same previously in this or that state, they are persons' (*Rational Thoughts on God, the World and the Soul of Man* (1725), §924).

a subject of a morally practical reason, is exalted above any price; for
as a person he is not to be valued merely as a means to the ends
of others, but as an end in himself, that is he possesses a *dignity* (an
absolute inner worth) by which he exacts *respect* for himself from all
other rational beings in the world.[2]

No philosopher has placed greater emphasis on the *ethical* character of the concept of a person and on its essential link to the concepts of *freedom* (hence *reason*) and *responsibility*, or had greater
influence in allocating such a pivotal role in the characterization of
our conceptual scheme to the concept of a person thus conceived.

It was not always so. The concept of a person originated from the
word *persona* – the mask (Greek *prosōpon*) worn by an actor in the
ancient world to signify the role he was playing.[3] Thence it was
naturally extended to the role a human being has in life. In the
writings of the Stoics, the idea of *persona* was associated with morality not via the notion of man as possessor of the powers of practical
reason, but rather via that of social role – what would later become
known as the ethics of 'my station and its duties'. Epictetus insisted
that 'to play well the assigned role (*prosōpon*) is your business but
to choose the role, the business of another'. Similar sentiments are
expressed by Cicero in *De Officiis*, where he compares the stage
personages created by the playwright with the character (role,
persona) that nature has assigned to each of us.[4]

The association of *persona* with the notion of a role spread to the
law courts. For the plaintiff and defendant are, by analogy with the
actor on-stage, playing clearly defined roles, and 'persona' became
used for these. The expression was rapidly extended to encompass
human beings standing in other characteristic legal relations, in particular *qua* possessors of *ius* (commonly translated as 'a right').[5] So

---

[2] Ibid., 6. 434f.

[3] The following historical observations are indebted to Adolf Trendelenburg,
'A Contribution to the History of the Word Person', written in 1870 and published
posthumously in *Kantstudien* (1907) and in translation in *The Monist*, 20 (1910),
pp. 336–63.

[4] Cicero, *De Officiis*, I – xxviii; cp. xxxi.

[5] Very much later, the concept of a legal person was extended to create the notion
of an 'artificial person' in law, such as a corporation or other institution that is
the bearer of legal rights and duties, and has legal responsibilities. This extended
concept of a person will not be discussed here.

in the *Institutes* I, §8, it is observed that 'every right of which we treat pertains to persons or to things or to lawsuits', and §9 adds: 'And indeed the highest division of persons in law (*Et quidem summa divisio de iure personarum*) is this, that all men are either freemen or slaves.' Here 'person' stands in contrast to things, and extends the original notion of *role* to signify *human beings* in general. (Thus used, the later Kantian proposition 'Human beings are persons' would be a trivial tautology.[6]) However, Roman law rapidly evolved to exclude slaves from the category of persons. Justinian's translators of the *Institutes* characterize slaves as *aprosōpos*, and from Justinian's codifications onwards, only the legally qualified man is a person. Slaves were characterized as things, and a person was defined as a man of civil status (*Persona est homo statu civili praeditus*).

Further complications were generated by Christian struggles with the doctrine of the Holy Trinity. Greek theologians had characterized the Father, Son and Holy Ghost as three *hypostases* with one divine *ousia* (nature or essence). The Latin translation of this generated severe difficulties, since *hypostasis* ('foundation' or 'standing under') is literally translated as *substantia*, which is also used to translate *ousia*. Tertullian, in *Adversus Praxeas*, suggested that the Holy Trinity consisted of three *persons* in one substance, remarking that he used this term for the purpose of distinguishing the Father, Son and Holy Ghost, not of separating them ('*Personae, non substantiae nomine, ad distinctionem non ad divisionem*').[7] It was of this doctrine that Augustine later candidly remarked in *De Trinitate*, 'We say "three persons" not because this expresses just what we want to say, but because we must say something.'

Boethius, in the sixth century, defined 'person' as 'an individual substance of rational nature'.[8] This detached the concept of a person from that of a role, and associated it with the array of capacities which

---

[6] It is noteworthy that this general usage exists in English to this day, in such turns of phrase as 'a young person', meaning a young man or woman, and in the slighting usage 'a person in trade' or 'a sort of secretary person down at the works' (*OED*).

[7] This generated further serious trouble, since translating back into Greek involved the word *prosōpon*, (mask or role), ascribing to the Trinity three *roles* performed by *one nature*, thus heretically denying separate individuality to the Father, the Son and the Holy Ghost.

[8] Boethius, *Liber de persona et duabus naturis contra Eutychen et Nestorium*, ch. 2.

Aristotle had emphasized as distinguishing humans from other animals.
This conceptual nexus was adopted (and modified) by Aquinas and
transmitted to early modern philosophy.

   In philosophy of the modern era, the concept of a person has been
the locus of much confusion. What precisely is a person? How is a
person related to the human being that is one? How is the person
related to the mind and to the body that a human being is said to
have? The confusion is unsurprising. On the one hand, the traditional
debate itself was entangled with religious commitments of questionable intelligibility concerning survival after death. On the other hand,
the family of concepts of person, body, mind and soul has been, and
in many ways remains, bewilderingly fluid. 'Person' can be used to
speak of a human being's personality, as in 'He is not the same
person as he used to be'. It can also be used to refer to the corporeal
features of a human being, specifically with regard to appearance and
dress, as in 'a fair person', 'comely of person', 'a pale, thin person
of a man' or 'in disregard of one's person and dress'. Thus used, it
approximates 'body'. Conversely, 'body' could also mean person, as
in 'A better body neyuer drunk wine' (1340); 'Every noble body ought
soner chese deth thene to do . . . thing that sholde be ayenst their
honour' (1475); 'the foolish bodyes say in their hertes: Tush there is
no God' (1653); and as late as 1771, 'The countess was a good sort of
body'. All that remains of this usage in current English (by contrast
with Scottish English) is 'somebody', 'anybody', 'everybody' and
'nobody'. To multiply confusion, the soul, like the body, is presented
as something a person has. But the word 'soul' could also mean living
thing in general, as in 'All maner of soulles yt crepe vpon earth' (1535),
or person – as in 'The number of British slain in 11 years was
112,000 souls' (1672), 'We have now pretty accurately ascertain'd
the Number of Souls . . . existing in England' (1724), and 'poor soul',
or 'a merry old soul'. Finally, 'mind', which likewise signifies something that a person is presented as having, can mean thinking people
too – as in 'The best minds [the most intellectually gifted people] in
Britain were gathered at Oxford', or 'Two minds [thinking people]
are better than one'.

   The sources of confusion, however, reach deeper. They are also to
be found in the grammar of first-person psychological predications
and their asymmetry with third-person ascriptions. For third-person
ascription of psychological predicates rests on behavioural criteria.
But first-person utterances do not. So we are prone to confuse the
absence of 'outer', behavioural criteria with the presence of 'inner',

mental criteria, to which the subject, it then seems, has privileged access. Confusion is further exacerbated by knowledge of curious experiences, such as 'out-of-the-body' experiences, and multiplied by religious doctrine and promises of an afterlife, which encourage the misconceived identification of the person with the mind or soul.

2. An unholy trinity: Descartes, Locke and Hume

The fluidity of the language in which the questions were posed is bewildering enough. The debate between the leading early modern philosophers magnified the confusion. It is instructive to examine the contours of that debate, for the difficulties with which we are still struggling are direct descendants of seventeenth- and eighteenth-century reflections. They can be resolved only by identifying ancestral confusions and eradicating them.

As we have seen, Descartes set the stage, claiming that a human being is not an *ens per se*, but a union of two one-sided things, a mind and a body. The self (the ego, the *res cogitans*), however, was conceived to be a unitary substance – a single one-sided thing, the essence of which is thought or consciousness.[9] The difficulties associated with the Cartesian conception are various. The first two turn on the intelligibility of the idea of an immaterial substance and its attributes.

(1) There are criteria (*constitutive*, not *inductive* evidence) for ascribing psychological attributes to human beings. They consist of what people do and say in the circumstances of their lives. If someone injures himself and groans or writhes, we say that he is in pain; if someone looks through the window and says, 'Oh, it is going to rain', we say that he thinks that it is about to rain; if someone turns white and trembles in the face of danger, we say he is afraid; and so forth.[10] If psychological attributes are ascribable to immaterial substances, we can ask the questions: On what grounds does it make sense to ascribe a given psychological attribute to an immaterial substance?

---

[9] It is noteworthy that Descartes does not invoke the term 'person' at all, but speaks rather of 'the I', of the mind or soul that he is.

[10] Of course, such evidential criteria are defeasible. In *some* circumstances, someone may be simulating or acting. But what is possible some of the time, or in some circumstances, is not possible all of the time or in all circumstances.

How are we to render intelligible to ourselves what it means for an immaterial substance to be thinking, fearing, hoping, imagining, something or other? What makes a given attribute an attribute of *this* immaterial substance? And if no satisfactory answers are forthcoming, this will call into doubt the intelligibility of the idea of such an immaterial substance.

Immaterial substances, according to Descartes, do not *behave.* They think, they judge and will – which are not forms of (corporeal) behaviour. Although they are held to *cause* the behaviour of their bodies associated with such mental acts, the evidential nexus that would warrant others ascribing mental attributes to them would have to be *inductive, analogical,* or an *inference to the best explanation,* rather than constitutive (criterial). For the Cartesian conception of mind and body holds there to be no *conceptual* connection between 'the inner' and 'the outer'. For the mind and the body are two independent entities that stand merely in a causal (external) relation to each other.

Inductive, analogical or other non-constitutive grounds for ascription of mental attributes to others presuppose non-inductive identifications. For all involve the correlation of the inner and the outer in one's own case as a basis of an inductive, analogical or explanatory inference from the behaviour of others to their mental attributes. This requires the independent identification of one's own mental attributes and the behaviour that is allegedly discovered in experience to be regularly correlated with it.

Identification of the behaviour, both in one's own case and in the case of others, is, it seems, unproblematic. But 'the inner', according to this conception, does not belong to the public domain. Only the subject, it seems, has access to it. So any inductive correlation of inner and outer has to be established by the subject in his own case. Only when that is established, can he go on to consider the ascription of psychological predicates to others. Accordingly, the Cartesian must propose *some basis* for the self-ascription of such predicates. Waiving, for the moment, any worries about its character (awareness, introspection, inner sense, etc.), this in turn would demand some means for assigning a meaning to, and explaining the meaning of, psychological predicates *independently of any conceptual nexus with behavioural manifestation.* For in order to take oneself to be in pain, to be thinking this or that, to be judging or willing, one must possess the concepts of pain, thinking, etc. But there can be no such means for assigning or explaining the meaning of these predicates, even in one's own case and for one's own subjective purposes. For private ostensive definition of mental predicates by reference to putatively private defining samples laid up in memory is incoherent.[11] It is incoherent to suppose that one might define concepts such as *pain, thinking, willing* by reference to mnemonic samples, as one explains the meaning of colour or length predicates by public ostensive definition employing colour charts or rulers. For memory images cannot satisfy the conditions required for something to be a sample. For there can be no criterion of identity for the putative mental sample. So a memory image can play no role in the rules for the use of mental predicates. Moreover, a mental image cannot function, as samples can and do, as an object for comparison. For there is no such thing as *comparing* the putative mental sample – the memory image – with what it may be a sample of in order to determine the identity or content of a current experience. One cannot juxtapose one's memory of a pain (or of thinking, seeing, etc.) with what one has in one's leg (or with what one is doing or experiencing) to determine whether the latter is a pain (is thinking or seeing), as one can juxtapose a sample of ultramarine with a curtain to determine whether the curtain is ultramarine, or a ruler with a piece of string to determine whether the string is 15 inches long.

Of course, we, by contrast with the dualist, apply to ourselves a distinctive range of psychological predicates without any grounds or criteria at all. We do not say that we are in pain or thinking on the basis of observation of our behaviour. But we do not say this on the basis of inner *observation* and *comparison with a mnemonic sample* either. Rather, we have a pain, and say so. We think, and we say that we are thinking. But we can do so only in so far as we have mastered the public, constitutive, behavioural criteria for applying such predicates to others. The groundless self-attribution of psychological predicates and their criterial other-ascription are two sides of the same coin, two aspects of the technique of using these familiar predicates. Their meaning is not given by a private ostensive definition, and they are not applied, either to oneself or to others, on the basis of comparison with a private sample.

(2) Officially, the identity of the mind just is the continued identity of one and the same immaterial substance. But we have been given no criterion of identity for immaterial substances. So there seems no

---

[11] See Wittgenstein, *Philosophical Investigations* (Blackwell, Oxford, 1953), §§243–315. For detailed elaboration of his private language arguments, see P. M. S. Hacker, *Wittgenstein: Meaning and Mind* (Blackwell, Oxford, 1990).

way to distinguish between one immaterial substance thinking all my thoughts at a given time and a thousand such immaterial substances thinking the very same thoughts. The difficulty is not epistemic, but logical. Nothing has been laid down to determine what would *count* as one such substance as opposed to a thousand. The problematic nature of the synchronic identity of the mind is mirrored by similar puzzlement over its diachronic identity. So, it seemed to Locke to matter not a whit, as far as one's own sense of identity over time is concerned, whether the substance in which Cartesian thoughts inhere be the same substance or not from day to day, as long as the thoughts – the variety of modes of consciousness – remain appropriately connected. And that is incoherent.

(3) Corresponding to the incoherences concerning mind (the ego or self) are the incoherences, noted in the previous chapter, concerning the body that a human being is said to have, coupled with the unwarranted denial that I – a human person – *am* a body, that is, an animate spatio-temporal material continuant. For the body that we are is, as it were, conflated with the body we have, which is conceived to be an *insensate* piece of biological machinery, animated, during our life, by the presence of the person *embodied* within it. The person, however, is in effect identified with the mind or soul. But, as we have seen, in one sense of 'body', a human being is a body and is a living organism (which is not something a human being *has*). In another sense, talk of the body a human being *has* is no more than a manner of speaking of an array of attributes of a human being, including bodily *sensations* (as long they are ascribed by means of verbs).

(4) Having bifurcated human beings into two conjoined substances, Cartesians had to explain how they interact. Notoriously, Descartes held the locus of interaction to be the pineal gland (now known as the pineal body, since it is not a gland). But if there is a mystery as to how an immaterial substance can interact with the body, it is not obviated by holding that it does so by interacting with the pineal gland or any other bodily part. This problem, as Descartes admitted to Princess Elizabeth of Bohemia, seemed insuperable. Strikingly, however, neuroscientists, until the mid-twentieth century, continued to speculate about the locus and mode of interaction of the mind with the brain.[12]

---

[12] So, e.g., the great Charles Sherrington, and his renowned pupils John Eccles and Wilder Penfield were all committed to mind–brain causal interaction. Eccles spoke

(5) The semantic consequences of dualism are far-reaching and unacceptable.

There is a clear commitment to the thought that all predicates predicable of human beings can be divided into two fundamental classes, predicates of the mind signifying the range of modes of consciousness, and predicates of the body signifying the range of physical attributes of insensate matter.[13] In natural languages there are numerous predicates that cannot be allocated to either of these, such as 'greeted', 'warned', 'sat down wearily', 'walked hurriedly'. But that is only because they are to be analysed, in a 'metaphysically perspicuous language', into mind predicates pertaining to an agent's knowledge, belief, perception and volition (Cartesian thoughts), and body predicates concerning physical movements caused by the mind. This programme of analysis has never been carried out. Nor can it be, since it involves a misunderstanding of the use of predicates of cognition, cogitation and volition. Voluntary action is not bodily movement caused by an act of volition of the mind, and to do something with understanding is not to accompany one's action with a simultaneous activity of understanding. There is similar incoherence when it comes to predicates such as 'is in debt', 'is the son-in-law of', 'is the President', 'scored a goal'. Such actions and relations are analysable not in terms of mental acts and bodily movements, but in terms of norm subjects – people – their relationships and their normative powers under constitutive norms of action.

Corresponding to this dichotomous account of predicates predicable of human beings is the equally unacceptable claim that the first-person pronoun is systematically ambiguous, sometimes referring to the body that a person has and sometimes referring to the person – that is, to the mind that he allegedly is. Moreover, when the predicate

of the 'liaison brain' and held one point of interaction to be the pyramidal cells of the motor cortex. And his philosopher friend Karl Popper held that the 'self plays on the brain, as a pianist plays on a piano or as a driver plays on the controls of a car' (K. R. Popper and J. C. Eccles, *The Self and its Brain* (Springer Verlag, Berlin, 1977), pp. 494f.; cf. p. 362). For detailed discussion, see M. R. Bennett and P. M. S. Hacker, *Philosophical Foundations of Neuroscience* (Blackwell, Oxford, 2003), ch. 2.

[13] Localized sensations are accordingly allocated to the mind as subject, their physical localization held to be uniformly in the brain, and their phenomenal localization construed as an 'as-if' that seems warranted by the phenomena of phantom-limb pains (see Descartes, *Principles of Philosophy*, I, 46, 67, and esp. IV, 196). A comparable view is defended today by J. R. Searle, who holds that pains are in the body image that is in the brain.

is allegedly 'mixed' (like 'sat down wearily'), then there is held to be a *double* reference. For what is meant is that I – the mind or person that I am – was weary, and that I – the body that I have – sat down. But this account of the semantics of the first-person pronoun is wildly implausible. There is no grammatical evidence to suggest any such ambiguity in the use of 'I'. Our common references to, and predications of, our body are misconstrued. The fact that there are some sentences in which 'my mind' can be replaced by 'I', such as 'My mind is confused', no more shows that 'I' and 'my mind' are co-referential than the fact that 'my sake' can be replaced by 'me', as in 'Do it for my sake', shows that 'me' and 'my sake' are co-referential. Similarly, the fact that 'I ache all over' is equivalent to 'My body aches all over' does not show that 'I' in the first sentence refers to my body, any more than the equivalence of 'My bank account is in the red' and 'I am in the red' shows that 'I' in the latter sentence refers to my bank account. Whether or not the first-person pronoun is usefully deemed a referring expression or a degenerate case of a referring expression (see pp. 266f.), it is evident that it never *refers* to a person's mind *or* to his body.

Descartes himself did not explicitly discuss personal identity at all. But Locke inherited the problems implicit in Cartesian dualism, and struggled mightily with them. By interiorizing the problem of the diachronic identity of a person and suggesting that the criterion of identity of a person lies in mnemonic continuity, he bequeathed a web of interrelated difficulties in which philosophers are still enmeshed. According to Locke, a person is 'a thinking intelligent Being, that has reason and reflection, and can consider it self as it self, the same thinking thing in different times and places'. So, to count as a person, a creature has to have or be able to have a sense of its own identity over time. Whence this awareness of identity?

> Since consciousness always accompanies thinking, and 'tis that, that makes every one to be, what he calls *self*; and thereby distinguishes himself from all other thinking things, in this alone consists *personal Identity*, i.e. sameness of a rational Being: And as far as this consciousness can be extended backwards to any past Action or Thought, so far reaches the Identity of that *Person*; it is the same *self* now as it was then: and 'tis by the same *self* with this present one that now reflects on it, that Action was done.[14]

---

[14] Locke, *Essay Concerning Human Understanding*, II. xxvii. 9.

He rightly held the concept of a person to be forensic, and further held (rightly or wrongly) that a condition of responsibility for one's past action is that one is conscious of, recollects, having done the action.

Inheriting the Cartesian identification of a person with a mind, and conceiving of substance in general as no more than an unqualified support of qualities, Locke saw no role for substance identity in identification of oneself as the person who did such-and-such in the past. Some substance, he held, was necessary, since consciousness, including consciousness of one's past experiences, must *inhere* in something or other – but not obviously in *the same* substance. All that is necessary for the identity of myself with the person who did this or that in the past, Locke held, is mnemonic connectedness. If I can remember catching a salmon on a certain occasion, then I am the same person as he who caught a salmon then. But Locke, countenancing relative identity, disconnected *being the same person* not only from *being the same substance*, but also from *being the same human being*. The identity of a human being consists in the identity of the same living creature. The identity of a person, by contrast, consists in the existence of the series of appropriately connected memories. In principle, these two may come apart – it is, according to Locke, conceivable that one might wake up 'in the body of a cobbler' – with all one's normal memories. We shall examine such puzzle cases below.

To suppose that the experiences of a person must 'inhere in' a substance is perfectly correct (though poorly expressed – it is a point of logic, not of super-physics, and the use of the phrase 'to inhere in' is an invitation to confusion). But to suggest that the substance that 'thinks in me' (as Locke put it) may change independently of my continued identity is incoherent. That incoherence stems from Locke's failure to grasp the logico-grammatical category of substance (see pp. 53f.). Confusion is further multiplied by supposing the human being to be distinct both from the person and from the substance that 'thinks in him'. The only truth of the matter here is that *person* is not a substance concept. It does not follow that the entity that qualifies as a person is not an individual substance of a certain kind – such as a human being.

Interiorization of the criteria of personal identity was a mistake. Our first question should be perfectly general, namely: 'What is it for A to be the same person as B?' This is a demand for clarification of the concept of a person and the associated constitutive conditions of identity. The second question should be couched in the third person, namely: 'What are the *evidential* criteria we employ to determine whether A is the same person as B?' This demands clarification of *how we tell* whether A is the same person as B. Such clarification is required *prior* to investigating the first-person case. For first-person mnemonic judgements of the form 'I am the person who V'd on such-and-such an occasion' involve no identification of a person. 'I V'd' is normally a memory utterance that rests on no evidential grounds.

Memory is not a source of knowledge, but retention of knowledge possessed. I can be said to remember breaking a leg on a past occasion, if and only if I broke a leg then and have not forgotten that I did. Consequently, memory is not *my criterion* for whether *I* am the same person as the little boy who broke his leg. If I remember breaking my leg on the relevant occasion, then I don't need evidence for my having done so – I already know. 'I remember . . .' does not answer the question 'How do you know?'; it deflects it. To say that I remember V-ing, I need make no judgement of identity. It is in effect to say that I V'd previously and knew that I was V-ing, and I still know that I V'd (have not forgotten my V-ing).[15] It does not allude to a way of finding out that I am identical with the V-er, but is a declaration that it is not necessary for me to find out. Of course, there are many episodes in a person's early life that he may indeed find out about, but this is precisely what is not disclosed by memory – although the discovery may stir the memory. Equally, that A remembers V-ing shows *us* that A is in fact the person who . . . ; that is, a memory avowal is *an* evidential criterion of personal identity *in the third-person case*. But it is not a necessary condition, and its validation *as correct* requires establishing that the human being was in the appropriate place at the appropriate time to do or experience what he avows he recollects doing or experiencing.

Locke's conception was rightly criticized by Butler, who observed that 'consciousness of personal identity presupposes and therefore cannot constitute, personal identity, any more than knowledge, in any other case, can constitute truth which it presupposes'.[16] In recollecting that I V'd yesteryear, what I remember is *my* V-ing. What I now know,

[15] In the case of psychological attributes that are such that it makes no sense to speak of the subject knowing or being ignorant that things are thus with him, to remember that one V'd, e.g., that one was in pain, amounts to having been in pain and knowing now that one was in pain because one was in pain (not because one then knew one was).

[16] Butler, *Analogy of Religion*, 1st Dissertation.

because I then knew, is that *I* V'd. My recollecting does indeed presuppose that I, who have not forgotten my V-ing, am the very person who V'd.

The supposition that the identity of a person, the 'sameness of a rational Being', *consists* in memory of past action and thought continues to play havoc with philosophical reflection. It is the source of the contemporary neo-Lockean idea that the determinant of personal identity is 'psychological continuity'. This is doubly confused. First, it is not true that psychological continuity, correctly understood, is necessary for the identity of a person over time. For it would be mistaken to suggest that an amnesiac is not the same person after his memory-destroying mishap as prior to it. He may indeed have little sense of who and what he is – that is, *little sense of his own identity* – but it does not follow that he is a different person from the man who had the accident. Secondly, the very idea of psychological continuity is incoherent when severed from the idea of a substance – in our case, the living human being – the psychological characteristics of which persist.

The second point requires some elaboration. Memory is knowledge retained. What is known (in the Lockean case in question) is known to a person. Knowledge is a diffuse array of abilities. To remember what one previously knew is to retain the cognitive abilities antecedently acquired. Personal or experiential memory is retained knowledge of what one did and of what befell one. Undoubtedly, it is an important, indeed partly constitutive, feature of human persons that their *sense* of their own identity turns to a large extent on their possession of a 'first-hand autobiography'. A normal human being can remember not merely that, for example, he caught a salmon on his twelfth birthday (which he may have forgotten and then learnt at second hand), but can remember catching it (*his* catching it) on that occasion. And if a person remembers catching a salmon on his twelfth birthday, then he is indeed the very same person as that triumphant young fisherman. This is a part of what is meant by 'psychological continuity', and it presupposes the independent constitutive conditions of personal identity.

Memory, being the retention of a complex ability (e.g. to answer such-and-such questions, to correct such-and-such mistaken assertions, to adduce such-and-such justifications), is not something that it even makes sense to *transfer*. I can tell you *what* I know, and then you too will know it. But I cannot transfer *my knowing*, not because it is too difficult, but because there is no such thing – it is a meaningless form of words. It was, therefore, misconceived of Locke to claim that

> That with which the *consciousness* of this present thinking thing can join it self, makes the same *Person*, and is one *self* with it, and with nothing else; and so attributes to it *self*, and owns all the Actions of that thing, as its own, as far as that consciousness reaches, and no farther.[17]

For consciousness (i.e. knowing, remembering, perceiving, etc.) can no more *join itself* with anything than length or weight can. Hence too, it cannot disjoin itself from one thing and join itself with another. So too, consciousness, remembering, etc., cannot be *transferred* from one human being to another. Attributes or qualities are not transferable – only shareable – baggage (and if I share my knowledge with another, I don't lose it).

Least of all can a person's knowing or remembering be transferred from the brain or body of one human being to that of another. Being abilities, they are not to be found *in*, and are not possessed *by*, brains or bodies that human beings have, but by human beings. The brain may indeed be the vehicle of our cognitive abilities, but an ability is not reducible to its vehicle. One may fantasize that by transferring bits of one brain to another brain one may transfer memories, and that by transferring all the putative engrams in A's brain to B's, one could transfer all A's memories to the brain of another – who would now enjoy 'psychological continuity' with B. That is mere science fiction (of which more below). But the most that could result is not that B would be A, but rather that B would seem to remember doing what A did.[18]

Locke's discussion contains elements that have to be taken into account in any elucidation of the concept of a person: namely, substance,

---

[17] Locke, *Essay*, II. xxvii. 17. He further added, in a very revealing mistake, that 'Upon separation of this little Finger, should this consciousness go along with the little Finger and leave the rest of the Body, 'tis evident the little Finger would be the *Person*, the *same Person*; and *self* then would have nothing to do with the rest of the Body.' A little finger is not a candidate for being a person, and consciousness can no more 'go along' with it than it can go along with a table; nor, as we shall see, can it go along with the brain.

[18] Neo-Lockeans at this point introduce a notion of 'quasi-memory'. For refutation of that conception, see D. Wiggins, *Sameness and Substance Renewed* (Cambridge University Press, Cambridge, 2001), ch. 7.

living animal of a given kind, self-consciousness, experiential memory, a sense of one's own identity, and liability to praise and blame. But, labouring in the shadow of Descartes, on the one hand, and in that of Christianity, on the other, interiorizing a question that requires exteriorization, and being hopelessly confused about the concepts of substance and attribute, he conjoined the pieces incoherently.

Hume inherited Locke's incoherences, and, while rightly rejecting his confused notion of a substance (see pp. 53f.), pursued them to their absurd consequences. His famous chapter 'Of Personal Identity' in the *Treatise* is remarkable for not really touching on the concept of a person or on the identity of persons at all. It is concerned only with puzzlement regarding the unity of experience and the putative inner constitutive criteria of diachronic identity of a subject of experience.

Hume denied that we are 'every moment intimately conscious of what we call our SELF' – that is, a simple immaterial entity that is the subject of our experiences. The only object which would approximate that specification, he argued, would be a constant and invariable *impression*, which would give rise to the *idea of the self*. But, he insisted, there is no such constant impression. For, 'when I enter most intimately into what I call *myself*, I always stumble on some particular perception or other . . . I can never catch *myself* at any time without a perception, and can never observe anything but the perception.'[19] Hence he concluded that what is called 'the self' is 'nothing but a bundle or collection of different perceptions which succeed each other with an inconceivable rapidity, and are in perpetual flux and movement'.

However, having abandoned the conception of an inner subject of experience (an immaterial substance that is the self), and the very concept of a substance in which attributes may be said to inhere, and consequently conceiving of impressions and ideas as distinct existences, Hume found himself faced with the problem of discovering a principle of unity that determines a series of experiences *as* the experiences that are *his*. Causal connectedness and the resemblances that he thought constitutive of memory (i.e. between an original impression and a subsequent idea that is a copy of it) seemed the only glue available to bond together the bundle of experiences. But such principles can be thought to unify a manifold only if it makes sense for the constituents of that very manifold *not* to be thus united. Causation

---

[19] Hume, *Treatise of Human Nature*, I. iv. 6.

and resemblance can provide no *real* (i.e. logical) *connection* between distinct existences (as Hume thought impressions and ideas to be). But that the 'perceptions' I have are *mine* is a real (logico-grammatical) connection, not an empirical one. For it makes no sense to query whether the experience I am now enjoying is really mine or perhaps someone else's, *a fortiori* to *find out* whether it is mine by detecting whether it stands in mnemonic or causal relations to my previous experiences. Hence Hume's candid confession of failure in the Appendix to the *Treatise*: 'All my hopes vanish, when I come to explain the principles, that unite our successive perceptions in our thought or consciousness. I cannot discover any theory which gives me satisfaction on this head.'

Hume was right to reject the confused Lockean conception of substance as support of qualities, but wrong to abandon this crucial categorial concept. He was right to hold that there is no such thing as a self that is the subject of experience and that one might encounter in introspection. But he was mistaken to suppose that this shows that there is no substantial subject of experience – which is, after all, the living human being. He was confused to treat experiences (impressions and ideas) as 'independent existences', since there can be no experiences that are not someone's experiences, any more than there can be qualities that do not qualify anything. It was incoherent to ask what unites *the series of experiences I have*, in virtue of which they are *mine*, and necessarily futile to search for a principle of unity in experience. Had he raised the question of synchronic unity of experiences (e.g. of my simultaneously seeing the view from the window, hearing what you are saying, feeling cold, and having a headache), the absurdity of his attempted answer might have been obvious to him. For my contemporaneous experiences can obviously not be *my* experiences in virtue of being related by resemblance (or memory). By focusing exclusively on diachronic unity, the absurdity of his question was concealed from sight. But it is absurd to search for a principle of unity to apply to the field of experiences one *has* in order to differentiate those experiences that are one's own from those that are not. For the experiences I *have* cannot but be *my* experiences. It is logically impossible for me to have an experience that is not mine, since 'my experience' = $_{df.}$ 'the experience I have'. So there is no work for a principle of unity or a principle of difference to do. In so far as it makes sense to ask what *makes* my current experience *my* experience, then, the only answer is that it is the experience that is exhibited in *my* behaviour – *if* I choose to manifest my experience or if I cannot but show it (as in the case of severe pain). But, of course, *I* do not take or avow my current experiences to be mine on any grounds whatsoever. Rather, others can ascribe such experiences to me on the grounds of what I say and do.

The incoherences of the Cartesian-empiricist tradition were brilliantly criticized, but not satisfactorily remedied, by Kant, even though, as we noted, he allocated to the concept of a person a pivotal role in his moral philosophy. As William James was later to remark on this long debate on personal identity, 'Terribly, therefore, do the sour grapes which those fathers of philosophy have eaten set our teeth on edge.'[20]

3. Changing bodies and switching brains: puzzle cases and red herrings

Since time immemorial, human beings have fantasized about metempsychosis, the transmigration of souls. A variant of the idea is patent in Locke's supposition of the intelligibility of the prince awakening 'in the body' of the cobbler, having retained all his memories. This thought has been given rein in fiction, both in Anstey's *Vice Versa* and Conan Doyle's short story 'The Keinplatz Experiment', and in more extreme form in fairy tales, such as 'Beauty and the Beast', and surrealist fiction, such as Kafka's 'Metamorphosis', where Gregor Samsa finds himself 'in the body' of a giant beetle. These fantasies are supposed to illustrate the transference of the mind – indeed, of the person, conceived as identical with his mind – from one body to another. Amusing or terrifying as these fictions are, it is doubtful whether they make sense. Like Escher etchings, it is not easy to see where the incoherence is rooted. That is part of their charm. In *this* sense of 'imaginable', imaginability is not a criterion of logical possibility. Whether the tale makes sense has to be submitted to at least as careful a scrutiny as Escher's etchings demand. To identify the incoherence in the former case is considerably more difficult than in the latter.

In the sense in which human beings *are* bodies, then, it is clear that a human person can no more *change* bodies than can a house, a tree, a cat or a dog. Ascription of properties to the body *of* a living human being, as we have seen, is merely an alternative way of describing the corporeal properties of the human person. In the sense in which

---

[20] W. James, *Principles of Psychology*, vol. 1, p. 366.

human beings *have* bodies, then, talk of the body a human being has is a *façon de parler* behind which lie the corporeal attributes of a human person. Hence there is a trivial sense in which a human being can change his body. If his body is fat, he can diet and lose weight – then he will have a thin body. If her body is ungainly and her nose unsightly, then she can have plastic surgery and emerge from it with a shapely body and an attractive face. So, in this sense, human beings *can* change their bodies – that is, change from having a fat and flabby body to having a fit and athletic one.

Obviously, this is not what is meant. Could one's mind not be transferred from one organism to another? Would this not involve changing one's body? I can give another the same pain I have. If I have a stomach-ache from eating bad oysters, and I give you the same oysters to eat and you then have a stomach-ache that you describe in the same terms as I describe mine, then you have the same pain as I.[21] I can 'give' you my thoughts and beliefs by telling you what I think and believe and giving you good reasons for thinking and believing likewise. Then, if you are reasonable, you will have the same thoughts

---

[21] It is true that your stomach-ache is in your body and mine is in mine, but that is no reason for thinking that you have a different stomach-ache from mine. Different people may have the same pain if the pain has the same phenomenal qualities, the same intensity and the same location. But what we call 'same location' (of pains) is precisely location in *corresponding* parts of their respective bodies (or are we to argue that only Siamese twins with pain at the point of juncture can have the same pain?). The subject of pain does not determine the identity of the pain. So *being had by A* is not a distinguishing property of the sensation that might differentiate it from B's sensation. Similarly, *being had by this curtain* does not differentiate the maroon colour of this curtain from the maroon colour of that one. The subject of such attributes is not a differentiating mark of the attributes.

Nor will it help to try to differentiate people's sensations in terms of types and tokens. It has been argued that your pain is a different token-pain from mine, just as the first occurrence of the word 'pain' in this sentence is a different token of that word from the second. But this is mistaken. Peirce's distinction between type-words and token-words is dependent on conventions of orthography (and is ill-defined to boot). The criterion for two inscriptions in a given language being different tokens of the same type-word is that they consist of the same letters. The type–token distinction cannot be extended to pains, any more than it can be extended to colours. If there is a pair of maroon curtains, then there are two curtains of exactly the same colour, not two token colours of the same type. One may say that the two curtains are qualitatively identical but numerically distinct, but one cannot say that of their colour. Similarly, if two people have a splitting headache in their left temple, which they sincerely describe in exactly the same way, they both have the same pain – neither numerically nor qualitatively the same, but just the same.

and beliefs. But that, no matter how extensive, involves nothing that could be described as 'changing bodies'. For one thing, giving another person the pain I have no more means that I cease to have the same pain than persuading another to think what I think means that I cease to think thus. But even if I were to cease having the pain I have when I ensure that you have the same pain, or if I were to cease thinking what I persuade you to think, it would not follow that you were gradually becoming me – no matter how many of my mental attributes or modes of my consciousness you acquire in *this* sense. It would merely mean that you were becoming more like me. But numerical identity is not a limiting case of similarity. Not even my psychological *Doppelgänger* is me.

Of course, when philosophers speak thus of transferring thoughts or memories from one person to another, they do not mean transferring *what* is thought or remembered. Rather, they entertain the fantasy of transferring the thinking or remembering. But it makes no sense to speak of transferring *my* thinking that *p*, *my* expecting that *q*, or *my* having a headache – understood as events, processes or states. For thus understood, these items are *dependent particulars*. The event of my feeling a twinge, as opposed to the twinge I feel (the sensation), is identifiability-dependent upon me – that is, on the substance change in which is constitutive of the event in question. The event of another person feeling the very same twinge is a different event, for it is a different person undergoing change. One can no more transfer a person's experiences thus than one can *transfer* a person's smiling or gesturing – although, to be sure, a person may have his mother's smile or his father's gestures.

Why can one person's mind not be transferred into another person's body? – After all, Locke, Anstey and Conan Doyle imagined it. The mind, I have argued, is not an entity of any kind, but an array of distinctive powers and their exercise. So it is not a kind of thing that could *migrate* or be *transferred* from one substance to another like an appendage; nor are character traits, tendencies and pronenesses of thought, feeling and behaviour that characterize individual human beings. It *is* possible to transform chemical elements, but, contrary to the alchemists of old, one cannot, *logically*, turn lead into gold by getting the yellowness of a quantity of sulphur and the shininess of brass to *migrate* into a bar of lead. The only sense in which my mind, understood as my mental attributes, can be 'transferred' is *qua* universals. That is, one can bring it about that another has whatever psychological attribute one has oneself (I can, without difficulty, bring it about that you believe something that I believe, that you have the same pain as I have, and so forth) – and perhaps one may fantasize about bringing it about that another has *all* one's psychological attributes (perhaps at the cost of the destruction of one's own brain). But if this is (remotely) intelligible, then there is no reason why there should not be multiple 'transfer' – not to one other human being, but to any number. But if multiple transfer is logically possible, then identity is excluded.[22]

Similarly, the body I have is not an entity that I inhabit or *occupy*.[23] To speak of the body I have is to speak of a certain range of my corporeal characteristics – and characteristics are not 'inhabitable' – certainly not inhabitable by minds, which are neither inhabitants nor occupants. The features of the body I have are *my* corporeal features – features of *the body I am*. But I cannot *inhabit* what I *am*. Nor can I change the body I am save in the innocuous sense mentioned above. The thought that one 'inhabits' the body one has arises from failure to grasp the logical character of the idioms of *having a body*. If one thinks of oneself as *inhabiting one's body*, it becomes difficult to resist the temptation of supposing that one stands in a direct causal relation to one's body. But although one may be the *indirect* cause of one's corporeal features (e.g. one's body may be fat because one is self-indulgent, or athletic because one takes exercise; one's leg may hurt because one stubbed one's toe, and one's body may be sunburnt because one spent too much time on the beach), one cannot be the *direct* cause of attributes of one's body. One may bring it about that one's body is covered in perspiration or in good trim – but to bring something about is always a matter of indirect causation. One may bring it about that one's arm moves, but one does so by moving it with one's other hand or by pressing it against a wall and then standing back and letting it rise. But to raise one's arm is not to cause it to rise (see pp. 154–7). If one further confuses the body one is with the body one has – that is, confuses the two different

---

[22] See Wiggins's 'Only *a* and *b* rule', in *Sameness and Substance Renewed*, pp. 96ff.

[23] Cp. C. M. Korsgaard. 'Personal Identity and the Unity of Agency: a Kantian Reply to Parfit', *Philosophy and Public Affairs* 18 (1989), p. 126: 'And, as things stand, it is qua the occupant of this particular body that I live a life, have ongoing relationships, realize ambitions, and carry out plans. So long as I occupy this body and live this life, I am this rational agent, the same one.'

forms of description – one may also think that one stands in a direct causal relation to the body one is. But that too is confused. For I am not the cause of my doing what I do. I may move, but in so doing I do not cause the body that I am – that is, myself – to move. Of course, I may make myself do things I don't want to do – but that signifies determination in the face of weariness, reluctance and disinclination, and is not a matter of causing anything.

Most of the philosophical fantasies of the late twentieth century differed from their ancestral forms, philosophical and fictional alike. Perhaps inchoately aware of the incoherences of 'transferring' memories and minds, perhaps convinced that *science* fiction is better than fiction, and more impressed by men in white coats than by God, the fantasy has involved transplanting brains, hemispheres of the brain, and other bits and pieces of cortical tissue.[24] These seem to ensure a firm material, causal, basis for the transference of memories and other features encompassed by Locke's 'consciousness'. For it was this material base that was conspicuously absent in the tales thus far considered.[25] Transferring hemispheres was proposed in jest by Swift in *Gulliver's Travels* (Part III, 'Voyage to Balnibarbi'). In the latter half of the twentieth century, as much serious effort was spent by philosophers on speculating about brain transfers and hemispherectomies as the medievals are said to have spent on speculating about how many angels can dance on the head of a pin, and to rather less purpose. How did this come about?

The idea of an immaterial substance lost favour among philosophers. Whereas Descartes had conceived of the person as identical

[24] Samuel Clarke, in *A Third Defence of an Argument made use of in a Letter to Mr Dodwell to prove the Immateriality and Natural Immortality of the Soul*, repr. in *The Works of Samuel Clarke, D.D.* (orig. publ. 1738; repr. Garland Press, New York, 1978), vol. 3, pp. 825–53), envisaged God transplanting one person's consciousness into another, or impressing upon a thousand men's minds the like consciousness I find in my own – all without brain transplants. He was not impressed by the idea, and would not have been any more impressed by the idea of scientists transplanting brains.

[25] Further stimulus to these fantasies was given by neuroscientists' misdescriptions of the results of commissurotomy. The abnormalities involved seemed to suggest that each half of the brain possesses a mind of its own. These misdescriptions were repeated by philosophers, and stimulated the thought of hemispheric transplants that would produce two 'descendants' of a given person. That Sperry and Gazzaniga misdescribed the data is shown, and the correct description is presented, in Bennett and Hacker, *Philosophical Foundations of Neuroscience*, pp. 388–92.

with the mind, it now became common to identify a person with his brain. The dependence of all the characteristic functions of human beings on their brain inclined many to suppose that the mind *is* the brain, or that it stands to the brain as the software to the hardware of a computer. We can lose our legs and remain the same person, lose our arms and remain the same person – the one thing we cannot lose is the brain (the limiting case of a mutilated human being). Or so it seemed. If the brain survives, appropriately nourished, in a vat, surely the person survives – or so it was argued. We are not, it was conceded, brains in vats – although we could be. But we are in fact *brains in skulls*. Philosophers, cognitive scientists, and cognitive neuroscientists proceeded to ascribe to the brain a large range of psychological predicates: for example, to think, believe, compute, calculate, perceive, remember, want, decide. Hence ancient fantasies about transferring minds or souls from one body to another took a materialist turn. Surely, it was argued, we can imagine transplanting brains from one skull to another, and if the patient wakes up after the operation with all his memories and traits of character intact, then he is the same old person in a different body.

Brain transplants are biologically impossible. Let as waive that, since they are not *logically* impossible. Nevertheless, the science fiction does not show that if A's brain is transplanted into B's decerebrate skull, then the resultant person, let us call him Aby, is actually A. That would be true only if a person were an embodied (enskulled) brain. But the brain is a part of the human being – an organ, not an organism. It makes no sense to apply psychological predicates such as 'thinks', 'remembers', 'perceives', 'imagines', 'wants', 'decides', 'feels happy', and so forth to the brain. It is a mistake to apply predicates that signify attributes of an animal as a living whole to its parts – a mereological fallacy.[26] Just as it is a mistake to ascribe the property of *keeping time* to the fusée of an eighteenth-century table clock, or the property of *flying* to the engine of an aeroplane, so too it is a mistake to ascribe to a person's brain the property of *thinking that it is raining* or of *deciding to take an umbrella*. As noted in chapter 8, Aristotle wrote: 'to say that the *psuchē* is angry is as if one were to say that the *psuchē* weaves or builds. For it is surely better not to say

---

[26] For elaboration, see Bennett and Hacker, *Philosophical Foundations of Neuroscience*, ch. 3, and A. J. P. Kenny, 'The Homunculus Fallacy', repr. in *The Legacy of Wittgenstein* (Blackwell, Oxford, 1984).

that the *psuchē* pities, learns or thinks, but that the man does these things with his *psuchē*.' This insight was echoed by Wittgenstein in *Investigations*, §281: 'only of a living human being and what resembles (behaves like) a living human being can one say: it has sensations; it sees; is blind; hears; is deaf; is conscious or unconscious'. It is human beings, not their brains, that have a stomach-ache; it is human beings who put their eye to the keyhole to see what is in a locked room, who cock their ear to listen better, who sniff to smell – not their brains. It is Leonardo, not his brain, who paints with such intense thought and concentration. It is Mozart, not his brain, who plays the piano with such feeling. It is human beings in the stream of life who manifest their powers in what they do and say, who exhibit their character traits in their behaviour. It makes no sense to ascribe such attributes to brains, for brains are not animals, and there is nothing that brains can do that could warrant ascribing such attributes to them.

What is true is that human beings would not have the powers they do but for their brains' functioning normally. It does not follow that the brain is the real possessor of those powers. We could not walk but for the normal functioning of our brain, but the brain is not the real walker. Nor is it the real thinker. Magritte might well have painted a brain on a pedestal and entitled it *Le Penseur* – but that would have been a joke. Human persons are not enskulled brains (they weigh more than 3 lbs, and are taller than 7 inches). *Contra* Descartes, we are not identical with our minds – but we are not identical with our brains either. Substituting the brain for the Cartesian mind remedies none of the deep conceptual incoherences in Cartesianism – it only conceals them under a deceptive veneer of misunderstood neuroscience.

Could we not coherently imagine a living brain in a vat, connected up to various bits of electronic hardware, seeing what is going on around it in the laboratory by means of prosthetic eyes, and responding to our questions by means of a computerized voice? Perhaps – but then it would not be the brain that sees, that reflects before it speaks, and speaks thoughtfully. It would be the complex being consisting of the living brain of a dead human being and the electronic machinery to which it is attached – a cerebroid. If one removes A's cortex, leaving his thalamus, basal ganglia, cerebellum and brain-stem intact, then A will be in an irreversible vegetative state. If one removes A's brain from his skull, then A is dead – as is evident if one examines A's remains on the operating table. Suppose that one could, miraculously, insert A's brain into B's skull, and that when Aby awoke, he asserted that his name was 'A', that he recollects doing a variety of things (that we know A did), that he has various plans for the future (that we know A had). Does this not show that Aby is A? No – no more so than if B had been hypnotized to forget everything about his own life and had been told that he was the subject of the biography that we know to be A's. But suppose that he also appeared to recognize all the people that A knew, and to know his way about all the places that A frequented – would that not show that Aby is really A? If you woke up tomorrow and seemed to recognize all the people and places I know, seemed to recollect everything I recollect – would that make you me? The transplantation of cerebral tissue is, so to speak, a red herring – we are so mesmerized by the bogus science that we follow a false trail.[27]

What is true is that our concept of a person is tailored to creatures like us. We can coherently imagine all manner of circumstances in which it would lose its grip, circumstances under which we would no longer know what to say. The Jekyll and Hyde phenomenon might become common. Multiple personality cases, with no mnemonic connection between the different personalities, might become ubiquitous. Pairs of human beings might find that they, as it were, alternate personalities and memories every day. Complete 'memory portfolios' (i.e. what is remembered, not the remembering of it) might be transferable from one human being to another at the press of a button. And so on. Our concept of a person would not be very useful to such creatures. But all this shows is that the concept of a person, like all our concepts, is of utility only against a background of constancies.

There are some methodological morals to this tale of philosophical confusion that resulted from science-fictional prestidigitations. In neuroscience, the investigation of brain injuries leading to varying degrees of catastrophic impairment of human faculties is a primary method for investigating the brain and its activities. Breakdowns shed light upon the normal case. The interminable debate within late twentieth-century Anglophone philosophy about brain transplants and personal identity laboured under a serious illusion. It was assumed

---

[27] Even if the fantasies of brain transplants do not show that the person is identical with the brain in the human body, does not the converse possibility of radical organ transplants show this? Could we not imagine progressively replacing all of a human being's organs *except* for his brain? And would he not remain the same person throughout? Perhaps so – but that does not show that the person is identical with the brain in his body. For the successfully transplanted organs *become* his organs, become parts of him, no less than is his brain.

that in *conceptual* investigations light can be thrown upon a problematic concept by close examination of cases in which the application of the concept becomes questionable. But that is mistaken. We cannot clarify the normal use of a word, and shed light on the concept it expresses, by looking at its abnormal use – at its contentious and problematic application to extreme cases that never occur. The most that we can hope to discover, if we are fortunate enough not to become confused, are various breakdown conditions. In the extreme case, neither the conditions for applying the predicate nor the conditions for withholding it are satisfied. So, for example, in cases of so-called blindsight one can neither say that the patient sees nor that he does not see.[28] This does not clarify the concept of vision, but only describes conditions under which it crumbles.

Similarly, the debates about brain transplants involved extensive consulting of what goes under the name of 'intuitions'. We are supposed to contemplate various empirically impossible circumstances of brain transplants and to consult our intuitions as to whether the resultant individual is identical with the person from whose body the transplanted brain was removed. It might be transplanted into the skull of his twin brother, or into that of a man of his age, or into the body of the emperor of China, or the body of a woman, a little boy or girl – and by consulting our intuitions as to whether the resultant person is identical with the person from whom the brain was taken, we shall obtain valuable data that will clarify the nature of personal identity.

It is far from obvious what 'intuitions' are supposed to be. Are they simply hunches? Or guesses? And why should hunches about truth be of any value in philosophy? Why should guesses about how to apply a rule to circumstances for which it was not designed be supposed to shed light on its application to cases for which it *was* designed? It is one thing to determine whether someone has mastered a concept by asking him to decide its applicability to normal (logically possible) cases, but quite another to try to determine whether a problematic case is indeed logically possible by asking someone who has mastered the concept to decide on its applicability in such abnormal, imaginary cases by consulting his intuitions.

---

[28] See J. Hyman, 'Visual Experience and Blindsight', in J. Hyman (ed.), *Investigating Psychology* (Routledge, London, 1991).

Light can be shed upon a concept by careful examination of the correct use of the word that expresses that concept in normal conditions of its application – not by consulting one's hunches about the truth or falsity of its application in abnormal cases. There is no room for intuitions in determination of a concept. And a competent speaker's judgement about the correct use of a word in normal circumstances is no hunch or guess, any more than is the competent chess-player's judgement about the rules of chess – he *knows* how the game is played. If in abnormal scenarios, such as science fiction fantasies, we do not know whether to apply or withhold an expression (e.g. 'same person as'), that is not a matter of ignorance that could be remedied by consulting one's intuitions. It is itself a *result* – namely, that the rules for the use of the expression do not go this far. What is then needed is not conceptual elucidation but reasoned legislation – which, for science-fiction fantasy, is pointless.

4. The concept of a person

The seventeenth- and eighteenth-century debate provided the framework within which the concept of a person was discussed by most philosophers, including analytical philosophers, until the Second World War and beyond.[29] That framework was radically defective, and it continues to be at the root of extensive confusions, some of which have just been mentioned. To avoid these incoherences, one must start afresh, rather than trying to weave the rotten strands of the Cartesian-empiricist tradition into yet another threadbare tapestry. Informed by our previous examination of the concepts of the mind and the body that human beings have, and well apprised now of the pitfalls that lie in the path, we shall start with a reminder of some commonplaces. Human beings are the only persons we know or are ever likely to know. Our concept of a person evolved above all as a concept applicable to human beings – social beings who are members of a moral community. It is clear enough that it is not a concept belonging to the physical sciences that concern themselves with matter in motion; but

---

[29] See e.g. R. Carnap, *The Logical Structure of the World* (1928), tr. R. A. George (Routledge & Kegan Paul, London, 1967), Part 4; H. P. Grice, 'Personal Identity', *Mind*, 50 (1941), pp. 330–50; A. J. Ayer, *The Problem of Knowledge* (Penguin Books, Harmondsworth, 1956), ch. 5. What broke the framework was Peter Strawson's discussion of the concept of a person in *Individuals* (Methuen, London, 1959), ch. 3.

this does not mean that it belongs to a science of immaterial substances. It is not a concept that finds its place in the biological sciences that study the behaviour of animals in general. It belongs to the moral sciences – to the study of man as a moral, social and cultural being. And it is at home in our daily discourse about ourselves and our fellow human beings.

Human beings are living organisms of a given type. We are language-using, culture-creating, self-conscious creatures that have a mind and a body. The latter, peculiar mode of self-characterization, as argued, is no more than a manner of talking of distinctive attributes of intellect, will and affection consequent on being a language-using animal, on the one hand, and of corporeal characteristics pertaining to appearance, physique, health and sensation, on the other. We are not two one-sided things, as Descartes suggested. But nor are we one two-sided thing – like a penny. We are multifaceted, like cut stones – partly opaque and riven with flaws. Being self-moving creatures with cognitive and volitional two-way powers, we can voluntarily act, take action and engage in activities. We could not be thinkers unless we were also doers, could not be observers unless we were also experimenters, could not be spectators of the passing scene unless we were also players in the unfolding play.[30]

Being rational, we can reason and act for reasons. So we have intentions, plans and projects that we pursue. Having a language, our cognitive powers endow us with the ability to retain the complex forms of knowledge that we can and do acquire. This includes experiential or personal memory. So we possess, as it were, an autobiography – we can tell the tale of our life as we remember it. Each human being traces a unique autobiographical route through the world, and the combination of genetic endowment, variable responsiveness to individual experience, and memory gives each human being a *personality* – with a unique combination of character traits, behavioural tendencies, an awareness of a unique past (pertaining both to inner and outer life) and of projects for the future. Our consciousness of our past itself typically incorporates an awareness of our family and social group, and of the form of life that contributes to the generation of our social identity and plays a crucial role in our conception of ourselves. So we have a sense (weaker or stronger) of our own identity, which may be more or less individualistic, or more or less tribal.

[30] See S. Hampshire, *Thought and Action* (Chatto & Windus, London, 1959), for illuminating development of this insight.

Being animate, we have needs and a good. Being rational, we can act for the reason that something is beneficial or detrimental, either to ourselves or to others. Being social, we grow to maturity within a community bound by norms of conduct and by common values. Being capable of reasoning about what is right or good, we can judge shared norms and values as reasonable or unreasonable, genuine or perverted. So we have, or are normally capable of having, knowledge of good and evil. So we are capable of doing good and evil. So we are persons, bearers of duties and obligations, and of rights and related normative powers. Because we internalize norms of conduct and can exercise our power of reasoning concerning the right and the good, we (normally) possess a conscience. A corollary of this is that we are subject to moral emotions of self-assessment, such as guilt, shame and remorse, as well as other-regarding emotions, such as resentment and indignation. We are answerable for our deeds. A condition of answerability is the possibility of explanation and self-understanding in rational terms – that is, by reference to the categories of reason-giving explanations.

The concept of a person is not a substance concept, as is the concept of a human being. It has been said by Peter Strawson to be a 'primitive concept'.[31] In so far as this means that it is not analysable as a combination of a subject of predicates of states of consciousness (P-predicates) and a different subject of corporeal predicates (M-predicates) – that is, of a mind and a body thus conceived – then it is surely primitive. For it is one and the same thing that is the subject of both kinds of predicate. But, of course, P-predicates are ascribable to a large part of the animal kingdom, to a large range of different substances (elephants, apes, monkeys, cats, dogs, etc.), none of whom, save for human beings, are persons. So, one may add that persons, unlike other developed members of the animal kingdom, are not only subjects to whom P- and M-predicates are ascribable, but are also *self*-ascribers of P-predicates (and M-predicates). Hence they are self-conscious, language-using creatures. This is true (of naturally developed, undamaged persons) – but then so too is much else characteristic of human beings that flows from mastery of a language. And it is doubtful whether the capacity for first-person use of P-predicates can be hived off from the numerous other powers characteristic of persons discussed above. Furthermore, the dichotomous division of predicates into P- and M-predicates is overly Cartesian.

[31] Strawson, *Individuals*, pp. 101f.

Many predicates ascribable to plants cannot be ascribed to inanimate objects (e.g. grows to maturity, flourishes, produces seed, dies), and others cannot be applied to animals either (e.g. grows in acid soil, bears fruit in autumn, has pink blossom). Many classes of predicates applicable to animals are inapplicable to plants (perceives, feels pain and pleasure, has desires, runs swiftly), and others are inapplicable to any known persons (e.g. has eight tentacles, lays a clutch of five eggs, has bright green plumage, hibernates, has kittens). The class of predicates uniquely applicable to human persons ranges far wider than the domain of psychological predicates, and many of the subclass of psychological predicates that human beings apply to themselves without criteria are applicable to other animals on the basis of criteria similar to those applied to other humans. It is true that human beings are subjects of P- and M-predicates and uniquely self-ascribers thereof. But it is perhaps more illuminating to say with Aristotle that we are unique possessors of a *rational psuchē*, over and above the powers of the sensitive *psuchē* that we share with other animals, and of the vegetative *psuchē* that we share with all living things.

Although we know of no persons other than human beings, usage does not restrict the application of this categorial term to human beings alone. If there be other creatures possessing the appropriate range of language-dependent rational powers grafted on to an appropriate animal nature, then they too are persons. To be a person is not to be a certain kind of animal, but rather to be an animal of one kind or another with certain kinds of abilities.[32] The nature of a person is rooted in animality, but transformed by possession of intellect and will. So the concept of a person qualifies a substance concept of an animal of such-and-such a kind, earmarking the individual of the relevant kind as possessing (or as being of such a nature as normally possessing) a distinctive range of powers, a personality, and the status of a moral being.[33]

[32] I disregard here the fanciful case of the cerebroid with an animal ancestry and a cerebro-mechanical future. It is unimportant, for it is a person only in a derivative sense, and sheds no more light on our concept of a person than does reflection on angels.

[33] This conception is sometimes characterized as 'animalism', but misleadingly so. The identity of a person depends upon the *kind* of animal that the person in question is, for 'person' is a qualification on a substance noun. We are, and the only persons we are ever likely to know are, *human persons*. Our identity as persons turns on our identity as *individuals* of the kind *human being*. If an 'ism' has to be bestowed, the appropriate and wholly unsurprising one is 'humanism'.

It is a moot point whether the idea of mechanical, artefactual persons is intelligible. Science fiction is replete with androids. But not everything that is, in this sense, imaginable, is logically possible. The issue turns not on artefactuality, but on biology. If advanced kinds of life can be artificially made, then, in principle there is nothing *logically* awry with the thought of manufactured animals with the necessary endowment to be or become persons. But the idea of androids is far more problematic. Such imaginary beings are not merely manufactured, they are machines. So they presumably do not grow, or go through the phases of life – knowing no childhood, youth, maturity or old age. They neither eat nor drink, and can take no pleasure in food or drink. They neither salivate nor digest, and neither urinate nor excrete waste products. They neither inhale nor exhale, are never short of breath, and cannot gasp in excitement or astonishment. Since they do not reproduce, they presumably have no sexual character or drive; hence too they neither lust nor enjoy sexual intercourse. In what sense, if any, are they really male or female? Lacking parents and bereft of procreative drives and powers, do they have a capacity for love? Can androids feel passions at all? In what sense, if any, are they by nature social creatures, belonging to a moral community? That depends on their author's tale and its coherence – which is rarely adequately elaborated. If the fantasy is amusing, it matters little whether it does or does not make sense. We stray here far beyond the bounds of application of our concept of a person. It is patent that it matters little what we say, since the rules for the use of the word 'person' do not extend to such cases. If any such cases were to arise, we should need to modify the rules in the light of logical, practical and ethical considerations. But they do not, and we need not.

I have argued that Locke was mistaken in supposing that experiential memory is a necessary condition of personal identity (since amnesia does not exclude continued identity). But since the concept of a person is linked with that of a rational being possessed of intellect and will, memory in general and experiential memory in particular are among the faculties that such a being is, unless damaged, endowed with. Locke confused this constitutive feature with a necessary condition of personal identity, which it is not.[34] Only if a creature can retain knowledge acquired, can it act for the reason that things are as it previously learnt they are. And only if such a creature can recollect its doings and undergoings, can it learn from

[34] See Wiggins, *Sameness and Substance Renewed*, ch. 7.

its own experience, amass first-hand evidence, reason from its past experience to anticipation of future eventualities, and act for the reason that things were thus-and-so with it previously. Without experiential memory, we would have no genuine autobiography to tell, but at best only factual and second-hand knowledge of our past. We would be like victims of severe aphasia who had to learn about their lives from records and tales of others, and (from day to day) could never remember learning it. We could not enjoy the intimate personal relationships that turn on shared experience recollected, on reciprocities and debts of reciprocity. Experiential memory is an open-ended matter – as one event is recollected in shared reminiscence, others flood forth, sometimes in delight and merriment, sometimes in embarrassment or shame. Shared experience recollected is constitutive of shared lives. Those with whom we share experience that we thus recollect are, in a deep sense, a part of our lives. A person's *sense of identity* depends on his remembering a substantial part of his auto-biography. It is not only normal, but the *norm*, for a person to have a sense of his own identity and a more or less substantial autobiography.

It is the norm that human persons do not completely change their looks and characteristic manner of expression, gesture, voice and into-nation contour. It is the norm that human persons have a determin-ate, characteristic personality, manifest in action and reaction, that recognizably persists throughout change. It is the norm that human beings possess rational powers of thought and action, have emotions that are to a greater or lesser degree determined by reasons and to a greater or lesser degree amenable to reason. Being by nature social creatures, being born into families and growing up under parental guidance, human beings naturally exist within a web of social and moral relations and commitments. All this, and much more, is famil-iar platitude – but it is platitude that needs to be borne in mind in reflection on the concept of a person. These complex regularities and these typical entanglements characteristic of humanity are the background against which we identify human persons. These features provide the characteristic grounds for re-identifying human persons, as we do, on the basis of their appearance, their voice, their behaviour and recollections. These normal persistences are part of what gives point to the concept of a person that has evolved to meet our needs.

Deviations from these norms are abnormalities in human life. They may afflict a human being from birth, they may be consequences of accident, and they may be the grim infirmities of senescence. Those thus afflicted are defective, perhaps irreparably damaged, human beings (they may be in a permanent vegetative state, but they are not vegetables). They lack the normal abilities that human persons possess, abilities characteristic of the species (cabbages, by contrast, are not lacking in anything and are not damaged). Our concept of a person is sufficiently complex, multifaceted, and flexible to accommodate such fearful deviations from the norm.

Index